ENGLISH IDIOMS

Sayings & Slang

Wayne Magnuson

Prairie House Books

Prairie House Books
Box 84007 Market Mall
Calgary, Alberta
Canada T3A 5C4

Phone 403-202-5438 or 403-241-3719
Fax   403-202-5437 or 403-547-9892
e-mail phbooks@telusplanet.net
web   www.idioms.ca

Fourth Printing 2001

This book is also available in CD format: ISBN 1-895012-19-8

Canadian Cataloguing in Publication Data

Magnuson, Wayne, 1938-
English idioms

Previous ed. has title: Canadian English idioms
ISBN 1-895012-09-0

1. English language—Canada—Dictionaries. 2.
Canadianisms (English)—Dictionaries.* I. Title. II. Title:
Canadian English idioms.
PE3239.M35 1995   423'.1   C95-910344-9

This book is also available from:

Educational Distributors Canada Inc.   Phone   403-251-3904
2423 - 98 Avenue S.W.   Toll Free 888-251-3977
Calgary, Alberta T2V 4S7   Fax   403-251-4105
                                        e-mail   esolomon@telusplanet.net

Printed and bound by Quebecor World Printpak, Calgary, Alberta, Canada.

Foreword

ENGLISH IDIOMS, Sayings & Slang, now in its fourth printing, is also available in CD format and on the Web. The idioms in this edition—over 5000 total—reflect conversational English in North America and around the world. Anyone who speaks English as a first language will be familiar with most of the idioms in this book.

What is an idiom? The root *idios* means one's own; hence *idiom* means one's own way of speaking, where *one* may be a person or a group. In a broader sense, any word used in a non-literal way is an idiom; for example, *out* in *find out.* The expressions *out of your head* and *die out* also use *out* in a special way, as does the saying *You can't make a silk purse out of a sow's ear.*

Like popular songs, idioms, particularly expressions, have their heyday, then fade and usually die. Many, such as *the tip of the iceberg,* live on as clichés. A few, like *putting on the ritz,* get recycled. The Roaring-Twenties expression *It's a Duesey!* (as beautiful as a Duesenberg roadster) thrived until the late 1940s. In the 60s, everything was *groovy;* in the 70s, we said *do your own thing;* in the 80s, we discovered *the bottom line;* in the 90s, we experienced *virtual reality;* today, we talk about finding our *spiritual path.* Born in the 1950s, *cool* is in a class by itself. It may always be cool to say cool.

Idioms Limited would be an appropriate title for a dictionary of phrases. Just when you think you've heard them all, somebody mentions *spankin' the pavement,* and you know you've missed a few. But this collection would be less complete without *friggin.* It would be a friggin shame, to say the friggin least, to omit this substitute for the F-word.

Which leads to my decision to include vulgar idioms. Swearing is integral to the way we talk—in the playground, at work, on the street—and cannot be ignored in a book of common phrases. People learning English as a foreign language can avoid embarrassment by noting that "bad" or impolite idioms have been identified with [B].

Nor have the foreign and off-beat idioms been overlooked. My informal research led to conversations with many colorful talkers, including an Ethiopian, who explained the meaning of *wekabi.* The expression *shuck on down to the fraidy hole* was donated by a lady from Nebraska, whose family knew the fear of tornadoes. Canadian journalist Chris Dornan contributed the German expression *dasein,* which describes people who blend into a group so well they all but disappear.

Idioms are well camouflaged. Like customs, they remain hidden until a visitor looks puzzled when we say someone is *under the weather* or *over the hill.* Such phrases come to mind readily and sound better than *sick* or *old,* but we don't realize how confusing they can be.

That's because many idioms are metaphors. One can be *up the creek* in business, at college or in romance. At some point in the history of exploration, the creek became a symbol for the wrong route, and the further up the creek one went, the worse it got. If one is *up the creek without a paddle,* it is quite serious.

And idioms impart culture. People who understand *the grass is greener on the other side of the fence* share not only a universal insight into human nature, but also the expression of this truth in English. Their cultural affinity is as certain (if not as strong) as the smaller number of people who understand the regional expressions *Bigfoot* and *road apple*.

My sincere thanks to those who suggested idioms, cajoled me or critiqued my efforts, especially to my family—Linda, Kari, Leanne, Paula and Taea—for their help and encouragement. I owe them *big time*.

But this book is dedicated to those who want to learn colloquial English: the idioms, sayings and slang.

Wayne Magnuson

How to use this book

The idioms, sayings and slang words are arranged alphabetically—like a dictionary. If you want to know the meaning of *cool*, look at the idioms that begin with **C**. Find *cool*, and read the meanings and the example.

Cross-references
Idioms that are similar to *cool* appear in bold-face print. You can find **groovy, hip, neat, together, way cool** and **with it** in their alphabetical places in this book.

Under A or T?
Idioms that begin with *a*, *an* or *the* are explained under **A** and **T** respectively. For example, *a golden opportunity* is defined under **A**, with a cross-reference from **G** (golden); *the last straw* is defined under **T**, with a cross-reference from **L** (last).

Impolite or Bad Idioms
Some of the idioms are inappropriate for use in public—wherever vulgar language would offend or embarrass. Impolite or bad idioms are marked with [B].

Not Listed?
If you hear or read an idiom that you can't find in this book, write the idiom and your address on a piece of paper and send it to ENGLISH IDIOMS, Sayings & Slang, Box 84007 Market Mall, Calgary, AB, Canada, T3A 5C4.

Idiom	Meaning	Example

A

Idiom	Meaning	Example
'at a boy (that a boy)	good work, well done	Whenever I win, Don says, " 'at a boy! Good game!"
'at a girl (that a girl)	good work, well done	When Judy gets good grades, her mom says, " 'at a girl, Judy!"
a babe in arms	a baby, a child who is **wet behind the ears**	Dar was just a babe in arms when we emigrated to Canada.
a bad taste in my mouth	a feeling that something is false or unfair, a feeling of ill will	I left the meeting with a bad taste in my mouth. There was a lot of dishonesty in the room.
a bad time	a lot of teasing, **a rough time**	The class gave him a bad time about his pink shorts.
a ball-park figure	a number that is near the total; approximate figure	Fifty is a ball-park figure. It's close to our class size.
a bar fly	a person who often goes to bars or lounges	Every evening Penny goes to *Lucifer's*. She's quite a bar fly.
a bar star	a girl who goes to bars to drink and find friends	Lola was known as a bar star at *Pinky's Lounge*.
a bare-faced lie	a deliberate lie, a planned lie	His statement to the police was false—a bare-faced lie.
a barnburner	an exciting game, **a cliff-hanger**	When the Flames play the Oilers it's a barnburner—a great game.
a barrel of laughs	a lot of fun, a person who makes you laugh	Let's invite Chang to our party. He's a barrel of laughs.
a basket case	a person who is very nervous, **in bad shape**	If Gloria has one more crisis, she'll be a basket case.
a bawling out	a scolding, a lecture, **an earful, catch it**	When I forgot to do my chores Dad gave me a bawling out.
a bed of roses	an easy life, a pleasant place to work or stay	Who said that retirement is a bed of roses?

Idiom	Meaning	Example
a bee in her bonnet	upset, a bit angry, **on edge**	Aunt Betsy was kind of cranky, like she had a bee in her bonnet.
a big-rig	a big truck, a semi-trailer truck	Do you have a driver's license? Have you ever driven a big-rig?
a big shot	an important person, a boss, **a big wheel**	On payday he spends money like a big shot, buying drinks for all.
a big wheel	a person with power, **a big shot**	Bing has been acting like a big wheel since he got promoted.
a big wig	an important person, a president etc., **VIP**	Barry is a big wig in Gulf Oil— a vice president or something.
a bird in the hand is worth two in the bush	having one is better than seeing many	When searching for a better job, remember *A bird in the hand*....
a bit at sea	a bit unsure, uncertain	He seems a bit at sea since his brother died. They were close.
a bit off/a bit mental	not rational, unbalanced, **one brick short**	Kate talks to the birds. Do you think she's a bit off?
a bitch [B]	a complaining woman, a woman who **nags**	What a bitch! She complains to us and criticizes her kids.
a bite to eat	a lunch, a snack	We can grab a bite to eat at the arena. They sell snacks there.
a black mark	a mark beside your name means you are bad	If you cause an accident, you get a black mark beside your name.
a blank look	eyes show that a person does not understand, **the lights are on but...**	When I called her name, she gave me a blank look, as though she didn't know me.
a blast	a great time, a lot of fun	The students were having a blast until the teacher walked in.
a blessing in disguise	a problem that becomes a benefit or advantage	The rainstorm was a blessing in disguise. It stopped the fire.
a blow job [B]	giving oral sex to a man, fellatio	If you want a blow job, you'll have to shower first.
a blowout	to win by a large score, **no contest**	"Did the Flames win?" "Ya, 11-2. It was a blowout."
a blowout	a flat tire, a tire that breaks suddenly	We were late because our van had a blowout on the freeway.

Idiom	Meaning	Example
a bone to pick	something to argue about, a matter to discuss	Joe sounded angry when he said, "I have a bone to pick with you."
a breath of fresh air	a nice change, a new presence	Having Lan around the house is a breath of fresh air—she's so nice.
a breath of wind	a breeze, a light wind	In the evening, the lake was calm. There wasn't a breath of wind.
a brick	a dependable person, a friend who always helps	Parveen helped me get through my divorce. She's a real brick!
a brick short	(See **one brick short of a full load**)	
a budding genius	a child who appears to be very intelligent	The newspaper described Pam as "a budding genius" on the violin.
a bull in a China shop	a big, reckless person in a room full of fragile things; **cramp your style**	Imagine a 300-pound football player at a tea party, and you have a bull in a China shop.
a bum rap	unfair blame, unjust sentence, **take the rap**	It was a bum rap. Eddie didn't steal those paintings.
a bummer	an unfortunate event, bad luck, **too bad**	"Somebody broke a window in his car and stole his stereo." "That's a bummer."
a bun in the oven	pregnant, expecting a baby	Mabel has a bun in the oven. The baby's due in April.
a bunch of malarkey	an untrue story, **a lot of bunk**, **bull**	"Do you believe what the psychic said about your future?" "No. It's a bunch of malarkey."
a bundle of nerves	a very nervous person; **uptight** person	May has so many problems— she's just a bundle of nerves.
a card	(See **such a card**)	
a case of	an example of, **it's a case of**	Look at Bosnia. That's a case of ethnic civil war.
a caution	a bold or shocking person, **no shrinking violet**	She *is* a caution! She told the judge he was all wrong.
a cheap drunk	a person who gets drunk on one or two drinks	Jo admits she's a cheap drunk. Her limit is two drinks.
a chicken in every pot	enough food for every family	No one will be hungry if there's a chicken in every pot.

Idiom	Meaning	Example
a chin wag	a conversation, a visit	The grandmothers were talking happily—having a chin wag.
a chip off the old block	a boy who is like his dad, **the apple doesn't...**	Eric is a chip off the old block. He's just like his dad.
a cliff-hanger	a game that is close until the end, **a barnburner**	Every election in this town is a real cliff-hanger—a close race.
a close call	close to danger or an accident	That was a close call. The train nearly hit the bus!
a close shave	very close to serious injury or death	The old man described his fight with the bear as a close shave.
a clutch hitter (baseball)	a batter who hits when runners are on base	Joe's a clutch hitter. He's batting .431 with runners on base.
a common thread	an idea or theme that is similar to others	There's a common thread in most of Berton's stories.
a contract out on	a contract that pays to have someone killed	There's a contract out on Mike. The boss doesn't like him.
a coon's age	many years, **a dog's age**	We haven't been out to the coast in a coon's age. It's been years.
a crash course	a short course that has the main facts and skills	He took a crash course in cooking and bought a cafe.
a crush on	sudden feeling of love or romance	Judy has a crush on Tim. See the way she looks at him.
a crying shame	a sad event, it is **too bad**	It's a crying shame that they didn't have fire insurance.
a cut above	superior, better	A scholar's work is a cut above. It's superior to the others.
a cut-up	a joker, a person who tells jokes and has fun	When Marsha goes to a party she's a real cut-up—a lot of fun.
a dead giveaway	a clear signal, an obvious sign	The smile on her face was a dead giveaway that she got the job.
a dead heat	a race that finishes in a tie for first, **dead even**	A photograph of the finish line proved that it was a dead heat.
a dead loss	a complete loss, **a write-off**	The spoiled meat was a dead loss. We couldn't eat any of it.
a dead ringer	a very close likeness, like a twin	Chad is a dead ringer for Mel Gibson. They look like twins.

Idiom	Meaning	Example
a different kettle of fish	different, not the same	A cult is not a religion. A cult is a different kettle of fish entirely.
a dime a dozen	very cheap, low priced, **dirt cheap**	He can remember when eggs were cheap—a dime a dozen.
a dog's age	a long time, 10-15 years, **a coon's age**	Mel! I haven't seen you for a dog's age—at least ten years!
a dog's breakfast	a mixture of many things, a hodgepodge	This book is a dog's breakfast. It contains a bit of everything.
a dog's life	a poor life, **hard times**	Without a job, it's a dog's life.
a double-edged sword	a device that can help you and hurt you	Truth is a double-edged sword. It can imprison me or set me free.
a downer (sadness)	an event or statement that causes sadness	News of the war was a downer. Most of the people dreaded war.
a downer (drug)	a drug that relaxes you, a sedative	Before bedtime he took a downer to help him relax and sleep.
a drag	a boring time, **a yawner**	Mary's party was a drag. We just sat around and talked.
a dressing down	a scolding, a lecture, **a piece of my mind**	Mother gave me a dressing down when I said bad words.
a drop in the bucket	a small part, a tiny piece, **the tip of the iceberg**	This donation is only a drop in the bucket, but it is appreciated.
a dust-up	a fight, a skirmish; **set-to**	The boys argued and had a little dust-up, but no one got hurt.
a fair shake	a fair deal, a just settlement	The insurance company gave us a fair shake—paid all our damages.
a falling-out	a disagreement, a break in friendship	Guy and Jean had a falling-out. They argued about religion.
a false move	a wrong move, a threatening action	A man with a gun said, "If you make a false move, you're dead."
a far cry	not similar, very different	This is good sherry, but it's a far cry from the amontillado.
a faraway look	the eyes show thoughts of a distant place or friend	When I mention horses, you get a faraway look in your eyes.
a fart in a windstorm	an act that has no effect, an unimportant event	A letter to the editor of a paper is like a fart in a windstorm.

Idiom	Meaning	Example
a fat lip	a hit on the lip, an injured lip	Stop bothering her or I'll give you a fat lip. I'll hit you.
a feather in your cap	an honor, a credit to you, **chalk one up for you**	Because you are Karen's teacher, her award is a feather in your cap.
a few bricks short of a full load	not sensible or logical, **not all there**	When Moe began eating bugs, we knew he was a few bricks short.
a fifth wheel	a useless object, an unnecessary device	The team already had two guards, so I felt like a fifth wheel.
a fighting chance	a fair chance, a good chance	If I can get a job interview, I'll have a fighting chance.
a fill-up	a full tank of gasoline, **fill her up**	We got a fill-up before we left Winnipeg. The truck needed gas.
a fine line	a close relationship, not much difference	Sometimes there is a fine line between love and lust.
a fine-toothed comb	a careful search, a search for a detail	She read the file carefully—went over it with a fine-toothed comb.
a firm hand	a person who will discipline people	The students in Grade 8 need a teacher with a firm hand.
a flash in the pan	a person who does superior work at first	I'm looking for a steady worker, not a flash in the pan.
a fleeting glance	a very brief look, a quick glance	A fleeting glance from Marilyn would make his heart beat wildly.
a fly on the wall	able to hear and see what a fly would see and hear	I'd like to be a fly on the wall in the Judge's chambers.
a fool and his money are soon parted	a fool will spend all his money quickly; **easy come, easy go**	After he had spent his fortune, he remembered this saying: *A fool and his money are soon parted.*
a foregone conclusion	a certain conclusion, a predictable result	That he'll graduate is a foregone conclusion. He is a good student.
a fraidy-cat	a child who is afraid to jump etc., **chicken**	"Ian's a fraidy-cat!" the boys shouted. "Ian's afraid to jump!"
a free hand	complete authority, freedom to control	The President gave Ms. Drake a free hand in choosing the colors.
a free-for-all	a fight without rules, **Donnybrook**	There was a free-for-all after the dance, and Brendan got hurt.

Idiom	Meaning	Example
a freeze on	a stoppage; a decision to stop spending, hiring etc.	Right now there's a freeze on hiring at the plant—no hiring.
a fresh pair of eyes	a different reader, one who has not seen the writing	A fresh pair of eyes may find many errors in this report.
a fresh start	starting again, a new life	In Canada, you will have a fresh start. You can begin a new life.
a full house (cards)	a pair plus three of a kind, e.g., 2 kings and 3 aces	In our last game of poker, you dealt me a full house.
a full plate	a busy schedule, a lot to do	Nancy has a full plate these days. She has two jobs and three kids.
a gaggle of geese	a flock of geese, a bunch of geese	A gaggle of geese met us as we drove into the farmyard.
a game one	a willing player, a **rough and ready** person	I can see that Bev's a game one. She plays hard and doesn't quit.
a ghost of a chance	a poor chance, not likely to happen	That car doesn't have a ghost of a chance. It's too slow!
a glow on	slightly drunk, **tipsy**, **catch a buzz**	When Myrna gets a glow on, she likes to dance real close.
a go	(See **it's a go**)	
a go-getter	an aggressive employee, a hard worker, **gung-ho**	What a go-getter! He finished the course a month before the others.
a golden opportunity	a good chance to succeed, a good investment	The Royal Hotel is for sale. What a golden opportunity!
a goner	something that is lost or **beyond help**	I thought he was a goner, but the cat came back. He's home.
a good egg	a good-natured person, **a good head**	Everybody likes Marsha. She's a good egg.
a good head	friendly, generous person; **a good egg**	Sean is a good head. He'll help at the food bank.
a good sport	a person who is fair and friendly	What a good sport! You never complain, even when you lose.
a grain of salt	(See **take it with a grain of salt**)	
a grain of truth	a bit of truth, **take it with a grain...**	There's not a grain of truth in what Brian says. It's all untrue.

Idiom	Meaning	Example
a grandfather clause	a written statement that protects a senior worker	They can't demote him because he has a grandfather clause.
a handful	a child who is difficult to manage	Jason is not easy to manage. He is a real handful for his mother.
a handout	free food or money, **freeload**	I'm not asking for a handout. I'll pay you back when I find work.
a hard day	a day full of hard work, **put in a hard day**	You look tired, Dear. Did you have a hard day at the office?
a hard row to hoe	a difficult task, many problems	A single parent has a hard row to hoe, working day and night.
a hard time	teasing or bugging, **a bad time**	Ken will give you a hard time about missing that free throw.
a hard-on [B]	an erect penis, a hard penis	When our dog gets a hard-on, he tries to crawl up my leg.
a hassle	a problem, a bother	The tax form is a hassle this year. It's difficult to understand.
a head start	a chance to start ahead of the other runners etc.	Give the smallest runner a head start. He can't run very fast.
a heavy day	a busy day, **a hard day**	At the end of a heavy day he likes to sit on the patio and read.
a helping hand	help with a job or task, **lend a hand**	May was always ready with a helping hand.
a hill of beans	a small amount, very little	The money he lost doesn't amount to a hill of beans.
a hit	a popular song or movie, an idea everybody likes	Remember the song *Michelle*? It was quite a hit.
a hit	a drug dose, drugs from a needle	When she's depressed, she'll do anything for a hit.
a hollow leg	space for a lot of drink, room for a lot of beer	Parl drank six bottles of beer. He must have a hollow leg!
a holy pile	a lot, very much, **tons**	To feed 20 people, you need a holy pile of spaghetti.
a hoot	a time of laughter, a good time, **a riot**	Last night we went to Maude's party. It was a hoot.
a horse of a different color	a different matter, a separate issue	If he wants to *buy* the land, that's a horse of a different color.

Idiom	Meaning	Example
a horse's ass [B]	a fool, a **jerk**	After three drinks he was acting like a horse's ass.
a hot hand	lucky in card games or at gambling	Walter's got a hot hand tonight. He's won four games of poker.
a hot number	a couple (or topic) that everyone is talking about	Paul and Rita are a hot number now. They're in love.
a hot ticket	a popular item, a product that people want	Anything with James Dean's picture on it is a hot ticket.
a hot topic	popular topic, **the talk of the town**	Sex is a hot topic. Sex will get their attention.
a hotdog	one who plays only for the crowd, a **show-off**	Eddie was a hotdog—always trying to excite the crowd.
a hothead	a person who gets angry easily; **hot tempered**	Phil, don't be such a hothead. Try to control your anger.
a hotshot	a person who displays; **show-off, showboat**	What a hotshot he is—showing everybody his new car.
a household name	a name everyone knows; name of a famous person	Mario Lemieux, the hockey star, soon became a household name.
a howling blizzard	a very bad snowstorm, a winter storm	A howling blizzard delayed us. It was snowing and blowing.
a humdinger	a beautiful car etc. a well-designed product	Dad, you should see this coupe. It's a humdinger!
a into g	(See **ass into gear**)	
a jim-dandy	a fine piece of work, a beautiful object	Mom, you should just see this saddle. It's a jim-dandy!
a keeper	something you want to keep for a long time	"Do you like my leather jacket?" "Ya, man. It's a keeper!"
a kept woman	a woman who is paid to live with a man	I'm tired of being a kept woman. I want to be free of him.
a lady-killer	handsome man; a man who charms the ladies; **hunk**	"Liam Neeson! He's gorgeous!" she said. "What a lady-killer!"
a leg up	a start, a beginning, **the first leg**	If I take a night class, I'll have a leg up on my diploma.

Idiom	Meaning	Example
a level playing field	a place where everyone has an equal chance, **level the playing field**	A level playing field includes equal pay for equal work for all men and women.
a lick and a promise	a hasty plan, a promise made without much thought	If you get married on a lick and a promise, you may need a lot of good luck.
a lift	energy, a positive feeling, **a shot in the arm**	When I need a lift, I watch *Oprah*. She makes me feel good.
a little bird told me	someone told me, one of your friends told me	"How did you know that I play chess?" "Oh, a little bird told me."
a little hair off the dog	(See **hair off the dog**)	
a little off	not quite sane, a bit crazy, **one brick short...**	When Clem started eating grass, we knew he was a little off.
a little off	not quite centered, not level	The picture above the table is a little off. Let's straighten it.
a little steep	a little high in price, too much money to pay	I'd like to buy that leather coat but the price is a little steep.
a long shot	a poor chance of winning, **a slim chance**	The Leafs winning the Stanley Cup—now that's a long shot.
a loose cannon	unpredictable employee, one who may embarrass	The President is sensible, but the Vice President is a loose cannon.
a losing streak	losing several times in succession	The Leafs are on a losing streak. They've lost seven games!
a lost cause	a goal or project that is not worth working for	That video store is a lost cause. It has never made a profit.
a lot of bunk	a lot of lies, a lot of **bull**, **a pack of lies**	The President's speech was a lot of bunk. It contained no facts.
a lot of falderal	a lot of foolish talk, **a lot of bunk**	When you hear me speak Latin, you'll think it's a lot of falderal.
a lot on the ball	intelligent, smart	Melvin may not look intelligent, but he's got a lot on the ball.
a lucky break	good luck, good fortune, **stroke of good luck**	Finding that money was a lucky break. It was our good fortune.
a lucky streak	winning several times in succession	Whenever I wear this ring, I have a lucky streak. I win every game!

Idiom	Meaning	Example
a man of few words	a man who says little; who uses few words	Chung is a man of few words, but when he speaks, people listen.
a man of the cloth	a minister, a priest, a clergyman	Being a man of the cloth, he has studied the Bible.
a mental block	a problem with learning a subject or concept	I have a mental block when I try to do algebra. I can't think.
a month of Sundays	a very long time, many days	It will take a month of Sundays to phone the students in our school.
a nail-biter	exciting game or movie; having much suspense	Have you seen the movie *The Fugitive*? It's a nail-biter.
a necktie party	a hanging, a lynching	If the men catch the outlaw, they want to have a necktie party.
a new broom sweeps clean	an employee works hard on the first day or two, **make a good impression**	After my first day working for Grandfather, he said, "A new broom sweeps clean."
a new lease on life	a feeling that life will be better, **a fresh start**	The promotion gave him a new lease on life.
a notch below	inferior, not as good	That bicycle is a notch below the Peugeot. It's not quite as good.
a nut case	a person who is crazy, **crackpot**	If you go to work in pajamas, people will say you're a nut case.
a pack of lies	many lies, **no truth to it**	What Gail is saying about Julie is a pack of lies. It's not true.
a pain in the ass [B]	a bother, a lot of trouble	Fixing that car every day is a pain in the ass.
a paper trail	a series of memos or letters that record events	A business merger leaves a long paper trail—many documents.
a party to that	a person who helps to do something bad	Jane said she didn't want to be a party to computer theft.
a pat answer	a planned or memorized answer, a **canned** answer	You won't get the job if you give a pat answer to every question.
a penny for your thoughts	tell me what you are thinking about	When I'm quiet, she will say, "A penny for your thoughts."
a penny pincher	a person who spends carefully, a thrifty person	He used to be a penny pincher, but now he spends freely.

Idiom	Meaning	Example
a perfect stranger	a person you have never seen, **a total stranger**	In New York, a perfect stranger asked her to sleep with him.
a pick-me-up	something that gives me energy or new life	On a hot afternoon, a glass of iced tea is a great pick-me-up.
a piece of ass [B]	sex, intercourse, **nookie**	If it's just a piece of ass you want, why don't you find a prostitute?
a piece of cake	easy to do, **a snap**, **no problem**	Solving the puzzle was easy. It was a piece o' cake.
a piece of my mind	my criticism of what you did, **a tongue-lashing**	If *my* son stayed out all night, I'd give him a piece of my mind.
a piece of tail [B]	(See **a piece of ass**)	
a pig in a poke	a risk, a gamble, **taking a chance**	If you don't test drive the car, you're buying a pig in a poke.
a pinch of coon shit [B]	very little or no value, worthless	That Rambler ain't worth a pinch o' coon shit. It's a lousy car.
a pinch of salt	a bit of salt, the salt held between thumb and finger	Hector uses a pinch of salt when he makes chocolate fudge.
a pinch to grow an inch	on your birthday, guests pinch you to help you grow taller	"Happy birthday, Sal. Here's a pinch to grow an inch!" "Ouch!"
a play on words	a pun, a word or phrase that has two meanings	When a man says he'll *give you a ring*, it may be a play on words.
a pocket of resistance	a small group resisting, a few people not **on side**	There's a pocket of resistance in one district. A few disagree.
a poker face	a face with no expression; showing no emotion	Judge Brady has a poker face. He doesn't show his emotions.
a pop	per person, per ticket	"How much are the tickets?" "Fifty dollars a pop."
a pretty penny	a lot of money, a high price	I bet she paid a pretty penny for that coat. It looks expensive.
a question of	the important factor, the issue	For them, it's a question of faith. They believe in the Bible.
a quickie	a quick game or visit, a short time of play	I love to play chess. Do we have time for a quickie before dinner?

Idiom	Meaning	Example
a quickstudy	a person who tries to learn much in a short time, **a crash course**	When my wife was elected to city council, I became a quickstudy in municipal politics.
a red-letter day	a special day, a memorable day	This is going to be a red-letter day. I found my lost keys!
a redneck	a person who is intolerant of other opinions and cultures, a bigot	If you ask a redneck he'll say, "Find a job or starve—and if you don't like it, too bad."
a regular guy	an average man, a good guy	David? Well, he's honest and easy to live with—a regular guy.
a riot	a lot of fun, a good time, **a hoot**	You should've gone to Maude's party. It was a riot!
a rip-off	unfair price or rule, priced too high	The price of drinks was a rip-off. A small Coke cost $3!
a roll in the hay [B]	making love, having sex	"Want a roll in the hay?" "Sure. Do you have a condom?"
a rough time	a lot of teasing, a lot of **bug**ging	Did your friends give you a rough time about your funny haircut?
a rough time of it	a time of stress or bad luck, **a tough time of it**	After the divorce he had a rough time of it.
a royal pain	a feeling of irritation, **a pain in the ass** [B]	When he brags about his wealthy family, he gives me a royal pain.
a run for your money	strong competition, an opponent	I should enter the election and give him a run for his money.
a sack of hammers	a dead weight, a heavy object	Don't throw me in the lake! I'll sink like a sack of hammers!
a score to settle	an argument to finish, **a bone to pick**	I have a score to settle with him. He owes me a month's rent.
a screw loose	a little bit crazy, **one brick short...**	Sometimes I think he has a screw loose—like when he eats paper.
a shadow of his former self	much lighter than he was before, very thin and weak	After twenty years in prison, he was a shadow of his former self.
a sharp tongue	a tendency to reply sharply or sarcastically	Karly is a beautiful girl, but her sharp tongue may be a problem.
a sharp wit	an ability to say funny things at the right time	Mr. Mills is 85, but he still has a sharp wit. His mind is quick.

Idiom	Meaning	Example
a shoe-in	the person who is certain to win, **a sure thing**	Ralph is a shoe-in to win the next election. He'll win easily.
a short one	a small drink, a small amount of liquor	"Can I pour you a drink?" "Yes. A short one, please."
a shot in the arm	energy, encouragement, **a lift**	Billy Graham's sermon was inspiring—a shot in the arm.
a shot in the dark	a wild guess, a try, **hazard a guess**	His answer was incorrect. It was a shot in the dark.
a sight for sore eyes	something or someone you are happy to see	Well, my friend, you are a sight for sore eyes. Good to see you!
a silver spoon...	(See **born with a silver spoon in his mouth**)	
a sitting duck	an easy target, a person who is easy to deceive	The old lady was a sitting duck for the salesman. It was an easy sale.
a slim chance	very little chance, not likely to happen	"Is it going to rain today?" "Maybe. There's a slim chance."
a slip of the tongue	a spoken error or mistake, a word that **slips out**	I said *brew* instead of *blue*. It was a slip of the tongue.
a slow day	not productive, not many customers	Tuesday is a slow day in the car market—very few sales.
a slug	a group, a bunch	A slug of bats hung from a rock jutting out of the cave's ceiling.
a snootful	a lot to smell or drink, **get wind of**	When the coyotes get a snootful of our campfire, they'll run.
a snow job	a false story, a phony deal, **a rip-off**	I knew it was a snow job. They said if I ordered some pens, I'd receive a new TV.
a snowball's chance in hell	little or no chance to succeed	If I write the test now, I won't have a snowball's chance in hell.
a soft touch	a person who will not refuse, **an easy mark**	Barry's a soft touch. Let's ask him for a loan.
a spot of tea	a small cup of tea, a drink of tea	When I visit Mrs. Smith, we always have a spot of tea.
a steal	a bargain; purchased for a very low price	How much did I pay for my new coat? Very little. It was a steal.
a stiff upper lip	(See **keep a stiff upper lip**)	

Idiom	Meaning	Example
a stitch in time saves nine	a small repair may prevent a large repair	I believe in maintenance. *A stitch in time saves nine.*
a stone's throw	a short distance, 25 metres	A deer came into the yard, just a stone's throw from our door.
a sucker for punishment	one who allows himself to be hurt or blamed	If I accept blame for a team loss, I'm a sucker for punishment.
a suicide pass (hockey)	a pass behind the player causing him to look back	Older players always stop when receiving a suicide pass.
a sure bet	certain to win, a good choice to **bet on**	The Lions are a sure bet in the final game. They'll win easily.
a sure thing	a predictable result, sure to happen	For them, success is a sure thing. They plan for success.
a sweet tooth	a need to eat candy, a craving for sugar	After dinner we'll serve mints. Daddy has a sweet tooth, eh.
a talking to	a scolding, a personal lecture	If he has a poor attitude, Dan will give him a talking to.
a tall one	a large drink of liquor, a strong drink	After he heard the bad news, he poured himself a tall one.
a tempest in a teapot	a lot of excitement about a small problem	The argument was over quickly. It was a tempest in a teapot.
a thorn in my side	one who causes pain, one who **bugs** me	He's always been a thorn in my side—always critical of me.
a three-bagger	a person who needs three bags over his head because he looks so scary	"What did he look like?" "He was at least a three-bagger. He also needed a bath."
a three-bagger (baseball)	a hit that allows the batter to run to third base	Molitor hit a three-bagger in the sixth game of the World Series.
a tich	(See **just a tich**)	
a token gesture	a small sign of thanks or recognition	To thank us, they put our names in the paper—a token gesture.
a tongue-lashing	a scolding, a lecture, **a talking to**	When Sis came home drunk, Dad gave her a tongue-lashing.
a total stranger	one you have never seen, **a perfect stranger**	"Can I give you a ride home?" "No. You're a total stranger."
a touch of	a little illness, minor symptoms	Mary's not feeling well today. She has a touch of the flu.

Idiom	Meaning	Example
a tough act to follow	a performance that is not easy to equal	Gail danced very well. That is a tough act to follow.
a tough call	a difficult decision, a hard choice	Was the goal scored before the game ended? It's a tough call.
a tough row to hoe	(See **a hard row to hoe**)	
a tough time of it	a time of stress or bad luck, **a rough time of it**	When Bev left home she had a tough time of it. She had no job.
a tower of strength	a person who helps you during a crisis, **a brick**	When my parents were killed in an accident, Harry was a tower of strength to me.
a wash	not owing each other, **even, square**	You owe me $20, but you gave me a CD, so it's a wash, eh.
a wash-out	a failure, **a lost cause**	No one attended the concert. It was a wash-out.
a way with words	natural ability to speak, **the gift of the gab**	Ask Viv to write the speech. She has a way with words.
a whale of a game	an exciting game, **a cliff-hanger**	When Canada played Sweden, it was a whale of a game.
a wild goose chase	a waste of time, a long chase without results	Oil exploration is sometimes a wild goose chase. It's uncertain.
a window of opportunity	an opportunity, a chance, **a golden opportunity**	Sometimes a problem is actually a window of opportunity.
a wolf in sheep's clothing	an evil person who looks innocent	The priest looked harmless, but he was a wolf in sheep's clothing.
a word to the wise is sufficient	a wise person understands when he hears a key word	I can't discuss the plan, but a word to the wise is sufficient: *progress*.
a yawner	a boring event, a book etc. that is not interesting	I went to the movie, but it was a yawner so I left.
A-OK	fine, better than average	This restaurant is A-OK. The food and service are good.
about time	nearly late, **high time**	It's about time you got here. We've been waiting a long time.
above and beyond the call of duty	much more than expected, **go the extra mile**	Her extra work was above and beyond the call of duty.

Idiom	Meaning	Example
above board	legal, not hidden, not **under the table**, not **underhanded**	Every action, every payment is above board. Customers respect that kind of honesty.
according to Hoyle	according to the rules, if we follow the rules	According to Hoyle, it's your turn to deal the cards.
ace in the hole	a hidden strength or talent	Sam's ace in the hole is honesty, which his clients soon discover.
Achilles heel	a weakness, a vulnerable place	Jewelry is my Achilles heel. I buy too much jewelry.
acid test	(See **the acid test**)	
act out	explain by movement and gestures	Watch—I'll act out the meaning of *pacifist*.
act up	misbehave, do bad things	She said that Kim was acting up at church—making noise.
act up	not work right, give pain or problems	My stomach is acting up today. I don't feel well.
actions speak louder than words	people judge by actions more than words, **practice what you preach**	Parents should remember that actions speak louder than words. Kids imitate their parents.
add fuel to the fire	cause more anger, aggravate a problem	He's angry. Telling him bad news will add fuel to the fire.
add insult to injury	add another negative, **make it worse**, **put your foot in it**	If you say his answer is wrong, and then say he can't understand, you've added insult to injury.
afraid so	sorry, but it is true; believe me, **yeppers**	"Did he spend all of our money?" "Yes, 'fraid so."
after all	after you consider all the facts, to be fair	Will you help me with English? After all, I helped you with math.
against all odds	not likely to happen, **slim chance**	Against all odds—poor weather, student pilot—we landed safely.
against the grain	against the natural way, **rub the wrong way**	Some words go against the grain. Their spellings aren't natural.
age before beauty	the older person should be allowed to enter first	"Age before beauty," she said as she opened the door for me.
ahead of the game	finished your work, paid all the bills, **caught up**	With all these expenses, we can't seem to get ahead of the game.

Idiom	Meaning	Example
ain't	isn't, is not; aren't, are not	"It ain't easy being green," said the frog.
air was blue	(See **the air was blue**)	
airhead	(See **an airhead**)	
all ears	listening carefully, trying to hear everything	When Dad mentioned hunting, I was all ears. I loved to hunt.
all eyes	watching carefully, staring	When the fire truck arrived, the children were all eyes.
all fired up	eager, enthused, **gung-ho**	Ian gets all fired up when he sees Kari. There's love in his eyes.
all goes well	have good luck, have no problems	I hope all goes well for you at college. I hope you succeed.
all hell broke loose	people did crazy things, everybody was fighting	When the fire alarm sounded, all hell broke loose.
all his marbles	normal, sensible	Dan talks to the door. I wonder if he's got all his marbles.
all in	very tired, exhausted, **dog tired**, **done in**	After the marathon, she was all in—completely exhausted.
all in a day's work	not extra work, just part of my duties	She said, "Thanks for the help." "All in a day's work," he replied.
all in all	generally, considering everything	All in all, it was a good holiday. We enjoyed our trip to Europe.
all it's cracked up to be	as good as the ads say, **live up to** the reports	The new computer isn't all it's cracked up to be. It's not so hot.
all over but the shouting	(See **it's all over but the shouting**)	
all over hell's half acre	all over the place, everywhere	I left the gate open, and the cows are all over hell's half acre.
all set	ready, prepared to start	"All set?" he asked, as she closed her suitcase.
all shook up	excited, nervous	Al gets all shook up when he sees Gina. He likes her a lot.
all spruced up	clean and dressed in your best clothes, **dress**ed **up**	The young farmers got all spruced up for the dance.
all teed up	the golf ball is on the tee, everything is ready	The parade is ready to begin. It's all teed up.

Idiom	Meaning	Example
all that jazz	all related things, other similar topics	They were talking about UFO's and all that jazz.
all the bells and whistles	a lot of extra features, lots of **goodies**, **loaded**	When Horst sold his business he bought a motorhome with all the bells and whistles.
all the livelong day	all day, lasting the whole day	Our canary sings all the livelong day—from dawn to dusk.
all the marbles	all the money, the top prize	How does it feel to be playing in the final—for all the marbles?
all the tea in China	(See **not for all the tea in China**)	
all things being equal	if things remain the same, if no surprises occur	All things being equal, we should sell all our bicycles by October.
all things to all people	satisfy everyone, **live up to**	Be yourself. Stop trying to be all things to all people.
all thumbs	clumsy, unable to hold it, fingers feel like thumbs	When I try to sew a button on my shirt, I'm all thumbs.
all walks of life	all occupations and lifestyles	As a salesperson, you will meet people from all walks of life.
all washed up	failed in business or career	Barry's all washed up. His business is bankrupt.
all wet	mistaken, do not know what you are talking about	You're all wet! You can't grow bananas in Saskatchewan.
all work and no play makes Jack a dull boy	do not work too long, take time for recreation, **take time to smell...**	When I picked up my overtime cheque, Karen reminded me that *All work and no play....*
all your eggs in one basket	depending on one plan or one investment, **hedge your bets**	If you invest all your money in one hotel, you'll have all your eggs in one basket.
all's fair in love and war	there are no rules to guide you in love or war, **that's life**	When your girlfriend leaves you for your best friend, remember, *All's fair in love and war.*
all's well that ends well	a happy ending is the most important thing, **the end justifies...**	Although we argued and fought, we are happy with the result. All's well that ends well!
all-out	all your effort, **go all-out**	We looked day and night for the lost girl. It was an all-out effort.

Idiom	Meaning	Example
an ace up your sleeve	an important card to play, an important fact to reveal	To survive, one needs an ace up one's sleeve—a special talent.
an airhead	a person who talks without thinking, a fool	Sally is such an airhead. She said that chicklets are baby chickens.
an apple a day keeps the doctor away	eat one apple each day for good health	Mom gave me an apple, saying, "An apple a day...."
an attitude	a negative personality, **some attitude**	If you don't show respect, they will think you have an attitude.
an axe to grind	a point to discuss or argue about	Jason had an axe to grind at the meeting—job security.
an earful	a lecture, a scolding, **a bawling out**	If Mom catches you smoking, you'll get an earful.
an easy mark	one who can easily be persuaded, **a soft touch**	Ask Charlie for a loan. He's an easy mark.
an even keel	good balance, stability	We need a steady manager, one who can keep an even keel.
an eye for an eye (a tooth for a tooth)	equal punishment or revenge	Canadian laws do not demand an eye for an eye.
an offer I couldn't refuse	an offer that contains a threat or force, a request that is a command	The border guards invited me to stay for further questioning—it was an offer I couldn't refuse.
an old hand at	a person with a lot of practice or experience	Tom's an old hand at cribbage. He's played since he was a boy.
an ounce of prevention is worth a pound of cure	prevent a problem so you don't have to solve it, **a stitch in time...**	Forest fires deserve an ounce of prevention: public education in campfire safety.
anal retentive	too concerned with detail, pedantic	Amy is anal retentive. She writes down everything the teacher says.
anchor you	make you feel stable or confident	When you have a crisis, your faith will anchor you.
and how	very much	The kids love pizza—and how!
and stuff	and other things or activities, et cetera	We were watchin' TV an' stuff, just hangin' out.
and that's that	that is final, that is the way it will be done	You will be home by 10 p.m., and that's that!

Idiom	Meaning	Example
and then some	with lots to spare, plus a few more	We invited everybody in town—and then some!
angels fear to tread	(See **where angels fear to tread**)	
another nail in your coffin	another cigarette; harmful substance	Every cigarette he smoked was another nail in his coffin.
ante up	put some money in the center of the table	As the dealer shuffled the cards, he said, "Ante up, boys."
any old thing	any word, any answer	When the teacher asks him a question, he says any old thing.
any way you slice it	(See **no matter how you slice it**)	
any word	any phone calls or letters, any reply	Any word from Dale? He should have called us by now.
anything goes	there are no rules; expect anything to happen	Anything goes during Stampede week. People do crazy things!
apple a day...	(See **an apple a day keeps the doctor away**)	
apple of his eye	(See **the apple of his eye**)	
armed to the teeth	prepared to fight or defend, having lots of evidence	By the time the trial began, the lawyer was armed to the teeth.
around the bend	crazy or insane, **off your rocker**	If I had to listen to that noise all the time, I'd go around the bend.
around the clock	twenty-four hours, **'round the clock**	Julie worked around the clock to finish her sewing project.
as a matter of fact	to state a fact, **in fact**, **to be perfectly honest**	The burrowing owl is a protected species. As a matter of fact, it's an endangered species.
as busy as a beaver	very busy, working steadily	When the teacher returned, the students were as busy as beavers.
as clean as a whistle	without any dirt or marks, smooth and clean	The hen squeezed, and out popped an egg as clean as a whistle.
as drunk as a skunk	very drunk, **polluted**, **sloshed**	You don't remember the party. You were as drunk as a skunk!
as far as I know	based on my knowledge, **to the best of my...**	As far as I know, the company will pay your travel expenses.
as if	unlikely, unbelievable	As if we'd leave for Banff without you. We'd never do that!

Idiom	Meaning	Example
as luck would have it	as luck is sometimes good and sometimes bad	By the time we arrived, as luck would have it, the fight was over.
as new	like new, **in mint condition**	For Sale: 1992 Mazda Miata, red, all options, low km, as new.
as poor as a church mouse	very poor, having little, **the wolf knocking...**	How can they refuse to help her? She's as poor as a church mouse.
as right as rain	(See **right as rain**)	
as scarce as hen's teeth	rare, uncommon, not many of them	Country doctors are as scarce as hen's teeth.
as the crow flies	the shortest distance between two places	The farm is about ten miles north-east of town, as the crow flies.
as useless as a fifth wheel	not useful, not needed, redundant, (four wheels are sufficient)	I sat there watching the four of them play bridge, and feeling as useless as a fifth wheel.
as useless as tits on a boar	not useful, not necessary, having no function	Our toenails are useless—as useless as tits on a boar.
ask for it	invite or deserve an attack	When you called him a thief, you asked for it. You made him mad.
asking price	a starting price, a price to begin negotiations	The asking price for the lot was $29,500. It sold for $28,000.
asleep at the switch	not alert, not watching, not **pay**ing **attention**	If you're asleep at the switch, you won't learn much in class.
ass [B]	buttocks, **backside**, **butt**	Those jeans fit you, but they're a little tight around the ass.
ass	fool, **dipstick**, **jerk**	Don't be an ass, Duddy. Stay in school and get your diploma.
ass into gear	moving, working, doing	After holidays, I'll get my ass into gear and paint the house.
ass over teakettle	falling over backwards, **head over heels**	The cowboy knocked him off his feet—ass over teakettle!
at a glance	with one look, a quick look	I could see at a glance that the car was unsafe. A wheel was loose.
at a good clip	fast, at a high speed	When you passed us you were going at a pretty good clip.

Idiom	Meaning	Example
at a loss for words	unable to think of a reply or something to say	When he asked why I wanted the vase, I was at a loss for words.
at a moment's notice	with little warning, **on short notice**	We may call you at a moment's notice—whenever we need help.
at all	in any way, **in the least**	"Are you sleepy?" "No. Not at all."
at bay	at a distance, away from you	The smoke keeps the mosquitoes at bay. They don't like smoke.
at fault	caused the problem, **to blame**	The judge will decide who's at fault—who caused the crash.
at first glance	when you first see it, when you notice it	At first glance, it looked like a cat—a large cat.
at first light	just before the sun rises, **at the crack of dawn**	At first light, the ducks would fly to the grainfields to feed.
at heart	with feeling for you, with you **in mind**	Believe me, she has your needs at heart. She cares about you.
at it again	doing it again, **back at it**	That dog is at it again—barking in the middle of the night.
at least	not very much, very little to ask	At least he could have phoned. He could have done that.
at liberty	free to speak or act, allowed to speak	Are you at liberty to tell us who won? Can you tell us?
at loggerheads	not agreeing, opposed to each other	They're at loggerheads over who owns the farm. They don't agree.
at loose ends	disorganized, unable to concentrate	I was at loose ends when the kids were fighting. I couldn't think.
at my wits' end	very tired and nervous, **at the end of my rope**	After a wedding and a funeral she was at her wits' end.
at once	at the same time, simultaneously	You can't do two things at once. You can eat or talk, but not both.
at once	now, immediately	Your mother said you should come in at once—immediately.
at peace	feeling peaceful, without worry	After talking about his problem he was at peace with himself.
at rest	stopped, not moving	Tie these ropes while the boat is at rest—before it moves.

Idiom	Meaning	Example
at sixes and sevens	not in agreement, arguing, **at loggerheads**	Parents and teachers are at sixes and sevens over sex education.
at stake	what you could lose or gain	If you're involved in a crime, your career may be at stake.
at the crack of dawn	at the first sign of light, **at first light**	At the crack of dawn he would rise, wash and go for a walk.
at the drop of a hat	without hesitation, quickly	He'll argue at the drop of a hat. He likes to argue.
at the end of my rope/ at the end of my tether	losing control of myself, **losing patience**	Babysitting five kids, I was at the end of my rope.
at the hands of	while competing against, when fighting	It was at the hands of his former student that he was defeated.
at the ripe old age	at a very old age; being unusually old	He could still play checkers at the ripe old age of ninety-eight.
at the top of her game	at her best, playing as well as she can	If Val's at the top of her game she can defeat Olga.
at the top of his voice	as loud as he can, shouting loudly	Ben called for help at the top of his voice. "Help!" he shouted.
at the wheel	driving a car, steering a car or truck	Who was at the wheel when the car went off the road?
at this point in time	now, at this time	At this point in time, ten cases of AIDS have been reported.
at will	freely, without restraint	He shared his feelings, speaking at will about his problems.
at your beck and call	serving you, doing everything for you	You don't have to be at his beck and call, doing whatever he asks.
at your fingertips	easy to find, ready to use	When I repair a car, I like to have all my tools at my fingertips.
attitude	(See **an attitude** and **some attitude**)	
away out of line	(See **way out of line**)	
away to the races	going without a problem, **smooth sailing**	When they approve our business loan, we'll be away to the races.
awesome	(See **totally awesome**)	
axe to grind	(See **an axe to grind**)	

Idiom	Meaning	Example

B

Idiom	Meaning	Example
babe	darling, honey, girlfriend	"Hi, babe. Want to sit with me?" "Sure, honey. I'd love to."
babe in arms	(See **a babe in arms**)	
baby blues	feeling sad when you are pregnant	After seven months, Karly had the baby blues. She was feeling sad.
baby boomer	a person born during the decade after World War II	Baby boomers will retire in the first decade of the 21st century.
back down	yield, not challenge, not **stand up to**	Ole won't back down from you. He's ready to fight.
back off	do not come closer, do not touch me	Back off, you animal! Don't touch me!
back on your feet	feeling better, recovered from an illness	When you're back on your feet, we want you to return to work.
back out	decide not to do it, **change your mind**	If you sign your name, you can't back out. You have to pay.
back teeth are floating	have to urinate, need to pee	Please watch for a rest room. My back teeth are floating.
back to square one	back to the first step, **start from scratch**	If you forget to do one of the steps, it's back to square one.
back to the drawing board	back to the beginning, **back to square one**	If this plan fails, it's back to the drawing board. We start again.
back to the grind	return to the job, go back to work	After New Year's, it's back to the grind—the old routine.
back up	go backwards, drive in reverse	I'll back up the truck so we can load it.
back you	support your decision, sign your application	His brother will back him if he needs financing.

Idiom	Meaning	Example
back yourself into a corner	put yourself in a bad position, have no escape	If you buy what you can't afford you back yourself into a corner.
backpack (business)	support, be the parent company	First, GM backpacked Saab. Then they bought the company.
backside	buttocks, **bum, buns**	When I was learning to skate, I fell a lot. My backside was sore!
backup	saving information on a computer disk	Don't forget to make a backup disk of all your computer files.
bad apple	bad one, rotten one	He's the bad apple in that group. He's always in trouble.
bad blood	bad feelings, a negative relationship	John and Fred are bitter enemies. There's bad blood between them.
bad breath	unpleasant smell from the mouth, **jungle mouth**	I've been eating garlic, so I may have bad breath.
bad date	a man who beats a prostitute, **john**	Viki had another bad date. A guy beat her and took her clothes.
bad news	troublemaker, someone who causes problems	Don't hire him. Everybody says he's bad news.
bad taste in my mouth	(See **a bad taste in my mouth**)	
badmouth	criticize, say bad things about, **put down**	Don't badmouth employers. Don't criticize your references.
bafflegab	confusing statements, jargon, political language	There was a lot of bafflegab in the speech, a lot of nonsense.
bag and baggage	everything you own, all of one's possessions	The next day, he moved into her apartment—bag and baggage.
bag lady	a lady who looks for food and bottles in the streets	Behind the restaurant, a bag lady was digging in the garbage cans.
bag of tricks	skills, methods, plans; devices to entertain	You need a large bag of tricks to teach the Grade 8 class.
bag some rays	sit or lie in the sunshine, have a sun bath	While you're swimming, I'm going to bag some rays.
bah	nonsense, it is not true	Bah! There is no tooth fairy!
bail me out	help me solve a problem, pay to get me out of jail	If they arrest me, will you bail me out—pay the bail money?

Idiom	Meaning	Example
bail out	quit, leave a project	Tom bailed out when Lan became Project Manager.
balance of power	(See **the balance of power**)	
ball her [B]	have sex with her, **lay** her	"Hey, Ted. Did you ball her?" "No. All you think about is sex!"
ball's in your court	(See **the ball's in your court**)	
ball-park figure	(See **a ball-park figure**)	
ballistic	(See **go ballistic**)	
baloney	false statements, **bull, bunk, hogwash**	Most of what the speaker said is a lot of baloney—untrue.
bam	a word to describe a hit or collision, **pow**	The car rolled down the hill and into the wall—bam!
bananas	very excited, nearly crazy	When we won the cup, the crowd went bananas.
bang [B]	have sex with, **lay**	"Did you bang her, Ted?" "If I did, I wouldn't tell you."
bang for your buck	fun for your money, value for your dollar	You get more bang for your buck at garage sales. They're fun!
bang on	exactly right, very true, correct, **spot on**	Your answer to Question 3 was bang on. It was correct.
bank on	depend on, **count on**	We were banking on more sales to pay for our marketing costs.
bar fly	(See **a bar fly**)	
bar hop	drink at many bars in one evening, **pub crawl**	Our wives were out late last night. They were bar hopping.
bar none	including all products or people, no exceptions	Apex is the best detergent, bar none.
bar star	(See **a bar star**)	
bare bones	only the necessary things, no extras, **stripped**	ACTION CLEAN is a bare-bones operation—a family business.
bare your soul	tell the public about your private experiences	To write a good novel, you may have to bare your soul.
bare-faced lie	(See **a bare-faced lie**)	

Idiom	Meaning	Example
barf	vomit, puke, **hork**, **throw up**	If I eat another hotdog, I'll barf. I'll be sick.
bark is worse than his bite	he sounds angry but he is not; do not be afraid of him	Baxter sounds mad, but his bark is worse than his bite.
bark up the wrong tree	look in the wrong place, do not expect it	If you expect money from him, you're barking up the wrong tree.
barnburner	(See **a barnburner**)	
bash	a wild party, a party where people are drunk and noisy	"Did you go to Tina's party?" "Ya. It was a noisy bash."
basket case	(See **a basket case**)	
bat a thousand	hit every time at bat, win every competition	I've had two interviews and two offers. I'm batting a thousand!
bat an eye	flinch or blink, show a sign of guilt or shame	When they asked him about the crime, he didn't bat an eye. His expression didn't change.
bat five hundred	hit half the times at bat, win half the competitions	If you solve five problems out of ten, you're batting five hundred.
bat her eyes	blink the eyes, blink in a sexy way	Verna just stood there batting her eyes, trying to look sexy.
bated breath	(See **with bated breath**)	
battleaxe	cranky woman, **bitch**	Marlene—that old battleaxe— is spreading lies about me.
batty	(See **drive me batty**)	
bawl me out	tell me I have been bad, scold me	If I fail math, Dad will bawl me out. He'll give me a lecture.
be my guest	have this chair, have that drink, **help yourself**	Be my guest. Sit here. I can find another chair.
be my undoing	be the cause of my failure; my **Achilles' heel**	Credit cards may be my undoing. My VISA balance is over $5000!
be off	leave, go, **off with you**	Be off, my dear, or you'll be late for work.
be there	be ready, be alert, **up for it**	The captain of the hockey team shouted to his mates, "Be there, guys! We have to win this game."

Idiom	Meaning	Example
be there for me	help me when I need it, be supportive, **stand by me**	"Will you be there for me?" she asked. "I need your support."
be there or be square	if you do not come we will think you are **square**	We're having a party at 7 on Saturday. Be there or be square!
be yourself	be natural, behave normally	Don't worry about what to say at the party. Just be yourself.
be-all, end-all	trying to be too great, **world beater**	The new manager thinks he's the greatest—the be-all, end-all.
bean pole	tall and thin, **string bean**	Carl is a bean pole—tall and skinny—just like his father.
bear down	try harder, **bite the bullet**	If you bear down a little, you can graduate this year.
bear the brunt	accept the most blame or responsibility	When we got in trouble, Ed bore the brunt of the blame.
beat a dead horse	continue to ask or try when there is no hope	They won't refund your money. You're beating a dead horse.
beat a hasty retreat	run away from, leave quickly	When the boys heard the siren they beat a hasty retreat.
beat around the bush	talk without telling the main point	Politicians often beat around the bush. They talk a lot but say little.
beat it	go, **get lost**	Beat it, kid! Get going! Leave!
beat the pants off	defeat by a large score, **blow you away**	Ho plays table tennis very well; she'll beat the pants off you.
beat the rap	have the charges removed or dropped, **get off**	Every time the burglar was caught he was able to beat the rap.
beat up	hit and injure, defeat badly	She cared for him when he got beat up, trying to case his pain.
beat up on	hit and injure, defeat in a fight	"Why does he beat up on people?" "Because his dad beat up on him."
beat your head against a stone wall	try an impossible task, work on a futile project	Preventing war is like beating your head against a stone wall.
beat your time	take away your girlfriend or boyfriend	I can't believe that your *friend* would beat your time.
beater	a car that is in poor condition, **clunker**	Why does he drive that old beater? He could buy a new car.

Idiom	Meaning	Example
beauty is in the eye of the beholder	each person has a different idea of what is beautiful, **one man's garbage...**	To him, the statue is elegant; to me, it's ugly. Beauty is in the eye of the beholder!
beauty is only skin deep	do not judge a person by physical features, **you can't tell a book...**	If you want to date a beauty queen, remember that beauty is only skin deep.
beck and call	(See **at your beck and call**)	
become of	happen to, **end up**	What became of Ko after he moved? How's he doing?
becomes you	looks good on you, is right for you, **suits you**	That perfume becomes you. It smells good on you.
bed down	lie down and sleep, find a place to sleep	After grazing in the valley, the deer will bed down on the hill.
beef it up	add more bulk, increase the size	"Does this doll look like Santa?" "Yes, if you beef it up a little."
beeline	(See **make a beeline**)	
been around	experienced, not naive, **wasn't born yesterday**	Margo's been around; she can work with the convicts.
been had	cheated, swindled, **taken in**	If he paid a hundred dollars for that radio, he's been had.
before you can say Jack Robinson	very quickly, **in a split second**, **in no time**	Before you could say Jack Robinson, the ghost was gone!
beg off	ask to be excused from duty, **get out of** a task	Some people volunteer to work and then they beg off.
beg to differ	have a different opinion, disagree with	When I stated the cause of the loss, he said, "I beg to differ."
beg your pardon	excuse me, please do not be offended	I beg your pardon, but I am using this phone booth.
beg your pardon?	what did you say? will you repeat what you said?	Beg your pardon? Did you say you are Paul Newman?
beggars can't be choosers	people who receive free things should not expect the best	When they complained about the shabby coats, he said, "Beggars can't be choosers."
behind bars	in jail, in prison, **in the slammer**	Behind bars, she didn't have much of a social life.

Idiom	Meaning	Example
behind the eight ball	behind schedule, not coping very well, not **up to par**	I'm behind the eight ball in my computer course. I need to study and practise.
behind the scenes	out of sight, unnoticed, **unsung hero**	This organization has many people who work behind the scenes helping us to succeed.
behind your back	where you cannot see, when you are not here	He says nice things to you, but criticizes you behind your back.
being there	being where good things happen, being in the right place at the right time	Caleb seems to succeed by just being there. Good things happen to him wherever he is.
believe my ears	(See **can't believe my ears**)	
believe my eyes	(See **can't believe my eyes**)	
bells and whistles	(See **all the bells and whistles**)	
belly up	not operating, bankrupt, **tits up**	Four car dealers went belly up during the recession.
belly up to the bar	sit close to the bar, find a chair at the bar	Belly up to the bar, boys. I'd like to buy you a drink.
bellyache	complain, whine	Don't bellyache about the referee. Just play your best.
below the poverty line	not earning enough to survive, very poor, **as poor as a church mouse**	If husband and wife are earning minimum wage, they're living below the poverty line.
belt you	hit you, punch you	I should belt you for saying that my sister looks like a dog.
bend over backwards	do anything to help, try to please, **go the extra mile**	They'll bend over backwards to find a room for you. They give excellent service.
bend the rules	change the rules to help, **look the other way**	Ed won't accept late reports. He won't bend the rules.
bend your ear	ask you to listen, **buttonhole you**	Carl, can I bend your ear for a minute? I have some news.
bend your elbow	drink beer or liquor, **tip a few**	Your eyes look red and tired. Bend your elbow last night?
benefit of the doubt	(See **the benefit of the doubt**)	

Idiom	Meaning	Example
beside myself	very upset, very worried, **at loose ends**	She was beside herself with grief when her sister died.
beside the point	off topic, not related, irrelevant	The brand of cigarette is beside the point. Smoking is the issue.
best foot forward	(See **put your best foot forward**)	
best interests at heart	thinking of a person's needs, **in mind**	When I give low grades, I still have your best interests at heart.
best laid plans	(See **the best laid plans**)	
best of both worlds	(See **the best of both worlds**)	
bet on	place a bet, gamble	I bet on the bay mare, and she won! I bet $20 on her.
bet on a lame rooster	bet on a loser, **fall for that**	If you vote for that guy, you're betting on a lame rooster.
bet you dollars to donuts	I will bet dollars, you bet donuts; **give you odds**	Ben is the fastest runner. I'll bet you dollars to donuts he wins.
better half	spouse, wife or husband	Bring your better half when you visit us. We'd like to meet her.
better late than never	it is better to arrive late than not to arrive	"You're an hour late," he said. "Better late than never," I replied.
better off	in better conditions: healthier or wealthier etc.	Are you better off renting an apartment than buying a house?
better than a kick in the ass [B]	better than punishment, not as bad as it could be, **don't knock it**	When I told him we had won $10 in the Lotto, he said, "It's better than a kick in the ass."
better the devil you know...	a new devil could be worse than the old devil	"Should we fire the coach?" "No—better the devil we know than the one we don't."
better to have loved...	(See **it is better to have loved and lost...**)	
between a rock and a hard place	in a difficult position, making a difficult choice, **Sophie's choice**	If I told the truth, I would lose my friend. I was between a rock and a hard place.
between sixes and sevens	(See **at sixes and sevens**)	
between the devil and the deep blue sea	in a difficult position, no place to go, **between a rock...**, **Sophie's choice**	If he ran, they would shoot him; if he stayed in the shop, the gas would kill him. He was between the devil and the deep blue sea.

Idiom	Meaning	Example
betwixt and between	not able to choose one or the other, ambivalent	Which should I choose—PC or Mac? I'm betwixt and between.
bevy of beauties	a group of beautiful women, a few **lovelies**	Mr. Gable returned to Hollywood and his bevy of beauties.
beyond help	lost, cannot be saved	Some addicts are beyond help. They don't want to be helped.
beyond repair	ruined, cannot be repaired, **a lost cause**	That copier is wrecked. It's beyond repair.
beyond the call of duty	(See **above and beyond the call of duty**)	
biff/biffy	washroom, bathroom, **the can, the john, the loo**	"Is there a biffy on the bus?" "Yes. There, at the back."
Big Apple	(See **The Big Apple**)	
big boys	powerful men in business, moguls, **big shots**	If you want to do business with the big boys, you need money.
big bucks	a lot of money, a high price	You'll pay big bucks to rent an apartment near the university.
big deal	important event, major happening	A small fire is a big deal because it can cause a lot of damage.
Bigfoot	a large ape-man living in the forests of western N. America; **Sasquatch**	Gary told me he saw Bigfoot's tracks in the sand beside the Kootenay River.
big mouth	someone who talks too loud, **loud mouth**	Every crowd has a big mouth— some guy who yells at the cops.
big picture	(See **the big picture**)	
big-rig	(See **a big-rig**)	
big shot	rich or important person, **VIP, big boys**	Randy's a big shot in the movie industry. He owns four studios.
big time	a lot, very much, **heavy duty**	You've helped me so much. I owe you big time.
big wheel	(See **a big wheel**)	
big wigs	important persons: judges, presidents etc., **VIP**	We've asked the big wigs to change their decision.
bigger fish to fry	more important people to meet or do business with	Don't bother fighting with him. You've got bigger fish to fry.

Idiom	Meaning	Example
bigger than life	heroic: stronger, wiser, uglier; **larger than life**	The characters in most novels seem to be bigger than life.
bigger they are...	(See **the bigger they are...**)	
bimbo	foolish girl, **an airhead**	Don't call any girl a bimbo, please.
birdbrain	a person with a tiny brain, **dumbo**	Hey, birdbrain. Why are you throwing money in the river?
birder	a bird watcher, one whose hobby is watching birds	Some birders were looking at an oriole in a poplar tree.
birds of a feather flock together	people with similar feelings and attitudes	Art and Don are birds of a feather. They like cars and football.
birthday suit	naked, nude, **in the buff**	"Do you wear pyjamas in bed?" "No. Just my birthday suit."
bit by bit	doing a small amount each time, **little by little**	Bit by bit, they rebuilt a church that was destroyed by bombs.
bit off	(See **a bit off**)	
bitch	complain, **grouse**	He tells me I'm always bitching, but I don't complain very much.
bitch [B]	(See **a bitch**)	
bite me [B]	I have no respect for you, **kiss off, blow me**	"Bite me! Take your list of whores and live with them!"
bite off more than you can chew	begin more tasks than you can complete	When I took the night class, I bit off more than I could chew.
bite the bullet	try harder, be tougher	Bite the bullet during exam week. Don't party; just study.
bite the dust	die, quit, lose, **kick the bucket**	Pete was 98 when he bit the dust. He lived for nearly a century.
bite the hand that feeds you	be unkind to the one who cares for you or pays you	If you criticize your employer, you bite the hand that feeds you.
bite your tongue	do not say that, you should not have said that	When I mention Dad's temper Mom says, "Bite your tongue."
biter (curling)	a rock that is touching the twelve-foot circle	The Heidt rink is lying four— one is a biter.

Idiom	Meaning	Example
bits and pieces	small pieces, **odds and ends**	Jack built our cabin with bits and pieces—leftover materials.
bitten by the same bug	have the same interest or hobby	My cousin and I were bitten by the same bug. We collect coins.
bitter end	(See **the bitter end**)	
blab	tell everybody, tell secrets	I told you I like Kevin, and you blabbed it to everybody.
blabbermouth	a person who tells everything, **loud mouth**	Sharon—that blabbermouth! She told the whole class I love Bill.
black eye	an eye injury that causes the skin to turn black	"How'd you get the black eye?" "Fighting—in a hockey game."
Black Friday	the day the stock market crashed (failed) in 1929	In the 1980s, there were days to remind us of Black Friday.
black mark	(See **a black mark**)	
black sheep	the bad one, the one who does bad things	He's the black sheep in that family—always in trouble.
black-listed	excluded, not be invited, not allowed to join	Gore was black-listed because he led the demonstration.
blast	(See **a blast**)	
blast you	scold you, yell at you	Ms. Zank blasted me for using her computer. She was angry.
blasted	**dad-blamed, darn, doggone**	Where's the blasted hammer? It's never here when I need it!
blasted	drunk, **loaded, plastered**	On her 40th birthday, she went to the bar and got blasted.
bleeding heart	one who begs for sympathy for victims, **have a soft spot...**	Hector is a bleeding heart for wolves. "Save the wolves," he tells people in his speeches.
blessing in disguise	(See **a blessing in disguise**)	
blind date	going out with a boy or girl you have not met	Kate met Jeff on a blind date. They got married a year later.
blind leading the blind	(See **the blind leading the blind**)	
blood from a stone	(See **get blood from a stone**)	

Idiom	Meaning	Example
blood is thicker than water	blood relationships are stronger than a marriage ceremony	When my wife supported her dad in a fight with me, I said, "So blood *is* thicker than water."
blood is up	excited, angry, ready to fight	Kerry is friendly, but when his blood is up, he's dangerous.
blood money	money paid to the relative of a murdered person, **dirty money**	The widow refused to take blood money from the men who murdered her husband.
bloody well	very truly, damn well	He bloody well knows my name because I bloody well told him.
blotto	exhausted, **bushed**	After studying for twelve hours, she was blotto—very tired.
blow a bundle	spend a lot of money, lose a lot of money gambling	When Al went to Vegas, he blew a bundle—he lost a lot of money.
blow a kiss	kiss your hand and blow across it, **throw a kiss**	Taea can blow a kiss, and she's only eighteen months old!
blow it	cause a big mistake, ruin it, **screw up**	Karen won't blow it this time. She'll skate a perfect program.
blow it out of proportion	exaggerate it, make it bigger than it should be	When Gretzky was traded, the media blew it out of proportion.
blow it up (photo)	enlarge it, magnify it	If you want to see details in the photo, blow it up.
blow job [B]	(See **a blow job**)	
blow me [B]	you are worth nothing, kiss my ass, **fuck off**	"You want me to support you by stealing? Blow me!"
blow me down	I am very surprised, I do not believe it	Well, blow me down, Olive. You can cook spinach, too!
blow me over	it is unbelievable; **far out**	He's over 50? Well, blow me over!
blow my cover	reveal my true identity, reveal my hiding place	With a false passport, I can enter Bali, if nobody blows my cover.
blow sky high	upset a lot of people, cause a scandal or riot	This government will blow sky high if people hear these tapes.
blow snakes (music)	play great jazz, improvise creatively	I went to hear jazz at the club, and Guido was blowing snakes.

Idiom	Meaning	Example
blow the lid off	reveal a story, tell some news, **break a story**	When the defendant confessed, it blew the lid off the murder trial.
blow the whistle	tell the teacher or the police, **squeal**	Jimmy knows we stole the keys, but he won't blow the whistle.
blow them away	defeat them badly, **kick butt**	The Russians blew them away in the first game of the series.
blow this joint	leave this building, **quit this place**	I'm sick of playing billiards. Let's blow this joint.
blow this popsicle stand	leave this place, **quit this place**	What a boring town! Let's blow this popsicle stand!
blow to kingdom come	explode and destroy, **blow up**	There's enough gas in the well to blow us kingdom come!
blow up	explode using a bomb or dynamite	They plan to blow up that old building because it's unsafe.
blow up	become angry, **lose your temper**	If you criticize Al, he'll blow up. He's very sensitive.
blow you away	defeat you easily, **beat the pants off**	You're going to play chess with Boris? He'll blow you away.
blow you out of the water	defeat you, humiliate you	If you challenge his leadership, he'll blow you out of the water.
blow your lid/stack/top	become very angry, shout, **lose your cool**	Don't blow your stack in front of the kids. It's a bad example.
blow your mind	amaze you, astound you, shock you	Watching films of the holocaust will blow your mind.
blow your stones [B]	ejaculate, **come**	There's more to it than blowing your stones. Sex is an art form.
blow your wad	spend all your money, **blow a bundle**	He blew his wad on some hand-made boots. They cost $700!
blowout	(See **a blowout**)	
blue	sad, depressed, **down, low**	"Are you blue, Dear?" "Yes. Jack left me."
blue in the face	weakened, tired after trying many times	I called that dog until I'm blue in the face. He won't come in.
blue-collar worker	someone who works at a trade, e.g., a plumber	The blue-collar workers will vote for Ed. He's a tradesman.

Idiom	Meaning	Example
blurt out	say without thinking, reply quickly	"I did it!" the boy blurted out, and he began to cry.
boarding (hockey)	checking into the boards, **chairman of the boards**	Boarding causes serious injuries to hockey players.
Bob's your uncle	no problem as "Bob," a powerful friend or relative, will do it or have it done	When I asked her to give your application to the president, she said, "Bob's your uncle!"
body language	body movements that show feelings	Your body language tells me that you're tense. Please relax.
boggle your mind	confuse you, **make your head spin**	These numbers boggle my mind. I don't understand them.
boiling mad	very angry, very upset, **hopping mad**	By the time the car started, Emil was boiling mad.
bolt from the blue	(See **like a bolt from the blue**)	
bomb out	fail, not succeed	Most engineers say the electric car is a failure. It bombed out.
bombed	drunk, **hammered**, **sloshed to the gills**	Fay was bombed before she got to the party. She was drunk.
bone dry	very dry, as dry as an old bone	Someone had drained the pool. It was bone dry.
bone of contention	point of disagreement, controversial point	Job security is the bone of contention in our discussions.
bone to pick	(See **a bone to pick with you**)	
bone up on	study, learn practise	I have to bone up on my French if we're going to Paris.
bonkers	crazy, insane, **nuts**, **wacko**	If you watch professional wrestling you must be bonkers!
booboo	(See **make a booboo**)	
boobs [B]	breasts, tits	Okay, she has lovely boobs. What about her personality?
boogie	go, walk, drive	Let's boogie on down to the store and rent a video.
book worm	one who reads a lot, **geek**	Sarah is quite a book worm. She loves to read history books.

Idiom	Meaning	Example
booked/booked up	no more space or rooms, no vacancy	The Royal Hotel is booked up. Every room is reserved.
boom box	portable radio, **ghetto blaster**	We can have music at the beach if you bring your boom box.
boot it	drive fast, **highball it, pedal to the metal**	If you boot it, Betty won't ride with you. She hates going fast.
boot up	start or switch on a computer	Wait until I boot up the Mac. Then we can print your letter.
booze	liquor, **hooch, moonshine**	I think Gus has been drinking. His breath smells of booze.
boozing buddies	friends who drink liquor and party together	In those days, Billy and I were boozin' buddies—pals.
born with a silver spoon in his mouth	born into a rich family, accustomed to wealth	Jason won't look for a job; he was born with a silver spoon....
bosom buddy	close friends, friends who grew up together	Don't criticize Brad, eh. He's my bosom buddy.
botch it	ruin it, do it wrong, **blow it**	When you bake bread for the first time, it's easy to botch it.
bottle drive	going to houses asking for pop and liquor bottles	The bottle drive was a success. The girls earned $350.
bottle man	a man who finds bottles in garbage cans or dumpsters	The bottle man walked down the alley pushing a cart full of junk.
bottle up	not talk about, keep in your mind	Don't keep all those feelings bottled up inside you. Talk!
bottom fell out	(See **the bottom fell out**)	
bottom line	the final number, the conclusion	The bottom line is this: we can't afford to expand.
bottom out	go down to the bottom, arrive at the low point	The recession will bottom out by the end of the year.
bottom rung	the first step, the lowest position	Jerry, my boy, in this company you start at the bottom rung.
bottoms up	finish your drinks, drink the remainder	"Bottoms up," said his friend. "It's time to go."
bounce back	recover from failure or sickness, try again	Lana has the flu, but she bounces back quickly.

Idiom	Meaning	Example
bow out	resign so someone else can serve, **step down**	When Dad sees that I can manage the firm, he will bow out.
bowl me over	surprise me, **blow me down**	Well, bowl me over! You've done your homework!
boy, oh boy	wow, oh man, **holy cow**	Boy, oh boy! I'm glad to see you!
boys will be boys	all boys are the same; boys are rough and noisy, **a chip off the old...**	When Steve came home with his shirt torn and nose bleeding, his father said, "Boys will be boys."
brain	(See **what a brain**)	
brain drain	emigration of intelligent people	If Canada's best professors move away, it's called a brain drain.
brain is fried	brain is very tired or ruined by drug abuse	After writing six exams, my brain was fried—too much studying!
brain storm	think of ideas together, **think tank**	Our family decided to brain storm the problem of wasting food.
branch office	an office in another location or city	Please contact our branch office in your town or city.
branch out	open a second office/store, expand a company	Business is very good. It may be time for us to branch out.
brand new/ brand spanking new	not used **at all**, just off the assembly line	Imagine a brand new Mercedes in an accident. What a shame!
bread	money, cash, **dough**	Hey, man, we need more bread if we're gonna buy cigarettes.
bread and butter	the main product, the source of profit	We sell a variety of parts, but the oil filter is our bread and butter.
breadbasket	stomach, belly	The ball hit him just below his chest—right in the breadbasket.
breadbasket	an area that produces grain, **wheatbelt**	Saskatchewan is a major wheat producer: Canada's breadbasket.
break a habit	stop doing a daily activity: drinking coffee, smoking	Laurie can't seem to break her habit of writing on her hands.
break a leg	good luck, have a good performance	"Break a leg!" she whispered as he walked on the stage.
break a promise	not do as you promised, **go back on** your word	Trudy never breaks a promise. She is very dependable.

Idiom	Meaning	Example
break a spell	cause a spell to stop, not be **under a spell**	I was captivated by her until she smoked. That broke the spell.
break a story	be first to tell a story, be first to tell some news	*The London Times* broke the story of Charles's confessions.
break a sweat	begin to sweat or perspire, **work up a sweat**	For exercise to be beneficial, the athlete must break a sweat.
break and enter	break a lock or window to enter illegally, B&E	They were charged with break and enter. They stole some cash.
break away	move away, go away from, stop doing or using	She tried to break away when the cult leader asked for her savings.
break curfew	stay out later than the rules allow	If you break curfew, the coach will remind you of the rules.
break down	fail, not operate, **out of order**	If that copier breaks down again I'm going to give it away.
break in	operate or drive slowly when it is new	When I bought my first new car, Dad said to break it in carefully.
break into	break a door or window to enter, **break and enter**	I couldn't believe that my son would break into a store.
break off	tell a friend that you wish to stop seeing him	She wonders if she should break off her relationship with Liam.
break out	escape, get away, **bust out**	He was shot trying to break out of prison—trying to escape.
break out	happen suddenly, erupt	A riot will break out if you don't talk to the strikers.
break out in a rash	have a rash appear on your skin	When the temperature goes over 30°, baby breaks out in a rash.
break the bank	spend all savings, leave no balance	One more expense this month will break the bank.
break the ice	relieve the tension, **put you at ease**	Andy likes to tell a joke to break the ice—to help everybody relax.
break the law/rules	not obey the law, commit a crime	If you rob a store, you are breaking the law.
break the record	do better than the previous record	The coach believes Bev can break the record in long jump.
break the silence	talk about a secret, tell people the truth	When he accused us of the crime, my brother broke the silence.

41

Idiom	Meaning	Example
break up	not date anymore, not be lovers anymore	Lan and Chan broke up last night. They had a bad quarrel.
break your fall	prevent serious injury when you fall	He fell from the roof, but a tree helped to break his fall.
break your heart	cause you to feel very sad and lonely	Marilyn broke my heart. She left me for a younger man.
breakdown	sudden health failure, **fall apart**	After his breakdown, he found an occupation with less stress.
breath of fresh air	(See **a breath of fresh air**)	
breath of wind	(See **a breath of wind**)	
breathe a sigh of relief	feel relieved after a time of worry	When we saw the children were safe, we breathed a sigh of relief.
breathe down my neck	watch everything I do, follow me as I work	It's difficult to work with him breathing down my neck.
brick	(See **a brick**)	
bridge the gap	help people communicate, mediate	When the staff and the manager fight, I try to bridge the gap.
bright	intelligent, brainy, **sharp**	I left the water running. That wasn't a very bright thing to do.
bright eyed and bushy tailed	frisky, lively, full of life	Perry is bright eyed and bushy tailed tonight. He looks rested.
bring an end to	(See **put an end to**)	
bring home the bacon	bring home a paycheque, support a family	Stan is disabled, so Louise brings home the bacon.
bring it off	manage it successfully, **carry it off**	Don't worry about the project. Mr. Ho can bring it off.
bring the house down	cause a lot of cheering or applause or laughter	If Kurt skates well in Calgary he'll bring the house down.
bring to a close	conclude, finish, **wrap up**	Now, to bring my presentation to a close, I'll tell you a story.
bring up	introduce, begin to talk about	Please bring up that point at the meeting. We can discuss it then.
bring up	vomit, puke	Did the baby bring up his breakfast? Let me wipe it up.

Idiom	Meaning	Example
bring you up short	cause you to stop and think, rebuke you	When I began to criticize Jan, Mother brought me up short.
broad	girl, woman, **chick**, **dame**, lovelies	Why do guys go downtown? They're lookin' for broads!
broad daylight	(See **in broad daylight**)	
broke	(See **flat broke**)	
broken dreams	plans that did not work, hopes that died	Their divorce will mean broken dreams for both of them.
brouhaha	shouting and fighting, melee, **Donnybrook**	After the dance, there was a brouhaha in the schoolyard.
brown nose [B]	try to please the manager, **suck up to**	Some guys brown nose their way to success. But is it success?
browned off	unhappy, a little bit angry, **ticked off**	Tran was browned off because we were late. She didn't like that.
brownie points	points for doing extra work for the manager	Bruno earns brownie points by offering to help the manager.
brush cut	short, level haircut— like a brush on top	Your brush cut looks great— nice and flat on top.
brush it off	not let it bother you, not be concerned	When Erik criticizes my family, I just brush it off and walk away.
brush up on	review, relearn or practise; **bone up on**	The teacher said I should brush up on my spelling—try to improve.
brush with the law	an illegal act, a minor crime	Judd told me about his brush with the law—a shoplifting charge.
brush-off	(See **give him the brush-off**)	
buck	dollar, **greenback**, **loonie**	When I earn some bucks, I'm going to buy a stereo.
buck up	be strong, be positive	Buck up, my friend. You will soon be finished with exams.
buckle down	work harder, try harder, **bite the bullet**	Next term I'm going to buckle down and get good grades.
buckle under	quit, lose, not try, **give up**	We're losing, but we won't buckle under. We won't quit.

Idiom	Meaning	Example
buckle up	fasten your seat belt, buckle your seat belt	Buckle up. Dad won't drive away until we fasten our seat belts.
budding genius	(See **a budding genius**)	
buffalo	frighten, bluff, intimidate	The director shouts a lot, but don't let him buffalo you.
bug (someone)	bother, irritate, **get to me**	That scraping noise bugs me. It's quite annoying.
build a better mousetrap	improve a common product	If you're not an inventor, you try to build a better mousetrap.
build up	increase, raise	Talking with Rudy will build up your confidence. He's positive.
built like a brick shithouse [B]	have a strong body, have a sturdy build	Tyronne plays football. He's built like a brick shithouse.
bull/bullshit/BS [B]	a story that is not all true, **balderdash**	His explanation is a lot of bull. Don't believe it.
bull in a China shop	(See **a bull in a China shop**)	
bully for you	you were lucky, **good for you**	When I beat Ed at cribbage, he says, "Bully for you!"
bum	buttocks, **backside**, **butt, rear end**	"Why did she slap your face?" "Because I pinched her bum."
bum rap	(See **a bum rap**)	
bum's rush	(See **the bum's rush**)	
bummer	(See **a bummer**)	
bump and grind (hockey)	bump other players and work to get the puck	To win hockey games we need players who bump and grind.
bump and grind	walk or dance in a sexy way	A seminude dancer was bumping and grinding under red lights.
bump into	meet by chance, **run into**	Do you know who I bumped into yesterday? Larry Mason.
bumper to bumper	a lane of vehicles with the bumpers nearly touching	Traffic on Memorial Drive was bumper to bumper at 4:30 today.
bun in the oven	(See **a bun in the oven**)	
bundle	(See **make a bundle**)	

Idiom	Meaning	Example
bundle of nerves	(See **a bundle of nerves**)	
bundle up	dress warmly, put on winter clothes, **rug up**	Be sure to bundle up if you go skating on the lake. It's cold!
bunk	false statements, rumors, **baloney, bull**	They claim that computers can think, but that's a lot of bunk!
buns	buttocks, **bum**	Tony said Rita has great buns.
burn a hole in your pocket	feel that you have to spend your money	If money burns a hole in your pocket, invest it.
burn out	use too much emotional energy, **breakdown**	Working too hard can cause a person to burn out.
burn the midnight oil	work or study very late at night	To become a doctor, you have to burn the midnight oil.
burn up	become angry, **lose your cool**	The coach was burned up when I got a penalty for holding.
burn your ass [B]	bother you, irritate you, **bug** you	You know what burns my ass? Doing my income tax.
burn your bridges	resign without notice, leave no way to return	He can't return to the company. He's burned his bridges.
burned	convicted or punished while involved in crime	Tony got burned when he was a drug dealer. He went to jail.
burning question	(See **the burning question**)	
bury the hatchet	stop arguing or fighting, **throw down your arms**	When will the English and the French bury the hatchet?
bush telegraph	street gossip, **through the grapevine**	Arne gets the news through the bush telegraph. People tell him.
bushed	very tired, **worn out**	After caring for five kids all day, Mom's bushed. She's exhausted.
bushwhack	stop you and rob you, **jump**, **mugged**	When he stopped to camp by the stream, two guys bushwhacked him—stole his money and horse.
business as usual	everything is normal, nothing has changed	The morning after the holdup, it was business as usual at the bank.
bust my butt	work very hard, **work my fingers to the bone**	She busts her butt to earn a good wage, and he spends it.

Idiom	Meaning	Example
bust out	escape, get away, **break out**	Hey, man. I can bust out of here if you have a rope.
busted	charged by the police, arrested	Shane got busted for trafficking. He sold cocaine to some kids.
busy as a beaver	(See **as busy as a beaver**)	
but good	completely, thoroughly, **and how**	If somebody hurts her, she'll get revenge, but good!
butt	buttocks, **bum, backside**	If you tell anybody that I like her, I'll kick your butt.
butt in	intrude, interrupt	When a salesman butts in, tell him to butt out.
butt of the joke	(See **the butt of the joke**)	
butt out	go away, **beat it, get lost**	We asked him to butt out so we could have a private talk.
butter fingers	unable to catch or hold, **cement hands**	When Anna dropped the ball, Shelly said, "Butter fingers!"
butter up	be nice to, **suck up to**	Butter him up before you ask to borrow his car.
butter wouldn't melt in his mouth	he is very calm and clear, he is a **smooth talker**	When he's talking to voters, butter wouldn't melt in his mouth.
button your lip	do not tell anyone, **on the QT**	Button your lip about the speeding ticket. Don't tell Dad.
buttonhole you	stop you and talk to you, **corner you** and bore you	At the meeting, Al buttonholed me and asked me to vote Reform.
buy a round	buy a drink for everyone at the table, **this one is on me**	When Gina was born, I bought a round for the team. Every player had a drink to honor our baby.
buy into	believe and support, agree to support, **come onside**	He will buy into our plan if the money goes to needy children.
buy out	buy a business and all the inventory	We knew his business was in debt, so we offered to buy him out.
buy that	believe that, **eat that**	He says he went to see his friends at the park. I can buy that.
buy the farm	die, **kick the bucket, pass away**	"Where's Henry?" "Oh, he bought the farm years ago—died of cancer, eh."

Idiom	Meaning	Example
buy time	request time to plan, ask for extra time	If we can just buy a little time, maybe the price will go down.
buy up	buy all of a product or all the shares in a company	At closing time, Abe comes in and buys up the last shares.
buzz off	go away, **beat it, get lost**	Next time he asks to borrow something, tell him to buzz off.
buzzed	slightly intoxicated, **tipsy**	Jane got buzzed on fermented coconut juice. She was happy!
buzzword	new word or expression, the latest jargon	*E-commerce, global village*—these were buzzwords of the 1990s.
by a country mile	by a long distance, by a wide margin	Black Beauty won the race by a country mile. She was far ahead.
by a long shot	(See **not by a long shot**)	
by all means	yes, please do it	By all means, come to the Learning Skills Center.
by and large	mostly, mainly, most of the time	By and large, chocolate is the favorite flavor.
by any means	any way or method, by doing any job	He survived by any means when he first came to Canada.
by any stretch...	(See **not by any stretch of the imagination**)	
by cracky	you listen to what I say, this is the truth, **by gosh**	This is serious, by cracky! We're lost and we have no water!
by dint of	as a result of, because of	By dint of her efforts alone, this family is happy and healthy.
by golly	I am surprised, impressed; **by gosh**	By golly! She did it. She made a cherry pie!
by gosh	what an experience, this is interesting, **by golly**	Well, by gosh! This is my first look at Niagara Falls!
by guess or by gosh	any way that is possible, by chance	How did I learn to speak French? By guess or by gosh, that's how.
by heart	memorized every word, **down pat**	Eva knew the speech by heart. She didn't look at her notes.
by hook or by crook	any way that is possible, **by any means**	He'll get that car—by hook or by crook! He'll get it somehow.

Idiom	Meaning	Example
by Jove	it happened, it is amazing	By Jove! We reached our goal. We sold 15,000 tickets!
by leaps and bounds	by large amounts, by a lot	The population of Calgary has grown by leaps and bounds.
by no means	not in any way, **not by any stretch...**	By no means is a car a good investment. It will depreciate.
by the same token	judging by the same rule, to be fair to both sides	By the same token, he should help with the housework.
by the seat of your pants	with little money, **a lick and a promise**	You can't operate a business by the seat of your pants.
by the skin of their teeth	by a little, barely	He won the election by one vote, by the skin of his teeth.
by the way	in addition to what I was saying, incidentally	By the way, I heard that Ed is resigning.
by word of mouth	by one person speaking to another, person to person, **through the grapevine**	News of his birth traveled by word of mouth. Soon everyone knew that Mary had a baby boy.
bye	good-bye	Bye, Mom. I love you.
bye for now	good-bye but I will see you soon	Bye for now. See you tonight at choir practice.

Idiom	Meaning	Example

C

Idiom	Meaning	Example
c'est la vie	that is fate, **that's life**	If you have bad luck some days, it's natural. C'est la vie!
Cabbagetown	a district in Toronto where European immigrants live	Restaurants in Cabbagetown serve European food.
cabin fever	feeling depressed because you have to stay inside	After three weeks of cold weather we all had cabin fever.
cackleberries	eggs, chicken eggs	Look! This hen laid five cackleberries!
call a spade a spade	say it in plain language; **straight goods**	Kris will report the facts. She's not afraid to call a spade a spade.
call attention to	ask you to read or notice, **draw attention to**	I would like to call attention to the student parking problem.
call for	require, ask for	This recipe calls for bee pollen. Where can we get that?
call his bluff	challenge his story, **give it to me straight**, **put up or shut up**	When I called his bluff about low profits, he admitted that the company made 11 million.
call it a day	not work anymore today, **call it quits**	I'm feeling very tired. I think I'll call it a day.
call it quits	stop doing something, quit what you are doing	The dust is bothering all of us. I think we should call it quits.
call it square	we do not owe each other, it is **a wash**, we are **even**	I bought the pizza; you bought the beer. Let's call it square.
call off	cancel, postpone	They called off the concert because the lead singer is sick.
call on	ask, request	I may call on you to speak at the meeting. Will you speak to us?
call tabs	collect money from bar customers	If customers are drunk, you call their tabs and ask them to leave.

Idiom	Meaning	Example
call the shots	make the decisions, decide what happens	Mr. Binks may be the president, but Ms. Barker calls the shots.
call up	phone, **dingle you, give me a ring,**	Call her up and ask her for a date. Go ahead, phone her.
calm before the storm	(See **the calm before the storm**)	
calm down	not be so upset, **chill out**	Please calm down, Mr. Tse. Your daughter is safe.
camel toes [B]	the folds of the vagina revealed by tight jeans	When Betty wears her old jeans you can see her camel toes.
can	(See **the can**)	
can	dismiss, **fire, let go**	He was canned for drinking liquor at work. They dismissed him.
can help it	can stop it, can prevent it	Abortion won't become legal if he can help it. He's against it.
can it	stop it, **knock it off**	Miss Schmidt heard a boy say, "Can it! Here comes the teacher."
can of worms	a controversial issue, an old problem	Gun control—let's not open that can of worms!
can't believe my ears	cannot believe what I hear, it is unbelievable	The cat is babysitting the kids? I can't believe my ears!
can't believe my eyes	cannot believe what I see, it is unbelievable	When you walked into that cafe, I couldn't believe my eyes.
can't have it both ways	you have to choose one or the other; cannot **have your cake...**	When children are allowed to make choices, they learn that they can't have it both ways.
can't help	cannot prevent, cannot stop	I can't help crying at weddings. They make me feel sad.
can't hold a candle	(See **hold a candle**)	
can't put my finger on it	cannot remember the exact words	I know the answer, but I can't put my finger on it.
can't put my hands on it	cannot remember exactly where it is	Your book is in my office, but I can't put my hands on it now.
can't see for looking	cannot see because I have been looking too long	Will you try to find my glove? I can't see for looking.

Idiom	Meaning	Example
can't see the forest for the trees	I am so close that I cannot see the whole picture or **the big picture**	I'm so involved in teaching that I've lost my view of education. I can't see the forest for the trees.
can't stand	does not like, hate	Don can't stand love songs. He thinks the words are silly.
Canada goose	getting goosed in Canada by a Canadian	"There," he said. "Now you've had your Canada goose."
canary	a person who tells the police, a **squealer**	Ken—that canary! He tells the boss who comes in late.
canned	prepared, memorized, **a pat answer**	His answers sound canned, like he memorized them.
Canuck	a Canadian, a citizen of Canada	When we visited Montana, a clerk called us "Canucks."
capture the imagination	cause a person to imagine a scene or character	The story of *Jacob Two-Two* will capture the kids' imagination.
car buff	a person who loves to repair or restore cars	Colin has been a car buff ever since he bought his first Ford.
card	(See **such a card**)	
card-carrying member	a regular member, a person on the membership list	Only card-carrying members will be allowed to attend the meeting.
carry a tune	sing well, sing in tune, **pipes**	Ask June to lead the singing. She can carry a tune.
carry it off	make it happen, **pull it off**	This project requires planning and skill, but he can carry it off.
carry on	continue, **keep on**	Carry on with your game. I'll wait until you're finished.
carry on	talk or act silly, not be sensible	They were kissing in church. Imagine carrying on like that!
carry out	do, complete, execute	Now that we have the loan we can carry out our plan.
carry the can	be responsible, see that the job gets done	The manager gets a big salary, but Mario carries the can.
carry the conversation	continue the conversation, continue talking to you	Visiting with Sally is easy. She carries the conversation!
carry weight	have influence, have power	Nina is a good reference; her name carries a lot of weight.

Idiom	Meaning	Example
carry your weight	do your share of the work, do enough work	If you carry your weight, you can work here for the summer.
cart before the horse	(See **the cart before the horse**)	
cascade (business)	allow information to flow down to the employees	Archie thinks we should control this information, not cascade it.
case in point	an example to support my point or thesis	Social democracy can succeed. Sweden is a case in point.
case of	(See **a case of** and **it's a case of**)	
cash and carry	pay cash and carry it out of the store (no deliveries)	The ad stated the terms of the sale: CASH & CARRY.
cash cow	a source of much money, a profitable resource	Alberta's cash cow—oil—is helping to balance the budget.
cash flow	money spent on the operation of a business	Calculate your weekly business expenses. That's your cash flow.
cash in	receive cash for bonds or poker chips; profit from	You're retired now. It may be time to cash in your bonds.
cash on the barrelhead	pay cash to the owner at the time of purchase; **cold, hard cash**	The old man said, "To buy my pony you'll have to pay $300 —cash on the barrelhead."
cash on the line	pay the full price in cash to the seller	I'll pay $200 for the bike—cash on the line.
cash up/cash out	count all the cash at the end of a business day	After you cash up, put the money in the safe and lock it.
cast a spell	use charm or spiritual power to change people	When Pavarotti sings, he casts a spell over his audience.
cast your vote	vote in an election, mark your ballot	Before you cast your vote, think carefully about the issues.
cat got your tongue	why do you not speak? **lose your tongue?**	Before I could reply, she said, "Cat got your tongue?"
cat's ass	(See **the cat's ass**)	
cat's meow	(See **the cat's meow**)	
cat's out of the bag	(See **the cat's out of the bag**)	
catcall	shouting disapproval or insults, heckling	The catcalls from the audience caused the speaker to pause.

Idiom	Meaning	Example
catch 22	the cause is the effect and the effect is the cause	It was catch 22. I needed my glasses to find my glasses.
catch a buzz	begin to feel intoxicated, begin to feel **high**	This is strong beer. You catch a buzz from drinking one bottle!
catch a cold (catch cold)	be sick with a cold, **come down with** a cold	I caught a cold while we were in Vancouver.
catch a glimpse	see for only a second, visible for a brief time	I caught a glimpse of Sue at the mall, but she didn't see me.
catch a plane/bus/train	go to the airport and get on the plane	After the meeting, you can catch the plane to Toronto.
catch a ride	ride with someone who has a vehicle, **get a lift**	When I go to church, I catch a ride with my neighbor Lila.
catch as catch can	no order, get what you can	The Clearance Sale was catch as catch can—each one for himself.
catch hell [B]	get a scolding or lecture, **get it**, **get shit** [B]	"Did you catch hell for cheating?" "Yes. The teacher lectured me and gave me zero on the exam."
catch it	get a scolding or lecture, **catch hell** [B]	Did you catch it for coming in late? Was your mom mad?
catch me doing that	see me doing that, find me doing that	You won't catch me skydiving. It's too dangerous.
catch on	learn how to do, **learn the ropes**	We need trainees who catch on quickly—people who learn fast.
catch on	get work, get a job, **hire on**	Maybe you can catch on with a survey crew for the summer.
catch some rays	have a sun bath, get a sun tan, **bag some rays**	When we get to Hawaii, you can catch some rays. It's sunny there.
catch some z's	sleep, get some rest, **crash**	Do you mind if I catch some z's on your couch? I'm sleepy.
catch the wave	join the trend, do what is popular	Condos are popular now. Should we buy one and catch the wave?
catch up	arrive later, **join you**	You go ahead. I'll catch up with you at the bus stop.
catch up on	do something that you have neglected	Ali can't go to the movie. He has to catch up on his homework.

Idiom	Meaning	Example
catch up with	revealed or exposed, **come back to haunt you**	When your lies catch up with you, it's embarrassing.
catch you at a bad time	visit or call when it is inconvenient	You look very sad. Did I catch you at a bad time?
catch you later	I will talk to you later, I will see you later	I have to leave now. Catch you later.
catch you off guard	surprise you, say what you do not expect	Did my comment about dog poop catch you off guard?
catch your death	become very ill, **catch a bad cold**	In this terrible weather, put on a coat or you'll catch your death.
caught dead	(See **wouldn't be caught dead**)	
caught flatfooted	not ready to respond, **mind in neutral**	Esposito was caught flatfooted by Lemaire's slapshot—an easy goal!
caught in the act	caught doing a crime, **caught with his pants down**	Two of the boys were caught in the act of vandalism. They were breaking car windows.
caught looking	be looking when you should have been acting	I was caught looking when he hit the ball. I just watched it.
caught red-handed	caught with evidence, **caught in the act**	The smuggler was caught red-handed with a kilo of cocaine.
caught up	busy with, involved	Maidra is caught up in church activities. She's very busy.
caught up	be finished, completed the required work	I want to get caught up on my cleaning before we have guests.
caught with his pants down	found doing a bad act, **caught in the act**	Percy was caught cheating— caught with his pants down.
caution	(See **a caution**)	
cave in	quit, be unable to cope, **fold**	One more crisis and I'll cave in. I'm very weary.
cement hands	awkward hands, **butter fingers**	Joey can't type; he's got cement hands.
chain letter	a letter that is copied and sent to other people	This letter says I will have bad luck if I break the chain.
chain of command	order of those in power, **line of authority**	If you are a lieutenant, the chain of command goes up and down.

Idiom	Meaning	Example
chain reaction	one event causing a sequence of events	Abe sold his shares, causing a chain reaction in the market.
chain smoker	a person who smokes one cigarette after another, **smokes like a furnace**	"Do all chain smokers die of emphysema?" "No, but most of them do."
chairman of the boards (hockey)	a player who controls play along the boards	In the 1970s Doug was chairman of the boards for the Hawks.
chalk one up for you	you have earned a point, you won that point/game	Good shot! I'll chalk one up for you.
chances are	it is quite possible, it may be	Chances are they're lost, and that's why they're late.
change for the better	improve, become better	My attitude has changed for the better. I'm more positive now.
change hands	change owners, be sold or traded	That condo changed hands three times in one year—three owners!
change horses in mid stream	change plans/methods after you have begun a competition or business	We're in the furniture business, not clothing. We can't change horses in mid stream.
change of heart	change from negative to positive	Now he seems friendly toward us. Has he had a change of heart?
change your mind	choose a different plan, change your decision	Please change your mind about leaving home. Please don't go.
change your tune	change your attitude, **change your mind**	If the price of a barrel of oil goes down, he'll change his tune.
character assassination	saying things that ruin a person's reputation, **muckrake**	"What did they say about him?" "It was mainly gossip and character assassination."
character density	number of dense people, number of dummies	If I join your company, the character density will decrease.
charge it	buy or purchase on credit, **put it on the bill**	The clerk said, "If you don't have cash, you can charge it."
charity begins at home	first help the needy in your own community; then help others	If you want to help the poor, remember that charity begins at home.
chaser	a soft drink to follow a hard drink, a weaker drink	The old man drank coffee as a chaser for the Irish whisky.

Idiom	Meaning	Example
chasing rainbows	trying to achieve an impossible goal	Many young actors are chasing rainbows—hoping for fame.
cheap	unwilling to spend money, not generous, **tight**	They refuse to buy the boy a decent suit. They're too cheap.
cheap drunk	(See **a cheap drunk**)	
cheap like borsch	not expensive, as cheap as vegetable soup	I didn't pay much for this jacket. It was cheap like borsch.
cheap skate	a person who does not pay his share, a **tight-ass**	That cheap skate can keep his money. I'll pay for the tickets.
cheat on	break a marriage promise, be unfaithful	He cheats on his wife. Now he's sleeping with a waitress.
check it out	inquire, **find out** about	Check it out. It may be a great opportunity.
check out	**find out** about, see if it is okay	Let's check out that Subaru we saw at Chong's Used Cars.
check over	look for errors in a paper, see if there are mistakes	I've written a letter of application. Will you check it over for me?
check that	look at that, **get a load of that**	When Rick saw the sports car, he said, "Check that!"
check up on	see if everything is fine or safe	He went to check up on the kids because they were crying.
check up on	supervise, watch to see if it is done correctly	They don't like a manager who is always checking up on them.
check your bags	give your luggage to the ticket agent	I would like to check my bags. Will you put them on the plane?
check-out	the counter where you pay for your purchases	The shoppers were lined up at the Canadian Tire check-out.
checkered career	career with failures, history of good and bad	His checkered career may ruin his chance of being elected.
checkup	doctor's examination, medical examination	If you aren't feeling well, go to the doctor for a checkup.
cheek	sharp reply, sarcasm, **lip**	When I called Mom a crab, she said, "No more of your cheek!"
cheek by jowl	beside, alongside, **side by side**	Jack and James fought cheek by jowl in World War I.

Idiom	Meaning	Example
cheeky	rude, impolite, **lippy, sassy**	Tara is too cheeky. She told her mom to stop flirting with men.
cheesecake	naked flesh, bare skin	The dancer provided lots of cheesecake—lots of bare leg.
cheesed off	upset, annoyed, **ticked off**	They were cheesed off when I said you wouldn't pay them.
cheesy	poor quality, **crappy, shabby**	The acting was pretty cheesy. The actors didn't know their lines.
cherrypicker (hockey)	a player who waits at center ice for a pass	Our coach told us about the cherrypicker on the other team.
chestnut	old favorite song, well-known story	Moira played the piano, and we sang old songs—old chestnuts.
chew him out	lecture him, scold him, **give** him **hell [B]**	My sister chewed me out for taking her car. She gave me hell.
chew the fat/ chew the rag	talk, visit, have **a chin wag**	I'll go and get the wine while you two relax and chew the fat.
chick	girl, woman	We were waiting for the bus, and this chick says, "Hi, boys."
chicken	afraid, scared, **yellow**	When it comes to heights, I'm chicken. I'm scared.
chicken in every pot	(See **a chicken in every pot**)	
chickens come home to roost	we cannot escape the consequences of our actions	We soon discover that lies return to their owner, just as chickens come home to roost.
chief cook and bottle washer	manager, supervisor	Hal is the chief cook and bottle washer for our school supper.
chill out	pause to gain control of your emotions, **cool off**	I think you should chill out before you see the supervisor.
chin wag	(See **a chin wag**)	
chintzy	unwilling to spend, **cheap, tight**	Don't be so chintzy with your time. Volunteer to visit seniors.
chip in	each one help to pay for, everybody pay a little	We should chip in and buy Sadie a gift when she moves away.
chip off the old block	(See **a chip off the old block**)	

Idiom	Meaning	Example
chip on his shoulder	in a fighting mood, looking for a fight	Ron has a chip on his shoulder. He's arguing with everybody.
chips are down	(See **when the chips are down**)	
chock full	very full, full to the top, **plump full**	The truck was chock full of paper to be recycled.
choke	be so nervous you cannot perform or do it well	Don't even think about choking when you make your speech.
chomping at the bit	eager to go, anxious to leave	If you mention camping, the kids will be chomping at the bit.
choose sides	help one side or team, **take sides**	Some of the students will dislike you if you choose sides.
choose up sides	choose people to play on two or more teams	Let's choose up sides and play a game of volleyball.
chops	lips and teeth, mouth	You need big chops to play the tuba, eh.
chow	food, something to eat	I'm starved. Let's get some chow.
chow	(See **ciao**)	
chow down	eat, have a meal	I'm hungry. Let's chow down before we go to the movie.
Christmas graduate	a student who leaves college at Christmas	Among the Christmas graduates last year was Gerard Kutz.
chromedome	bald person, **silkhead**	A chromedome can tell you the the advantages of being bald.
chuck it	put it in the garbage, **junk it**	We used to say *chuck it*, but now we say *recycle it*.
ciao	good-bye, see you later	Ciao, Tony. See you in Rome.
circles around you	much better than you, **no contest**	Why do you play cards with her? She can play circles around you.
circular file	garbage can or wastebasket, **file 13**	A lot of memos go in the circular file. They're garbage.
clam	dollar, **buck**	He paid a hundred clams for that radio.
clam up	stop talking, become quiet	Why do you clam up when we mention Judy? Why so quiet?

Idiom	Meaning	Example
claptrap	nonsense, trivia, **bull**	I heard what the psychic said. What a lot of claptrap!
claws are showing	show resentment or envy or jealousy, **if looks could kill**	When you talked about Carla, your claws were showing. Do you dislike her?
clean cut	well groomed, clean, neat	We're looking for clean-cut boys to work as waiters.
clean up	pick up garbage, put away clothes or toys, wash	Lorne, please clean up the mess in your bedroom.
clean up on	defeat, beat, **whip you, wipe you**	Little Chad cleaned up on big Clint. Chad is quite a fighter.
clean up your act	do it better, do it legally, **get your act together**	I've missed classes, failed tests. I need to clean up my act.
clean up your plate	finish eating all the food on your plate, **eat it up**	You may leave the table after you've cleaned up your plate.
clear as a bell	easy to hear or understand, clearly audible	We heard him say it. He said *no*, clear as a bell.
clear as mud	not understandable, confusing	Mr. Lee explained the formula. Then he said, "Clear as mud, eh?"
clear out	leave, go, get out, **take off**	When the gang arrived, we cleared out. We left in a hurry.
clear out	sell at a low price, sell at a discount	We're clearing out last year's stock at 20% off.
clear the air	explain, talk about a problem openly	His statement will clear the air. It will prevent more confusion.
clear up	explain, discuss so everyone understands	Let's clear up the matter of the missing keys. Were they stolen?
clear your head/mind	relax so you can think clearly	After an argument I need time to clear my head, to become calm.
click in	become aware, realize, **dawn on, hit me**	It didn't click in that he was hurt until I saw the blood on his shirt.
cliff-hanger	(See **a cliff-hanger**)	
climb the walls	feel upset or stressed, **go bonkers, go crazy**	On the first day of school, the teacher was climbing the walls.
close a deal/sale	complete a sale to a customer	Vi knows how to close a sale. She's a good closer.

Idiom	Meaning	Example
close call	(See **a close call**)	
close shave	(See **a close shave**)	
close to the vest	hidden, covered, not showing your cards	Walter plays close to the vest. He doesn't let me see his cards.
clotheslined (hockey)	lifted by a bodycheck, hanging in the air	Orr was clotheslined just as he crossed the line. What a check!
clued in	aware, **in the know**, **with it**	"How do you get clued in?" "You watch and listen, man."
clueless	not informed, ignorant, not **with it**	When I don't know the answer, I try not to look clueless.
clunker	a car that is in poor condition, a **beater**	Uncle Blair has bought another clunker—an old Pontiac.
clutch hitter (baseball)	(See **a clutch hitter**)	
clutz	(See **klutz**)	
cock and bull	nonsense, **bull**, **BS** [B]	Do you believe that cock-and-bull story about Bigfoot?
cocky	proud, **smart-ass**	"Why is Len acting so cocky?" "He won the frisbee contest."
cocoon	stay inside your home to feel comfortable and safe	We don't want to go out tonight. We feel like cocooning.
coffee talk	conversation while having coffee, **water-cooler...**	I don't believe Sally's pregnant. It's just coffee talk, just gossip.
coin	money, loot, **dough**, **serious coin**	Wait till I get some coin. Then we can travel.
coin a phrase	(See **to coin a phrase**)	
cold call	a visit to an employer or customer without an appointment	Sam got a job by making cold calls—by knocking on doors and asking for work.
cold, hard cash	actual money, dollar bills; not a cheque or credit card	No cheques—I want cold, hard cash for that car.
cold turkey	abruptly, completely, not gradually	Barb stopped smoking, cold turkey. No plan, no program.
coldcock	punch without warning, **jump**	Buddy coldcocked the pitcher— hit him when he wasn't looking.

Idiom	Meaning	Example
collect my thoughts	think calmly and clearly, organize my thoughts	She was glad when the kids left so she could collect her thoughts.
collecting dust	not used for a long time, idle, **gathering dust**	"Where's the silver tray?" "On the shelf, collecting dust."
come [B]	have an orgasm, ejaculate	Some women fake an orgasm— they pretend to come, eh.
come across	seem to be, appear to be	You came across as being angry, not just disappointed.
come across	discover, find	I came across an antique basin in the attic. It was in a box.
come across	give, pay, **pay up**	They came across with $250— half the money they owe us.
come across [B]	consent to have sex, **get laid**, **go all the way**	You kiss me as though you're going to come across, but then you say no.
come again	what did you say? **beg your pardon?**	When I asked Grandpa if he liked the soup, he said, "Come again?"
come alive	become lively, cheer, applaud	As the players skated onto the ice, the crowd came alive.
come around	begin to co-operate, believe, **come onside**	When he reads the report, he'll come around. He'll believe us.
come back to haunt you	cause you to feel guilty or ashamed	Lies will come back to haunt you, remind you of the past.
come by	find, get, obtain	How did you come by that vase? Where did you get it?
come clean	tell the truth, admit everything, **own up**	The police asked him to come clean about the money—to tell them everything he knew.
come down hard	punish hard, **throw the book at**	The teachers come down hard on cheating. They suspend cheaters.
come down to earth	be realistic, **get your head out of the clouds**	If she'd come down to earth, if she'd stop dreaming about fame, she could pass her exams.
come down with	become sick, become ill	Brenda came down with the flu. She's very sick.

Idiom	Meaning	Example
come hell or high water	no matter what happens, **by any means**	I'll buy that ranch, come hell or high water. I'm determined.
come home to roost	(See **chickens come home to roost**)	
come into	inherit, receive as a gift	When her father died, she came into a lot of money.
come into play	affect, influence, be a factor	In sales, all of your skills come into play. You use them all.
come into your own	be your natural best, **find your voice**, **realize your potential**	After five years in medicine, he came into his own. He became an excellent doctor.
come naturally	able to learn easily, have natural ability	Playing the piano seemed to come naturally to Susan.
come of	happen, result, develop	Peter liked Mia, but nothing ever came of it—no romance.
come of age	become old enough to vote or go to the bar or fight in a war	On my 18th birthday, Dad said, "Now that you've come of age, here's a set of keys to the car."
come off	happen as planned, succeed	The band wanted to produce a CD, but it didn't come off.
come off it	I do not believe it, **you're kidding**	You had a date with Cybill Shepherd? Come off it!
come on	cheer, encourage	Come on, Mat, you can do it! You can ride that bull!
come on	do what we ask	Come on, tell us a story. Please?
come onside	come on our team, be on our side, **buy into**	We want to persuade Vi to come onside. We want her to join us.
come onto	talk to in a sexual way, **make advances**	In the car he started coming onto her. He said he wanted her.
come out in the wash	become clear later, **when the dust settles**	We will soon know who did it. It will all come out in the wash.
come out with	say, tell, **blurt out**	Then she comes out with a dirty joke and nobody laughed.
come through	complete the task, do what is expected	We're hoping that Ron will come through with high grades.
come to	regain your senses or consciousness	A few minutes after the accident, he came to. He opened his eyes.

Idiom	Meaning	Example
come to	involves, includes	When it comes to dessert, I like raisin pie.
come to a head	come to a climax, result in a fight	Things will come to a head when the family discusses the will.
come to grips with	accept the truth, **face facts**	I am finally coming to grips with my divorce. I'm accepting it.
come to terms	agree, sign an agreement, **settle it**	We hope they can come to terms before the court date.
come to terms with	accept that it is true, **face facts**	She helped the boy come to terms with the death of his father.
come to the point	say what is important, **get to the point**	When you make a speech, come to the point quickly.
come to think of it	now that I remember it, a thought has just come	Come to think of it, I was the one who suggested marriage.
come unglued	lose control, **fall apart**	If Tina doesn't stop worrying, she'll come unglued.
come up	happen, occur, **crop up**	In this job we never know what will come up. One customer wanted to buy an ostrich.
come up with	think of, compose	Can you come up with the answer to my question?
come-on	invitation to romance, **give her the eye**	She's giving Rex the come-on, smiling at him **and stuff**.
coming out of our ears	having too many, having too much	Everybody brought salad. We had salad coming out of our ears!
coming out of your yin yang	having far too many, having far too much, **tons**	If we learn all the idioms in this book, we'll have idioms coming out of our yin yang!
coming up roses	doing very well, succeeding,	Since I met Ty, life is wonderful. Everything's coming up roses!
common sense	the ability to make logical decisions; **horse sense**	It is because she has common sense that we ask her opinion.
compare notes	compare what we saw and heard	We haven't had a chance to compare notes on Pat's wedding.
conk out	quit, not work any more, sleep, **give out**	The TV conked out just after the movie started.

Idiom	Meaning	Example
consarned	darn, **blasted,** **dingbusted, friggin**	The consarned battery is dead. How unlucky!
contract out on	(See **a contract out on**)	
cook	play good jazz, play music with skill and inspiration	The Boss Brass was cookin' last night. What a great band!
cook your goose	finish you, ruin you, **your goose is cooked**	If you borrow too much money, you'll cook your goose.
cool	fine, sophisticated, **hip,** **groovy, neat, together,** **way cool, with it**	"Do you know any cool guys?" "Yes. There's one in my class. Would you like to meet him?"
cool it	stop it, be good, **knock it off**	The students cool it when the principal walks in.
cool off	control your emotions, **chill out, calm down**	I better cool off before I talk to the kids. I'm still angry.
cool under pressure	calm during a crisis, able to perform well when you must do it	Jo was very cool under pressure. When the judge asked questions, she answered clearly and calmly.
cool your heels	wait for a judgement, serve a detention	Chad is cooling his heels in the Remand Center—the city jail.
cooler heads prevailed	sensible people spoke, violence was avoided	There was nearly a riot, but cooler heads prevailed.
coon's age	(See **in a coon's age**)	
cop	policeman, **fuzz, pig**	I know this cop on the Calgary Police Force—he's a nice guy.
cop out	an excuse, not trying, not doing your share	Instead of speaking, he showed a video. What a cop out!
copacetic	agreeable, fine, **go along with, OK**	Don is copacetic. He agrees with our plans.
corked	intoxicated, drunk, **plastered, sloshed**	Grant got corked last night and walked home. He couldn't drive.
corner the market	become the main supplier, have a monopoly	Japanese automakers are trying to corner the luxury car market.
corner you	insist that you listen, **buttonhole you**	If Helmer corners you, tell him you have to go to the bathroom.

Idiom	Meaning	Example
corny	obvious humor, unsophisticated humor	The farmer said his cows are moody today. Now *that* is corny!
cost a pretty penny	cost a lot of money, had a high price	Elvis bought a new pink Cadillac. I bet that cost a pretty penny.
cost an arm and a leg	cost a lot of money, is very expensive	That fur jacket must have cost her an arm and a leg.
cost you	require much money or emotional stress or time or energy	Caring for a child will cost you— cost you a lot. But it's worth every minute, every tear.
cotton to that	believe in that, do that, **relate to that**	City folks play cards on Sunday, but we don't cotton to that.
cotton-picking	thieving, **doggone flippin, ruddy**	Get your cotton-pickin' fingers off that bike! Don't touch it!
couch potato	a person who watches a lot of TV	If I watch four hours of TV every day, am I a couch potato?
cough up	pay your share, pay a debt, **pay up**	Come on, Tony. Cough up. You haven't paid anything.
couldn't believe my ears	(See **can't believe my ears**)	
count on	depend on, rely on	We can count on Tanya. She always comes to choir practice.
count your chickens before they hatch	depend heavily on plans, spend money that you have not received	Politicians have learned not to "count their chickens" before the election.
course you can	you can do it, believe it, **of course you can**	"I don't think I can learn this." "Course you can, son."
courseware	computer program that teaches a course	We sell courseware to schools all over North America.
courtesy of	from, given by, donated by	The doughnuts are courtesy of Harry's Bakery.
cover for me	make an excuse for me, do my work	I may be late for work today. Will you cover for me?
cover up	hide it, **sweep under the carpet**	He can't cover up his mistake because people know about it.
cover your ass [B]	protect yourself by having documents signed etc.	If you discipline or dismiss an employee, cover your ass.

Idiom	Meaning	Example
cover-up	hiding something from the authorities or media	The reporter heard about the cover-up of police brutality.
cow pie	cow shit [B] cow dung	Watch where you step. There are cow pies everywhere. Oops!
cow tow	do as someone wishes, **brown nose, suck up to**	Marie won't cow tow to anyone. She's proud and independent.
cowpoke	a cowboy, a man who works on a ranch	Three cowpokes were herding some cattle down the road.
Cowtown	Calgary, Alberta; a town where cows are sold	The Calgary Stampede is the pride of Cowtown. Y'all come!
crack a book	study, read a textbook	Sean passed that exam without cracking a book.
crack down on	stop, not permit, not allow	The police began to crack down on speeders in the school zones.
crack me up	make me laugh hard, **split a gut**	Robin Williams cracks me up when he tells a story.
crack of dawn	(See **at the crack of dawn**)	
crack shot/salesman etc.	a person who is highly skilled at shooting etc.	Marvin has developed into a crack salesman. He's excellent.
crack the line-up	earn a place on a team, **make the team**	He's a good basketball player, but can he crack the line-up?
crack this case	solve a crime, discover who is guilty	David will crack this case; he's a thorough investigator.
crack under the strain	become irrational or hysterical due to strain, **go around the bend**	Mother was a strong person. She never cracked under the strain of raising ten children.
cracked	crazy, **nuts, wacko**	He must be cracked. He mailed a letter to himself.
crackers	crazy, **bonkers, nuts**	Don't worry about me. I've been crackers all my life.
crackpot	a person who is strange or weird, **wacko**	Some crackpot wrote a letter to him threatening his family.
crackup	collision, crash	Drinking and driving causes a lot of crackups.
cramp your style	cause problems for you, cause stress for you	If we can't buy a Corvette, will it cramp your style?

Idiom	Meaning	Example
crank issue	a topic that causes anger, **can of worms**	The Premier raised a crank issue and then went on holidays.
crank it up	turn up the volume, louder please	Hey, Karen, crank up the radio. That's a great song.
crank out	make, write, manufacture	Can you crank out a few jokes for our school newspaper?
crap	lies, **bull**, **BS**	He told us that history books contain a lot of crap—BS.
crappy	poor quality, junky, **shabby**	What a crappy camera! Look at these terrible pictures!
crash	go to bed, go to sleep	Sometimes Don crashes on our sofa and sleeps for hours.
crash a party	go to a party uninvited, **horn in**	Bo and his friends crashed our party. They came uninvited.
crash course	(See **a crash course**)	
crawl on my hands and knees over broken glass just to see her photo	do anything to be closer to her, **worship the ground she walks on**	I'm so in love I'd crawl on my hands and knees over miles of broken glass to see her photo.
crawling with	having many of them, **oodles**, **scads**	The hotel was crawling with police. I couldn't count them.
crazy about	like a lot, **mad about**	Dad's crazy about sports. He really loves baseball.
crazy like a fox	crafty while appearing foolish or dumb, **play the fool**	In the debate, he was crazy like a fox. He praised his opponent for being clever and ruthless.
cream of the crop	best of the group, the finest ones	Only the cream of the crop will be invited to the interviews.
cream you	hit you, knock you down, **knock you flat**	If Jon discovers you lied to him, he'll cream you. He'll hit you.
creep	strange person, pervert, **weirdo**	What a creep! He looks like a stray dog!
crocodile tears	false tears, phony sadness	Her crocodile tears don't fool me. She just wants sympathy.
crop up	happen, occur, **come up**	I'm planning to go to Montreal unless something crops up— like an airline strike.

Idiom	Meaning	Example
cross my heart and hope to die	promise sincerely	I'll pay you back on Friday, cross my heart and hope to die.
cross paths	meet, encounter	We'll cross paths again, I'm sure. Until then, good luck.
cross someone	go against someone, insult someone	People are afraid to cross Phil because he has a violent temper.
cross that bridge when I come to it	make that decision when it is necessary, do not **jump the gun**	If interest rates begin to drop, I can buy bonds, but I'll cross that bridge when I come to it.
cruising for a bruising	inviting a fight, **asking for it**	The new kid was cruisin' for a bruisin'—insulting everybody.
crummy	poor quality, **lousy, shabby**	We cancelled the picnic because of the crummy weather.
crunch	(See **the crunch**)	
crush on	(See **a crush on**)	
crux of the matter	(See **the crux of the matter**)	
cry her heart out	cry a lot, sob, **cry your eyes out**	Poor girl! She's crying her heart out because he hasn't called her.
cry in your beer	be sad as you drink beer, regret as you drink beer, **cry the blues**	Go to college. Get your diploma. Or someday you'll be crying in your beer.
cry me a river	you can cry a lot but you will not get my sympathy, **crocodile tears**	When he complained about how much he had to pay his chauffeur, I said, "Cry me a river, guy."
cry over spilt milk	cry about small accidents, cry instead of doing	Children drop things and break them. Don't cry over spilt milk.
cry the blues	complain because your friend or lover has gone	Lan is crying the blues because Bing left her for another woman.
cry your eyes out	cry a lot, cry hard, **cry her heart out**	The little boy was lost and scared, and crying his eyes out.
crying shame	(See **a crying shame**)	
cup of tea	favorite activity, choice of entertainment	A holiday in the Yukon is not her cup of tea.
cup runneth over	feeling too full of love or joy or happiness	My cup runneth over whenever I listen to Mother Teresa.

Idiom	Meaning	Example
curl your hair	shock you, disgust you	The man described the accident. It was enough to curl your hair!
curtains	the end, the death, **the last of**	If we clear-cut Canada's forests, it's curtains for the lumber industry.
cushy	soft, luxurious, comfortable	They had a cushy life in their beautiful home beside the ocean.
cuss	curse, say bad words, **air was blue**	The little boy had learned to cuss. He said *damn* and *hell* a lot.
cut	defined, clearly visible	Neil's muscles are well cut. They ripple when he moves.
cut above	(See **a cut above**)	
cut and dried	simple, not complex, **open and shut**	For me, the choice was cut and dried. I chose the Peugeot.
cut corners	use less material, use less than required	If we cut corners, we'll produce a low-quality product.
cut from the same cloth	from the same family, very similar	Ty and Ed are cut from the same cloth—both are serious and quiet.
cut him off [B]	not have sex with him, not **make love** to him	If he doesn't buy me a car, I'll cut him off—no **nookie**!
cut it	do the job, satisfy, **work**	Red and brown just don't cut it. They look ugly together.
cut it out	stop it, do not do that, **knock it off**	When the kids began throwing dirt, we told them to cut it out.
cut losses	quit the project and accept the financial losses	If the stock price goes down, sell them and cut your losses.
cut me to the quick	hurt me, cause me to feel sad	I was hurt when she called me a cow. She cut me to the quick.
cut my teeth on	learned as a young person, learned as I grew up	Yes, I can tie a bow knot. I cut my teeth on string and ropes.
cut off	not allowed to do it any more, stopped from doing	We have to cut off beer sales at 12 midnight. No more sales.
cut off	drive in front of, swerve into your lane	That jerk cut me off! He swerved into my lane!

Idiom	Meaning	Example
cut off	interrupt, prevent from talking, **shut down**	The chairman cut me off in the middle of my question. "You're out of order," he said.
cut off your nose to spite your face	make your problem worse, hurt yourself because you dislike yourself	If you abuse drugs to forget a problem, you are cutting off your nose to spite your face.
cut out for	have natural ability for, be suited to	I guess I'm just not cut out for bull riding. I'm not good at it.
cut rate	second class, sold for less than full price	We bought some cut-rate lumber and built a shelter for the boat.
cut the cheese [B]	let off gas, fart, **pass wind**	Then somebody cut the cheese, and everybody laughed.
cut the crap [B]	stop telling lies, do not **BS**, no more **bull**	Will somebody tell him to cut the crap and give us the facts.
cut the mustard	do the job properly, **cut it**	If I'm too old to cut the mustard, maybe I should retire, eh.
cut to the chase	tell the exciting part, **get to the point**	George, please, cut to the chase. We're tired of the story already.
cut you down to size	make you feel smaller; not as important	The foreman cut him down to size by calling him a laborer.
cut you to ribbons	defeat you in an argument, embarrass you in a contest	That professor will cut you to ribbons if you question his facts.
cut your own throat	hurt yourself, be **your own worst enemy**	By overspending, you will cut your own throat.
cut-up	(See **a cut-up**)	
cute as a bug's ear	petite and pretty, adorable	Have you seen her little sister? She's cute as a bug's ear.
cutting edge	the latest technology, **state of the art**	This picture is the cutting edge— the best in the TV industry.

D

Idiom	Meaning	Example
dad-blamed	damned, **darn**, **dingbusted**	The dad-blamed fishing line is tangled! It's in knots!
damaged goods	abused, in poor condition	One man described prostitutes as *damaged goods*.
damn it [B]	it is very annoying or frustrating, **darn it**	Damn it! That cigarette smoke is making me ill.
damned if you do and damned if you don't	you are blamed if you do it and blamed if you do not, **between the devil...**, **can't have it both ways**	If you offer to help, he refuses; if you don't offer, he complains. You're damned if you do, and damned if you don't.
dampen your spirits	reduce your enthusiasm, cause you to lose interest	Losing one game didn't dampen her spirits. She's full of hope.
dark horse	the competitor that could surprise us and win	The dark horse in the World Cup is Ireland. They could win it all.
dark side	bad side of a person, the evil part of our nature	Most people try to hide the dark side of their personality.
darken a church door	attend church, go to a church service	He never darkens a church door except to attend funerals.
darn	damn, **ruddy**	35° is hot—too darn hot!
darn it	oh no, not again, **nuts**, **rats**	Darn it! I locked my keys in the car.
darn my luck	my luck is poor, I am unlucky today	My bread is in the oven and the power goes off. Darn my luck!
darn right	that is right, yes, **you betcha**	"Do you believe in ghosts?" "Darn right I do! I just saw one!"
darn tooting	that is true, I agree, **darn right**	"They still talk about the winter of 1907, don't they, Helmer?" "Darn tootin'! It was a *cold* one!"

Idiom	Meaning	Example
dasein	blending into a group, not distinct or unique	How to describe Anna? Dasein— she seems to disappear in a group.
dash off a note/letter	quickly write a note or letter and send it	Josi dashed off a note to her cousin in Toronto—in English.
date	boy and girl go to a movie etc., **go out with**, **see**	Tong has been dating May since they met at Christmas.
dates you	tells your age; when you were born	Knowing that song dates you. It was popular in the 1950s.
dawn on me	cause me to think of, occur to me, **hit me**	It didn't dawn on me that they're twins until I saw them together.
day in, day out	every day, daily	Day in, day out, she walked to work. I saw her every morning.
day one	(See **from day one**)	
dead as a doornail	dead, showing no signs of life, **stone dead**	It's only a stuffed bear. It's dead as a doornail.
dead certain	very certain, very sure, **positive**	He's dead certain that Ming is the man who talked to him.
dead even	having the same score, tied, **dead heat**	After six events in the decathlon, the two men were dead even.
dead giveaway	(See **a dead giveaway**)	
dead heat	(See **a dead heat**)	
dead in the water	not competitive, not qualified to compete, **haven't got a hope**	When you're job hunting, if you don't have a resume you're dead in the water.
dead last	the last runner or competitor	It doesn't matter if you come in dead last. Just finish the race.
dead loss	(See **a dead loss**)	
dead meat	finished, terminated, **done for**	If you're caught driving drunk in Sweden, you're dead meat.
dead on	accurate, correct, **spot on**	When you said our sales would double, you were dead on.
dead ringer	(See **a dead ringer**)	
dead set against	strongly opposed to, **down with**	She's dead set against abortion as a means of birth control.

Idiom	Meaning	Example
dead tired	very tired, **blotto, zonked**	After fighting the fire, they were dead tired—exhausted.
dead to the world	sleeping, in a deep sleep, **sound asleep**	I was dead to the world when the phone rang and woke me.
dead wrong	clearly wrong, mistaken	I was dead wrong about the word: it's *prejudice,* not *prejudism.*
dead-eye Dick	a person who can shoot accurately	We call him *Dead-eye Dick.* He can shoot the dot off an *i.*
deadbeat	a person with no desire to work, **good-for-nothing**	Lana, are you going to marry that deadbeat? He's no good!
deadhead	a person who has damaged his brain with drugs	It's too bad, really, but Marvin is a deadhead—too much cocaine.
deal me in	deal cards for me, please; I want to play cards	Deal me in, Walter. Deal me a winning hand.
death row	the prisoners who are to be executed or **put to death**	The priest wants to visit the prisoners on death row.
death warmed over	(See **look like death warmed over**)	
death wish	saying you want to die, inviting death	To challenge the Mafia would be a death wish. It would be suicide.
deathbed	(See **on your deathbed**)	
deck him	knock him down, **cream you**	Tony decked him in the first round of the boxing match.
deep, dark secret	very private information, **on the QT**	I'll tell you all—except my past. That's a deep, dark secret.
deep six	in a six-foot-deep grave, **pushing up daisies**	If you overdose on coke, you're deep six, man.
deked out of his jock	tricked out of position, **outplayed**	Mario skated in on the goalie and deked him out of his jock.
Denver boot	a wheel block that stops a car from moving	Greg was drunk, so the police put a Denver boot on his car.
deserve credit	deserve praise or thanks, **give her credit**	David deserves credit for finding the lost keys. Thank you, boy.
devil-may-care	carefree, wild, **on a lark**	Employers won't hire people with a devil-may-care attitude.
dibs	(See **first dibs**)	

Idiom	Meaning	Example
dick [B]	penis, **dink**, **dork**, **hoo-haw**	With all these winter clothes on, I can't find my dick.
did good	did well, did a good job, **done good**	I watched you ride that horse— you did real good!
did yourself proud	did a good job, did well, **did good**, **done good**	That was a great dinner, Nora. You did yourself proud.
diddly-squat	nothing, not a penny	For all that work, he gave me diddly-squat—not even thanks.
die down	gradually stop, diminish, **drop off**	When the laughter died down, I found my false teeth, put them in my mouth, and said, "Excuse me."
die for	want very much; **in the worst way**	I'm dying for a cup of coffee! I'll have an Espresso, please.
die hard	change slowly, continue to be strong, **you can't teach...**	Some men still want to be the head of the family. Old beliefs die hard.
die off	become extinct, all of them die	That type of horse died off before humans appeared.
dig/dig it	like, enjoy, relate to	Ole digs the Beatles. His favorite song is *Norwegian Wood*.
dig a little deeper	try harder, give a little more	The coach asked the team to dig a little deeper, to give their best.
dig deep	give more money, **dig a little deeper**	We'll all have to dig deep if we hope to achieve our goals.
dig in	begin to eat, **eat up**, **help yourself**	Dig in, everybody. There's lots of food.
dig in their heels	hold their position, not yield or move	If we discuss money, he digs in his heels. "No raises," he says.
dig it up	dig the garden, dig to uncover a buried object	Remember where you bury the treasure, because some day you may want to dig it up.
dig your own grave	cause your own failure, **cut your own throat**	When you criticize the manager, are you digging your own grave?
dig yourself in	make it worse, say or do something that aggravates	When he insulted the policeman, I said, "Don't dig yourself in."

Idiom	Meaning	Example
digs	apartment, house, **pad**	I'm having a party so everybody can see my new digs.
dilly-dally	go very slowly, pause too much	Sarah, you come straight home from school. Don't dilly-dally.
dime a dozen	(See **a dime a dozen**)	
dimwit	one who is slow to respond or **catch on**	I felt like a dimwit when I couldn't remember her name.
ding-a-ling	fool, **airhead**, **jerk**	What a ding-a-ling! She expects me to *pay* for a phone book!
dingbat/ding-dong	strange person, **nerd**, **weirdo**	That dingbat wanted me to take off my clothes!
dingbusted	damn, **blasted**, **consarned**, **darn**	I couldn't reach the dingbusted switch to turn on the light.
dingle you	phone you, call you, **give me a ring**	I'll dingle you when I get back from Chicago. What's your number?
dink [B]	penis, **dork**, **hoo-haw**	Did you wash your hands after you touched your dink?
DINKS	married couples who have Double Income No Kids	Our travel packages are purchased mainly by DINKS.
dipstick	a person who seems to be stupid, **dimwit**	When Todd is nervous, he acts like a dipstick—like a fool.
dirt cheap	very cheap, not expensive	Cherries are dirt cheap in B.C. during the summer.
dirt file	record of failures and bad actions	Every time we have a fight, you haul out my dirt file.
dirty dog/dirty rat	immoral person, liar, **scum**, **slime bucket**	You dirty rat! You stole my truck and used my credit card!
dirty money	stolen money, money obtained illegally	We believe the donation from the Mafia is dirty money.
dirty thirties	1930s, when drought caused hardship on the prairie; **hungry thirties**	During the dirty thirties, soil drifted into the ditches and crops wouldn't grow.
dirty work	unpleasant tasks, difficult work	I do the dirty work—fight for the puck—and he scores the goals.
dis	insult, criticize, **put down**	If you dis me, I won't help you with your math.

Idiom	Meaning	Example
discombobulate	upset, excite, agitate	That whistle discombobulates my dog. He barks and howls.
discretion is the better part of valor	be sensible when you are brave; be courageous but not reckless	In all your battles, be brave but not foolish. Discretion is the better part of valor.
dish it out	criticize, complain	Jay can dish it out, but she gets mad if you criticize her.
disk jockey (DJ)	radio announcer who plays recorded music	Clare became a disk jockey with a radio station in Moose Jaw.
ditch him	leave him, **lose him**, **give him the slip**	I tried to ditch him at the mall but he held on to my hand.
do	(See **hairdo**)	
do (a speed)	travel at a speed, drive at a speed of	We were only doing 50 km per hour. That's the truth.
do a 180	turn around and go in the opposite direction, **U-turn**	When the boy on the motorcycle saw the police car, he did a 180 and sped off.
do a favor	help someone who asks, do a task for someone	Ben offered to do me a favor if I ever need help.
do a gig	play music for a dance or concert	Our band is doing a gig at Bijo's tonight. We play from 10 till 2.
do a number on	deceive, fool, **taken, taken in**	They did a number on us when we bought this car. It's not reliable.
do away with	throw out, dispose of	We want to do away with nuclear weapons—to dispose of them.
do drugs	use drugs, **take drugs**	They don't hire people who do drugs. No way.
do it the hard way	use a poor method, **go against the grain**	Don't start a fire with stones. That's doing it the hard way.
do lunch	have lunch together, eat lunch	We'll do lunch tomorrow, OK? Do you like salads?
do me in	kill me, **knock me off**	I hope no one wants to do me in. I want to live a few more years.
do or die	last chance to win, **it's now or never**	It's do or die. If we lose this game, we'll be out of the series.

Idiom	Meaning	Example
do the honors	do the task for the leader, **fill in for** the leader	The Mayor can't speak to us, so Mr. Kelly will do the honors.
do the town	celebrate or party all over town	On July 1, we'll do the town. We'll really celebrate.
do the trick	solve the problem, help, **that's the ticket**	If you need a lubricant, Vaseline will do the trick.
do time	be in prison, be in a penitentiary	He's doing time for sexual assault. He's in for five years.
do unto others as you would have them do unto you	treat people the way you would like to be treated	This is The Golden Rule: "Do unto others as you would have them do unto you."
do up	lace, tighten the laces	Do up your skate laces, please. I will help you tie them.
do with	would like, want	I could do with a cold drink. I'm hot and thirsty.
do without	manage without, not have, **make do**	We did without meat all winter. We became vegetarians.
do you follow	do you understand? do you see how it operates?	Turn the key left to lock, right to unlock. Do you follow?
do you mind	do you care? does it matter?	Do you mind if I sit on your desk? Does it bother you?
do your own thing	do it your own way, do what you feel, **let it all hang out**	I like managers who let me do my own thing—who respect my way of doing things.
do your part	do your share, do your job	We did our part to help the food bank. We donated cereal.
do your utmost	do as much as you can, do whatever you can	Pat did his utmost to save her, but she fell into the pool.
do yourself proud	do something that you are proud of	You did yourself proud when you helped the refugees.
do-dad	an object with a name you cannot remember, **do-funny**	A little do-dad on the back of the carburetor was sticking. That was the problem.
do-funny	a thing with a funny name, **thingamabob**	You put the do-funny on the lever, and you're finished!
dodge a bullet	avoid a failure or loss or injury	Kevin dodged a bullet. He got a "D" on the final exam.

Idiom	Meaning	Example
doesn't add up	is not logical, does not **make sense**	One shot was fired, but three cows are dead. It doesn't add up.
doesn't mince words	does not say nice words when complaining, **call a spade a spade**	When Greta is angry she doesn't mince words. She tells you what is bothering her.
doesn't wash	is not believable, is not logical, does not **make sense**	His explanation doesn't wash. If a millennium begins at year 1, how does he account for the first year?
dog days of summer	the hottest days of summer, midsummer	We like to watch baseball during the dog days of summer.
dog eat dog	vicious competition, everybody for himself	Will education prepare us for the dog-eat-dog world of business?
dog in the manger	a person who will not share something he does not use or need	He's a dog in the manger about his office space. He doesn't use it, but he won't let us have it.
dog it	be lazy, not work	Bill admits he's been dogging it lately. He lacks energy.
dog me	follow me, bother me	His failure in politics dogged him for the rest of his life.
dog tired	very tired, exhausted, **all in**, **done in**	Janis was dog tired after the series. She played every game.
dog's breakfast	(See **a dog's breakfast**)	
dog's life	(See **a dog's life**)	
dolled up	in a party dress, with hair styled, **gussied up**	When Lisa gets all dolled up, Harry becomes very romantic.
don't borrow trouble	do not invite their trouble; we have enough trouble	When I said I was going to help my neighbor get a divorce, Pat said, "Don't borrow trouble."
don't count your chickens before they hatch	do not expect all plans to be successful, wait until you get the final results	"Look at the sales I'm going to make this month—over 50!" "Don't count your chickens...."
don't eat that	do not accept that, do not believe that	After hearing the report, Ben said, "Don't eat that, guys."
don't get mad; get even	do not waste your energy on anger, do get revenge; **actions speak louder...**	To the victims he said, "Don't get mad. Get even. Report this to the police."

Idiom	Meaning	Example
don't get me wrong	do not misunderstand; **take it the wrong way**	Don't get me wrong; I love literature, but I hate poetry.
don't get smart with me	show more respect, do not **talk back**	If you ask why, she'll say, "Don't get smart with me."
don't give me any of your lip	do not **talk back**, do not refuse to do what I ask	When the boy swore, she said, "Don't give me any of your lip."
don't give me that line/story etc.	do not tell me that false story	Don't give me that line about a cure for the common cold.
don't go away mad; just go away	do not be angry, but leave; you are not welcome here	He said to the heckler, "Don't go away mad; just go away."
don't hand me that	(See **don't give me that**)	
don't hold your breath	it is not going to happen soon, be prepared to wait	The City will repair the street but don't hold your breath.
don't knock it	don't be negative, it could be worse	"I only got a *C* for my report." "Don't knock it. I got a *D*."
don't know him from Adam	do not know who he is, have never met him	The man says he knows me, but I don't know him from Adam.
don't know the first thing about it	do not know anything about it	I can't fix a transmission. I don't know the first thing about it.
don't know the half of it	do not know all the facts, have not heard all of it	Yes, they got divorced, but you don't know the half of it.
don't know whether you're coming or going	you are confused, you do not understand, **go in circles**	If you believe the cult leaders, you won't know whether you're coming or going.
don't know which end is up	are confused, are **mixed up**	After talking to four bureaucrats, I didn't know which end was up.
don't know which side your bread is buttered on	do not know what is really important, have not learned much about life	If you refuse the assistance, you don't know which side your bread is buttered on.
don't know your ass from a hole in the ground [B]	you are ignorant, you are mistaken, **mixed up**	He said one member of the cult was so confused he didn't know his ass from a hole in the ground.
don't look a gift horse in the mouth	do not be critical of a gift, be grateful for a gift	Don't evaluate a gift. Don't look a gift horse in the mouth.
don't make a mountain out of a molehill	do not cause a big fuss about a small problem	So I scratched the car. Don't make a mountain out of a molehill.

Idiom	Meaning	Example
don't make me laugh	do not be ridiculous, **don't give me that line**	When I said I wrote the novel, he said, "Don't make me laugh."
don't make waves	do not do anything that will cause problems	Our company has changed a lot. Don't make any more waves.
don't mention it	it was no trouble, **no problem**	"Thanks for the ride," I said. "Don't mention it," he replied.
don't push your luck	do not try to get too much, do not ask for more	If Mom says *maybe*, don't push your luck. Be patient.
don't put all your eggs in one basket	do not invest all the money in one company	Balance your investments. Don't put all your eggs in one basket.
don't rock the boat	do not cause a change, do not upset anybody	If the team is winning, don't rock the boat. Don't change anything.
don't sweat it	do not worry about it, **you can't saw sawdust**	If you did your best but didn't win a medal, don't sweat it.
don't think so	do not believe it is so, think not	"Do you have dandruff?" "I don't think so."
done for	defeated, beaten, hopeless	We were done for until Tim hit a home run and we won the game.
done good	did well, performed well, **did good**	After watching the race, his dad said, "You done good, Son."
done in	very tired, **dead tired, all in**	After the roundup, the old-timer was done in—exhausted.
done it all	had a lot of experience, done every activity	We need a manager who's done it all—done all the jobs.
done to a turn	cooked or baked until very tasty	The steaks were done to a turn—brown and juicy.
done with it	finished using it, not using it	Just leave the pen on my desk when you're done with it.
Donnybrook	a fight involving many people—especially in a game of hockey	The Flames and the Oilers had another Donnybrook last night—a bench-clearing brawl.
door to door	going from one house to the next house	We went door to door asking for donations for the team.
dork [B]	penis, **dick**, **hoo-haw**	"Does your dork shrink after you've been swimming?" "Ya. That's natural."

Idiom	Meaning	Example
double or nothing	double the first bet and if I win, I owe nothing	After losing the first bet, I said, "Double or nothing this time?"
double take	look again in disbelief, **can't believe my eyes**	She did a double take when Clint Eastwood walked into the store.
double-cross	break a promise, **cheat on** someone	He promised not to tell you, but he did. He double-crossed me.
double-edged sword	(See **a double-edged sword**)	
double-talk	confusing talk, **bafflegab**	His explanation of the Premier's decision was a lot of double-talk.
dough	money, dollars, **moola**	Did you get some dough? We need money to buy groceries.
doughhead	someone who does not think before acting	Don't ever call him a doughhead again. He's my boyfriend.
dove	a person who wants peace, pacifist	The doves complained when the US built more nuclear weapons.
down	sad, depressed, **low**	She's been down ever since her cat died. She misses her cat.
down a peg	(See **take him down a peg**)	
down and dirty	not polite, rude, vulgar	The next song is down and dirty. It's called *Snake's Pad*.
down and out	poor and unlucky, bumming and boozing	When he was down and out, he went to the Salvation Army.
down for the count	defeated by an opponent, out of the contest	Chad was down for the count. He couldn't get up.
down home	simple but good, old fashioned	Hey, Ma. I can't wait to taste your down-home cookin'.
down in the dumps	sad, not happy, depressed, **down in the mouth**	Shelly was down in the dumps until her boyfriend arrived.
down in the mouth	looking sad, having a sad face, **sad sack**	You'd be down in the mouth, too, if you'd just lost your job.
down my throat	(See **shove that down my throat**)	
down on his luck	not lucky lately, not happy or positive	With no money and no job, Ragnar was down on his luck.
down pat	memorized, just right	Flora had her speech down pat. She had practised it many times.

Idiom	Meaning	Example
down the drain	lost, wasted, squandered	His fortune went down the drain when he began to gamble.
down the garden path	(See **lead you down the garden path**)	
down the hatch	down the throat and into the stomach	Another pickled egg went down the hatch. Yum!
down the line	in the future, later, **down the road**	Down the line, we'll meet again and laugh at our argument.
down the road	dismissed, **fired**	Disagree with the boss and you'll soon be down the road.
down the road	in the future, in a few years	We plan to have an office in both cities—but that's down the road.
down the tubes	lost or gone, ruined, **up the creek**	You have to advertise, or your business will go down the tubes.
down to a T	perfectly, exactly, **down pat**	Sharon is wonderful in the play. She has her part down to a T.
down to brass tacks	(See **get down to brass tacks**)	
down to earth	humble, not proud, **salt of the earth**	I like Mrs. Wilson because she's so down to earth, so natural.
down to the wire	to the last minute, near the end	The first two games went down to the wire—very close scores.
down under	Australia, New Zealand etc.	Next year I'm going down under for my holidays—New Zealand.
down with	do not support, stop that plan, **not**	"Down with the sales tax!" they shouted. "Down with the tax!"
downer (sadness)	(See **a downer**)	
downer (drug)	(See **a downer**)	
downhearted	sad, unhappy, **down**	"Are you downhearted, my dear?" "No. Just quiet, my love."
downplay	say it is not important, **soft pedal**	They tried to downplay the fact that smoking caused the fire.
downside	(See **the downside**)	
downtime	time needed to repair a machine	When you own a computer, you have to expect some downtime.

Idiom	Meaning	Example
draft dodger	a person who runs away from military service	American draft dodgers came to Canada in the 1970s.
drag	(See **a drag**)	
drag race	two cars racing from a stop light	"Did you see the drag race?" "Ya. The Corvette won."
drag your feet	work too slow, prevent progress	They're dragging their feet. Tell them to work faster.
drag it out	take a long time to finish, speak for a long time	When James tells a ghost story, he drags it out for an hour.
drag on	go for a long time, last for hours or days	The funeral dragged on and on—for three days!
dragged through a...	(See **look like I was dragged through a knothole**)	
drain the swamp	remove what prevents a clear view of the problem	If I were manager, my first step would be to drain the swamp.
drat	oh no, **nuts**, **rats**, **scrut**	Drat! I've lost the key. How can we get into the apartment?
draw a blank	not be able to think of an answer, **mind go blank**	For some reason, I drew a blank when the professor questioned me.
draw a sober breath	be sober, not be drunk	They say he hasn't drawn a sober breath since his son was killed.
draw attention to	ask people to notice; show or display to people	If you wear a short skirt, you draw attention to your legs.
draw first blood	attack first, be first to hit or win	The Jets drew first blood in the series, winning game one 5-4.
draw it to my attention	tell me about it, cause me to be aware of it	Spelling *is* a problem. Thanks for drawing it to my attention.
draw the line	stop, refuse to do it	When it comes to drugs, he draws the line. He won't touch them.
draw their fire	get attention while a friend moves or escapes	You draw their fire while I move behind them. You distract them.
draw upon	recall and use, remember	At university, I drew upon my knowledge of Russian history.
drawing card	entertainment to attract people, **loss leader**	The community hired a comedian as a drawing card for the fair.

Idiom	Meaning	Example
dream on	you are not being realistic, **get your head out...**	You expect me to buy you a Corvette? Dream on!
dress down	(See **a dressing down**)	
dress down	dress in casual clothes, dress informally	It's a library party, so dress down. Wear something casual.
dress rehearsal	the last rehearsal before the performance, **dry run**	All actors must come to the dress rehearsal—our last practice.
dress up	dress in your best clothes, put on **glad rags**	Everybody got dressed up for the banquet. Roy wore his new suit.
dressed fit to kill	dressed in party clothes, **dolled up**, **dress up**	In walks Erica, dressed fit to kill. She looked terrific!
dressed to the nines	dressed in high fashion, **gussied up**	Here I am in jeans. Everybody else is dressed to the nines.
drink like a fish	drink a lot of liquor every day	If Hal is coming to visit, buy lots of beer. He drinks like a fish.
drink up	drink your wine etc., **bottoms up**	Drink up, my friends. It's Buddy's birthday!
drink you under the table	drink more liquor than you, drink and not **pass out**, **put you away**	After three glasses of beer, you're nearly drunk. I bet I can drink you under the table!
drips and drabs	(See **in dribs and drabs**)	
drive a hard bargain	pay a low price, negotiate firmly	When buying land, Cal drives a hard bargain. He pays low prices.
drive around	drive a car up and down the streets, **tooling around**	At night we drove around town, looking for something to do.
drive it home	make a message clear, say it so they understand	When you talk about safe sex, drive it home. Stress safety.
drive me batty	cause me to be insane, **drive me crazy**	The noise from that motorcycle is driving me batty!
drive me crazy	cause me to feel crazy, **bug** me a lot	That TV commercial drives me crazy! It's on every channel!
drive me to the edge	cause me to be nearly mad or insane	When those chipmunks sing, it drives me to the edge!
drive me up the wall	cause me to feel anxious; go **around the bend**	I won't babysit for the Kaplans. The kids drive me up the wall.

Idiom	Meaning	Example
drive standard	shift gears on a car or truck	Can you drive standard? My car has a five-speed transmission.
drive you	hit you, punch you, **cream you**	If you get pushy, he'll drive you. He's got a bad temper.
drive you nuts	cause you to feel crazy, **drive you crazy**	Working for Harry will drive you nuts. He's a perfectionist.
drive you to distraction	cause you to lose thoughts, **drive me up the wall**	Her continual chatter will drive you to distraction.
drive you to drink	cause you to drink alcohol or want to be drunk	His critical attitude will drive you to drink. I had to resign.
drop	stop taking a subject, withdraw, **drop out**	You wouldn't drop English! It's the key to other subjects.
drop a bundle	lose money by gambling, **lose your shirt**	I dropped a bundle at the track last night. I lost every bet.
drop a hint	suggest, give a sign	When he was hungry, he'd drop a hint, like point at the fridge.
drop a line	write a letter, send a postcard	Be sure to drop us a line from Paris. Tell us about your trip.
drop a log [B]	have a bowel movement, **take a shit** [B]	What a smell! Open a window after you drop a log, eh.
drop a name/drop names	pretend you know famous people, **name dropper**	He was dropping names at the interview—Klein, Clinton, etc.
drop back	run slower than before, run further behind	Our horse dropped back to fourth place and lost the race.
drop behind	run further behind, **lose ground**	Our party has dropped behind in the polls. We're in second place.
drop charges	withdraw complaints, not **press charges**	I realized it was an accident, so I dropped the charges.
drop dead	you are badly mistaken, **go to hell** [B]	If you think I'm getting on that motorcycle, you can drop dead.
drop her/him	leave her, not date her anymore, **tube her**	She wouldn't quit smoking, so I dropped her—told her it was off.
drop him like a hot potato	leave him, not associate with him	If she finds out you're not rich, she'll drop you like a hot potato.
drop in	visit, go to see, **drop over**	When you come to Edmonton, be sure to drop in for a visit.

Idiom	Meaning	Example
drop in the bucket	(See **a drop in the bucket**)	
drop it	stop talking about it, do not say any more	When I mentioned his accident, he told me to drop it.
drop like flies	dying in great numbers, falling dead on the floor	When a pox infected the tribe, people were dropping like flies.
drop off	deliver, drive and leave a parcel	I'll drop off the parcel today. What's your address?
drop off	go to sleep, doze, **fall asleep**	I only dropped off for a second. I was awake for the news.
drop off	reduce, diminish, **slip, slow down**	Sales have dropped off recently. Maybe we should advertise.
drop out	quit, stop attending	I have decided not to drop out of school. I'm going to continue.
drop out of sight	disappear, not be seen for awhile	After the scandal, he dropped out of sight. I haven't seen him.
drop over	visit, come and talk	Our friends dropped over last night for a cup of coffee.
drop your drawers	take your pants down, remove your shorts	Don't you hate it when you have to drop your drawers for a nurse?
drop your gloves (hockey)	remove your gloves to fight with your fists	Don't drop your gloves in this game. There's no fighting.
drop-in	visitor, one who **drops in**	He was a drop-in at the Seniors' Center. He liked to go there.
drown your sorrow	drink until the sadness goes away	Jay drowned her sorrow in wine. Then she had a headache.
drum up	create interest in, recruit, find some customers	We have a million widgets to sell. Let's drum up some customers.
dry out	stop using alcohol, **on the wagon**	She's drying out at a treatment center. It's a four-week program.
dry run	complete rehearsal, **walk through**	Let's do a dry run of our play so I can add the background music.
dry up	stop talking, be quiet	I wish he'd dry up. He talks too much.
dubs	everyone pays for his own food; **Dutch treat**	If we go to the cafe, it's dubs. We each pay for our own treat.

Idiom	Meaning	Example
ducks in order	organized, planned; each person knows his job	I have to get my ducks in order before the sale on Tuesday.
due north	straight north, directly north	Follow the winding road west to the junction; then go due north.
duke it out	fight with your fists, punch each other	Gerry wanted to duke it out with the referee—tried to punch him.
dumbbell	one who does not think, **airhead, knucklehead**	What a dumbbell I am! I locked the keys in the car.
dumbo	a person who acts stupid, a fool, a **dipstick**	Hey, dumbo! You're driving on the wrong side of the road!
dump her/him	leave her or him, **drop her, tube her**	Sid and Marie had a fight, so he dumped her and began seeing me.
dump on	unload the dirty jobs, give what is left over	They dump on Karen too much. They give her the large classes.
dumpster diving	searching in the garbage to find bottles etc.	No. This college does not offer a course in dumpster diving.
durn	(See **darn**)	
dust	ruined, dead, **done for, toast**	If you smuggle drugs into the US, you're dust. You'll go to jail.
dust bunny	ball of dust on the floor, dust that looks like fur	On Saturday morning I vacuum up the dust bunnies before I go out.
dust devil	small whirlwind, twister	Dust devils seemed to follow us as we walked across the field.
dust-up	(See **a dust-up**)	
Dutch treat	everyone pays for his/her own lunch etc.; **dubs**	When we go for eats, let's go Dutch. That's fair, eh.
duty calls	it is my duty, I must do a task	"Duty calls," he said, opening a book to begin his homework.
dying seconds	(See **the dying seconds**)	
dying to know	wants to know, is very curious	Amy is dying to know the name of the guy in the leather jacket.

Idiom	Meaning	Example

E

Idiom	Meaning	Example
each to his own	(See **to each his own**)	
eager beaver	a person who wants to work	Joan is the eager beaver in this class. She likes to work.
eagle eyes	a person who can see details or errors	We call him *Eagle Eyes* because he finds so many lost golf balls.
ear candy	music that is pleasant, beautiful music	The theme music in the movie *Out of Africa* is ear candy.
ear to the ground	(See **keep your ear to the ground**)	
earful	(See **an earful**)	
early bird	(See **the early bird gets the worm**)	
ears pinned back	told to behave, disciplined	The rowdy kid needs his ears pinned back. Tell him to behave.
ease up	work or play slower, **take it easy** on	Ease up on the younger players, eh. Don't work them too hard.
ease up	not push as much, reduce the pressure, **let up**	You can ease up on the gas pedal when we reach 100 km per hour.
easy as pie	very easy to do, **piece of cake**	That math problem is easy as pie. I'll show you how to do it.
easy come, easy go	if we get things free we do not worry when we lose them	As Ming was spending his lottery money, he said, "Easy come, easy go."
easy pickings	an easy task or job, **piece of cake**	It was a multiple-choice test— easy pickings if you studied.
easy street	an easy life, a life with lots of money to spend	Win five million dollars and we'll be on easy street.
easy time of it	not much work to do, an easy life	While living with his wealthy aunt, he had an easy time of it.

Idiom	Meaning	Example
eat crow	admit you were wrong, **take back** what you said	When I lost the bet, I had to eat crow—admit I was wrong.
eat humble pie	admit I did not play well, feel humble after defeat	Ben had to eat humble pie after he finished fourth in the race.
eat it up	finish eating some food, eat all of the food	That's a good boy. Eat it up and then you can go out to play.
eat it up	believe a story, **eat out of the palm...**	The children were eating it up— every word the teacher said.
eat like a horse	eat a lot, **pig out**	Barney eats like a horse. He has a monstrous appetite.
eat my hat/shirt	be very surprised or shocked if it is true	If the Vancouver Canucks win the Cup, I'll eat my hat!
eat out	eat at a restaurant, eat at a cafe	On Friday evenings we eat out, usually at a Greek restaurant.
eat out of the palm of your hand	do whatever you ask, obey you, **win the hearts**	If you tell the children a story, you'll have them eating out of the palm of your hand.
eat that	believe that, **buy that**, **swallow that**	After listening to the UFO scientist, my uncle said, "Are we supposed to eat that?"
eat up	begin to eat, continue to eat, **dig in**	Eat up, folks. We have lots of pancakes.
eat you for breakfast	defeat you easily, **have you for breakfast**	In a game of racquetball he'll eat you for breakfast. He's quick.
eat you out of house and home	eat all your food, **pig out**	Our son's team came to dinner and ate us out of house and home!
eat your fill	eat until you are satisfied, eat as much as you can	Eat your fill. You won't have another meal till we get home.
eat your heart out	envy my prize, wish that you had one	When Kurt won the Porsche, he said, "Eat your heart out, guys."
eat your words	regret what you said, admit you were wrong	He told me the answer, and I had to eat my words. I was wrong.
eating you	(See **what's eating you**)	
edgy	nervous, cranky, **touchy**	You're kind of edgy today. Did you sleep well last night?

Idiom	Meaning	Example
egg me on	encourage me, tell me to do it	I didn't want to steal the exam, but they egged me on.
egg on my face	embarrassed, outsmarted	I made a deal with Jake and ended up with egg on my face.
ego trip	feeling of self importance, feeling superior	If you tell him he played well, he'll go on an ego trip.
eh	you understand, you know what I am taking about	There were three boys but only two girls, eh.
eke out a living	earn or grow enough to survive	On the small farm we were able to eke out a living.
elbow room	room to move among people, space in a crowd	On the streets of Hong Kong there wasn't much elbow room.
electronic superhighway	a computer network, **Internet**	We can find more information on the electronic superhighway.
end justifies the means	(See **the end justifies the means**)	
end of the line	(See **the end of the line**)	
end up	where you stop or finish, the end of a journey	We often end up sleeping at Ty's house. His mom doesn't mind.
enough is enough	it is time to stop, **enough already**	"Enough is enough!" she said after my sixth piece of pie.
even	we do not owe each other, **a wash**, **call it square**	I owe you $20, but I gave you a haircut, so we're even.
even keel	(See **keep an even keel**)	
even so	regardless, no matter	"He doesn't need the money." "Even so, I must repay the loan."
even up	equal parts, equal pieces for each person	They split the profits even up— 50% to each partner.
even-steven	equal work or achievement, evenly matched	After one lap, Karim and I were even-steven. It was a tie race.
every trick in the book	every method or device, every way of doing it	If you want to find boys, Keiko knows every trick in the book.
every walk of life	every occupation, all lifestyles	People from every walk of life attend our church.
everything but the kitchen sink	almost everything, **the whole works**	We put everything in his truck, everything but the kitchen sink!

Idiom	Meaning	Example
everything from soup to nuts	a lot of food or things, a variety of groceries	His shopping cart was full. He had everything from soup to nuts.
everything old is new again	fashions and trends are repeated or revived	Hey, if miniskirts are back, everything old is new again!
ex	former wife or husband; girlfriend or boyfriend	His ex got the Mercedes; he got the truck.
exit stage left	departure, **gonzo**, **outa here**	When that bull got loose, I did an exit stage left!
expand your horizons	experience or discover new ideas or goals or cultures	Travel, read, discuss—expand your horizons!
eye candy	something that is nice to look at, a beautiful object	She was eye candy. I've never seen a more beautiful car!
eye for an eye	(See **an eye for an eye**)	
eye of a needle	(See **the eye of a needle**)	
eye of the storm	(See **the eye of the storm**)	
eye to eye	(See **see eye to eye**)	
eyes glaze over	eyes express disbelief or "I've heard this before"	When I told him I'd pay the rent *next* week, his eyes glazed over.
eyes peeled	(See **keep your eyes peeled**)	

Idiom	Meaning	Example

F

'fraid so	(See **afraid so**)	
F-word	(See **the F-word**)	
face facts	accept the truth, deal with reality, **come to grips**	If we face facts, we can see that one salary is not enough.
face the music	face the results of our actions, be responsible	If you damage the car, you must face the music—pay for repairs.
face up	admit that you did it, **own up**	If Karl caused the problem, he'll face up. He'll admit it.
fag/faggot	gay or homosexual man	Sean is a fag; he admits it.
faint of heart	timid, not courageous, **chicken, lily-livered**	Sky diving is not for people who are faint of heart.
fair game	legal to hunt or shoot or criticize, **open season**	An elected politician is fair game for criticism.
fair shake	(See **a fair shake**)	
fair-haired boy	favorite boy, favorite man	He's the fair-haired boy in this office. They think he's perfect.
fake it	create the parts you forget, **fudge it, make up**	If he forgets the words, he fakes it. He thinks of new words.
falderal	(See **a lot of falderal**)	
fall apart (at the seams)	not be able to cope or manage, **come unglued**	After his wife died, he fell apart. He lost interest in everything.
fall asleep	begin to sleep, **drop off**	Don't fall asleep while we're in church. It's embarrassing.
fall behind	not be able to run as fast, **drop behind**	You will fall behind in your work if you miss a day of school.
fall for	begin to love, **fall in love** with	When I was in Grade 8, I fell for Miss Kramer. She was beautiful.

Idiom	Meaning	Example
fall for that	believe that, **eat that**	Surely you're not going to fall for that story. It's nonsense.
fall in line	do as others are doing, obey orders	Although Barry doesn't like the new rules, he'll fall in line.
fall in love	begin to love, feel romantic about	Michael and Rose have fallen in love. They're very happy.
fall into a trap	be tricked, be deceived	When the lawyer asks you questions, don't fall into a trap.
fall into my lap	find without looking, receive without asking	Reg got another job offer today. Things seem to fall into his lap.
fall off the wagon	become drunk again, return to a bad habit	The old man fell off the wagon. He got drunk last night.
fall on deaf ears	talk to people who will not listen, **really deaf**	If you talk to the workers about management's problems, your message will fall on deaf ears.
fall on your sword	quit, resign, **pull the pin**	I know I caused the problem, but I won't fall on my sword. They'll have to fire me.
fall short	not able to do as well as planned	I'm falling short of my career goals because I've been ill.
fall through	not happen, not succeed, not **come off**, not **pan out**	His plans to write a novel fell through because he didn't get a government grant.
fall through the cracks	not be included, **leave out**	These children fell through the cracks. They didn't learn to read.
fall to pieces	be unable to talk or reply, be overwhelmed	When I see Mario, I just fall to pieces. He's so handsome!
fall-out	harmful effects, continuing effects	We still feel the fall-out from his negative speech on abortion.
fallen woman	prostitute, **hooker**	The priest was trying to save the fallen women in his parish.
falling in love	beginning to feel love, being in love	They say that falling in love is wonderful—marvellous!
falling-out	(See **a falling-out**)	
false move	(See **a false move**)	

Idiom	Meaning	Example
familiarity breeds contempt	a friend may dislike you if you do not respect his or her privacy	Don't call Margaret *Maggie*. Remember, familiarity breeds contempt.
family jewels	(See **the family jewels**)	
family tree	chart of ancestors, record of parents' forefathers	Bo is helping me to research my family tree—my ancestors.
famous last words	a prediction that is false— the opposite happens, **twist of fate**	"We don't need a spare tire. We never have flat tires on this car." "Sure. Famous last words!"
fancy footwork	neat maneuvers, clever moves	You did some fancy footwork to answer their questions. Bravo!
far cry	(See **a far cry**)	
far out	unbelievable, fantastic, **wow**	When I wear my bikini, he says, "Far out!"
fart around [B]	play instead of work, **goof off**, hang out	When we were kids we used to fart around at my uncle's store.
fart in a windstorm [B]	(See **a fart in a windstorm**)	
fast friends	close friends, permanent friends	Sue and I became fast friends when we were in Grade 4.
fast lane	(See **life in the fast lane**)	
fast track	the quickest route or path, **short cut**	There is no fast track to success in the field of photography.
fat cat	rich or wealthy person, **rolling in it**	They're the fat cats in our town. They've got tons of money.
fat chance	very little chance, not likely	Me? Type 100 words per minute? Fat chance!
fat lip	a hit on the lip, an injured lip	Where'd you get the fat lip? Did somebody hit you?
fate is sealed	destiny was known, fate was determined	When you said you loved me, that's when your fate was sealed.
feast your eyes on	enjoy looking at, **get a load of**	I opened a box of diamonds and said, "Feast your eyes on these!"
feather a pass (hockey)	pass a puck accurately but softly	Nilsson could feather a pass better than the other players.
feather in your cap	(See **a feather in your cap**)	

Idiom	Meaning	Example
feather your nest	make a comfortable place, prepare your future place, **nest egg**	Charles became a professor and began to feather his nest at the University of Manitoba.
fed up	tired of, disgusted with, **had enough**	He's fed up with their laziness. I think he's angry with them.
feedback	reply, response, reaction to a plan, **splashback**	"What is the feedback on our plan to cut education funds?" "Negative. People disapprove."
feel a draft	feel the air from someone who is talking too much	When Jake talks too much, Pete asks, "Does anyone feel a draft?"
feel blue	feel sad, **down, low**	When Mara goes away, Don feels blue. He's lonely and sad.
feel for	feel sympathy or pity for someone	I feel for kids who are homeless. I want to help them.
feel free	feel that you may do it, **by all means**	Feel free to use the library. You can read and study there.
feel myself	(See **not feeling myself**)	
feel the pinch	feel a little bit poorer, feel there is less money	Now that we have only one income, we feel the pinch.
feeling bum	feeling lazy or negative, lacking energy	I'm feeling kind of bum today. I didn't sleep well last night.
feeling good	a little bit drunk, **buzzed, had a few**	After drinking a few beers Pat was feeling good.
feeling his oats	feeling energetic, feeling strong	Look at that cowboy dance! He's feeling his oats tonight.
feeling no pain	half drunk, **half-corked, half-shot**	After three drinks of rum, Alex was feeling no pain.
fence sitter	a person who supports both sides in an argument, **middle ground**	Many politicians become fence sitters because they want to please everyone.
fend for yourself	be independent, care for yourself	Soon you'll know the city, and you can fend for yourself.
fender bender	minor car accident, collision	I had a little fender bender with your car, Dad—just a scratch.
fever breaks	fever stops, fever begins to go down	His fever broke last night. He's going to be alright.

Idiom	Meaning	Example
few and far between	very few, rare, **the odd one**	Canada still has timber wolves, but they are few and far between.
fib	small lie, **white lie**	"What's a fib, Dad?" "It's a lie. It's the same as a lie."
fickle finger of fate	(See **the fickle finger of fate**)	
fiddlesticks	oh no, **darn**, **nuts**, **rats**, **shucks**	Fiddlesticks! I forgot to get the mail!
fifth business	an unimportant player, an extra member	You are fifth business, Dunny. Anyone can play your part.
fifth wheel	(See **a fifth wheel**)	
fight fire with fire	fight with the same weapon the enemy uses	If he uses statistics, you use statistics. Fight fire with fire!
fight tooth and nail	fight hard, fight like an animal	Canadian women fought tooth and nail for the right to vote.
fighting chance	(See **a fighting chance**)	
figure out	analyze and understand, discover why	Can you figure out why the car stalled? Is the gas tank empty?
figurehead	a person who calculates but does not control	Shamir is just a figurehead; if you want a decision, see Ali.
file 13	the garbage can or wastebasket	This letter goes in file 13—in the can in the corner.
fill her up	fill the tank with gasoline, **fill-up**	He drove up to the gas pumps and said, "Fill 'er up, please."
fill his shoes	do his work as well as he does	If Mia leaves, it won't be easy to fill her shoes. She does two jobs.
fill in	complete by writing, write in the spaces	Fill in the blanks, please. Then give the form to Ms. Kiraly.
fill in for me	do my job, do my work	Will you fill in for me while I'm away? Just answer my phone.
fill me in	tell me the details, tell me more	Fill me in when I get home. I'd like to hear what happened.
fill out	complete by writing, **fill in**	Fill out the application, sign it, and mail it to the college.

Idiom	Meaning	Example
fill the bill	do the job, **fill the gap**, **serve the purpose**	If we need an extra cashier for the sale, Bert will fill the bill.
fill the gap	fill an empty space, help where there is work to do	Pam filled the gap when I got injured. She played in my place.
fill up	fill to the top	You fill up the salt shaker, okay?
fill your face	eat, put a lot food in your mouth, **pig out**	Imagine yourself in a chocolate factory, filling your face!
fill-up	(See **a fill-up**)	
filthy lucre	money, dollars	Filthy lucre—that's what people want—cash, moola, lettuce.
filthy rich	very rich, wealthy, **rolling in it**	She was filthy rich after she got married. She was a millionaire.
find a way around	find a way not to pay, avoid a rule, **get around**	If you want to find a way around a tax law, talk to Sammy.
find fault	look for faults and mistakes, criticize	I don't want to be around a guy who is always finding fault.
find my tongue	think of something to say, think of a reply	When she told me she had AIDS, I couldn't find my tongue.
find out	discover, learn	We found out he was a member of a cult. His sister told us.
find your voice	discover your personal style	Write, write, write until you find your voice—your own style.
find your way	find the correct path or road	A bus driver will help you find your way. Ask for directions.
find yourself	be surprised by what happens to you	If I don't brush my teeth, I may find myself without friends.
fine-toothed comb	(See **a fine-toothed comb**)	
fine-tune	cause it to work very well, cause it to run smoothly	Sandro fine-tuned my Peugeot. Now it purrs like a kitten.
finger	accuse, blame	He was fingered for the crime, but he didn't steal anything.
finish off	eat the remaining amount, eat the last piece	The kids finished off the cake when they got home.
finish off	kill, strike the final blow	The spider finished off the fly and began to eat it.

Idiom	Meaning	Example
finishing touch	the final move, the act that completes the task	As a finishing touch, the baker added a maraschino cherry.
fink	fool, **jerk, nerd**	You fink! You sat on my pizza!
fire	dismiss from a job, terminate employment	"What happened to Larry?" "He got fired for stealing funds."
fire away	ask questions, comment, criticize, **shoot**	After speaking for gun control, he invited the men to fire away.
fired up	enthusiastic, motivated, **gung-ho**	The boys are fired up and ready to play. They're really excited.
firm hand	(See **a firm hand**)	
first and foremost	first and most important, firstly	The speaker began by saying, "First and foremost...."
first class	high quality, excellent	Pam's meals are first class. She's an excellent cook.
first come, first served	whoever comes first gets served first	If tickets are selling on a first-come basis, let's buy ours now.
first crack at	first turn, first chance to do it	I want first crack at solving the problem. I want to try first.
first dibs	first person to use it, first chance to use it	When we get to the motel, I get first dibs on the shower.
first down/first and ten	first try to gain ten yards (in football)	The Lions have a first down on their own 35-yard line.
first hand	being there to see or hear it, **in person**	I want to see the Pantheon first hand. I want to see its dome.
first light	(See **at first light**)	
first off	first on the list, the first thing to do	First off, we should define the problem. Then we can solve it.
first up	first on the list, the first thing to do	On our list of things to do, the broken copier is first up.
fish and company stink after three days	fish should be eaten while it is fresh, and guests should not stay too long	Grandfather had this sign on the wall of his garage: *Fish and company stink after three days!*
fish for a compliment	hint that he wants a compliment	If Al mentions cars, he's fishing for a compliment on his Jaguar.

Idiom	Meaning	Example
fit as a fiddle	very fit, in good physical condition	Uncle Doug is fit as a fiddle. He does aerobic exercises.
fit to be tied	very angry, mad, **see red**	He was fit to be tied when you said the accident was his fault.
fits and starts	moving unevenly, stop and go	The new crew worked in fits and starts, not at a steady pace.
fix you	punish you, **get even**, **get you back**	"I'll fix you," he shouted at us. "I'll build a fence to keep you off my property!"
fix your wagon	hurt you, **get back at**, **get revenge**	If you make him angry, he'll fix your wagon. He'll get revenge.
flag a cab	wave at a cab driver to come, **hail a cab**	The bus was late, so we flagged a taxi that was going by.
flake	phony, not real	The salesman was a flake. What he said was phony.
flake out	lie down and sleep, **conk out**	Grant flaked out on the couch after lunch. He was really tired.
flap your gums	talk, speak, **gab**	Don't just stand there flapping your gums. Help with supper.
flash a smile	smile at someone for only a second	Andy flashed a smile at me when the teacher asked to see his work.
flash in the pan	(See **a flash in the pan**)	
flat	not motivated, lacking energy, not **up for it**	In the second game, the team was flat. They lacked energy.
flat broke	having no money, **out of** cash	By the end of my first term at university, I was flat broke.
flat out	as fast as possible, pedal to the metal	Scott was driving flat out most of the way—over 180 km per hour.
flatfoot	policeman, a constable who walks the streets	Ted is a flatfoot in Regina. He works for Regina City Police.
flatfooted	(See **caught flatfooted**)	
flatliner	a person who does not show changes in his/her feelings	Our doctor is a flatliner. His face shows no joy, no sorrow.
flattery will get you nowhere	saying nice things will not help you, **kiss the blarney stone**	When I complimented Anna on her hair, she said, "Thanks, but flattery will get you nowhere."

Idiom	Meaning	Example
fleeting glance	(See **a fleeting glance**)	
flew the coop	departed, left home	Brian flew the coop last night. He packed a suitcase and left.
flip	be surprised, **freak out**	Mom nearly flipped when I told her we got married.
flip you for it	flip a coin to decide who pays	When our food check arrived, Al said to me, "I'll flip you for it."
flip your lid	become angry, **blow your stack**	If you get another speeding ticket, Dad will flip his lid.
flip-flop	change of opinion, move to the other side	We often see politicians do a flip-flop after they're elected.
flipping	**consarned, darn, friggin,**	If you don't like the flippin' rules, you don't have to play.
floor it	push the gas pedal down, **pedal to the metal**	Buddy floors it from every stoplight. He drives too fast.
floor you	surprise you, shock you, **bowl you over**	The odor from a turkey farm is enough to floor you.
Florida green	yellow traffic light, amber warning light	Oops! I just drove through a Florida green. Any cops around?
flunk out	fail a school program, fail a course	If you flunk out of college, you will have to find a job.
fly by the seat of your...	(See **by the seat of your pants**)	
fly in the face of	contradict, be opposite to	These errors fly in the face of our reputation for accuracy.
fly in the ointment	small problem, troublesome detail	The fly in the ointment is that a boy saw you kissing Lola.
fly low	drive a vehicle very fast, drive so fast you nearly fly	On the freeway I was flying low —going over 200 km per hour.
fly off the handle	become angry suddenly, **lose your temper**	After Charlie flew off the handle he apologized for his temper.
fly on the wall	(See **a fly on the wall**)	
fly-by-night	bad, dishonest, not to be trusted	He put his money in a fly-by-night company and lost it all.

Idiom	Meaning	Example
fold	quit, stop operating	The store folded during the recession—went bankrupt.
follow the rules	read the rules and do what they say, **toe the line**	If everybody follows the rules, we'll have fewer accidents.
follow through	do what you promise, **see it through**	If you promise to help, try to follow through.
food for thought	ideas worth considering, interesting suggestions	Your comments on Quebec have given me food for thought.
fool and his money...	(See **a fool and his money are soon parted**)	
fool around	play, play around, **goof off, horse around**	We don't fool around in her class. She's very strict.
fool around	have sex with someone who is not your spouse, **have an affair**	Rita asked Jon for a divorce. She knows he's been fooling around.
fool you	trick you, deceive you	Paul was fooling you. He owns a Ford, not a Ferrari.
foot the bill	pay all of the expenses, **pay the shot**	It's not right for Dad to foot the bill for your trip to Vegas.
footloose and fancy-free	carefree, not committed, **devil-may-care**	When the kids moved out, we were footloose and fancy-free!
for a dog's age	a long time, 10-15 years, **in a coon's age**	We haven't seen Aunt Sophie for a dog's age—for years.
for a song	for a little money, for a low price	Look at this sweater. I got it for a song at a second-hand store.
for all the tea in China	(See **not for all the tea in China**)	
for better or worse	during good times and bad times, **through thick and thin**	When you marry someone for better or worse, you hope for better but prepare for worse.
for crying out loud	before I start crying, **for gosh sake**	For cryin' out loud will you stop playing those drums!
for dear life	to save your life, because a life is in danger	When the bear stood up on its hind legs, we ran for dear life.
for good	forever, permanently	Remember, a tattoo stays on your skin for good—forever.
for good measure	adding enough or a bit more than required	For good measure, we added a a bottle of wine to the punch.

Idiom	Meaning	Example
for goodness sake	for the good of everyone, please	For goodness sake, don't drive so fast! The roads are icy.
for gosh sake	for god's sake **for goodness sake**	For gosh sake! Where did you get that monstrous hat?
for heaven's sake	for the sake of everyone, **for goodness sake**	For heaven's sake, don't give her a teapot. She has four!
for kicks	for fun, for enjoyment	"What do you guys do for kicks?" "I play computer games."
for laughs	for fun, for amusement	For laughs, we watch old movies.
for long	for a long time, for many minutes or days	She wasn't in the water for very long—just a couple of minutes.
for love nor money	not for any reason, never, **no way**	I won't skydive for love nor money. It's too dangerous.
for openers	as a first activity, to begin	For openers, let's discuss the budget. It's very important.
for Pete's sake	for the good of "Pete" and everybody	For Pete's sake, don't talk when your mouth is full of food!
for sure	yes, certainly, **no doubt**	I'll pay you back tomorrow for sure. I promise.
for the birds	poor quality, **crummy**, **the pits**	It was a beautiful wedding, but the food was for the birds.
for the fun of it	for fun, for a good time, **for laughs**	"Why did you take my bike?" "Just for the fun of it."
for the life of me	it is a mystery to me, **why in the world**	For the life of me, I don't know why she stays with him.
force of habit	from habit, because of a habit	She still cooks enough food for five people. It's force of habit.
forever and a day	for a long time, for an eternity	This treaty will last forever— forever and a day.
forget it	do not continue, stop it, I do not want it, **drop it**	I'm not interested in joining the club. Forget it.
forget your manners	forget to be polite, forget to say *please* etc.	When I reached in front of Mac, he said, "Forget your manners?"
foregone conclusion	(See **a foregone conclusion**)	

Idiom	Meaning	Example
fork over	pay, **pay up**	They said, "Fork over, man. Pay your share of the bill."
found money	money found on the street, money saved by nature	Wind power is like found money. I save what I paid for electricity.
found out	discovered, caught	If you cheat on the exam, you'll be found out. They'll see you.
four-letter word	bad word, profanity: damn, hell, shit, etc. [B]	He gave a good speech, but he used a lot of four-letter words.
frame	cause you to look guilty, **set you up**	He framed you. He lent you his car, then reported it as stolen.
frame of mind	mood, mental attitude, **state of mind**	I'm not in the right frame of mind to listen to your poem.
frazzled	having tired nerves, **going in circles**	I'm frazzled! Gift shopping takes all my nervous energy.
freak/freak out	show surprise or disbelief, **flip, go ballistic**	Mom will freak when I tell her we're married.
free-for-all	(See **a free-for-all**)	
freebie	a free ticket etc., a sample	Some drug companies advertise through freebies—free pills.
freeload	receive free food or rent, **a handout**	Do social programs encourage freeloading? It's a good question.
freeze wages	keep wages the same, not increase wages, **dig in their heels**	To control spending, the board is going to freeze our wages— no salary increases for one year.
freeze-up	when the lakes and ground freeze (November)	We want to dig the hole for the basement before freeze-up.
fresh	(See **get fresh**)	
fresh legs	players who are rested, players who are not tired	"We need fresh legs out there!" the coach yelled. "They're tired!"
fresh out	do not have any, all **used up**	I wish I could lend you some rice, but I'm fresh out.
fresh pair of eyes	(See **a fresh pair of eyes**)	
fresh start	(See **a fresh start**)	
freshen up	wash your hands etc., use the washroom	If you want to freshen up, you can use our bathroom.

Idiom	Meaning	Example
friends with	a friend of, a good friend	"Are you friends with Carla?" "Yes. She's my best friend."
friggin	damn, fucking [B], **cotton picking**, **darn**, **flipping**	Then the friggin string broke and the friggin marbles fell all over the friggin floor!
frightened to death	very afraid, **scared spitless**, **scared stiff**	She said she was frightened to death when she heard the shot.
from day one	from the beginning, from the first day	From day one, Carol has been a good employee.
from hand to mouth	poor, spending every cent on necessities	They lived from hand to mouth, never enjoying luxury or travel.
from hunger	poor quality, poor taste, **the pits**	Tanya can sing, but her hair style is strictly from hunger.
from pillar to post	from one problem to another	After getting fired, he went from pillar to post—more bad luck.
from rags to riches	from poverty to wealth, from bum to millionaire	She went from rags to riches when she gambled in Vegas.
from scratch	(See **start from scratch**)	
from soup to nuts	(See **everything from soup to nuts**)	
from square one	(See **back to square one**)	
from the bottom of my heart	sincerely, with deep feeling	For your kindness, I thank you from the bottom of my heart.
from the frying pan into the fire	from bad to worse	I went from farming to fishing— from the frying pan into the fire!
from the get-go	from the beginning, **from day one**	First, a dog has to learn who's boss—right from the get-go.
from the horse's mouth	(See **straight from the horse's mouth**)	
from the word go	from the beginning, from the start	You knew I worked for the KGB. You knew it from the word go.
from time to time	once in awhile, occasionally	They visit us from time to time—every year or two.
front man	one who performs before the star goes on stage	Mick is the front man for Dolly. He sings before she does her act.

Idiom	Meaning	Example
front me	lend me money for now, **put up the money**	If you will front me, I can buy the car and then repay you.
front runner	leader, one of the best	With this new model, Nissan will be a front runner again.
frosty Friday	(See **that'll be the frosty Friday**)	
fuck off [B]	go, get out of here, **get lost, take off**	When I asked him to move his truck, he told me to fuck off.
fuck that noise [B]	that is not a good idea, **down with** that plan	"Let's return the TVs we stole." "Fuck that noise. Let's sell 'em."
fuck up [B]	cause a mistake, **make a booboo, screw up**	If you fuck up, don't worry— but learn from your mistakes.
fucked by the fickle finger of fate [B]	feel that luck is against you; cheated by fate	A flood ruined my business. I was fucked by the fickle finger of fate.
fuddle duddle	**fiddlesticks, nuts, phooey, rats,**	I did not use the F-word. I said, "Oh, fuddle duddle!"
fudge it	create, **fake it, make up**	If you can't remember a name, fudge it. Answer every question.
full blast	as loud as possible, **pull out all the stops**	When we got home, the kids had the stereo on full blast.
full blown	all the symptoms, every sign	It often takes years for the virus to develop into full-blown AIDS.
full of herself	impressed with her own work, too proud of herself	The actor was proud—too full of himself—during the interview.
full of it [B]	full of lies, full of shit, full of **BS**	You're full of it if you think I took that watch. I am not a thief.
full of piss and vinegar [B]	lively, full of encrgy	That little kid is full of piss and vinegar. He won't sit still.
full out	as fast as you can go, **flat out, full tilt**	He was skating full out, but he couldn't catch Messier.
full plate	(See **a full plate**)	
full steam ahead	as much power as we have, **full throttle**	I told the Captain about the ice, but he said, "Full steam ahead!"
full strength	not weakened or diluted, **straight up**	Did John Wayne drink bourbon full strength? Without water?

Idiom	Meaning	Example
full throttle	gas pedal to the floor, **pedal to the metal**	He drove the Mercedes at full throttle on the freeway.
full tilt	as fast as possible, **flat out**	Were you going full tilt when you passed us—as fast as it would go?
full up	full, no more room	This bus is full up. We'll have to wait for the next one.
fun and games	a good time, a lot of fun	"How was the office party?" "Oh, fun and games!"
funny in the head	a little crazy, not rational, **a little off**, spinny	Poor Mike. He's been funny in the head since his horse died.
funny money	counterfeit money, fake money	Don't accept any funny money. We can't spend it.
funny stuff	tricks, pranks, **monkey business**	"No more funny stuff," said the principal as we left his office.
fuss over	care for too much, **pay** much **attention** to	Bertha's always fussing over her cats. She even warms their milk.
future looks bright	future looks good, success will come to you	Vi was promoted to Department Head. Her future looks bright.
fuzz	policemen, **cops**, **pigs**	The boys ran away when the fuzz drove up in a patrol car.

Idiom	Meaning	Example

G

Idiom	Meaning	Example
gab	talk, visit, **flap your gums**	Mom and Maria were gabbing as they played cribbage.
game for anything	ready to try anything, **a game one**, **gung-ho**	If you're going to the moon, I'll go. I'm game for anything.
game one	(See **a game one**)	
game over	finished, complete; the chance is gone	If you've signed the contract, it's game over. You can't change it.
gang up on	several go against one, many fight one	Three boys ganged up on Willie and knocked him down.
garage kept	in good condition, kept in a garage when not in use	This car has been garage kept. The body's excellent.
gash	girls, **broads**, **chicks**, **lovelies**	We can't have a party without gash. Let's phone some girls.
gather dust	not being used, sitting on a shelf, **collecting dust**	That old coffee tray has been gathering dust for years.
gear up	prepare, get ready, find equipment and supplies	After we print this manual we have to gear up for a novel.
gee	oh, well, **gosh**, **wow**	Gee! What happened to your hair? Did you cut it yourself?
gee whiz	**golly gee**, **gosh darn**, aw **shucks**	Gee whiz, Miss Julie. I'd never do anything to hurt you.
geek	strange person, scholar, **book worm**, **nerd**	Allan reads a lot and stays by himself. He's kind of a geek.
geez	**darn**, **gee whiz**, **gosh**	Geez, I hate mosquitoes!
geezer	old man, old person, **old coot**	On one street there was an old geezer begging for money.
geezer gap	the differences between people aged 60 and 80	The word *senior* includes everyone in the geezer gap.

Idiom	Meaning	Example
Generation X	people born in the 1970s; a generation that wanted to change the **work ethic**	Generation X said that the jobs disappeared as they graduated from high school and university.
get a bang out of	enjoy, have fun, **get a kick out of**	Ms. Lau gets a bang out of playing bingo. She loves bingo.
get a charge out of	enjoy, is amused by	Ming gets a charge out of Pam's memos. They're humorous.
get a fix	use some drugs; **a hit**	He'll shake until he gets a fix. He's addicted to heroin.
get a fix on	calculate, determine, **figure out**	We should get a fix on the office expenses—the total per month.
get a grip	be realistic, be serious, **get serious**	You expect to get A's without studying? Get a grip!
get a grip on yourself	control yourself, do not be so emotional	When he cried, she said, "Get a grip on yourself, Dear."
get a handle on	understand, **find out** about	We have to get a handle on the parking problem—get the facts.
get a hold of	talk to, phone	I tried to get a hold of Pierre when I was in Montreal.
get a kick out of	get some enjoyment, laugh, **get a bang out of**	I get a kick out of the way he skates. He's fun to watch.
get a laugh	cause people to laugh	Your jokes always get a laugh.
get a life	change your lifestyle, **get it together**, **get with it**	He never goes out—just stays at home and watches TV. I wish he would get a life!
get a lift	get a ride, **catch a ride**	I can get a lift with Brian. He's driving to Moncton.
get a load of that	look at that, **check that out**, **feast your eyes**	When Marilyn stepped out of the taxi, he said, "Get a load of that!"
get a move on	go quickly, **vamoose**	We're late! Let's get a move on!
get a rise	get an answer, get a response	Can you get a rise out of him? He doesn't answer me.
get a shot	get a needle from a doctor	You are sick. Maybe you should get a shot of penicillin.
get a shot at	shoot at, see the target you want to shoot at	The buck was partly hidden. I couldn't get a shot at it.

Idiom	Meaning	Example
get a ticket	receive a note stating you parked or drove illegally	If you park your car on the sidewalk, you'll get a ticket.
get after	scold, lecture, **give you hell** [B]	Mom got after us for smoking. She told us it was a bad habit.
get ahead	make progress, succeed	Do you want to get ahead in this world? Do you want to succeed?
get along	co-operate, **give and take**	Joey gets along with everybody. He is very co-operative.
get along	cope, live, manage	I don't know how I'll get along without you. How will I manage?
get along	go, do not stay here	Get along now. Go home, please.
get around	visit friends and places, socialize	With a full-time job and three kids, I don't get around much.
get around it	avoid rules or laws, **find a way around**	You must obtain a business license. You can't get around it.
get around to	do, work at, complete	I haven't got around to calling him yet. I haven't had time.
get at	suggest, imply	When you said I was slow, what were you getting at?
get at it	do it, **get busy**, **get to it**	Well, this work has to be done. Let's get at it.
get away with	not obey the rules, not **get caught**	He gets away with speeding, but the police will soon catch him.
get axed	be fired, be dismissed	He got axed for stealing funds.
get back at	return an insult, **get revenge**	If you don't apologize, he'll get back at you. He's quite angry.
get blood from a stone	do an impossible task, **beat your head against...**	You'll get blood from a stone before you get money from Ed.
get burned	be caught, get blamed, **get into trouble**	I got burned for helping Bev with her divorce. They blamed me.
get busy	begin to work, start to do, **get at it**	Get busy and cut the grass before your father comes home.
get by/scrape by	have just enough money, **make do**	I can get by on very little money, if necessary. I can be frugal.

Idiom	Meaning	Example
get carried away	become too emotional, **go overboard**, **go too far**	When the kids play hockey, their parents get carried away, yelling at the referees and fighters.
get caught	found doing something, **caught in the act**	Did Vi get caught driving without a licence? Did she **get a ticket?**
get caught up	do unfinished work, learn what you missed	I have to get caught up on my studies. I missed two classes.
get down to brass tacks	become serious about it, **knuckle down**	As soon as I'm feeling better I'll get down to brass tacks.
get down to business	work seriously, not waste time or effort	"Let's get down to business," he said. "We have much to do."
get even	do the same thing to someone, **get back at**	When he loses a game, he wants to get even. He wants to win.
get fingered	be accused, be blamed	He got fingered for taking the money because he had the key.
get fresh	act in a sexual way, **come onto her**	When he's had a few drinks, he tries to get fresh with me.
get going	go, start moving, **get lost**	When I stopped to rest, he said, "Get going. Get out of here."
get good wood on	shoot the puck hard, hit the ball squarely	Clark got good wood on that shot, but he missed the net.
get hell [B]	receive a scolding, **catch hell** [B], **get it**	He got hell for breaking a glass. Mrs. Fisk told him he was bad.
get high	feel good, have a special feeling	I get a natural high from jogging. I feel happy and free.
get him back	get revenge, **get back at**	Lyle wants to get me back for seeing Betty. He's jealous.
get home	arrive at home, come home	I'm going to bed when I get home. I'm sleepy.
get in deeper	cause you more trouble, **dig yourself in**	Telling another lie will only get you in deeper—make it worse.
get in my face	confront me, stand in front of me	When I try to talk to Jodi, her boyfriend gets in my face.
get in on it	benefit from it, **take advantage of** it	Baymart is having a half-price sale, and I want to get in on it.

Idiom	Meaning	Example
get in on the ground floor	be there at the start, be one of the first	If I get in on the ground floor at MING'S, I'll advance quickly.
get in your hair	(See **in your hair**)	
get into her pants [B]	have sex with her, **lay her** [B]	He wants to get into her pants, but she won't let him.
get into trouble	do bad things, **break the law**	When he's with the Subway Gang he gets into trouble. He's bad.
get it	understand, know what is funny	"Get it? Do you get the joke?" "Yes. Ha ha. Ha ha ha."
get it	be scolded or punished, **get hell** [B]	I really got it for taking my brother's car. He was furious.
get it off your chest	talk about a problem, complain	He can get it off his chest at the meeting. He can complain there.
get it on	kiss and hug in a sexual way, **make out**	The phone rang just when they were getting it on.
get it over with	do it quickly, finish it before it becomes worse	"If you want a divorce," he said, "let's get it over with."
get it straight	understand it, **catch on**, **figure out**	She doesn't know the difference between boys and girls. I hope she soon gets it straight.
get it together	become organized, be effective	I'll get it together this term. I'll improve my grades.
get it together	get a well-balanced life; become happy, successful	She's getting it together. She's trying to live a meaningful life.
get laid [B]	have sex, get her/him into bed	Most guys take you out expecting to get laid, right?
get lost	go, leave, **beat it**	They told me to get lost, to go home to Mommy.
get mad	become angry or cross, **lose your cool**	When she gets mad, I leave the house. She has a bad temper.
get me down	cause me to feel negative; to feel **down**	What gets me down is the way government wastes our money.
get my drift	understand my meaning, **dig me**	I don't think of you as a sister, if you get my drift.
get my kicks	get my enjoyment, have my fun	I get my kicks from coaching kids' teams. I enjoy doing that.

Idiom	Meaning	Example
get off	not have to pay, not be convicted, **get out of**	If he's guilty, how did he get off? Why isn't he in prison?
get off a few good ones	tell a few jokes, say a few funny lines	When Rob spoke at our wedding he got off a few good ones.
get off my back	stop criticizing me, **get off my case**	If he criticizes you again, tell him to get off your back.
get off my case	stop criticizing me, **check up on**	I told the manager to get off my case—to stop criticizing me.
get off on	like to do, enjoy	He gets off on bowling. He loves to knock over those pins.
get off the ground	succeed at first, begin successfully	For a new product to get off the ground, you need about $5000.
get off to a good start	begin with success, start with confidence	In Math 201, it's important to get off to a good start.
get off your high horse	do not act like you are better than everyone else	Colin acts so superior! Tell him to get off his high horse.
get on in years	getting older, **over the hill**	When Mother broke her hip, she was 77—getting on in years.
get on it	do it now, **get at it**, **get to it**	Mr. Jarvis wants his car repaired by noon, so let's get on it.
get on my good side	(See **on my good side**)	
get on my nerves	bother or irritate me, **bug** me	Her questions get on my nerves. They're too personal.
get on with it	continue working or speaking	When I paused, he said, "Get on with it. Tell the rest of it."
get on your horse	move, get started, **get a move on**	Get on your horse or you'll be late for work. It's nearly 8!
get out	I do not believe it, **you're kidding**	Your father played hockey with Bobby Orr? Get out!
get out of	avoid doing, not have to do	You can get out of gym class if you say you have a headache.
get out of my face	go away, I am **sick of** you	I didn't ask for your advice. Get out of my face!
get out of the road	move, do not stand there	"Get out of the road!" he yelled as he rode his bike down the hill.

Idiom	Meaning	Example
get out of town	you are mistaken, do not expect us to believe you	You saw a Martian? Get outa town! I don't believe it.
get out of your hair	leave, not bother you, **get lost**	Let me ask one more question; then I'll get out of your hair.
get over	travel, go to visit	We hope to get over to the island when we go to Vancouver.
get over	forget, stop worrying about	We can help her get over the accident by listening to her.
get real	try to see what is really happening, **get serious**	He wants five million dollars to play hockey? Tell him to get real.
get reamed out	(See **ream out**)	
get revenge	hurt someone who hurt you, **get even**, **pay him back**	Do you want to get revenge, or do you want to discuss the problem and forgive him.
get rid of	discard, throw away, **do away with**	First, we have to get rid of the money. Where can we hide it?
get rolling	move, go, drive away	If you have to be home by noon, we should get rolling.
get screwed	receive unfair treatment, **ripped off, taken in**	I got screwed when I bought this condo. I paid too much for it.
get serious	do not joke, be serious, **pay attention**	When we discussed water safety he told us to get serious.
get shit [B]	get a scolding or a lecture, **catch it, get hell** [B]	He got shit for drinking beer in school. The principal was mad.
get something out of	learn from, benefit from	We always get something out of her class. We learn something.
get the drop on	be quicker to start, **get the jump on**	Stu's very quick. In faceoffs, he gets the drop on his opponents.
get the finger [B] (get the bird)	get a bad sign, see the middle finger	Bad drivers get the finger when they cut in front of Randy.
get the green light	get approval, **it's a go**	Don't start construction until we get the green light from the City.
get the hang of	learn to do, know the first steps	I'm getting the hang of algebra. I can solve the easy problems.

Idiom	Meaning	Example
get the jitters	become nervous, begin to shake	When I get up to speak, I get the jitters and I can't think clearly.
get the jump on	start faster than the others, **quick on the draw**	Ben got the jump on the other runners. He led by one stride.
get the lay of the land	check the conditions, **size up** the situation	Before I sell insurance in a town, I like to get the lay of the land.
get the lead out	move faster, hurry, **move it, shake a leg**	The coach told me to get the lead out—to get moving.
get the picture	understand, see the way it is	After Jack explained his plan, he said, "Get the picture?"
get the point	understand the idea or the message	Did you get the point of his talk? What was the main idea?
get the word out	tell the message, **spread the word**	The easiest way for us to get the word out is on the Internet.
get the wrinkles out	improve, revise	When they get the wrinkles out of the electric car, I'll buy one.
get this monkey off my back	stop a bad habit, be rid of a problem or **hangup**	I have to get this monkey off my back. I have to stop gambling.
get this show on the road	begin to do something, **get down to business, get rolling**	After a lot of talk about how to drill a well, the boss said, "Let's get this show on the road."
get this straight	understand what is said, **get the picture**	Let me get this straight. You say there's a moose in your bathtub?
get to first base	do the first step, complete the first stage	He was hoping for a kiss, but he didn't get to first base.
get to it	do it now, do not delay, **get to the point**	After listening to her babble for awhile, I said, "Please get to it."
get to me	bother me, **bug** me	The sound of the fan gets to me. It's too loud.
get to the bottom of	get the facts, find the cause	Did you get to the bottom of the problem? What is the cause?
get to the point	say what is important, **come to the point**	When answering questions, get to the point. Be direct and brief.
get to the root of the problem	find the cause, **get to the bottom of**	We got to the root of the problem. The children are afraid of the dog.

114

Idiom	Meaning	Example
get together	come to visit, **have you over**	We should get together at Easter. Would you like to visit us?
get under my skin	bother me, **bug me, get to me**	Don't let Bob's teasing get under your skin. Don't let it bother you.
get up a head of steam	generate enough power to move, get **up to speed**	If I get up a head of steam, I can knock down the door.
get up on the wrong side of bed	be grouchy or cranky, get **off to a bad start**	Did you get up on the wrong side of bed? Are you in a bad mood?
get wind of	hear about, **find out** about	Did she get wind of our plan? Does she know about it?
get with it	become aware, learn how, **in the know**	Leni, a friend at work, told me to get with it or I'd lose my job.
get worked up	feel upset, become angry	He gets worked up about unions. He hates protests and strikes.
get you back	(See **get back at**)	
get you down	cause you to feel sad, cause you to be **down**	Do Mondays get you down? Do you hate going back to work?
get your act together	become organized, **get it together**	Bill is getting his act together. He's not late anymore.
get your back up	become upset, **get mad**	Tim gets his back up when you criticize his work. Be careful.
get your buns over here	come here quickly, **on the double**	Wade, get your buns over here and sign your name.
get your dander up	annoy or bother you, **bug** you	Do barking dogs get your dander up? Does barking irritate you?
get your feet wet	try to do it, attempt it, **try your hand at**	To become a lawyer, learn the theory; then get your feet wet.
get your goat	annoy you, **bug** you, **get to me**	Don't let Jason get your goat. He teases everybody.
get your head out of the clouds	be more realistic, **come down to earth**, **get real**	You can dream at home, but please get your head out of the clouds when you come to work.
get your head together	begin to think clearly, **get your act together**	I need a holiday to get my head together—to think clearly again.
get your hopes up	cause you to be hopeful, **pin your hopes on**	Now don't get your hopes up, but I plan to appeal your conviction.

Idiom	Meaning	Example
get your jollies	(See **get your kicks**)	
get your kicks	enjoy yourself, **have fun**	How do you get your kicks? Do you sing? Dance? Travel?
get your knuckles rapped	be punished, **get hell, get shit** [B]	If I forget to register my guns, I'll get my knuckles rapped.
get your mind around	understand, comprehend, **wrap your mind around**	He explained DNA, but I can't get my mind around it.
get your shirt in a knot/ get your shit in a knot [B]	want to hurry or rush, **hurry up**	If we asked Pop to hurry, he'd say, "Don't get your shirt in a knot!"
get your shit together [B]	become organized, make a plan and follow it	A counsellor can help you get your shit together. Talk to one.
get your way	do what you want to do, **have it your way**	You used to get your way with Mom and Dad. They trusted you.
get your wires crossed	get the wrong meaning, communicate poorly	We got our wires crossed. I said *someday*, and you heard *Sunday*!
get yours	be hurt, get hit or injured	After the fight he said, "You'll get yours! Just wait!"
get-go	(See **from the get-go**)	
get-up	clothes, strange clothing, weird costume	A vest with jogging pants! Are you going out in that get-up?
get-up-and-go	energy, vitality	I feel so lazy. I have no get-up-and-go.
getting on in years	(See **get on in years**)	
ghetto blaster	portable radio, **boom box**	Loud rock music came from a ghetto blaster on the steps.
gift of the gab	(See **the gift of the gab**)	
gild the lily	decorate a beautiful object, improve a **work of art**	Decorating that Scotch pine would be gilding the lily.
gimme a break	do not tell me to do that, that is unreasonable	You expect me to spell every word correctly. Gimme a break!
girl Friday	girl employee who does a variety of office jobs	Jan is our girl Friday. She does the important jobs in our office.
git	go, leave, **get going, get lost**	When the cat dug in his flower garden, he said, "Git! Go on!"

Idiom	Meaning	Example
give 110%	work harder than required, do more than asked	If we want to win this game, everyone has to give 110%.
give a black eye	cause a loss of respect for a person or organization, **pride goeth before a fall**	When a priest is convicted of sexual assault, it gives the Catholic Church a black eye.
give a damn/shit [B]	care about, **give a hoot**	Look at his hair. He doesn't give a damn about his appearance.
give a hoot	care; show interest, show concern	The problem with Julio is that he doesn't give a hoot about family.
give a little	be flexible, do not be so firm	When you discuss the divorce terms, try to give a little.
give an arm and a leg	give a lot, pay a lot, **give my eye teeth**	She'd give an arm and a leg to have her baby back.
give an inch	concede a little bit, compromise, **let up**	We asked Dad to change his rule, but he wouldn't give an inch.
give and take	win and lose, give something to get something	Marriage works on a give-and-take basis—more give than take.
give head [B]	give oral sex to a man, perform fellatio	Can you catch AIDS from giving head?
give her	use more power, **give it all you've got**	If the foreman wants us to work faster, he yells, "Give 'er!"
give her credit	say that she helped or contributed	Give Jane credit for staying with Tarzan all these years.
give her shit [B]	try hard, play hard, go fast, **give her**	Give 'er shit, guys. We can beat this team.
give her the eye	look at her with interest, **come-on**	At the school lunch table, Kevin would smile and give her the eye.
give him a taste of his own medicine	do to him what he does, **an eye for an eye**	If Jim is sarcastic, give him a taste of his own medicine.
give him an inch and he'll take a mile	give him a little freedom and he will take a lot	He lacks self-discipline. Give him an inch and he'll take a mile.
give him enough rope and he'll hang himself	allow him enough freedom and he will hurt himself or be caught	If he's bad, give him enough rope and he'll hang himself. The police will stop him.
give him the brush-off	turn away from someone, reject someone	When Don asked Jane for a date, she gave him the brush-off.

Idiom	Meaning	Example
give him the evil eye	look fierce or evil, stare in a bad way	When I testified in court, the prisoner gave me the evil eye.
give him the slip	leave him, **ditch him**	We gave him the slip while he was in the washroom.
give in	not try anymore, yield	Emily always gives in; she won't disagree with me.
give it a rest	do not say that anymore, stop complaining	Give it a rest, eh. All you talk about is religion.
give it a whirl	try to do something, **try your hand at**	When I saw the others dancing, I decided to give it a whirl.
give it all you've got	try very hard, do all you can	When I say "push," give it all you've got.
give it the once-over	look at it quickly, **look it over**	When I drove by the house, I gave it the once-over. It's nice!
give it to him	lecture him or hit him, **tell him off**	If he touches me again, I'm really going to give it to him!
give it to me straight	give me the facts, do not **beat around the bush**	"I have some bad news, man." "Tell me. Give it to me straight."
give it your best shot	do the best you can, try your hardest	If you want to win, you have to give it your best shot.
give me a bad time	tease me, **bug** me, **give me a rough time**	I wish you wouldn't give me a bad time about my low grades.
give me a break	give me a chance to win, **gimme a break**	When we play tennis, give me a break. Don't play your best.
give me a call	phone me, **ring me**	I'll give you a call when I have a minute. I have your number.
give me a dingle	phone me, call me, **give me a ring**	Give me a dingle sometime. My number's in the phone book.
give me a hand	help me, **lend a hand**	Please give me a hand with this math problem. I can't solve it.
give me a hint	tell me part of the answer, say a word to help me	I can't guess the name of your new boyfriend. Give me a hint.
give me a lift	give me a ride, **pick you up**	Can I give you a lift to school? Want to ride with me?

Idiom	Meaning	Example
give me a lift	give me a happy feeling, cause me to feel better	Pat's jokes give me a lift. When I laugh, I feel much better.
give me a ring	phone me, call me, **ring me**	Give me a ring when you get home from work, eh.
give me the creeps	cause me to feel scared or uncomfortable	Damon looks like a ghost. He gives me the creeps.
give me the third degree	question me carefully, **haul up on the carpet**	The police ask a lot of questions. They give you the third degree.
give my eye teeth	give something valuable, **give my right arm**	Does he like me? I'd give my eye teeth to know if he likes me.
give my right arm	give something valuable, **give my eye teeth**	What a voice! I'd give my right arm to be able to sing like that.
give no quarter	not co-operate or concede, **drive a hard bargain**	When he negotiates a contract, he gives no quarter. He's firm.
give notice	give a letter that says you are leaving or quitting	If I want to leave the position, I give them two weeks notice.
give off an odor	smell, have an odor	After sitting in the sun, the dead fish gave off a strong odor.
give out	break, stop operating, **conk out**	After three hours of steady use, the pump gave out. It just quit.
give them a hand	clap your hands, applaud	Let's give them a hand, folks. They sang very well.
give them what for	give them a lecture, scold them, **give you hell**	After the team lost a game, the coach gave 'em what for.
give up	stop trying, not try any more	I give up. I can't remember who invented the telephone.
give up the blue line (hockey)	let opponents cross the blue line before you check them	If we give up the blue line, they will get more shots on goal.
give up the ghost	stop hoping after a long time	When will she give up the ghost? Her son has been gone for years.
give you a boost	cause you to be confident, encourage you	Winning that award will give her a boost. It will encourage her.
give you a hard time	tease you, criticize you, **bug** you, **hassle** you	Did the class give you a hard time about losing their papers?
give you a line	tell you a false story, **hand you a line**	Don't believe him. He's giving you a line about being wealthy.

Idiom	Meaning	Example
give you a ribbing	tease you, **bug** you, **give you a hard time**	When I got stuck in the lake, my friends gave me a ribbing.
give you a rough time	tease you, **hassle you**	The players gave me a rough time about scoring on my own goalie.
give you a run for your money	compete with you, try to defeat you	I'm not the best skier, but I'll give you a run for your money.
give you an out	give you an excuse, allow you to **beg off**	You don't have to work. Your sore back will give you an out.
give you flack	tell you what you did wrong, criticize you	He gave me flack for smoking in his car. The smell bothers him.
give you hell [B]	lecture you, scold you, **tie into** you	She'll give you hell if you come late to her class, so be on time.
give you odds	if I lose the bet, I pay you more money than you bet	I'll give you odds that Montreal will win. I'll bet $2; you bet $1.
give you shit [B]	lecture you, be angry with you, **give you hell**	If you spend too much money he'll give you shit.
give you static	criticize what you did, **give you flack**	He gave me static for failing the exam. He said I can do better.
give you the axe	fire you, dismiss you, **get the axe**	"Why did they give her the axe?" "For stealing company money."
give you the benefit...	(See **the benefit of the doubt**)	
give you the boot	fire you, dismiss you, **down the road**	If you drink liquor at work, they'll give you the boot.
give you the gears	fool you, tease you, **josh** you, **pull your leg**	When Dad said you would have to pay for cleaning the carpet, he was giving you the gears.
give you the runaround	(See **the runaround**)	
give you what for	lecture you, **give you hell**	If you miss hockey practice, the coach will give you what for.
give your best	(See **give it your best shot**)	
glad rags	best clothes, **dress clothes**	I'll come to your concert. I'll do my hair and put on my glad rags.
glassy eyed	dazed, not alert	When I saw him he was glassy eyed. I think he was drunk.

Idiom	Meaning	Example
glitch	fault, problem, **snag**	That printer is full of glitches. It isn't working right.
glom onto	grab, take	Don't leave any donuts around, or Bubba will glom onto them.
gloss over	cover faults or errors, **cover up**	Jill won't gloss over your errors. She'll tell you about them.
gloves are off	(See **the gloves are off**)	
glow on	(See **a glow on**)	
glowing terms	(See **in glowing terms**)	
glued to the set	watching TV, interested in a TV show	Jack loves sports. He's glued to the set every Saturday.
gnashing of teeth	anger, complaining	When the hospital closed, there was much gnashing of teeth.
go against the grain	oppose the natural way, **do it the hard way**	Moe has always been perverse— always going against the grain.
go all the way (sports)	win a final series, win the cup or trophy	If the Leafs beat us, they'll go all the way.
go all the way (sex)	have intercourse, **make love**	"When I go all the way, I want to feel loved," she said.
go all-out	do your best, **give it all you've got**	He'll go all-out at the Olympics. He wants to win a medal.
go along with	agree to, co-operate with	If you go along with the crime, you'll be as guilty as they are.
go along with	pretend you do not know, **play along**	If we have a surprise party for Kay, will you go along with it?
go ape	become extremely excited, **go bananas**	The girls would go ape when they saw the Beatles.
go around the bend	(See **around the bend**)	
go around with	be friends with, **hang out** with	At the time, I was going around with a girl named Diane.
go at a good clip	(See **at a good clip**)	
go back on	reverse a decision, **break a promise**	Mat wouldn't go back on his word. He's very dependable.

Idiom	Meaning	Example
go bad	spoil, become sour	Milk will go bad if it's left in the sun. It will taste sour.
go ballistic	become very upset, **freak out**	When I told Mom I was pregnant she went ballistic.
go bananas	become very excited, act crazy, **go nuts**	When Elvis swiveled his hips, the girls went bananas.
go berserk	become insane, **go crazy**	With ten kids, it's a wonder the poor woman didn't go berserk.
go bonkers	lose control of emotions, **freak out**, **go crazy**	He went bonkers because there was too much pressure at work.
go by the boards	become less important, be neglected or omitted	When he returned to school, his social life went by the boards.
go crazy	lose control, **go bananas**, **go wild**	If I don't leave this place I'll go crazy! It's boring here.
go down	lie down, go to bed, go to sleep	Our baby goes down early— and gets up early.
go down for the third time	drown, die, fail	In Calculus 101, I'm going down for the third time. I'm failing.
go down on [B]	give oral sex to a woman or a man	"Do you want to go down on me?" she whispered.
go downhill	fail and lose, **down and out**	It's too bad. After getting out of prison he just went downhill.
go downtown [B]	have intercourse, **go all the way**	If I go up to your room, it doesn't mean you can go downtown.
go easy on	do not ask him to work hard, **ease up on**	Go easy on Billy, please. He's not well today.
go easy on	do not take too much, use less	Go easy on the jam, please. Leave some for me.
go figure	you find the answer, the answer is *no*	He said he quit smoking, then he asks for a cigarette. Go figure.
go for	believe, accept	I said I was late because of a flat tire, but Dad didn't go for that.
go for	admire, desire	Burt goes for Dolly, but Dolly doesn't like Burt.
go for a spin	go for a ride in a car, **take a drive**	Clyde stops the car and says to Bonnie, "Want to go for a spin?"

Idiom	Meaning	Example
go for broke	try your hardest, **go all out**	On my last jump I'll go for broke. I'll beat my best mark.
go for it	try it, attempt it	When he asked if he should climb the tree, we yelled, "Go for it!"
go great guns	(See **going great guns**)	
go haywire	break, not work properly, **break down**	They said they fixed the car, but it went haywire again the next day.
go hog wild	have a wild celebration, **go wild**	When the Stampeders won the Grey Cup, the fans went hog wild.
go hungry	not have enough to eat, continue to be hungry	We may be poor, but we never go hungry.
go in circles	walk around but not work, work in confusion	I'm going in circles. I have to stop and plan my work.
go into detail	give details in a story or report	Don't go into detail right now. Just tell us how much it costs.
go jump in the lake	go away and do not return, **take off**	If he expects us to write a 50-page report, he can go jump in the lake.
go like crazy	work fast and hard, be very busy, **like crazy**	We've been going like crazy trying to feed fifty people!
go like stink	go fast, accelerate quickly	That Mustang goes like stink. It's a fast car.
go mad	become insane, **go crazy, go nuts**	If he doesn't stop playing those drums, I'll go mad.
go nowhere fast	not be able to advance, be stuck where you are	Without a diploma, you'll be going nowhere fast.
go nuts	become insane, **go bonkers, go crazy**	If another mosquito bites me, I'll go nuts!
go off half-cocked	speak without thinking, rush into action	Dar is sensible, but he goes off half-cocked when he plays ball.
go off the deep end	do something strange, **go overboard**	Now don't go off the deep end and hit somebody.
go on	happen, occur, **what's going down**	What's going on here? Why is your bike in the bathtub?
go on	it cannot be true, **you're kidding**	"Ted drove the car into the lake!" "Go on! Ted wouldn't do that!"

Idiom	Meaning	Example
go on about	talk steadily, ramble, **run off at the mouth**	"What was he saying?" "Oh, he was going on about taxes and the price of wheat."
go one better	do more, hit harder, **outdo yourself**	If he gives her candy, I'll go one better and give her flowers.
go out of your mind	(See **out of your mind**)	
go out of your way	do special things to help, **put yourself out**	Hilda went out of her way to help us when Dad was sick.
go out on a limb	promise too much, risk, **take a chance**	Don't go out on a limb. Don't say the company will pay for it.
go out with	be a boyfriend/girlfriend, **date, see**	Jerry asked me to go out with him. I think he likes me.
go over	read, practise	Did you go over your notes? Are you ready for the quiz?
go over	be liked, be accepted	Free drinks will go over with the students. They'll like that idea.
go overboard	do it too much, **go off the deep end**	He goes overboard if he likes a girl—buys her flowers every day.
go places	succeed, do well, **make it big**	When Percy got his degree, we knew he was going places.
go public	tell the public, tell a reporter	If he goes public, everybody will know that we had an affair.
go soft	be gentle, be considerate	I've learned to go soft when I return papers with low grades.
go steady	**date** only one person, **go out with** only one	Tony and Pearl are going steady. They're faithful to each other.
go straight	change from a criminal to a law-abiding citizen	When he's released from prison he plans to go straight.
go strong	(See **going strong**)	
go the distance	finish the race, complete the course	If Mat begins a project, he'll go the distance—he'll complete it.
go the extra mile	work longer or harder than expected, **give 110%**	If you are willing to go the extra mile, you can be the top student.
go the way of the dodo	become extinct like the dodo bird, **die off**	If we don't protect our language, it will go the way of the dodo.

Idiom	Meaning	Example
go through	say, read, **run through**	Could you go through the steps one more time, please.
go through the roof	become very angry, **blow your stack**	Mr. Tse will go through the roof when he sees all these mistakes.
go to any trouble	work to make us welcome, **put yourself out**	Please don't go to any trouble for us. Don't change your plans.
go to bat for	help someone by talking to managers or authorities, **put in a good word for**	Uncle Bob works for the City. If your tax bill is too high, maybe he'll go to bat for you.
go to great lengths/ go to any lengths	do whatever is necessary, never **give up**	Cynthia will go to any lengths to find a dress designed by Voz.
go to hell [B]	leave, go, **drop dead, take off**	When I asked him to move his car, he told me to go to hell.
go to hell in a handbasket	waste one's life, become careless and immoral, **ignorance is bliss**	We don't get involved in issues. We're wasting our lives and going to hell in a handbasket!
go to pieces	(See **fall to pieces**)	
go to pot	(See **gone to pot**)	
go to town	(See **going to town**)	
go to trouble	(See **go to any trouble**)	
go to your head	(See **let it go to your head**)	
go too far	become too excited, **get carried away**	Some soccer fans go too far. They fight and cause damage.
go under	fail, be unable to continue, **go bankrupt**	Companies that can't make loan payments will go under.
go up in smoke	burn, be destroyed in a fire	You need fire insurance. What if your condo goes up in smoke?
go wild	act wild, run and squeal etc.	When the teacher leaves the room, the kids go wild.
go with the flow	do what others do, do what helps everybody	Don't always try to be different. Go with the flow sometimes.
go without	not have any, not have money, **do without**	When Dad lost his job, we had go without steak.

Idiom	Meaning	Example
go wrong	choose wrong answers, **make a mistake**	Where did we go wrong with our budget? Did we miscalculate?
go-getter	(See **a go-getter**)	
go-round	a turn, a try, a cowboy's ride	In the second go-round, he scored a 79, better than his first try.
god awful	ugly, **shabby**	I won't wear that god-awful suit! It looks like a garbage bag!
God rest his soul	(See **rest his soul**)	
going down	(See **what's going down**)	
going gets rough	(See **the going gets rough**)	
going great guns	working very well, **going strong**	We were going great guns till our goalie got hurt. Then they scored.
going rate	(See **the going rate**)	
going strong	doing well, succeeding	The party was going strong— lots of dancing and laughter.
going to town	working or talking hard, protesting, **sound**ing **off**	One man was really going to town, speaking against taxes.
gol dang/gol darn	frustrating, **dad-blamed, darn**	The gol dang cord is tangled. It's full of knots.
golden age	best years, time of most prosperity	He said the decade after World War II was Canada's golden age.
golden opportunity	(See **a golden opportunity**)	
golden rule	(See **the golden rule**)	
golden years	65 years of age or older, **sunset years**	Dad is retired now, enjoying his golden years.
golly	oh, **gee, gosh**	Golly! I've never seen so much snow.
golly gee	oh, **gee whiz, wow**	Golly gee! Nobody ever did that to me before.
gone to pot	in poor condition, neglected, **run down**	The farmyard had gone to pot. There was junk everywhere.
gone to the dogs	not well maintained, in very poor condition	My garden has gone to the dogs. It's full of dandelions and weeds.

Idiom	Meaning	Example
goner	(See **a goner**)	
gonzo	gone, not here, **out of here**	On June 30, school's finished and I'm gonzo!
good afternoon	hello, **hi**, **good day**	Answer the phone this way: "Good afternoon, Ko speaking."
good and dead/mad/sick	very dead or mad or sick etc.	That rodeo bull was good and mad. He tried to gore the rider.
good bet	good team or horse or person to bet on	The Leafs look like a good bet to win the series. They should win.
good day	hello, **good morning**, **good afternoon**	"Good day, Mrs. Hardy." "How do you do, Mr. Lane."
good egg	(See **a good egg**)	
good for a loan	willing to lend money, able to lend money	Let's ask Mike for some money. He's usually good for a loan.
good for you	good work, **'at a boy**, **good on you**	When Dad saw my high marks, he said, "Good for you, Nick."
good going	good work, **'at a girl**, **way to go**	Good going, Judy! You passed the exam!
good golly	oh, **gosh**, **wow**	Good golly, Miss Molly. You are the prettiest girl in the county!
good gravy	oh, how surprising, **gosh**	Good gravy! I've got BINGO! I won!
good grief	what a shame, oh no, **too bad**	Good grief! You're injured! Your hand is bleeding!
good hands	skilful hands; ability to pass, catch, shoot etc.	He's not a fast runner, but he's got good hands.
good head	(See **a good head**)	
good morning	hello, hi, **good day**	We said, "Good morning, Miss Keele," as we entered the room.
good on you	that is good, you did good work, **good for you**	If you can tie a kangaroo down, good on ya, mate!
good riddance	good that someone or something goes away	When the manager resigned, we all said, "Good riddance!"
good show	that is good, you performed well	Good show, I say. Jolly good show! Let's see another trick.

Idiom	Meaning	Example
good sport	(See **a good sport**)	
good wood on it	(See **get good wood on it**)	
good-for-nothing	not useful, useless	I'll be glad when we sell that good-for-nothing truck.
goodies	cookies, candy, cake, etc.	Grandma always had a plate of goodies on the table for us.
goodies	accessories: air, cruise, sun roof, etc.; **loaded**	He likes the Buick because it has a lot of goodies.
goodness gracious	oh my, oh dear, **gosh**	Goodness gracious! That sauce is hot!
goof off	play, **fool around**, **horse around**	We were goofing off in the hall before class—joking and stuff.
goof up	do it poorly, **screw up**	If I goof up again, I'm going to use a different typewriter.
goose egg	zero, no score, **skunked**	They got three goals. We got the goose egg.
goose is cooked	chance is gone, plan has failed, **game over**	If we don't win this game, our goose is cooked.
goose it	press the gas pedal down, **pedal to the metal**	When a car tries to pass us, don't goose it. Slow down.
goosed	(See **Canada goose**)	
gosh	oh, **gee**, **golly**, **wow**	Gosh! I didn't know you had a twin sister!
gosh darn (gol darn)	frustrating, **darn**, **friggin**	Where is that gosh-darn pen? Who took my pen?
gospel truth	(See **the gospel truth**)	
got a corner on	got most of the business, **corner the market**	Bata's got a corner on the shoe business in Ontario.
got a crush on	feel romantic about, **sweet on**	Wayne's got a crush on Miss Kramer. He loves Miss Kramer!
got a light	got a match, have a cigarette lighter	I lost my matches. Have you got a light?
got guts	have courage, have **nerves of steel**	She's got guts to try skydiving. It's a dangerous sport.

Idiom	Meaning	Example
got him covered	point a gun at him, prevent him from going	"I've got you covered!" the boy said, pointing a toy gun at me.
got it bad	feels it very much, has **a case of**	Poor Jenny. She loves Stuart. She's got it bad for him.
got it coming	deserve to get hurt, should **get hell** [B]	If you drive drunk, you should be punished—you've got it coming.
got it in for	dislike, is unkind to, is **on my case**	I think Mr. Yee's got it in for me. He's very critical of my work.
got it made	be happy and successful and rich	Brandy's got it made: she has a career, wealth and a loving family.
got my eye on	am interested in, want to to know him/her or buy it	A Corvette? No. I've got my eye on a Fiat Spyder.
got my hands full	am very busy, **plate is full**	I'd like to help with your project but I've got my hands full.
got no business	do not have the right, have no claim	Charlie's got no business telling us how to manage our farm.
got rocks in your head	have no sense, make bad decisions	If he swims with sharks, he's got rocks in his head.
got the balls [B]	got the courage, **got what it takes**	He wants to enforce gun control, and he's got the balls to do it.
got the blues	feel sad, **feel blue**	Zora's got the blues because her lover was untrue.
got the hots for	desire, feel passion for	She's got the hots for Tony. See how she touches him.
got the rags on [B]	menstruate, **have your period**	Lana doesn't feel like going out tonight. She's got the rags on.
got what it takes	got what is needed, **got the balls** [B]	We need a person to manage the office. Ko's got what it takes.
got you by the balls [B]	got you so you can't move; can't quit or **back out**	If you signed the contract, they've got you by the balls.
got you cornered	make it difficult to move or answer	"I've got you cornered," he said, pointing at the checker board.
got your number	know how to manage you; how to **get her way**	She's got your number, Bill. You'll do anything she asks.

Idiom	Meaning	Example
gotcha (got you)	tricked you, defeated you	When I don't know the answer, he says, "Gotcha!"
gotches	men's shorts, men's underwear	Uh oh, no clean gotches. It's time to do my laundry.
grab a bite to eat	eat a lunch or meal, **have a bite**	We were so busy we didn't have time to grab a bite to eat.
grab a chair	sit down, **have a seat, take a load off your feet**	After I introduced everybody, I said, "Grab a chair and sit down."
grain belt	a region or area that produces cereal crops	The grain belt got very little rain this year. The land is dry.
grain of salt	(See **take it with a grain of salt**)	
grand slam	a **home run** with runners on all bases, a major score	It was 5-1. Then Carter hit a grand slam and tied the game, 5-5.
grandfather clause	a written statement that protects an employee	They can't demote him; he has a grandfather clause.
granola	a person who believes in less government and a natural way of living	Pat is mostly granola. She wants to join a commune, grow gardens and protect the environment.
grapevine	(See **through the grapevine**)	
grass is greener...	(See **the grass is greener on the other side of the fence**)	
gravy train	a profitable product, **the rest is gravy**	In 1928, coal was Alberta's gravy train.
grease my palm	pay me, give me money	If you want good service, grease his palm. Give him a tip, eh.
greaser	a young man with greasy hair, a hoodlum, a **hood**	Two greasers were hanging out behind the school.
greasy kid's stuff	heavy hair dressing, thick hair oil	None of that greasy kid's stuff on my hair. I use a natural product.
greasy spoon	small cafe that serves greasy food	I eat at the greasy spoon. The food ain't great, but it's cheap.
great guns	(See **going great guns**)	
Great One	(See **The Great One**)	
great Scot	**good gravy, gosh, heavens**	When Dale gets excited, he says, "Great Scot!"

Idiom	Meaning	Example
great shakes	(See **no great shakes**)	
Great White Hope	(See **The Great White Hope**)	
Great White North	(See **The Great White North**)	
Greek to me	(See **it was Greek to me**)	
green stuff	dollars, money, **lettuce, moola**	In those days we had plenty of green stuff, so I bought a Lexus.
green thumb	good gardener, naturally good with plants	Willie is the green thumb in our group. He's the gardener.
green with envy	envious, wishing to have someone else's property	How I wish I owned your Acura. I'm green with envy.
greenback	American dollar, money, **buck**	If we're going to Vegas, we need our pockets full of greenbacks.
grey area	unclear topic, vague statement	There are many grey areas in the legal system—many vague laws.
grey power	the large numbers of seniors or older people	An increase in life span causes an increase in grey power.
grim reaper	(See **The Grim Reaper**)	
grind to a halt	stop with regret and problems	If he quits, the project will grind to a halt. It depends on him.
grinding halt	unplanned stop, forced stop	When Andy lost his job, their marriage came to a grinding halt.
groaty to the max	very nice, **way cool, totally awesome**	That bike is groaty to the max. I love those wide tires!
groovy	stylish, **cool, neat, with it**	That's a groovy T-shirt, man. I like the purple parrot.
ground me	keep me at home, not allow me to go out	If I don't pass all my subjects, my parents will ground me.
grounded	not allowed to go out, forced to stay in	Pam was grounded for a week because she stayed out all night.
Group of Five	(See **The Group of Five**)	
Group of Seven	(See **The Group of Seven**)	
grouse	complain, **bitch**	The mayor said everybody's grousing about high taxes.

Idiom	Meaning	Example
grow on you	you like it more each day, gradually like it more	In time, you will appreciate Lang's poetry. It grows on you.
grow up	live during childhood, become a young adult	He grew up on a farm in Alberta. He was a farm boy.
grow up	become mature, accept responsibility	Grow up, Jerry. Put away that water pistol and act like an adult.
grunge	dirt and grease, grime	Let's remove the grunge from the motor. It's really dirty.
grunge (music)	alternative rock music, distorted sound of rock	When we visited Seattle, every radio station was playing grunge.
grunge (fashion)	youth clothing designed for grunge music fans	The kids go to parties dressed in grunge. That's cool.
guard is down	not ready for a fight, not protecting yourself	I wasn't ready for her criticism. My guard was down.
gun down	shoot, kill with guns	He was gunned down as he left his apartment—shot in the back.
gun it	step on the accelerator, **floor it, goose it**	When a car tried to pass him, he gunned it. He sped away!
gung-ho	very enthusiastic, very interested	Barb's gung-ho about our trip to Greece. She's excited about it.
gussied up	groomed and dressed for a party	Sally was all gussied up when Jim arrived for their date.

Idiom	Meaning	Example

H

Idiom	Meaning	Example
hack/hacker	writer, journalist, computer guru	Some hack wrote a story about the mayor's son being on drugs.
had a bellyful	had too much, do not want to receive any more	I've had a bellyful of the Reborn Party. What a bunch of bigots!
had a belt	had a drink of alcohol, **had a couple**	Ragnar had a belt or two at the tavern in town.
had a couple	had two or more drinks of alcohol, **tipsy**	She was laughing a lot—like she'd had a couple.
had a few	a little drunk, **buzzed**	He staggered a bit when he walked—like he'd had a few.
had better	should, ought to	I'd better call and explain why we didn't attend the reception.
had enough	endured, **fed up**, **put up with** a lot	After ten minutes of his talk, she's had enough. She leaves.
had his bell rung	hit hard, bodychecked, **knocked out**	Pat had his bell rung by No. 4. He was unconscious for awhile.
had it	had too much of, frustrated with, **fed up**	I've had it with politicians who waste our money. It's sickening.
had it	worn beyond use, **shabby**, **wear out**	My bike's had it: the frame's broken and the gears slip.
had it up to here	upset too many times, **had enough**	I've had it up to here with his smoking! Yuk!
had the bird	worn or broken, **wear out**	These shoes are full of holes. They've had the bird.
hail a cab	wave your hand to stop a cab, **flag a cab**	We missed the bus, so we hailed a cab.
hair off the dog that bit you	remedy that uses the cause, **fight fire with fire**	The theory of penicillin is to use the hair off the dog that bit you.

Idiom	Meaning	Example
hairbrain	not sensible, irrational, crazy, **kooky**	Eric is talking about a hairbrain plan to train ants as employees.
hairdo	hairstyle, coiffure	Did you see Eileen's hairdo? She looks lovely in tight curls.
hale fellow, well met	friendly man, **good head, jolly good fellow**	Bert is a social person—always hale fellow, well met.
half-assed [B]	incomplete, half missing	There's a guy at the door with a half-assed invention for sale.
half-baked	not well planned, not developed	Satellite schools? Sounds like a half-baked idea to me.
half-cocked	(See **go off half-cocked**)	
half-corked	half drunk, **buzzed, feeling no pain**	Andy was at the bar for awhile. He's half-corked.
half-cut	(See **half-corked**)	
half-hearted	using half your ability, not giving enough effort	He made a half-hearted attempt to find our luggage: one phone call.
half-lit	(See **half-corked**)	
half-pint	a child, a person who is half the size of an adult	When you were a boy—just a half-pint—your hair was yellow.
half-shot	(See **half-corked**)	
half-snapped	(See **half-corked**)	
half the battle	half of the task completed, half of the job done	You've done the research for the report. That's half the battle.
ham	humorous person, comedian, **joker**	When you imitate John Candy, you're quite a ham.
ham hands	large hands, huge hands	When the coach saw my big hands he called me *Ham Hands*.
ham it up	act funny and tell jokes, **play the ham**	Robbie likes to ham it up when he talks to a group—he tells jokes.
hammer and tongs	angrily, furiously, **tooth and nail**	The two men were arguing— going at it hammer and tongs.
hammered	very drunk, **pissed, sloshed**	You were hammered, so I took your keys and drove you home.

Idiom	Meaning	Example
hand down	told by the elders to the children	The story about the loon was handed down for generations.
hand in	give to the teacher or manager, **turn in**	If we hand in an essay before it's due, teacher gives us a 5% bonus.
hand in hand	related, together	Math and science go hand in hand. They're related subjects.
hand me down	clothes that belonged to an older family member	Bobby said he's tired of wearing hand-me-down clothes.
hand out	give to the class or audience, **pass around**	Cory, please hand out the song books—one to each member.
hand over	give them to me, **fork over**	Hand over the keys to the safe— give them to me now!
hand over fist	as fast as possible, one after the other	The T-shirts are selling hand over fist. Everybody wants one.
hand to mouth	(See **from hand to mouth**)	
hand you a line	tell you a false story, **give you a line**	Some politicians try to hand you a line about how busy they are.
handful	(See **a handful**)	
handle herself	protect herself, **been around**	Dolly has worked with men before. She can handle herself.
handout	page of information for students	If you want to know more about Brazil, read the handout.
handout	(See **a handout**)	
hands are tied	be unable to act because others are in control, **out of our hands**	I'm in favor of public health care but my hands are tied. I have to wait for a government decision.
hands down	easily, **no contest**	The captain of the team said, "We won hands down—6 to 1."
hands on	practice doing a task by working with your hands	In shop class, we get hands-on experience in car maintenance.
hands up	put your hands above your head, **reach for the sky**	"Hands up, everybody!" the thief shouted as he entered the bank.
hang around	stay near, be with, **hang out**	Don't hang around with that gang. They steal cars.

Idiom	Meaning	Example
hang in there	continue, persevere, be patient, **keep on**	Hang in there until the doctor comes. He'll relieve your pain.
hang loose	be calm, relax, do not be **uptight**	In Hawaii, they tell the tourists to hang loose—to relax.
hang on	wait, **hold on**	Hang on a second. I have one more question to do.
hang on every word	listen carefully to every word that is said	When Dr. Frye spoke, we would hang on every word. We listened.
hang out	play with, be with, **spend time** with	Cal hangs out with Aaron. They go to the gym every day.
hang ten (surfing)	let your toes hang over the edge of the surf board	When you get tired of standing on the board, just hang ten.
hang tough	continue to try, be strong and determined	As we returned to the field, the coach said, "Hang tough, guys."
hang you out to dry	defeat you, convict you, **throw the book at**	If you're caught shoplifting, they'll hang you out to dry.
hang your hat	live here, live with us	You can hang your hat here for awhile—until you rent a room.
hang-up	a fear or phobia, a personal problem	For me, marriage is a hang-up. I can't commit to one person.
hangover	feeling ill or nausea the day after you are drunk	Is it true that vodka doesn't cause a hangover?
hanky-panky	unfair deal, cheating, **underhanded** plan	There is no hanky-panky in the contract we signed. It's okay.
happy as a box of birds	joyful, very happy	When we go to the lake, the kids are as happy as a box of birds.
happy as a clam/lark	very happy, carefree	When Tim is working on his car, he's happy as a clam.
happy as a pig in shit [B]	very happy, contented	"Does Caleb like farm life?" "He's happy as a pig in shit."
happy camper	a person who is happy most of the time	Jack's a happy camper today. He's smiling and whistling.
happy hour	an hour (or hours) when bar drinks are cheaper	Adam has invited me to the lounge for happy hour.
happy motoring	have a good trip in your car	The slogan of the auto club is *Happy Motoring!*

Idiom	Meaning	Example
hard as nails	tough, not sympathetic	The lawyer was as hard as nails. He felt no pity for anyone.
hard at it	working hard, **busy as beavers**	When the foreman returned, the workers were hard at it.
hard copy	printed page(s), paper with printed words or pictures	You can check your work on the computer screen, but it's easier find errors on hard copy.
hard day	(See **a hard day**)	
hard done by	overworked, asked to do too much	With all the help Bonnie gets, she's not hard done by.
hard feelings	unfriendly feelings, resentment	After the argument, Bill said, "I hope there are no hard feelings."
hard line	statement or policy that a person refuses to change	The principal takes a hard line on school attendance. I must attend.
hard liquor	strong liquor (rum etc.) with 40 % alcohol	The bar was serving beer, wine and several kinds of hard liquor.
hard nosed	firm, tough; refusing to lower his price or standard	Ms. Bond is hard nosed. If you plagiarize, you fail the course.
hard of hearing	not able to hear very well, partly deaf	Now that Grandpa's in his 80s, he's quite hard of hearing.
hard on me	makes me work hard, **tough on me**	That job was hard on me. My back is sore from the lifting.
hard pressed	challenged, faced with a hard task	They'll be hard pressed to find a person who doesn't drink coffee.
hard put	unable to answer easily, **stump me**	He was hard put to answer the questions on cold fission.
hard row to hoe	(See **a hard row to hoe**)	
hard stuff	(See **hard liquor**)	
hard times	a time of poverty and drought and famine	We endured hard times in the 1930s. We were all poor.
hard to believe	not easy to believe, difficult to believe	It's hard to believe that you're a grandfather. You look so young.
hard to get	(See **play hard to get**)	

Idiom	Meaning	Example
hard to swallow	hard to accept, **hard to take**	She said, "He has custody of the children. It's hard to swallow."
hard to take	difficult to tolerate, **hard to swallow**	Her cruel words hurt me. Her sarcasm is hard to take.
hard up	poor, unable to pay, **in the poor house**	After the war, our family was so hard up we couldn't buy meat.
hard-on [B]	(See **a hard-on**)	
hardware	computer machines and accessories	The printer is an important part of your computer hardware.
harum-scarum	careless, disorganized, **pell-mell**	Tag is a harum-scarum kind of game—no rules or referee.
has a mind of his own	(See **mind of his own**)	
has the cat got your...	(See **cat got your tongue**)	
has the makings	has the potential, has the ingredients	Darcy has the makings of a good teacher. He explains things well.
has-been	someone who has been skilled or famous	Bobby now plays on a team of has-beens: The Old Timers.
hash it over	talk about it, discuss it, **talk it over**	If I mention the lawsuit, he says, "We can hash it over later."
hassle	(See **a hassle**)	
hassle me	bother me, **bug** me, **give me a bad time**	If you hassle me about my kinky hair, I'll cut it all off.
hat in hand	humble, almost begging	If he doesn't find a job in town, he'll return to us, hat in hand.
hat trick	one player scoring three goals in one hockey game	Brad scored a hat trick in the game against the Blades.
hatchet man	the man who does the bad jobs: firing, layoffs etc.	Uh oh, there's Jake, the hatchet man. Who's getting fired now?
hats off	a tribute or honor; praise and thanks	And hats off to Mr. Singh for co-ordinating the volunteers.
haul ass [B]	do it, hurry, **get going**	If you want a magazine, haul ass. You can buy one at the drugstore.
haul up on the carpet	questioned, disciplined, **give me the third degree**	If you don't obey every rule, you will be hauled up on the carpet.

Idiom	Meaning	Example
have a ball	enjoy the activity, **have a blast**, **have fun**	We had a ball at Yolanda's party. It was lots of fun.
have a bite	eat lunch, eat some food	We can have a bite at a restaurant after we finish shopping.
have a blast	have a great party; enjoy the dance etc.	"How was the dance?" "Super! We had a blast!"
have a boo	go to the bathroom, go to **the can**	Let's stop at the next service station so Cory can have a boo.
have a boo	have a look, **have a peek**	Have a boo with my binoculars. You can see one of the planets.
have a case of	be sick from, have a disease	I was in bed. I had a bad case of the flu.
have a chair	please sit down on a chair, **have a seat**	"Please have a chair," my aunt said, and the man sat down.
have a clue	know about the answer, know about the topic	I didn't have a clue about the answer to Question 2.
have a conniption	become very upset, **have a fit**	Stop playing your violin, or Mom will have a conniption!
have a crush on	(See **got a crush on**)	
have a drag	draw smoke through a cigarette, **have a puff**	I'm out of cigarettes. Can I have a drag of yours?
have a fit	become very excited, **have a conniption**	Promise me you won't have a fit if I fail math.
have a fix	take some drugs, **get a fix**, **shoot up**	After he's had a fix, he's happy. The heroin satisfies his need.
have a flat	have a hole in a tire, have a flat tire	If you have a flat, phone a service station for help.
have a fling	live a wild life as a young person	Dad, did you have a fling when you were young?
have a go	try to do, attempt	You have a go at this puzzle. See if you can solve it.
have a good time	be happy, enjoy yourself, **have a blast**	You should come to the party. We'll have a good time.
have a heart	do not be cruel, have some feeling	Have a heart when you coach the kids. Be gentle with them.

Idiom	Meaning	Example
have a hitch in your getalong	limp, walk with a limp	Since he broke his ankle, he's had a little hitch in his getalong.
have a laugh	laugh, chuckle	Phan and Lo had a laugh about their early birthday parties.
have a leak [B]	urinate, **take a pee** [B]	When you go camping, it's okay to have a leak in the woods, eh.
have a look-see	look at something, look for something	Pete thinks he can find the cow. He went to have a look-see.
have a mind to	am considering, may do this	I have a good mind to tell his wife he's been with a prostitute.
have a puff	(See **have a drag**)	
have a say	be allowed to state a view, help to make the decision	Only the investors will have a say in the price of the product.
have a seat	sit down, please be seated, **have a chair**	The farmer pointed to a chair and said, "Have a seat."
have a shot at	have a chance or a try, qualify to compete	If Scotty wins this fight, he'll have a shot at the boxing title.
have a sip	have a small taste, drink through a straw	Can I have a sip of your cherry drink? Just a little sip?
have a smash	have a drink of liquor, **have a sip**	Here, Jon. Have a smash of the brandy before it's all gone.
have a soft spot for	have a caring feeling for, have sympathy for, **feel for**	I've always had a soft spot in my heart for Martha. She was so kind to me as a child.
have a whiz	go to the toilet, visit **the john**	We were so busy we didn't even stop to have a whiz!
have a word with you	talk to you, discuss with you	As I left the room, Mr. Lee said, "May I have a word with you?"
have an affair	see a lover who is not your spouse, **fool around**	"Liz is having another affair." "Who is she seeing? Bart?"
have an attack	feel sudden pain from a disease or illness	She can hardly breathe. I think she's having an asthma attack.
have an inkling	know, be aware of, **have a clue**	I didn't have an inkling that you loved him. I didn't know.
have at me	criticize me, scold me, **give you hell** [B]	Every time I come home late, my parents have at me.

Idiom	Meaning	Example
have designs on	want to take away from, envy, covet	I have no designs on your job. Believe me. I don't want it.
have fun	enjoy an activity or event, **have a good time**	Did you have fun at the party? Did you enjoy it?
have half a mind to	(See **have a mind to**)	
have it both ways	let it go and still have it, **have your cake...**	You can't be married and single. You can't have it both ways.
have it coming	deserve it, **ask for it**	If you get fined for driving too fast, you have it coming.
have it in for	(See **got it in for**)	
have it in hand	be able to control it, have it **under control**	A fire started in the kitchen, but it's okay. We have it in hand.
have it made	have achieved success, have everything you want	Viv has a new home, two cars and a career. She has it made.
have it out	argue, fight, **settle it**	Jake and Dan had it out. They argued for more than an hour.
have it your way	do what you want to do, **get your way**	Have it your way. Choose the movie *you* want to see.
have my ears lowered	get a haircut, have my hair cut	When my hair is long, I go and have my ears lowered!
have my eye on	(See **got my eye on**)	
have my work cut out	have a difficult task to do; a problem I must solve	Our goal is to win the cup, so we have our work cut out for us.
have nookie	have sexual intercourse, **have sex, make love**	All he wants to do is have nookie—all the time!
have one on me	have a drink and I will pay for it, **this one is on me**	Put your money away, please. Have one on me.
have sex	have sexual intercourse, **make love**	She said that it's dangerous to have sex with several partners.
have the balls [B]	(See **got the balls**)	
have the final say	make the final decision, **call the shots**	The children want a pony, but John has the final say.
have the floor	it is your turn to speak to the group	You have the floor, Mai. Please tell us about your idea.

Idiom	Meaning	Example
have things in hand	(See **have it in hand**)	
have to	must, cannot avoid	Jill *has* to go to the meeting. She's the president.
have to go	need to visit a washroom, have to **whiz**	Can we find a washroom? I have to go.
have to go some	must try harder, have to improve	You'll have to go some to get an *A*. It's a difficult course.
have to hand it to you	must admit that you can do it, **give** you **credit**	I have to hand it to you. You did every problem correctly.
have what it takes	(See **got what it takes**)	
have you for breakfast	defeat you easily, **cut you to ribbons**	Don't try to beat the gangsters. They'll have you for breakfast.
have you over	invite you to visit us, **drop over**	When we move into our new home we want to have you over.
have your cake and eat it, too	have something after you have eaten or spent it, **have it both ways**	You want to spend your money and still have it. You can't have your cake and eat it, too!
have your period [B]	menstruate, **got the rags on**	I get stomach pains when I have my period. Do you?
haven't got a hope	do not have a good chance of succeeding	If you don't study for exams, you haven't got a hope.
haven't got a hope in hell	have no chance to win or succeed or survive etc.	If the parachute doesn't open, I haven't got a hope in hell.
haven't got the stomach for it	dislike it, do not enjoy it	She likes to dissect frogs, but I haven't got the stomach for it.
haven't seen hide nor hair	have not seen a person, have seen no sign of him	We haven't seen hide nor hair of Jack since he borrowed $1000.
havoc strikes	problems happen, crises occur suddenly	Farmers plant their crops, and havoc strikes in hailstones.
hawk	a person who likes war; wants to **make war**	The hawks were pleased when the US declared war on Iraq.
haywire	(See **go haywire**)	
hazard a guess	guess at the answer, take a **shot in the dark**	How many beans are in the jar? Do you want to hazard a guess?

Idiom	Meaning	Example
he who hesitates is lost	if you hesitate you may not get another chance	If you want to marry Ko, ask her. He who hesitates is lost.
head (headbanger)	a person who uses drugs, **junkie**	That school has no heads. Not one student is using drugs.
head and shoulders	superior, better, **a cut above**	Her work is superior—head and shoulders above the others.
head honcho	boss, foreman, manager	Who's the head honcho here? I have a package for him—or her.
head in the clouds	dreaming, wondering, not practical	Shelly is a daydreamer. She's got her head in the clouds.
head in the sand	unable to see, unwilling to look	The minister hasn't noticed their poverty. His head is in the sand.
head is spinning	mind is confused, **boggle your mind**	The lawyer asked me so many questions my head was spinning.
head on	directly, without hesitation	Lynn meets her challenges head on, but Vera tries to avoid them.
head out	leave, depart	We should head out soon. We have a long way to go.
head over heels	in love with, **crazy about**	Lan's head over heals for Chan. She's crazy about him.
head up	lead, manage	Rod will head up the project. He can get the job done.
headhunter	a person who looks for professional employees	The headhunters are looking for good computer programmers.
heads or tails	choose one or the other, which side of the coin?	"Heads or tails?" the gambler asked as he flipped the coin.
heads will roll	people will be dismissed, people will be fired	When the manager hears about the damage, heads will roll.
health nut	a person who eats health foods and does exercises to become healthy	Gary is a health nut. He eats fruit and granola, and jogs five to ten kilometres every day.
hear me out	listen to all that I have to say, do not interrupt me	Please, hear me out. Wait until I finish before you comment.
heart is in the right place	people who encourage you even if they cannot help	Max is too old to help us now, but his heart's in the right place.
heat is on	(See **the heat is on**)	

Idiom	Meaning	Example
heaven forbid	we should not do it, we are not permitted	Grandma said, "Heaven forbid! Don't play hockey on Sunday!"
heaven help us	we are facing a crisis, we need a lot of help	Heaven help us if we have an accident with Dad's Mercedes.
heavens	goodness, oh dear, **gosh**	Heavens! You weren't supposed to arrive until Friday!
heavens to Betsy	oh no, **heavens**	Heavens to Betsy! I can't find my purse!
heavy	very serious, not fun	War is a heavy topic because it involves death and destruction.
heavy day	(See **a heavy day**)	
heavy duty	very difficult, demanding	I have to work hard at math. It's a heavy-duty course.
heavy going	difficult part, hard work, **tough going**	I'm glad we have Al on our team. He likes the heavy going.
heavy heart	sad, sorrowful	It was with a heavy heart that he attended his father's funeral.
heck	hell, **shucks**	She asked me to come in, but heck, her boyfriend was there.
hedge your bets	bet safely, bet on two or more horses etc.	If you hedge your bets, you have a better chance of winning.
hell bent for election	going fast, determined to get somewhere	There goes Joe, driving hell bent for election—always in a hurry.
hell to pay [B]	angry people to face, questions to answer	When I come in at 4 a.m. there's hell to pay.
hell's half acre [B]	(See **all over hell's half acre**)	
hellish [B]	bad, awful, unfair	If we have to pay our medical bills, it's a hellish arrangement!
help out	help someone, **lend a hand**	The Wongs are good neighbors —always willing to help out.
help yourself	please take some, **dig in**, **eat up**	Help yourself to hamburgers. Don't wait to be served.
helping hand	(See **a helping hand**)	

Idiom	Meaning	Example
hemming and hahing	saying "ahem...ah" while thinking of what to say, **beat around the bush**	When we asked him about the missing money, there was a lot of hemming and hahing.
here's mud in your eye	here is a toast to you, **drink up**	It's good to have a drink with you. Here's mud in your eye.
hey	listen, I am calling you	Hey, Ron. Where are you going?
heyday	best years, **in your prime**	In his heyday, Pele was the best soccer player in the world.
hi	hello, **howdy**	Hi, Kelly. How are you?
hi there	hello, **hi**	Hi there. Do you know the way to Monterey?
hick	rural person, **local yokel**, **rube**	Wearing overalls and a straw hat, he looked like a hick.
hidden agenda	secret plan to control the meeting or decisions	The board has a hidden agenda. We don't know their real plans.
hidden talent	a talent or skill you do not show very often	Oh, you play the harmonica! Got any more hidden talents?
hide nor hair	(See **haven't seen hide nor hair**)	
high	drunk, feeling happy after using a drug, **stoned**	Look into his eyes to see if he's high. Are his eyes clear?
high	(See **natural high**)	
high and mighty	better than other people, snobbish, **upper crust**	After she married the judge, she acted kind of high and mighty.
high-five	celebrating by slapping each other's raised hand	After scoring a goal, the players exchanged high-fives.
high handed	superior, above other people	We don't like managers who are high handed—high and mighty.
high hopes	expecting the best, hoping for success	Todd has high hopes for his son, including a college education.
high on the hog	having expensive things, in luxury	If I win the lotto, we'll live high on the hog—in a mansion!
high roller	a person who spends a lot on gambling and betting	This is a game for high rollers. You need a hundred grand to play.
high strung	nervous and sensitive, easily upset	Jacqueline won't speak in public because she's very high strung.

Idiom	Meaning	Example
high time	late, past due, **about time**	It's high time you got a job, Ty. What kind of work do you like?
high-hat	proud, snobbish, pompous	Cynthia looks high-hat, but she's really very friendly.
highball it	drive fast, **boot it**	The big truck was highballin' it, speeding down the freeway.
higher than a kite	drunk, **high**, **sloshed**	Don't let him drive—he's higher than a kite.
highfalutin	proud, pretentious	We need a musician, not some highfalutin rock star!
hightail it	leave in a hurry, run away	If the bull gets loose, you hightail it for the house.
hill of beans	not very much, very little	What I lose in the poker games doesn't amount to a hill of beans.
hip	sophisticated, **cool**, **groovy**, **with it**	It's not hip to say *doll*. You got to say *chick* now.
hire on	get work, get a job, **catch on**	Norm was hired on as a roughneck with an oil company.
his nibs	a man who acts high class, **His Royal Highness**	We were having fun till his nibs walked in and told us to be quiet.
his own man	independent man, one who makes his own decisions	Ken will do his job, but he does it his way. He's his own man.
His Royal Highness	the king, His Majesty	His Royal Highness would like you to play your lute for him.
history	fired, dismissed, gone, **down the road**	If you refuse to do a job, you're history, pal.
hit	(See **a hit**)	
hit and miss	some right and some wrong, **trial and error**	Hiring good help is still a hit-and-miss procedure.
hit and run (baseball)	a play in which the batter tries to hit as the base runner runs	On the next pitch, the Mets tried a hit and run, but the batter missed the ball.
hit and run (traffic)	an accident in which the driver leaves the scene of the collision	Was your car involved in a hit-and-run accident? Did you fail to stop after hitting someone?

Idiom	Meaning	Example
hit home	become very meaningful, affect you personally, **touch you**	When they see hungry Canadian children on TV, the message about poverty will hit home.
hit it off	relate well, be friends immediately	Gus and Bert seem to hit it off. They've been talking for hours.
hit man	hired killer, a person who is paid to commit murder	The hit man who killed the president is a terrorist.
hit me (card games)	give me another card; yes, I'll have another one	The old man looked at his cards carefully, then said, "Hit me."
hit me	the meaning becomes clear to me, I understand	It hit me later that she was a teacher, not a student.
hit me	tell me, say it now, **give it to me straight**	When I said it was bad news, he said, "Hit me. Let's have it."
hit me for a loan	ask to borrow money, ask me for a loan	Hit me for a loan on payday. Then I'll have some money.
hit me with your best shot	shoot or hit as hard as you can, **sock it to me**	Hit me with your best shot. Serve the ball as hard as you can.
hit my funny bone	cause me to laugh, **crack me up**	The word *pollywog* always hits my funny bone. Ha ha ha, ha ha.
hit on	think of, **come up with**	Ko was a nurse until she hit on the idea of selling jewelry.
hit on	talk to in a sexual manner, **come onto**	When he hit on a waitress, we asked him to stop.
hit rock bottom	feel very unfortunate, feel very depressed	After his farm was seized, he hit rock bottom—lost all hope.
hit speeds of	travel at speeds of, **do (a speed)**	The stolen car was hitting speeds of 120 km per hour in the city.
hit the bar	go to the bar to buy some drinks	Every night after work he hit the bar and stayed for hours.
hit the books	begin to study, **crack a book**	Exams begin next week. It's time to hit the books.
hit the bottle	drink liquor, get drunk to forget problems	When Laura left him, he hit the bottle, drinking to forget her.
hit the brakes	step on the brakes in a car or vehicle, try to stop	When I saw that the other car couldn't stop, I hit the brakes.

Idiom	Meaning	Example
hit the ceiling	become very angry, **lose your cool**	The third time we were late for class, she hit the ceiling.
hit the ground running	be able to work effectively when you begin a new job, **self-starter**	We need someone who can hit the ground running, a person who needs no training.
hit the hay	go to bed, **crash**	After supper he hit the hay. He was exhausted.
hit the high notes	sing high notes, play high notes	Can you hit the high notes on your trumpet? High C?
hit the nail on the head	say the right word, suggest a good idea	Your comment hit the nail on the head. You spoke the truth.
hit the road/trail	travel, leave	Let's hit the road early. We have many miles to go.
hit the skids	begin to fail, **go downhill**	After losing his job and his wife he hit the skids—became a bum.
hit the spot	taste right, is satisfying	Sometimes tea hits the spot. It satisfies me.
hit town	arrive in town	It was 2 a.m. when we hit town.
hitch in your getalong	(See **have a hitch in your getalong**)	
hobnob	associate with, be a friend of	Per likes to hobnob with artists because he likes to draw.
Hobson's choice	accept what is offered or you get nothing; **Sophie's choice**	If I don't agree to accept half the money, it will all go to charity. It's a Hobson's choice.
hogwash	false statements, **bull, bunk, hot air**	He told you I have a pet python? That's a lot of hogwash!
hoity-toity	a bit snobbish, **high and mighty**	Pamela is a classy lady, but she is not snobbish or hoity-toity.
hokey Dinah	**gosh**, **holy cow, wow**	Every time you hit the ball, Wendy says, "Hokey Dinah!"
hold a candle	do as well, compare with, **measure up**	The Buick is nice, but it can't hold a candle to the Cadillac.
hold a grudge	stay angry for a long time, **bad blood**	He gets mad, but he never holds a grudge. He forgives easily.
hold a meeting	organize and conduct a meeting	The club will hold a meeting on Monday at 7:30 p.m.

Idiom	Meaning	Example
hold down	keep, stay at	He has shown that he can hold down a job. He's reliable.
hold her liquor	drink but not get drunk, **hold your drinks**	Thelma can hold her liquor. She looks sober after five drinks.
hold it	stop, this is important, **hold on**, **wait a minute**	"You and I will swim over to—" "Hold it! I can't swim. I didn't agree to swim anywhere!"
hold me responsible	say that I am responsible, **carry the can**, **lay the blame**	Because I'm the cashier, the manager holds me responsible for missing cash.
hold on	wait, do not begin, we are not ready	Hold on! We haven't fastened our seat belts.
hold out for	wait to get full price, **drive a hard bargain**	He'll hold out for the full price of his car. He'll wait.
hold that over my head	remind me of my mistake, judge me by a failure	My parking ticket—is he going to hold that over my head?
hold the fort	manage until we return, **look after** things	The manager asked me to hold the fort while he was gone.
hold the phone	wait a minute, let me think about it	"Dad, I'm going to quit school." "Hold the phone! Let's talk."
hold the purse strings	control how much is spent, decide when to spend	He does the talking, but she holds the purse strings.
hold up	stall, not be able to go, be unable to continue	The plane was held up because of a snowstorm—delayed an hour.
hold up	use a gun in a robbery, **mugged**	A robber held up the store and took the money from the till.
hold up	cope, not cry, not lose control of your grief	Teri has endured a lot of pain. How's she holding up?
hold water	be logical, be sensible	He can't be in two places at once. His story doesn't hold water.
hold you up	delay you, cause you to be late	Did the traffic hold you up? Is that why you were late?
hold your drinks	drink liquor but not be rude or foolish	You may be able to hold your drinks, but you can't drive my car.
hold your hand	help you when you are afraid, baby-sit you	When you go to college, who's going to hold your hand?

Idiom	Meaning	Example
hold your horses	wait a minute, **hold on**, **hold the phone**	When I said the accident was his fault, he said, "Hold your horses!"
hold your mouth the right way	if you shape your mouth the right way you can do it, **the way you hold...**	"I can't tie a reef knot." "Sure you can—if you hold your mouth the right way."
hold your nose	accept it but not like it, **look the other way**	This plan is better than no plan, so hold your nose and vote for it.
hold your own	be equal to the others, **keep pace**	She can hold her own with the best skiers. She's excellent.
hold your tongue	be polite, do not **talk back**	When your father is talking, you hold your tongue. You be quiet.
hold-out	a person who does not agree	There are two hold-outs, but both people are willing to negotiate.
holding the bag	left alone to finish the work or be responsible	Mom says we leave her holding the bag—to finish jobs alone.
hole in one (golf)	hit the ball from the tee into the cup in one stroke	There's a $50 prize for a hole in one at the Pines Golf Course.
hole up	hide and wait, find a place to stay until it is safe	The robbers were holed up in a motel on Hastings Street.
hollow leg	(See **a hollow leg**)	
holy cow	that is exciting, **geez, gosh, wow**	Holy cow! That car just about crashed into us!
holy Moses	that is amazing, **gosh**, **holy Toledo, wow**	Holy Moses! What a lot of birds! There must be a million!
holy pile	(See **a holy pile**)	
holy smoke	what a sight, **holy cow, wow**	Holy smoke, he was weird! He had purple hair!
holy Toledo	how exciting, **holy Moses, wow**	Holy Toledo, he has big muscles! They're huge!
home free	finished a job, free to go home or away	Two more newspapers to deliver and we're home free—finished.
home run (baseball)	the batter scores a run on one hit (See **grand slam**)	I remember the game when Rusty hit three home runs.
honesty is the best policy	telling the truth is the best plan, honesty **pays off**	Above the teacher's desk is this sign: *Honesty is the best policy.*

Idiom	Meaning	Example
honky	white person, Caucasian	Then this honky gave us a ride. Some whites are nice, eh.
hoo-haw [B]	penis, **dork, prick**	"Yes, I've seen a hoo-haw," she said. "I have three brothers."
hooch	liquor, **booze, homebrew, screech**	Arne brought a bottle of hooch to the dance.
hood	teenage boy involved in crime, hoodlum	Ron looks like a hood, but he's a good boy—and a good student.
hook up with	join, travel together	In Calgary, I hooked up with a guy from Montreal.
hooker	prostitute, **fallen woman**	As I walked along 3rd Avenue, a hooker asked me if I was lonely.
hoosegow	(See **in the slammer**)	
hoot	laugh, **laugh your head off, split a gut**	When I said I live in Moose Jaw, he hooted. He laughed at me.
hop up	increase the power, **supercharge, tweak**	"What are you driving?" "A hopped-up Ford. It flies!"
hopes dashed	plans ruined, dreams lost	Her hopes were dashed when she failed the entrance exam.
hopping mad	very angry, **hot**	She was hopping mad when you laughed at her wig.
hork	vomit, puke, **barf, throw up**	Somebody horked on the floor of my car! Yuk!
horn in	interfere, intrude, **butt in**	We were playing a game of tag, and the big guys tried to horn in.
horny [B]	ready for sex, wanting to have sex, aroused	How come you're never horny when I am?
horse around	play, joke, **fool around, goof off**	Don't horse around in the lab. You could spill some acid.
horse feathers	lies, false stories, **bull, a bunch of malarkey**	When she told her dad she saw a ghost, he said, "Horse feathers!"
horse of a different color	(See **a horse of a different color**)	
horse sense	being sensible, logical; **common sense**	He's got horse sense to rent a condo before he buys one.

Idiom	Meaning	Example
horse shoes up his ass [B]	very lucky, always winning	He's got horseshoes up his ass! He won six games of bingo!
horse's ass [B]	(See **a horse's ass**)	
horseplay	just having fun, **fooling around**	Don't worry. The boys aren't fighting. It's just horseplay.
hose it down/ hose it off	spray with water from the hose, **wash down**	If the rubber mat is muddy, lay it on the sidewalk and hose it off.
hoser	Canadian guy, neighbor	Hey, hoser. What're you doin' in my garden?
hot	angry, mad, **pissed** [B]	She was really hot when you said her wig was crooked.
hot air	false talk, bragging, **bull**, **hogwash**	Steve brags about winning the marathon, but he's full of hot air.
hot and bothered	upset, getting angry, ready to speak angrily	You know that Dad gets hot and bothered when you stay out late.
hot goods	stolen products, items obtained illegally	I won't buy a watch from him because he sells hot goods.
hot hand	(See **a hot hand**)	
hot off the press	paper that has just been printed	As the boy handed me the paper he said, "Hot off the press!"
hot on the trail	following the trail, looking for evidence	The police are hot on the trail of the bank robbers.
hot on your heels	following close behind, not far behind	If you begin to run, the bear will be hot on your heels.
hot potato	(See **drop him like a hot potato**)	
hot stuff	very popular person, very sexy person	When Arlana was in high school she was hot stuff—very sexy!
hot tempered	quick to become angry, **lose your temper**	He's hot tempered—very impatient and often angry.
hot ticket	(See **a hot ticket**)	
hot topic	(See **a hot topic**)	
hot under the collar	upset, becoming angry, **hot and bothered**	It's only a joke. Don't get hot under the collar.

Idiom	Meaning	Example
hotdog	cooked wiener inside a long bun	Two hotdogs with mustard, please. And two coffees—black.
hotdog	(See **a hotdog**)	
hothead	(See **a hothead**)	
hotshot	(See **a hotshot**)	
household name	(See **a household name**)	
how about that	that is interesting, **you don't say**	How about that! We ran ten kilometres!
how are you doing	are you feeling fine? is life good to you?	How are you doing, Chan? I haven't seen you for awhile.
how are you fixed for	do you have enough? how many do you have?	How are you fixed for diapers? May I borrow one?
how are you getting along	are you able to do it? are you **okay**? **how are you doing**	"How are you getting along at the new school, Gail?" "Fine. I like my subjects."
how are you making out	are you able to do the job? have you made progress? **how are you doing**	The manager came to my office and said, "How are you making out? Finished the report?"
how come	why? how do you explain it?	How come you're going home? Don't you want to play?
how do you do	hello, nice to meet you, **good day**, **howdy**	"Mr. Grant, I'm Ken Blair, the new bank manager." "How do you do, Mr. Blair."
how do you like them apples	do you like this better? do you like that choice? **tough bananas**	If you don't like the bed, you can sleep on the floor. How do you like them apples?
how does that grab you	how do you feel about that?	A holiday in Greece—how does that grab you?
how goes it	is your life good? **how are you doing**	"How goes it?" said my friend. "Not bad," I replied.
how goes the battle	are you winning the battle of life? are you **okay**?	"How goes the battle?" Jo asked. "I win and I lose," Pat replied.
how it plays out	how it happens, how it ends how it **pans out**	The new policy is supposed to improve sales, but we'll see how it plays out.

Idiom	Meaning	Example
how so	explain how, **how come**	When I told him the game was cancelled, he said, "How so?"
how time flies	how quickly time passes, how short the time seems	How time flies when I visit you. The hours pass too quickly.
how you hold your...	(See **the way you hold your mouth**)	
how's that again	what did you say? **come again**	When Grandpa doesn't hear me, he says, "How's that again?"
how's tricks	is life okay? are you learning new skills?	When Andy sees me, he always says, "How's tricks?"
howdy	hello, good day, **how do you do**	The old cowboy says, "Howdy, ma'am," when he meets a lady.
huh	what did you say? pardon?	"Did you wash your ears?" "Huh?"
humdinger	(See **a humdinger**)	
humongous	huge, very large	My uncle has this humongous dog. It's as big as a calf.
hungover	having a headache after drinking liquor, **hangover**	The next day he was hungover so he rested and drank coffee.
hungry thirties	(See **dirty thirties**)	
hunk	a gorgeous man, a very attractive male	Matty thinks Robert Redford is a hunk. She dreams about him.
hunker down	get ready to lift or work, prepare to make an effort	To achieve our sales goals, we all have to hunker down.
hurl	vomit, puke, **barf**, **hork**, **woof your cookies**	After eating two raw eggs, she hurled—all over my sheepskin!
hurt my feelings	make me feel sad, offend me	You hurt my feelings when you said I waddle like a duck.
hurry up	do it quickly, **make it snappy**	Hurry up with the dishes. We want you to play cards with us.
hush up	do not talk, be quiet, **keep quiet**	"Mommy, there's the man who kissed you!" "Hush up, child."
hushed up	not talked about, **keep a secret**	In the 1950s, if a teen-age girl got pregnant, it was hushed up.
hyah	hello, **hi**, **hi there**	Hyah, Bill. What's new with you?

Idiom	Meaning	Example

I

I'll be a monkey's uncle	I cannot believe it, I must be dreaming	When Farley won the new car, he said, "I'll be a monkey's uncle!"
I'm afraid so	(See **afraid so**)	
icing on the cake	a bonus, extra benefit, **the rest is gravy**	We've sold enough tickets to pay for the trip. This money from the Elks Club is icing on the cake!
idiot lights	warning lights on the instrument panel of a car	Kim wants a car with gauges, not idiot lights.
if looks could kill	the look on your face was evil or hateful	If looks could kill, I'd be dead. Are you mad at me or something?
if a mussel doesn't open don't eat it	if you force things to happen you may regret it, **leave well enough alone**	If you force a child to talk, you may regret it. As they say, *If a mussel doesn't open, don't eat it.*
if my memory serves me correctly	if I can remember well, if I have a good memory	Your name is Jose—if my memory serves me correctly.
if only	I wish, we wish	If only we'd phoned before we came. There's nobody home!
if that doesn't beat all	that is the best/biggest/ worst I have ever seen	Fifty people in a phone booth— if that doesn't beat all!
if the shoe fits, wear it	if there is a lesson for you, learn it	When I listen to you preach, I wonder if the shoe fits me.
if you can't cut it, you can't stay	if you cannot do the work you will have to leave; **shape up or ship out**	When I complained about long days, the foreman said, "If you can't cut it, you can't stay."
if you can't stand the heat, get out of the kitchen	if you do not like the pressure, you can leave; **if you can't cut it, you can't stay**	In the boardroom someone had written on the flip chart *If you can't stand the heat, get out of the kitchen!*

Idiom	Meaning	Example
if you're born to hang, you won't drown	fate controls how we die; we do not control the time and cause of our death	After rescuing the swimmer, he said to me, "If you're born to hang, you won't drown."
if you're not with us you're against us	if you do not support us you are against us; **can't have it both ways**	War divides us into allies and enemies. If you're not with us, you're against us.
ignorance is bliss	ignorant people have nothing to worry about	The teacher said, "Ignorance is bliss—until you write exams."
in a bad way	feeling sad or **downhearted**	After the accident, Val was in a bad way. She was very depressed.
in a big way	with a lot of style and expense	Pam does things in a big way. She hired a band for her party.
in a big way	very much, a lot	My son likes to play computer games—in a big way!
in a bit	in a minute, within a short time	"Can we go?" asked the girl. "In a bit," her mother replied.
in a coon's age	in many years, for a long time, **for a dog's age**	Hello, Uncle Henry! I haven't seen you in a coon's age!
in a family way	pregnant, **a bun in the oven**	Carey's in a family way. She's due to have her baby soon.
in a fix	in a bad situation, **in a jam**	Without matches or food, the lost boys were in quite a fix.
in a flap	worried or upset, in a hurry	Kate is in a flap again. Her dog is sick.
in a flash	very quickly, **in no time**	If you're in trouble, Superman will be there in a flash.
in a flutter	(See **in a tizzy**)	
in a funk	in a bad mood, frustrated, **in a snit**	Rick is in a funk today because Muriel hasn't called him.
in a jam	in a difficult position, in trouble	I was in a jam. I had no money to pay the rent.
in a jiffy	in a minute, very soon, **in a sec**	When Dad says he'll be there in a jiffy, he means 20 minutes.
in a pickle	in a difficult situation, **in a jam**	When the motor on our boat quit, I knew we were in a pickle.

Idiom	Meaning	Example
in a pig's ass [B]	not true, unbelievable, **bull, full of it**	You wrote *War and Peace*? In a pig's ass!
in a pinch	in a difficult situation, **in a jam**	I was in a pinch because I had no money to pay for the meal.
in a rut	always doing it the same way, never changing the method or style	After ten years in the same job with the same manager in the same building, he was in a rut.
in a sec	in a second, very soon, **in a jiffy**	Wait. I'll be there in a sec.
in a slump	not performing well for several days	Wayne's in a slump. He hasn't scored a point in four games.
in a snit	upset, worried, **in a stew**	Ms. Mak is in a snit because she lost her cat.
in a split second	in less than a second, **in a flash**	In a split second, the cat twisted and landed on its feet.
in a stew	concerned and upset, **in a tizzy**	Dad gets in such a stew when Mom is sick. He really worries.
in a tight spot	in a difficult position, **in a pinch**	Mom told me to go, and Dad told me to stay. I was in a tight spot.
in a tizzy	upset, flustered, **in a flap**	Aunt Lottie gets in a tizzy when she can't find her wig.
in agreement	believing or feeling the same things	When we discuss Canadian unity, we're in agreement.
in any way, shape or form	in any way, **at all**, **in the least**	Winning the award didn't affect her in any way, shape or form. She hasn't changed at all.
in bad faith	not sincere, not really trying to agree	The workers accused management of bargaining in bad faith.
in bad shape	not feeling well, **out of it**	The day after the party I was in bad shape. How my head ached!
in black and white	written and signed, **in writing**	If they say the car is guaranteed, get it down in black and white.
in brief	briefly, without giving details	In brief, all flights have been cancelled.
in broad daylight	easy to see, not trying to hide	The man undressed right there on the street—in broad daylight.

Idiom	Meaning	Example
in cahoots	like partners, helping each other	I think the judge and lawyer are in cahoots—working together.
in charge	responsible for, **in control**	Who's in charge here? Who is the manager or supervisor?
in clover	becoming wealthy, receiving lots of money	We were in clover! We bought a ranch, a car, and a house in town.
in cold blood	without feeling, without mercy	He's accused of killing a **Mountie** in cold blood.
in control	able to manage, **in charge**	Mr. Blum is not in control of his pets. They run all over town.
in deep shit [B]	in bad trouble, likely to be punished	If you shoot a bear in a national park, you are in deep shit, man.
in deep trouble	in serious trouble, sure to **catch hell**	Driving without a licence could get you in deep trouble.
in dire straits	in debt, having no money	If we don't get a good crop this year, we'll be in dire straits.
in dribs and drabs	a few at a time, **little by little**	Many came to the sale, but they arrived in dribs and drabs.
in fact	to state a fact, **as a matter of fact**, **to be perfectly honest**	Some people think of gravity as a cause of falling; in fact, gravity often prevents us from falling.
in full flight	going full speed, **flat out**	The cyclist was in full flight when he passed the cars.
in glowing terms	with much praise, **praise you to the skies**	Your manager spoke of you in glowing terms. He praised you.
in good faith	sincerely, hoping to reach a fair agreement	The union president said that he always bargained in good faith.
in good hands	cared for by a friend, with a trusted person	If Darlene is caring for your dad, he's in good hands.
in hand	able to control, **under control**	Some fans began fighting, but the police have things in hand.
in heaven's name	if we think of heaven, **for heaven's sake**	Why in heaven's name did we come to Canada? It's cold here!
in her good graces	being liked by her, doing what she likes	If you are in her good graces, you will be invited to her tea party.

Idiom	Meaning	Example
in his good books	among those he likes, on his list of good people	She's in his good books because she praised his painting.
in hock	in debt, owing money, having a large mortgage	We were in hock after buying the property. We had a large debt.
in keeping with	following the rules or customs	Refunds are not in keeping with company policy. No refunds.
in leaf	having new leaves, growing leaves	Poplar trees were in leaf, wild roses in bloom.
in love	feeling romantic love, **fall in love**	Peter's in love with Wendy, but Wendy's in love with Tom.
in mind	thinking of, remembering, **keep you in mind**	When she wrote the story about the lawyer, she had you in mind.
in mint condition	in new condition, **as new**	The Nash was in mint condition. It looked like a new car.
in my care	for me to protect, **under my wing**	The children were in my care when the dog chased us.
in my good books	among the people I like, **on my good side**	To get in my good books, you can help me with my homework.
in no time	very soon, **in a sec**	We'll be there in no time. We have less than a kilometre to go.
in no uncertain terms	definitely, clearly, **call a spade a spade**	They told us about sex and drugs in no uncertain terms.
in one ear and out the other	not listening, hearing but not **paying attention**	The kids don't listen to me; it's in one ear and out the other!
in one fell swoop	in one action, in one attack, **at once**	Our TV ad is effective. In one fell swoop we create doubts about the other products and sell our own.
in order	to make it possible, to help it happen	In order to win, we have to work as a team.
in over your head	unable to win, competing against better players	If you play chess against Boris, you'll be in over your head.
in person	being there yourself, **first hand**	Dad saw the wall come down. He was there in person.
in place	in the correct position or location, available	Be sure to have the money in place before you buy a house.
in point of fact	(See **in fact**)	

Idiom	Meaning	Example
in seventh heaven	in a very good mood, feeling very happy	When Smitty asked me to marry him, I was in seventh heaven.
in step	doing things in a similar way, together	Are you in step with our youth? Do you understand how they feel?
in stir	(See **in the tank**)	
in stitches	laughing hard, **crack me up**	I was in stitches before she finished telling the joke.
in store for	in the future, going to happen	Carlos didn't know what was in store for him in Canada.
in stride	(See **take it in stride**)	
in the back of my mind	in my memory, **in your mind's eye**	In the back of my mind I could see our dog—asleep by the fire.
in the bag	drunk, **loaded**, **sloshed**	Two drinks and she'll be in the bag. She gets drunk easily.
in the bag	already won or decided, **a sure thing**	Don't worry. The game is in the bag—we'll win easily.
in the ball park	close, near the total	My offer wasn't even in the ball park. He wanted $500, not $300.
in the black	showing a profit, in a sound financial position	After one year our company was in the black—showing a profit.
in the boonies	out of town, out in the country	Lan lives in the boonies—fifty kilometres from Calgary.
in the buff	naked, nude	At our house, we walk around in the buff. Nude is natural, eh.
in the dark	unaware, not informed	I was in the dark about the trip to Ireland. No one told me.
in the doghouse	having your friend or spouse angry at you	I'm in the doghouse. I forgot her birthday and she's mad at me.
in the drink	in the sewer, lost	If you leave your ring on the sink it will soon be in the drink.
in the drink	failing, bankrupt, **up the creek**	In the drink—that's where I'd be without you. A total failure.
in the driver's seat	controlling events or decisions, **in charge**	Money and talent will put you in the driver's seat—in control.

Idiom	Meaning	Example
in the fast lane	(See **life in the fast lane**)	
in the flesh	the person (not a photo or recording of the person)	Julia was there—in the flesh, standing right in front of me!
in the gutter	having dirty thoughts or ideas	Pornography puts his mind in the gutter—lusting after flesh.
in the hole	having lost money when gambling or investing	By the time he left the poker game he was $500 in the hole.
in the hoosegow	(See **in the slammer**)	
in the know	informed, knowledgeable	Ask Joan about global warming. She's in the know.
in the lap of luxury	living in comfort, living **high on the hog**	If I win the lottery, we'll be rich. We'll live in the lap of luxury.
in the least	in any way, **at all**	Oil prices went up, but the price of gas didn't change in the least.
in the long haul	after several years, for the long term	In the long haul, you'll earn more money if you have a degree.
in the long run	planning for the future, looking many years ahead	In the long run, real estate is a good investment.
in the lurch	facing a problem alone, **holding the bag**	True friends won't leave you in the lurch, will they?
in the making	developing, growing	Raj is a talented pianist. Is he a Glenn Gould in the making?
in the meantime	for now, meanwhile	Someday I want to own a yacht. In the meantime, I have a canoe.
in the money	wealthy, rich, **loaded**	If my lottery number is drawn, I'll be in the money.
in the mood	feeling that you want to do something	I'm in the mood for pizza. Let's order a large one—loaded!
in the nick of time	nearly too late, **just in time**, **under the wire**	They jumped from the burning boat in the nick of time—just before it sank.
in the nude	naked, **in the buff**	Sleeping in the nude has advantages and disadvantages.
in the offing	ready to happen, soon to be	A great event was in the offing: the discovery of penicillin.

Idiom	Meaning	Example
in the picture	part of the scene, a factor	As Mr. Martin lost the election, he's not in the picture.
in the pink	looking and feeling healthy and happy	Last time I saw Barb, she was in the pink. She looked great.
in the poorhouse	poor, having little money, **as poor as a church mouse**	In 1936, they were in the poorhouse. They couldn't grow crops, and nobody had a job.
in the red	showing a financial loss, losing money	Last year our business was still in the red—still showing a loss.
in the road	blocking the way, preventing movement	We'll have to move the table. It's in the road.
in the running	competitive, could win, **give you a run for...**	With ten games remaining, the Expos are still in the running. They have a chance to win.
in the slammer	in jail, in prison, **behind bars**	Marv's been in the slammer four times. He knows prison life.
in the tank	in jail, in prison, **in the slammer**	While he was in the tank, he studied science and history.
in the throes	in the middle of some work, **caught up** in a process	We're in the throes of repairing an old house. What a job!
in the wink of an eye	very quickly, **in a split second**	In the wink of an eye, the coin disappeared from the man's hand.
in the works	in the plans, to be built	I've heard there's a housing project in the works.
in the worst way	very much, a lot	Hal wants a Porsche in the worst way. He loves sports cars.
in these parts	in this part of the country; **neck of the woods**	We haven't seen a bear in these parts for years.
in time	before the deadline, within the time limit	The cheque arrived just in time. We flew to Hawaii the next day.
in touch	phone or write a letter, **keep in touch**	Have you been in touch with your family in China?
in tough	in a difficult battle, against a tough opponent	If you play Ivan in the tennis tournament, you'll be in tough.
in trouble	accused, arrested, punished	If you steal, you'll be in trouble. You'll be arrested.

Idiom	Meaning	Example
in tune	believing the same, **on the same wavelength**	He's in tune with our religious beliefs. He believes in God.
in tune (music)	at the correct pitch, not sharp or flat	It was an excellent concert. Even the children sang in tune.
in two shakes (of a lamb's tail)	very soon, in a couple of seconds, **in a sec**	I'll be with you in two shakes. I just have to turn off the lights.
in writing	written and signed, **in black and white**	The company guarantees this pen for life. I have it in writing.
in your bad books	one of the people you do not like	If I don't agree with you, I'll be in your bad books, right?
in your corner	hoping you will win, **on your side**	Hey, man, I'm in your corner. I'll help you get your diploma.
in your face	placed in front of you, right in front of you	Every time I turn on the TV, that ad is in my face. I'm sick of it.
in your hair	bothering you, **bug**ging you	If you have too many kids in a class, they get in your hair.
in your mind's eye	in a picture in your mind, in your memory	In my mind's eye, I can see her face—clearer than a photo.
in your prime	during your best years, when you are strongest	When he was in his prime, he played professional soccer.
in's and out's	(See **the in's and out's**)	
in-crowd	(See **the in-crowd**)	
information leak	(See **leak**)	
inhale	eat quickly, **wolf down**	I rushed home, inhaled my lunch and drove to the airport.
inside information	facts available to those inside an organization	I can get inside information. My friend works for the FBI.
inside joke	a joke that is understood by only those who work or play together, **shop talk**	"Would you like to buy some of our **liveware**?" I asked. She frowned. "Never mind," I said. "It's an inside joke. Ha ha."
inside out	(See **know inside out**)	
inside story	(See **the inside story**)	
inside track	(See **the inside track**)	

Idiom	Meaning	Example
Internet	a system of computers, **World Wide Web**	If you want to know more about any topic, get on the Internet.
into fitness/dancing etc.	involved in fitness etc., enjoying a hobby	They're really into fitness. They exercise and jog a lot.
into hock	(See **in hock**)	
into the sauce	drinking alcohol, **off the wagon**	Uncle has been into the sauce. I can smell liquor on his breath.
into the tank	into business failure, into bankruptcy	Two companies went into the tank because of free trade.
into thin air	disappearing like a ghost, vanishing like steam	When I moved closer, the flying saucer vanished into thin air.
invite you over	(See **have you over**)	
iron out	solve, **work it out**	She ironed out the problem with the school. Jeff is back in class.
irons in the fire	very busy, **plate is full**	I can't help with your project. I have too many irons in the fire.
is that so	is that true? **no kidding**	Every time I tell Mr. Pratt some news, he says, "Is that so?"
is you is, or is you ain't my baby	are you my love? I want to know if you love me	Pearl is singing to Toby: "Is you is, or is you ain't my baby?"
it ain't over till it's over	a game is not finished until time has expired, **never say die**	A few fans stayed to watch the end of the game. "It ain't over till it's over," one man said.
it ain't over till the fat lady sings	an event is not finished until the final bell, don't **give up**	The tying goal was scored in the final second. It ain't over till the fat lady sings!
it appears to me	this is what I see, I believe this happened	It appears to me that this car swerved to avoid a collision.
it couldn't happen to a nicer person	it is just, it is right; the person earned it	"I won the *Biggest Jerk* award." "It couldn't have happened to a nicer guy! Ha ha."
it figures	it is logical, it appears so, it **makes sense**	"The owner must have started the fire," said Sherlock. "It figures," said Watson.
it goes with the territory	some problems are natural in some jobs or places	There's more crime in the cities. It goes with the territory.

Idiom	Meaning	Example
it goes without saying	it is obvious, **needless to say**	It goes without saying: we want equal pay for equal work.
it has your name on it	we saved this one for you, it is yours	There's a steak on the grill, and it has your name on it.
it is better to have loved and lost than never to have loved at all	you are a better person if you have loved someone— even for a short time	Old and alone, the woman often thought of a saying: *It is better to have loved and lost....*
it makes no difference	it does not matter, either way is okay	"Should we have tea or coffee?" "It makes no difference to me."
it never fails	it always happens, **time and again**	It never fails—when I get in the shower, the phone rings.
it occurs to me	this thought comes to my mind	It occurs to me that we won't meet again until Christmas.
it phased me out	it caused me to feel uneasy, **throw you**	I was nervous when you did the bungee jump. It phased me out.
it seems to me	it is my opinion, it is my view	It seems to me that Don expects us to phone him every week.
it strikes me	this is clear to me, this is my impression	It strikes me that we share many interests and activities.
it takes one to know one	one type of personality recognizes the same type	"Elizabeth is such a fool!" "Takes one to know one."
it was Greek to me	I could not understand what was said; it was like a foreign language	When he asked me what I had learned about DNA, I replied, "I don't know. It was Greek to me."
it works	it is right, it looks nice, it is a good style	If you place the vase over there and the statue here, it works.
it's a case of	it is an example of, it is **a case of**	With Bud, it's a case of too much love. His wife smothers him.
it's a go	it is approved, we can begin	After Ty read the fax, he said, "It's a go! Our proposal won!"
it's a jungle out there	the world is dangerous, the world is cruel	"Why can't I walk home alone?" "Because it's a jungle out there."
it's a snap	it is easy to do, it is **a piece of cake**	You should try making a paper plane. It's a snap.
it's a toss-up	they are equal, toss a coin to decide	It's a toss-up. It's difficult to choose. Both ideas are good.

Idiom	Meaning	Example
it's all over but the shouting	the contest is finished but the cheering continues	"The Blue Jays won," he said. "It's all over but the shouting."
it's been a slice (of life)	it has been an experience, it has been interesting	On the last day of work, Pam said, "It's been a slice, Mag."
it's beyond me	I do not understand why, it does not **make sense**	It's beyond me why they don't get married. They're in love.
it's cold/hot	the weather is cold/hot, **it's raining**	In January it's cold in Edmonton but hot in Chile.
it's in the bag	(See **in the bag**)	
it's not a question of	it is not a factor, it is not important	It's not a question of money. We can afford to buy a TV.
it's not what you know, it's who you know	references are important, **Bob's your uncle**	In politics, it's not what you know, it's *who* you know.
it's now or never	do it now or not at all, **he who hesitates is lost**	If we're going to have a family, it's now or never. We can't wait.
it's over/ it's over with	it is finished, it is done	When the trial ended, she said, "I'm glad it's over with."
it's raining/snowing	the weather is rainy or snowy	Whenever we visit Vancouver, it's raining.
it's up to you	it is your decision, you choose	I can't tell you which program to choose. It's up to you.
it's your move	now you move or speak, **it's your turn**	She jumps three of my checkers and says, "It's your move, Bud."
it's your turn	now you play, **it's your move**	Now it's your turn, Willie. Hit the ball to Daddy.
itchy feet	ready to go, anxious to leave	As we talked about the trip, I could see that Dad was getting itchy feet.

Idiom	Meaning	Example

J

Idiom	Meaning	Example
jack me around	tell me lies, **play games**	Don't jack me around, man. I need to know who took my car.
jack of all trades	a person who has many skills	She's a carpenter, plumber and cook—a jack of all trades.
jam	play jazz, practise music in a small group	After the concert, a few musicians started to jam.
jam/jam out	not come to the party etc., **back out**	Kai jammed last night because her cousin came to visit her.
jam session	informal practice session for musicians, **jam**	After the symphony rehearsal, a few of us had a jam session.
jam tart	a phony person, a pretender	That jam tart! He teaches writing but he hasn't written anything.
jazz up	add color or interest, add an accessory	It's a nice coat, but I'm going to jazz it up with a red scarf.
je ne sais quoi	I do not know what it is, it is a special something	She has a special quality, this lady, a certain je ne sais quoi.
jeepers	oh, **gee whiz, gosh**	Jeepers! I don't know what to say.
jerk	fool, **dipstick, fink**	Stop acting like a jerk! Stop squeezing mustard on me!
jerk me around	not be honest with me, **jack me around**	Don't jerk me around. I want to know if you've seen my child.
jerk off [B]	masturbate, **pull your wire** [B]	"If jerking off is a sin, I know a lot of sinners," said the old man.
jewels	(See **the family jewels**)	
jibberish	nonsense, **bafflegab, bunk**	Did he say *disregardless*? I wish he wouldn't talk jibberish!
jig is up	(See **the jig's up**)	
jim-dandy	(See **a jim-dandy**)	

167

Idiom	Meaning	Example
jimminy crickets	**geez**, **gosh**, **holy cow**	Jimminy crickets, it was hot! It was 39 degrees Celsius!
jive-ass [B]	one who tries to look cool, **cool cat**, **show-off**	What a jive-ass! Give him a mic, and he thinks he's Elvis.
jock	athlete, student who plays on school teams	Doug is a jock—he plays golf and baseball.
Joe Who	Joe Clark—a Canadian politician	When was Joe Who the Prime Minister of Canada? 1979?
joe-job	a routine task, a chore that nobody wants to do	If you're the junior employee, you'll have to do the joe-jobs.
jog your memory	do or say something to help you remember	This photo of your dog may jog your memories of the old days.
John Henry	signature, signed name	To give you a refund, we need your John Henry on this form.
john	(See **the john**)	
Johnny on the spot	being ready to help, being there when needed	When I need a ride, you're always here—Johnny on the spot.
Johnny-come-lately	a man who has not lived or worked there very long	"Who is she going with now?" "Oh, some Johnny-come-lately."
join up	enrol, enlist, **sign up**	The Army needed volunteers, so Milo joined up.
join you	meet you, **catch up** with you	You go to the game directly from work. I'll join you at the arena.
joke around	play and tell jokes, **fool around**	They were joking around after class—rapping and laughing.
joke is on you	(See **the joke is on you**)	
joker	a person who tells jokes and likes to laugh	Jerry is some joker! He makes everybody laugh.
joker	a stranger, a person who does something unusual	Some joker stopped and asked me if I knew the way to heaven.
jolly good fellow	a good person, a person being honored	At Jim's farewell party we sang *For He's A Jolly Good Fellow*.
josh	fool, tease, **kid**	Quit joshin' me. Be serious.

Idiom	Meaning	Example
juice	electricity, electrical power	This heater uses a lot of juice— 1500 watts.
jump	surprise and overpower, attack without warning	The gang attacked him in the alley. They jumped him.
jump [B]	have sex with, **bang, screw** [B]	"Did you jump her, Ted?" "Is that all you think of—sex?"
jump at the chance	be ready to try if you have the opportunity	If I was asked to play with their band, I'd jump at the chance.
jump for joy	jump up and down because you are happy	When their horse won the race, they jumped for joy.
jump in the lake	(See **go jump in the lake**)	
jump in with both feet	become totally involved, **go whole hog**	Ken gets involved in his work. He jumps in with both feet.
jump queue	go to the front of a line of people waiting for service, **horn in**	If somebody jumps queue in front of Dad, he tells them to go to the back of the line.
jump ship	go to work for the other team—the competition	The company asked me to sign a form saying I wouldn't jump ship.
jump start	use cables to start a car, **kick start**	One cold morning my dad helped me to jump start my car.
jump the gun	act too soon, leave early	A good chef waits until the food is cooked. Don't jump the gun.
jump through hoops	do all the required steps, **red tape**	To get a student loan, I had to jump through a lot of hoops.
jump to conclusions	form conclusions before you have all the facts, **jump the gun**	If you see a wrecked car and say that the driver was drunk, you are jumping to conclusions.
jumping Jehoshaphat	**holy cow**, **jimminy crickets, wow**	"Your VISA balance is $63,756." "Jumping Jehoshaphat! Is it?"
jungle mouth	smelly breath, unpleasant smell on the breath	Most people have jungle mouth when they wake up, eh.
junk	illegal drugs: dope, acid etc.	He tried to smuggle junk into Canada. He hid drugs in his shoes.
junk food	snack food, food with little nutritional value	They eat junk food for lunch— chips, candy and pop.

Idiom	Meaning	Example
junk it	throw it away, put it in the garbage	If a pen is leaking, junk it. Throw it away.
junk mail	advertisements and commercial letters	On her mail box she wrote a sign: *NO JUNK MAIL!*
junkie	a person who does junk or drugs; **head**	"What is a junkie?" "A person who uses bad drugs."
jury-rig	make a substitute, improvise	When we don't have a fuse, Dad jury-rigs one with silver paper.
just a smidgeon	just a little, just a small amount	"Would you like more cream?" "Just a smidgeon, please."
just a titch	just a tiny amount, **just a smidgeon**	"Is that piano too heavy?" "Just a titch."
just about	nearly, almost	We just about fell into the lake. Our canoe nearly tipped over.
just as soon	would prefer to, wish to	I'd just as soon forget the fight with Dwen, eh.
just ducky	just fine, wonderful, **peachy**	"Bill, my mother is coming to live with us." "That's ducky, just ducky!"
just in time	not quite late, **in the nick of time**	Superman arrived just in time to save the girl from burning.
just passing through	(See **pass through**)	
just-in-time	when the manufacturer or seller is ready, not before	T-Max has requested just-in-time delivery of the engine parts.

Idiom	Meaning	Example

K

Idiom	Meaning	Example
kaput	broken, ruined	We have a car, but it won't go. The motor is kaput.
keep a lid on it	not tell others, **keep it quiet**	The judges know who won, but they have to keep a lid on it.
keep a low profile	not go out much, **lay low**	He plans to keep a low profile until the trial is over.
keep a promise	do what you promise to do	You can depend on Vern to keep a promise. He's reliable.
keep a secret	not tell anyone, **keep it to yourself**	Children can keep a secret better than adults.
keep a stiff upper lip	do not cry, do not be afraid	When Arthur left Tag, Dad said, "Keep a stiff upper lip, Dear."
keep a straight face	not smile or laugh, have a **poker face**	When you said I was your uncle, I couldn't keep a straight face.
keep an even keel	be steady, be calm and sensible	Customer Service needs people who can keep an even keel.
keep an eye on	watch to prevent harm, **watch out for**	Fred, will you keep an eye on the children? I'm going to the store.
keep an eye open	(See **keep an eye out**)	
keep an eye out	watch for, look for, **keep your eyes peeled**	Keep an eye out for Helen at the school reunion. You may see her.
keep an open mind	be fair to all opinions, avoid prejudging	I keep an open mind when I talk to you—open to all opinions.
keep fit	exercise to be healthy, **look after** your body	You'll feel better if you keep fit —if you exercise regularly.
keep in good shape	care for your body, be fit, **keep fit**	You keep your body in good shape. You look fit.
keep in line	obey the rules, conform, **stay in line**	The manager expects us to keep in line, not cause problems.

Idiom	Meaning	Example
keep in touch	phone, write a letter	Please keep in touch with us when you move to the city.
keep it down	be quiet, do not be noisy, **pipe down**	Dad called to us, "Keep it down, eh. We're trying to go to sleep."
keep it quiet	do not tell anyone, **keep a lid on it**	I have a new job, but keep it quiet because I haven't told my boss.
keep it to yourself	do not tell anyone, **keep a secret**	If I tell you what she said, will you keep it to yourself?
keep it up	continue doing it, maintain this quality	Good work, Joe. If you keep it up, you'll soon be a manager.
keep on	continue, do it more	We asked him to stop phoning us, but he kept on doing it.
keep on trucking	continue to go or work, **carry on**	Len has a sign on the door of his big-rig: *Keep On Truckin, Man!*
keep out	do not come in, stay outside	There was a sign on the gate: PRIVATE — KEEP OUT!
keep pace	go as fast, **keep up**	Our company keeps pace with the leaders. We're near the top.
keep quiet	do not talk, **shut up**	Will you please keep quiet. You've said enough.
keep tabs on	watch and write notes, **keep track of**	Who keeps tabs on expenses? Who has the receipts?
keep the ball rolling	continue the work, encourage us to continue	Reg will keep the ball rolling. He won't allow the work to stop.
keep the faith	believe in what we know, do not doubt	When we parted, John said, "Keep the faith, eh."
keep the wolf from the door	keep us fed, prevent hunger	This cheque will keep the wolf from the door. We can buy food.
keep them straight	know the difference, be able to identify them	Mo, you have so many relatives. How do you keep them straight?
keep to yourself	be alone, not associate with people	When I'm feeling sad, I keep to myself. I like to be alone.
keep track	check, count	Keep track of the time you work at the computer. Keep a record.

Idiom	Meaning	Example
keep under wraps	keep something hidden, not show or talk about	Details of the program were kept under wraps until the election.
keep up	go as fast as the others, **keep pace**	In typing class, I can't keep up. I can't type as fast as the others.
keep up the good work	continue to do good work, **'at a boy**	I like to hear my supervisor say, "Keep up the good work."
keep up with the Joneses	buy what the neighbors buy, **keep pace**	I can't afford to keep up with the Joneses. I'm not rich!
keep up with the times	be aware of new methods and trends, **stay abreast**	Reading newspapers will help you keep up with the times.
keep you going	provide money or food or energy, **get by**	If you can't stop for lunch, drink some juice to keep you going.
keep you honest	keep you from lying, cause you to be truthful	Your child's questions will keep you honest. You can't lie to kids.
keep you in mind	remember you or your request, think of you	If we have any job openings in sales, I'll keep you in mind.
keep you on track	tell you what to do, remind you of the topic	The instructor will help to keep us on track. She'll remind us.
keep you posted	send or phone the news to you, inform you	I'll be in Korea for six months, but I'll keep you posted.
keep your cool	stay calm, not become excited	Can you keep your cool during an emergency, or do you panic?
keep your distance	do not come too close, respect a person's space	Keep your distance or she'll accuse you of harassment.
keep your ear to the ground	listen for news, listen for gossip	Keep your ear to the ground. You'll hear about drug dealers.
keep your eyes peeled	look or watch carefully, watch for	Keep your eyes peeled for birds. Watch for animals, too.
keep your head	think clearly, do not **lose your head**	Try to keep your head during a crisis. Try to think clearly.
keep your head above water	survive, have just enough to live, **get by**	With a part-time job, I was able to keep my head above water.
keep your nose clean	stay out of trouble, **toe the line**	Keep your nose clean, and you'll get out of prison sooner.
keep your nose to the grindstone	continue to work hard	Keep your nose to the grindstone and you'll pass the final exam.

Idiom	Meaning	Example
keep your shirt on	be calm, do not rush me, **don't get your shirt...**	When we asked Dad to hurry, he'd say, "Keep your shirt on."
keep your word	do as you promise, **keep a promise**	You can depend on him. He always keeps his word.
keeper	(See **a keeper**)	
keester	buttocks, **backside, bum, rear end**	We laughed when Lan fell off the horse and landed on her keester.
kept woman	(See **a kept woman**)	
kettle of fish	(See **a different kettle of fish**)	
kick a habit	stop a habit, **shake a habit**	A person needs discipline to kick a habit like drinking.
kick ass [B]	scold, lecture, **give you hell**	The coach will kick ass if we don't go to practice.
kick butt	defeat badly, **blow them away**	The Cougars beat us last week. Let's kick their butt tonight!
kick at the cat	a turn, a try, **have a go**	It's your kick at the cat. See if you can solve the puzzle.
kick back	relax, sit back and put your feet up	I'm going to kick back on the deck for a couple of hours.
kick myself	be angry at myself, regret my choice	I could kick myself for selling that car. I wish I hadn't sold it.
kick start	use battery cables to start a car, **jump start**	The battery was dead so we got a tow truck to kick start our car.
kick the bucket	die, **buy the farm, pass away**	Charlie finally kicked the bucket. He had cancer, you know.
kick the weed	stop smoking, **kick the habit** of smoking	It's hard to kick the weed after smoking for twenty years.
kick up a fuss	complain, **make a scene**	Jon will kick up a fuss if he doesn't get paid on time.
kick up your heels	celebrate, go to parties, **have fun**	After you've written your exams you can kick up your heels.
kicking around	lying around here; is here or there or somewhere near	"Do you have a hammer?" "Ya, there's one kickin' around here somewhere."

Idiom	Meaning	Example
kid	joke, fool, tease, **josh**	I was kidding when I said the mosquitoes are as big as bats.
kid you not	tell the truth, not joke	There were three large circles in the field, I kid you not.
kill a penalty (hockey)	prevent a goal while your player has a penalty	Team Canada killed a penalty near the end of the game.
kill an elephant	do too much, do ten times more than necessary, **overdo it**	He asked you to adjust the carburetor, not rebuild the motor. Don't kill an elephant!
kill for	do anything to get it, **in the worst way**	Lea would kill for a date with Mat. She really likes him.
kill me	cause me to laugh a lot, **crack me up**	Your jokes kill me. They're so funny I nearly die laughing.
kill off	kill all, kill every one	The oil killed off the ducks in the bays along the coast.
kill ourselves laughing	laugh hard, **hoot**, **split a gut**	When the teacher wasn't looking we killed ourselves laughing.
kill the goose that lays the golden eggs	lose or destroy the source of wealth	If we pollute the environment, we kill the goose—we lose it all.
kill time	wait, **put in time**, **time to kill**	He was killing time waiting for a plane, so he phoned a friend.
kill two birds (with one stone)	get two with one try, do two jobs on one trip	If you sell and advertise at the same time, you kill two birds....
killer instinct	wanting to defeat the opponent	Mel is a fine tennis player, but he lacks the killer instinct.
killing me	hurting me, causing pain	These new shoes are killing me. Can we stop and rest?
kiss ass [B]	be nice to get favors, **brown nose**	I won't kiss ass to get a job. I refuse to be a slave.
kiss curls (hair style)	flat curls on the forehead or in front of the ears	Teddi can't go out until her kiss curls are dry.
kiss it off	not deal with it, **put** it **off**	We're fighting for equal pay. We won't let them kiss it off.
kiss of death	an action that results in failure or loss	His TV speech was a disaster— the kiss of death for his party.

Idiom	Meaning	Example
kiss off	go, **get lost**, **take off**	When he's angry with me he says, "Kiss off!"
kiss that one goodbye	say it is lost or stolen, **down the drain**	Hank borrowed your new pen? You can kiss that one goodbye.
kiss the blarney stone	say a lot of compliments, **flattery will get you...**	You always say that I look nice. Did you kiss the blarney stone?
kit and caboodle	everything, all the stuff, **the whole shebang**	The canoe tipped, and it all fell in the river—kit and caboodle!
kitty bar the door	play defensively, play only to prevent a goal	In the third period we played kitty bar the door and won 4-2.
kitty-corner	the diagonally opposite corner of an intersection	The Bay is kitty-corner from the drugstore.
klutz	a clumsy person, one who makes careless mistakes	What a klutz I am! I poured sugar in the salt shaker!
knee high to a grasshopper	small or short, the size of a child	When we lived in Oslo, you were just knee high to a grasshopper.
knock	criticize, **put down**	Don't knock the teacher. She's trying to help us learn.
knock against	(See **the knock against**)	
knock around with	be friends with, **hang around** with	Lynn used to knock around with us. She was our friend.
knock flat	knock down, knock over	The flag pole was knocked flat— hit by a truck.
knock it off	stop it, do not do that	When we teased the bull, Dad told us to knock it off.
knock me over with a feather	I was very surprised, I could not believe it, **blow me down**	When she told me she was married to my ex-husband, you could have knocked me over with a feather.
knock off	remove, kill	One by one, the wolves were knocked off—shot by hunters.
knock out	hit a person until he is unconscious, **out cold**	You punched him very hard. You knocked him out.
knock the wind out of his sails	cause him to slow down, cause him to quit, **knock him down a peg**	If you tell him his letter is full of errors, you'll knock the wind out of his sails.

Idiom	Meaning	Example
knock them down, drag them out	fighting, brawling, **Donnybrook**, **no holds barred**	After the game, a few soccer fans began to fight. It was a knock-em-down-drag-em-out brawl.
knock up [B]	become pregnant, **in a family way**	She doesn't want to get knocked up, so she uses a contraceptive.
knock you down a peg	say you are too proud, **put him in his place**	If you are too cocky, Don will knock you down a peg.
knock you out	amaze you, **blow your mind**	You should see *The Phantom of the Opera*. It'll knock you out.
knock your socks off	surprise you, perform better than you expect	This music will knock your socks off! It's rock and roll!
knocked out	eliminated from a competition or series	Our team was knocked out during the semi-final games.
knockout	stunning appearance, beautiful body	When Jackie wears that red party dress, she's a knockout.
know better	know you should not do that	Why did you take the candy? You know better than to steal.
know inside out	know a method well, know an occupation well	After 30 years in real estate, he knows the business inside out.
know like the back of your hand	know an area well, know every feature of the land	I lived here for years. I know this town like the back of my hand.
know the first thing...	(See **don't know the first thing about**)	
know the ropes	know how, have much experience, **learn the ropes**	Good managers know the ropes. They have skills and experience.
know the score	know what is happening, **in the know**, **know your stuff**	The leader of the party should know the score. He or she should be well informed.
know where we stand	know our position, know if we have a chance, **leave me hanging**	The Department hasn't replied to our application for assistance, so we don't know where we stand.
know which end is up	know where you are, know what to do next	With so many problems, he doesn't know which end is up.
know which side your bread is buttered on	know who pays your salary, have **common sense**, **bite the hand that feeds...**	If you refuse extra work, you don't know which side your bread is buttered on.
know your stuff	know a lot, know facts, have the answers	In calculus, Tara knows her stuff. She can solve difficult problems.

Idiom	Meaning	Example
know your way around	know how to survive, be **worldly wise**	To live on the street, you have to know your way around.
knuckle down	work harder, achieve more	If you knuckle down and study, you can pass this exam.
knucklehead	one who does not think, **doughhead**	What a knucklehead! He made the same mistake ten times.
kooky	crazy, **hairbrain**, **nuts**	Just because I eat insects doesn't mean I'm kooky.

Idiom	Meaning	Example

L

lady-killer	(See **a lady-killer**)	
laid back	relaxed, casual	*Lenny's Place* is a laid-back kind of restaurant—casual.
laid bare	exposed, open for everyone to see	During the trial, details of his personal life were laid bare.
laid off	to be told by the manager that your job is cancelled	Billy was laid off because there's not enough work at the plant.
laid up	sick, injured, not able to work	Kelly was laid up for two weeks with a very bad cold.
land on your feet	be ready to work, be ready for action, **hit the ground running**	We're looking for employees who land on their feet after facing a problem or challenge.
lap of luxury	(See **the lap of luxury**)	
lap up	welcome, appreciate	She laps up their compliments. She loves their praise.
lard butt/lard ass [B]	a person with fat buttocks, a person with a big **bum**	When I was young and chubby, my brother called me lard butt.
larger than life	larger or prettier than people we know; **bigger than life**	In American movies, everything seems larger than life. Buildings are taller, women are sexier.
last but not least	the last one on the list but not the least important	Last but not least is Carla, winner of the spelling contest.
last call	last chance to buy a drink or come in for supper	Dad stood on the back porch and shouted, "Last call for supper!"
last hurrah	last big event for an old person	Frank is planning one more TV concert—his last hurrah.
last legs	(See **on his last legs**)	
last resort	last hope for assistance, last chance to succeed	I will call the police only as a last resort—only when I'm desperate.

Idiom	Meaning	Example
last straw	(See **the last straw**)	
last-ditch	last try, desperate attempt, **last resort**	In a last-ditch attempt to save the marriage, he bought her a BMW.
late bloomer	a person who is slow to mature or succeed	Kelly is not doing well in math, but she may be a late bloomer.
laugh up your sleeve	laugh secretly at someone, **behind your back**	He tried to please her, unaware she was laughing up her sleeve.
laugh your head off	laugh loud and long, **crack me up**, **hoot**	When Jerry tells a joke, I laugh my head off. He is so funny!
laugh yourself sick	laugh until you ache, **split a gut**	When I listen to Mandy's jokes, I laugh myself sick.
laugh yourself silly	laugh and laugh, **laugh your head off**	One girl said something funny, and we laughed ourselves silly.
laughing	fortunate, lucky, rich etc.	He has a full scholarship to go to university. He's laughing.
laughing stock	(See **the laughing stock**)	
laundered money	stolen money that has been invested or donated	Do Mafia companies donate laundered money to the church?
lay [B]	have sex with, **get laid** [B]	Chuck brags about all the girls he's laid, but I don't believe him.
lay a trip	suggest guilt or blame or duty	Don't lay a trip on me about low grades. I'm studying hard.
lay down your arms	stop fighting, **bury the hatchet**	It's time to lay down your arms. Stop fighting with your sister.
lay down your life for	die for, be killed for	Doug was killed in World War II. He laid down his life for Canada.
lay eyes on	see, look at	She says she's my sister, but I've never laid eyes on her before.
lay it on	compliment, praise, **butter up**	The salesman is praising the new Camry. He's really laying it on.
lay it on the line	be truthful, **straight goods**	You can lay it on the line. I want to know if I passed or failed.
lay low	stay out of sight; **out of circulation**	The escaped prisoner planned to lay low for a few days.

Idiom	Meaning	Example
lay of the land	(See **get the lay of the land**)	
lay off	not be able to employ any longer, **let go**	NSU laid off 50 employees because there's not enough work.
lay off	stop doing it, quit it, **cut it out**	I think I'll lay off coffee. I'm getting too much caffeine.
lay on	provide, supply	The chefs lay on lots of food at the banquet. It's a feast!
lay over	stay overnight while traveling	On the way to Winnipeg, we usually lay over in Regina.
lay rubber	spin a car's wheels, **drag race**	He likes to drive fast. He lays rubber at every intersection.
lay the blame	blame, say who is **at fault**	When he fails a test, his mom lays the blame on the teacher.
lay the lumber	hit with a hockey stick, slash with a hockey stick	The losing team started to lay the lumber on our best players.
lay waste	damage, wreck, plunder	The Vikings raided Scotland's coast, laying waste the villages.
lay you	bet you, **give you odds**	I'll lay you ten to one that Marc uses steroids. I'm sure he does.
lazy bones	lazy person, a person who does not want to work	If you don't want to work, we'll call you lazy bones.
lead a life	have a style of living, have a way of life	With your career and children, you lead a busy life.
lead pipe cinch	certain of the result, **foregone conclusion**	The Jets are a lead pipe cinch to win the game. They're better.
lead you down the garden path	tell you a false story, **give you a line**	He said the trip to Paris was free. He led me down the garden path.
lead you on	promise good things, pretend to be good	I know you love Jo, but she was leading you on. She loves Paul.
leaf out	grow new leaves, **in leaf**	She trimmed the branches before the trees began to leaf out.
leak	allow people to know, tell the media	Details of the program were leaked to a newspaper.
leak	(See **have a leak**)	

Idiom	Meaning	Example
lean times	times of poverty, **hard times**	During lean times they sold eggs for 50¢ a dozen.
learn the lingo	learn the language, know the idioms	To work in the computer industry you have to learn the lingo.
learn the ropes	learn the first steps, learn the basics, **know the ropes**	He wants to learn the ropes, to learn how to play jazz.
learn your place	learn to know where and when to speak	When I was young, kids learned their place; they showed respect.
leave me hanging	leave me wondering what happened	You begin a story, but you don't finish it. You leave me hanging.
leave no stone unturned	look everywhere, **look high and low**	In our search for Mom's wedding ring, we left no stone unturned.
leave out	not include, discard	Leave out the cracked dishes. We'll throw them away.
leave out in the cold	not invite, exclude	Kim didn't receive an invitation. She was left out in the cold.
leave the door open	allow people to reply, invite a response, **feel free** to reply	If you offer to provide answers to their questions, you leave the door open for a reply.
leave well enough alone	if you do more you could cause more trouble	If I cause a problem, I apologize. Then I leave well enough alone.
leave you holding the bag	leave you to do the work or finish a difficult job	He left me holding the bag. I had to finish the work by myself.
leave you in the lurch	leave you with a problem, **fend for yourself**	The bride didn't go to the church. The groom was left in the lurch.
leave yourself open	not protect yourself, allow people to hurt you	By coming late to work, he left himself open to discipline.
led to believe	be told, be given information, **lead you down...**	"Were you led to believe that the car was in good condition?" "Yes. They said it was fine."
left holding the bag	(See **leave you holding the bag**)	
left in the lurch	(See **leave you in the lurch**)	
left out in the cold	(See **leave out in the cold**)	
left over	remainder, what is not used or not eaten	We bought too much ice cream. There are two pails left over.

Idiom	Meaning	Example
left, right and center	in every direction, everywhere	There were soldiers everywhere— left, right and center.
leftovers	food not eaten at the previous meal	After the Christmas feast they ate leftovers for a few days.
lefty	left-handed person, **southpaw**	The ignition switch in most cars is not designed for a lefty.
leg work	walking, going to visit customers or voters	The kids delivered the notices— they did the leg work.
leg up	(See **a leg up**)	
lemon	a car with many problems, a car of low quality, **seconds**	When the American companies began to make small cars, there were a lot of lemons for sale.
lend a hand	help someone, **give me a hand**	Our neighbors lend a hand when we have too much work to do.
lesser lights	people who are not as talented, not **superstars**	We owe our success to the lesser lights on our team—the workers.
lesser of two evils	both are bad but one is not as bad as the other	Neither person can be trusted. Choose the lesser of two evils.
let a fart [B]	allow gas to escape, fart, **pass wind**	If I let a fart in this tiny room, we won't be able to breathe.
let down	not do as expected, disappoint someone	Don't let the team down. Please come to the game.
let George do it	let him or her do the job, wait for someone to do it	If his attitude is *let George do it,* he won't succeed in our firm.
let go of	release, allow to be free, **part with**	Please let go of my hand now. I want to leave.
let her rip	release or start suddenly, go with full power	When you want him to dump the load, just say, "Let 'er rip!"
let it all hang out	relax, be natural	When we go camping, we let it all hang out. We really relax.
let it be	leave it alone, do not touch it	When a cat is sick, let it be. Don't pet it or pick it up.
let it go to your head	become too proud, have a **swelled head**	So you won the golf tournament. Don't let it go to your head.
let me have it	tell me, do not wait to tell me	If you want to criticize my work, go ahead. Let me have it.

Idiom	Meaning	Example
let off	not have to pay or do, **get off**	Kyle was involved in the crime, but they let him off.
let off steam	express concern, **sound off**	Hec is letting off steam again. He wants to save the wolves.
let on	show, say, reveal, let others believe	Don't let on that you know me. Our friendship will be a secret.
let one	(See **let a fart**)	
let sleeping dogs lie	do not create problems, leave things alone	Don't tell them the price of gas will rise. Let sleeping dogs lie.
let the cat out of the bag	tell people, **the cat's out of the bag**	People know we plan to elope. Who let the cat out of the bag?
let the chips fall where they may	let it happen naturally, do not control everything	We've done all we can to win the the election. Let the chips fall....
let the good times roll	let the party begin, let us enjoy our time together, **the more the merrier**	Uncle Harry welcomed us to the reunion. Then he said, "Let the good times roll!"
let up	not do it as much, **ease up**	If the rain lets up, we'll go to the park.
let you down	(See **let down**)	
let you have it	scold you, shout at you, hit you, **tell you off**	If you tease him about his girlfriend, he'll let you have it.
let yourself go	relax, be natural, **let it all hang out**	"Let yourself go," the leader said. "Share what you are feeling."
let yourself go	not groom yourself, become sloppy	If you let yourself go, your wife may lose interest in you.
lettuce	money, **dough**, **moola**	A billion dollars is a lot of lettuce! It's more than I need.
level the playing field	make it equal for everyone, **a level playing field**	If we train all employees, we help to level the playing field.
level with you	be honest with you, **the straight goods**	Peter will level with you. He'll tell you what the doctor said.
lick and a promise	(See **a lick and a promise**)	
lick your wounds	become healthy again, recover from a defeat	After losing the election, he went home to lick his wounds.

Idiom	Meaning	Example
lickety-split	moving fast, **boot it, hell bent for election**	The train is going lickety-split, at least sixty miles an hour!
lie down on the job	stop working, refuse to work	Yes, I take long coffee breaks, but I would never lie down on the job.
life in the fast lane	a fast-paced life, living or working in a large city	We tried life in the fast lane—in Toronto—but Seth didn't like it.
life is just a bowl of cherries	life is just wonderful, life is grand	When Anne is happy, she says, "Life is just a bowl of cherries!"
life is not all guns and roses	life is not all war and love, life is not like the movies, **come down to earth**	After World War II, some people had to learn that life is not all guns and roses.
life of the party	(See **the life of the party**)	
life on the edge	(See **live on the edge**)	
life you lead	the way you live, lifestyle; **lead a life**	The life we lead here is based on respect for human rights.
lifer	a person who has been sentenced to life in prison	The lifers all sit at the same table in Hampton Penitentiary.
lift a finger	help someone, do anything to help	Loki is my friend, but he didn't lift a finger when I needed help.
lift my spirits	cause me to be happy, **give me a lift**	Music will lift our spirits. Let's listen to some Mozart.
light at the end of the tunnel	a sign of progress, feeling hopeful because you will soon be finished	After four years of study, I could see light at the end of the tunnel. I would soon graduate.
light in the loafers	homosexual, gay, **fag**	Just because he likes to sew, you think he's light in the loafers.
light up	light a cigarette, begin to smoke	As Ken left the school, he lit up. It was okay to smoke outside.
lighten up	relax, do not be so serious	Lighten up, Charles. Try to see the humor in life.
lighthearted	humorous, joking	His lighthearted approach to life is popular with students.
lights are on but...	(See **the lights are on but nobody's home**)	
like a bat out of hell	very fast, **go like stink**	When Harriet is late for work, she drives like a bat out of hell.

Idiom	Meaning	Example
like a bolt from the blue	like a sign from heaven, like a flash of light	Like a bolt from the blue, I got the idea to shave my head.
like a dirty shirt	always there—like shirts that need to be washed	If you have a garage sale, Jim will be there like a dirty shirt.
like a hot potato	(See **drop him like a hot potato**)	
like a ton of bricks	heavily, with force, like a very heavy object	Check your safety rope! If it breaks you'll fall like a ton of bricks.
like crazy/like mad	a lot, very much, **to beat the band**	She laughed like crazy whenever Earl told a joke.
like dog's breath	not pleasant, not popular	This plan smells like dog's breath. It's a bad plan.
like father, like son	sons are like their fathers, **a chip off the old block**	This is Fred, and this is Fred, Jr. Like father, like son.
like hell [B]	not likely, **no way, not**	"It's a goal!" said the referee. "Like hell it is!" said the goalie.
like hell [B]	fast, **go like stink**	That dog can run like hell.
like it or lump it	if we do not like it, that is too bad; **tough bananas**	This is the supper Dad cooked for us—like it or lump it.
like nobody's business	a lot, busily, **like crazy**	The squirrel was eating nuts— chewing like nobody's business.
like the devil	quickly, too fast to see, **like hell**	The disease spread like the devil. Soon his whole leg was swollen.
like the wind	fast and smooth, **like the devil**	You can't catch that deer. It can run like the wind.
lily-livered	cowardly, **chicken, wimpy**	Bull riding is not a sport for lily-livered folks. It's not for wimps.
line of authority	people in order of power, **chain of command**	The line of authority goes from our manager up to the president.
line up	form a line of people, form a queue	College students have to line up to buy their text books.
lingo	(See **learn the lingo**)	
lip	rudeness, **cheek**	No more of your lip, boy. I won't allow you to be rude.
lip off	talk without respect, **talk back**	Did you hear him lip off the police? He called them pigs.

Idiom	Meaning	Example
lips are sealed	will not talk about it, **mum's the word**	I won't tell anybody you love the coach. My lips are sealed.
lippy	rude, impolite, **cheeky, sassy**	If you get lippy with me, I'll give you extra work to do.
liquored up	drunk, having drunk too much liquor, **sloshed**	I wish Pa wouldn't get liquored up when he goes to town.
listen up	listen carefully, **pay attention**	The coach said, "Listen up, guys. This is important."
little bird told me	(See **a little bird told me**)	
little by little	a little progress each time you try, **bit by bit**	Little by little, we saved our money to buy this house.
little white lie	(See **white lie**)	
live and let live	live your life and let others live their lives	Pop's approach to life is simple and fair: live and let live.
live by	follow, use as a guide	My husband and I live by two principles: honesty and trust.
live it up	live wild, go to a lot of parties, **have a fling**	When I move to the city, I'm going to live it up—have fun.
live off	earn enough money to pay expenses	Can we live off the profit from selling your garden flowers?
live on	have to pay rent and buy food etc.	What will we live on if you don't have a job?
live on the edge	live in danger from drugs or disease or crime	When Bill played in the NHL, he was living on the edge.
live up to	be as good as people said you would be	Live up to your own standards. Set your own rules.
liven up	cause more activity or excitement	Let's invite Jerry to our party. He'll liven things up.
liveware	people who use computers, computer students	Our school has more liveware than computers!
living daylights	(See **the living daylights**)	
loaded	having many extra devices or accessories	That Buick is loaded, including a sun roof.

Idiom	Meaning	Example
loaded	drunk, inebriated, **sloshed**	After his fifth drink of rum, he was loaded. He was staggering.
loaded	wealthy, rich, **moneybags**	To own a jet, you would have to be very wealthy—loaded.
loaded to the hilt	fully loaded, packed to the top	The trailer was loaded to the hilt—full of our belongings.
local yokel	resident of a town or rural community, local resident	We were lost, so we stopped and asked a local yokel for help.
lock, stock and barrel	everything, **kit and caboodle**	They took everything in the shed—lock, stock and barrel.
lock you up	put you in prison, put you in a mental hospital	If you sell cigarettes to children, the police will lock you up.
log off	exit from a mainframe computer system	Before you log off, be sure to save the work you completed.
log on	enter a mainframe computer system	When you log on, you have to type in your password.
lollygag	be idle, be listless, **waste time**	Hank isn't busy today. He's just lollygagging around the house.
long and the short of it	(See **the long and the short of it**)	
long arm of the law	(See **the long arm of the law**)	
long for	wish for, want very much	Kelly longs for her home in the mountains. She's homesick.
long gone	departed earlier, not here now	Albert was long gone by the time the RCMP arrived.
long in the tooth	old, aged, **over the hill**	Jack is a good pitcher, but he's long in the tooth—too old.
long johns	winter underwear—with long sleeves and legs	If you are going cross-country skiing, put on your long johns.
long time no see	I have not seen you for a long time	When I got off the bus, Grandpa said, "Long time no see."
loo	(See **the loo**)	
look after	care for, **take care of**	He really looks after his car. It's in very good condition.
look daggers	look angry, look with hateful eyes	Ginny looked daggers at me when I kissed her boyfriend.

Idiom	Meaning	Example
look down on	look as if you are better, look superior	Do some Americans look down on people from Canada?
look down your nose at	look at a person as though he is not as good as you	Just because he's rich he looks down his nose at us.
look high and low	look everywhere, **leave no stone unturned**	We've looked high and low for that watch, but we can't find it.
look into	investigate, find the facts, **get to the bottom of**	The principal will look into the attendance problem and see what is causing it.
look like death warmed over	appear to be sick, look pale or weak	Mom is not feeling well. She looks like death warmed over.
look like he was dragged through a knothole	appear to be very tired, **burn out**, **run down**	After a divorce and a funeral, Anne looked like she'd been dragged through a knothole.
look out	be careful	Look out! That knife is sharp.
look out for	watch, protect, **look after**	Please look out for your sister. She needs your protection.
look out for number one	help yourself first, get enough for yourself	You can look out for number one as well as help your friends.
look over	check, examine, look at	I've looked over the report. It contains the data we need.
look over your shoulder	look to see who is following you	He's always looking over his shoulder to see who's after him.
look the other way	try not to notice, **turn the other way**	The officer saw the liquor, but he looked the other way.
look up/look it up	find it in a book	Please look up the word *guru*.
look up a dead horse's ass [B]	do a worthless task, do a pointless exercise, **pissing into the wind**	If they want a tax-free society, they may as well be looking up a dead horse's ass!
look up to	admire, idolize	Ian looks up to his brother. He respects James a lot.
looking up	(See **things are looking up**)	
loonie	Canadian one-dollar coin	I bought this rose for one loonie!
loony bin	mental hospital, **nut house**	If you ride that giraffe downtown they'll put you in the loony bin.

Idiom	Meaning	Example
looped	drunk, **loaded**, **smashed**	You were looped last night. You don't remember what happened.
loose cannon	(See **a loose cannon**)	
loose ends	unfinished tasks, **odds and ends**	"Finished making the dress?" "Almost—just some loose ends."
loose ends	(See **at loose ends**)	
loose ends	(See **tie up loose ends**)	
lord it over	be the boss of, dominate a person/group	When we were boys, my older brother tried to lord it over me.
lose a family member	experience the death of a member of the family	Poor Sadie. She lost her mother last year and a brother this year.
lose count	forget how many you counted, **lose track**	There were so many falling stars that I lost count.
lose favor	lose a person's approval, **in your bad books**	If you lose favor with reporters, you may lose the election.
lose ground	slide back, lose power, **fall behind**	Every day we lose ground in the battle to save the environment.
lose him	get away from him, **ditch him**	I can lose him at the mall— among the shops and people.
lose it	become angry, **lose your cool**	When he criticized you, I started to lose it. I almost hit him.
lose it	lose the ability to think clearly, become forgetful	After 35 years of teaching, he was losing it. He was confused.
lose my train of thought	forget my order of thoughts or words	Don't interrupt me because I may lose my train of thought.
lose out	lose a chance, fail to **take advantage of**	If I don't apply now, I'll lose out. This is my last chance.
lose patience	not be patient any longer, **out of patience**	Mom is losing patience with us because we don't obey her.
lose sight of	forget about, not remember the purpose	Let's not lose sight of why we're picking berries—to make pies.
lose time	waste time, **fall behind**	We lost time when the car stalled. We were delayed.

Idiom	Meaning	Example
lose track	forget how many you have, **lose count**	He tried to count the number of birds, but he soon lost track.
lose your appetite	not feel hungry anymore, lose the desire to eat	If a bug crawled out of your apple would you lose your appetite?
lose your cool	lose control of emotions, **lose your temper**	Don't you ever lose your cool? Don't you ever get angry?
lose your head	lose your ability to think clearly	If you become lost, don't lose your head. Be sensible.
lose your marbles	lose control of your mind, **lose it**	When people grow old, do they lose their marbles?
lose your mind	lose control of your mind, go **out of your mind**	If you continue to use drugs, you'll lose your mind.
lose your shirt	lose most of the money you invested	He invested in condominiums and nearly lost his shirt.
lose your temper	become angry, **get mad**	When you lose your temper, the children become frightened.
lose your tongue	be unable to think what to say, **cat got your tongue**, **mind goes blank**	It's embarrassing to lose your tongue when you're standing in front of an audience.
lose your touch	lose some of your skill, **lose it**	"I'm losing my touch," he said, looking at his drawing.
losing it	losing the ability to think or remember, not **sharp**	I think I'm losing it. I can't add or multiply without a calculator.
losing streak	losing game after game, losing a series of games	The Jays are on a losing streak. They've lost four games straight.
loss leader	a low-priced item to bring customers to a store	The loss leader at SuperStore is a package of coffee for 99¢.
lost cause	(See **a lost cause**)	
Lotus Land	British Columbia (west coast of Canada)	They went to Lotus Land for a holiday—to Vancouver.
loud mouth	one who talks about things he should not	When Bart was a boy, he was a loud mouth. He told our secrets.
lousy	poor quality, in poor condition, **shabby**	Everything works except the lousy printer. It's broken.
love at first sight	sudden love, love begins when people first meet	When Jessica met Ryan, it was love at first sight.

Idiom	Meaning	Example
Love Bug	Volkswagen *Beetle,* *The Bug*	I'd love to go for a ride in your Love Bug.
love conquers all	love is strong enough to overcome all problems	When the family was reunited, Mom said, "Love conquers all."
love is blind	people do not see the faults in their lovers	She can't see his bad habits because love is blind.
love is where you find it	love happens, love is not planned, **it is better to have loved...**	My family thinks Peter is too old for me, but I think love is where you find it.
love them and leave them	love them but not stay with them	When Claude was touring Europe, he'd love 'em and leave 'em.
lovelies	ladies, women, girls, **chicks**	When we docked at Rome, we met three lovelies and went dancing.
lovelife	the romantic part of your life, your intimate life	"How's your lovelife?" "Great! I met a wonderful lady."
Lovers' Leap	a cliff where lovers jump into a canyon together	Let's drive up to Lovers' Leap and look at the stars.
low	sad, depressed, ill, **down**	I've been feeling kind of low lately—it's the bad weather.
low-ball him	offer him a very low price for his car, house etc.	If his price is too high, low-ball him. Offer him a very low price.
low-down	bad, evil, not nice	Stealing from that old woman was a low-down thing to do!
lowdown	**(See the lowdown)**	
lowlife	a person without morals or humanitarian values	What a lowlife! He sold drugs to children.
luck of the draw	**(See the luck of the draw)**	
luck of the Irish	**(See the luck of the Irish)**	
luck out	have good luck, **a lucky break**	She lucked out at the casino. She won a thousand dollars.
lucky break	**(See a lucky break)**	
lucky dog	a lucky person, someone who has just won a prize	When I told Bill I won the car, he said, "You lucky dog!"

Idiom	Meaning	Example
lucky streak	a series of lucky wins, **string of good luck**	He lost the bet on the sixth race, and his lucky streak ended.
lump together	put together, place in the same category	They lumped us all together— young, old, rich, poor.
lush	alcoholic, **tank, wino**	Joni was a lush when she met me. Now she doesn't drink at all.

Idiom	Meaning	Example

M

mad about	like a lot, **crazy about**	Olga's mad about Yorgi. She loves him too much!
mad about	angry about, **pissed off** [B]	He's mad about the lost key. He told me I was careless.
mad as a hatter	strange, eccentric, batty, **plumb loco**	If you wear that pink wig, people will think you're mad as a hatter.
mad hatter	strange, unusual, **wacko**	Jo lives in a mad-hatter place. Her friends walk around nude and sing songs about heaven.
made for each other	be natural mates, be very compatible, **soul mates**	Bob and Alice are made for each other. They're happily married.
mainstream	common, familiar, of the majority	Smoking isn't as common now. It isn't a mainstream activity.
major	big, huge, main	"Is money a problem?" "Ya. Major."
make a big deal of it	complain a lot, **make a mountain...**	Whenever Todd dances with me, Brenda makes a big deal of it.
make a clean breast of it	tell all you know about it, admit what you did	The man went to the police and made a clean breast of his crime.
make a clean sweep	win all games in a series	The Jets made a clean sweep of the series—won all four games.
make a big to-do	complain too much, **make a federal case...**	If the waiter makes a mistake, don't make a big to-do about it.
make a booboo	cause an error, **make a mistake, screw up**	"I made a booboo." "Don't worry. We can fix it."
make a bundle	earn a large profit, **make a lot of money**	Manfred made a bundle selling real estate. He's rich.
make a difference	affect or change it, **tip the scales**	Even a small donation will make a difference. It will help us.

Idiom	Meaning	Example
make a face	wrinkle your face until it is ugly	Chad made a face at me and stuck out his tongue.
make a false move	reach for the phone or a gun, try to run away	"Make a false move and I'll shoot your buttons off," the boy said.
make a federal case of it	make it too important, **make a mountain**...	Okay, so I used your hair dryer! Don't make a federal case of it.
make a fuss	cry or complain, **throw a tantrum**	If I don't hold the baby, it will make a fuss. It will cry.
make a go of it	earn enough money to pay the bills, live well	With both of us working, we were able to make a go of it.
make a good impression	meet and talk to strangers so they like you	Penny made a good impression on my parents. She is so polite!
make a killing	earn a big profit, **make a bundle**	If you buy gold now, you'll make a killing when the price goes up.
make a life for yourself	live a good life; have a job, home and family	So you want to make a life for yourself in Canada. That's good.
make a mistake	give a wrong answer, **make a booboo**	Learn from making a mistake. Learn how *not* to do it.
make a mountain out of a mole hill	make a problem bigger, exaggerate a problem	I spent $50, not $500! Don't make a mountain out of a mole hill.
make a name for yourself	become well known, become famous	Martin Luther King made a name for himself—and for freedom!
make a pass	show that you feel romantic toward someone	Julie made a pass at me. She sent me a love note and smiled at me.
make a pitch	try to sell, try to persuade	She handed him her resume and made a pitch for the job.
make a point of	remember to do, act with a purpose, **make sure**	Uma made a point of telling me about the meeting. She wants us to come.
make a scene	complain too loud, **kick up a fuss**	If she doesn't let Denis ride in the shopping cart, he makes a scene.
make a silk purse...	(See **you can't make a silk purse out of a sow's ear**)	
make a splash	advertise with style, open with balloons and prizes	When Tom opened his Toyota dealership, he made quite a splash.

Idiom	Meaning	Example
make advances	try to kiss or touch, **come onto**, **get fresh**	"If he doesn't make advances, should I?" Shelly asked.
make amends	apologize to someone you have hurt, **make up for**	What can I do to make amends for opening her personal mail?
make an entrance	enter with style, enter with a flourish	When the duchess attends an event she likes to make an entrance.
make an offer	offer money to buy; write what you will pay for something	"Your price is too high." "Well, make an offer. What do you think the car is worth?"
make believe	imagine, pretend, **make up**	"Let's make believe we are baby elephants," I said to the children.
make do	use whatever you can find, substitute, **jury-rig**	When our kids don't have toys, they make do with pots and pans.
make ends meet	pay the bills, have enough to pay the expenses	Although the Millers are poor, they make ends meet.
make every effort	do everything possible, **bend over backwards**	Our employees make every effort to please our customers.
make faces	(See **make a face**)	
make friends	act in a friendly way, become a friend of	Sally makes friends easily. People seem to like her.
make fun of	tease, laugh at	Ko is angry because you made fun of him. You teased him.
make good	do as promised, **follow through**	When I get paid, I'll make good my promise to buy you dinner.
make good time	travel quickly, not be delayed, not **lose time**	Driving to Saskatoon, we made good time. It took only five hours.
make hay while the sun shines	work while the weather is good, work while we have time and helpers	There's a demand for our product, and we have a large stock. Let's make hay while the sun shines!
make headway	progress, **get ahead**	With Freda's help, we made headway. We learned to write.
make it	go or come, attend	Can you make it tonight? Can you come to the meeting?
make it better	improve it, help it	When a child is hurt, sympathy will help to make it better.

Idiom	Meaning	Example
make it big	succeed, be one of the best	Roch made it big as a singer. He's very successful.
make it snappy	be quick, **hurry up**	I'll have a Coke, please, and make it snappy!
make it worse	hinder, cause it to be worse	Stepping on the brakes will only make it worse. The car will skid.
make light of	make a joke about, **make fun of**	I was hurt when you made light of my poem. You laughed at it.
make love	embrace in a loving way and have intercourse	I can't describe how I feel when we make love. It's breathtaking!
make me do it	cause me to act, force me to do it	I didn't want to steal the watch. The devil made me do it.
make me sick/mad etc.	cause me to feel sick or mad etc.	It makes me sick the way he talks about war all the time.
make mention	talk about, **bring up**	No one made mention of his research—not one word!
make mincemeat of	defeat badly, demolish, **blow them away**	The heavyweight champ made mincemeat of the young boxer.
make money	work for wages, earn a profit	You can make money in real estate. You buy low, sell high.
make my day	do something to help me enjoy this day	Go ahead, kiss me, and make my day!
make myself clear	say it clearly, say it so you understand	Her sister said, "Do *not* wear my clothes. Do I make myself clear?"
make no bones about it	admit it, speak openly about it	She's in love with her student. She makes no bones about it.
make of it	know what it is, identify it, **make sense of it**	Do you see that bright light in the sky? What do you make of it?
make off with	take away, take without permission	The boys made off with his toys. They took all his cars and trucks.
make out	do, finish, **end up**	How did you make out when you played the Rebels? Did you win?
make out	kiss and hug, **get it on**, **make whoopee**	Keith and Dawn were making out in the back seat of the car.
make room	create a space, move **out of the way**	Please make room so Miss Munro can walk to her car. Move, please.

Idiom	Meaning	Example
make sense	appear to be logical or sensible	Renting a car makes sense to me—if it's not too expensive.
make sense of it	understand it, fathom it, see how it happened	He is my father, but I am not his son. Can you make sense of it?
make something of it	(See **want to make something of it**)	
make something of yourself	be successful, be respected for your skill and honesty	I want to choose an occupation and make something of myself.
make strange	be afraid of a stranger, cry when a stranger comes	Ali makes strange when we have visitors. He cries and tries to hide.
make sure	be certain, check carefully	Make sure you mail the letter. It must be sent today.
make the bed	arrange the sheets and blankets on a bed	Please make the bed before you eat breakfast.
make the grade	do acceptable work, **measure up**	To make the grade, you have to complete the training program.
make the most of it	do the best you can, **seize the opportunity**	When you speak, make the most of it. Persuade them not to fight.
make the team	become a member of the team	Paul will make the soccer team. The coach will choose him.
make tracks	hurry, move quickly, **vamoose**	We better make tracks or we'll be late for dinner.
make trouble	cause a fight, **make waves**	Don't make trouble, eh. Don't start an argument or a fight.
make up	create, imagine	He likes to make up stories— you know, fiction.
make up	be friends again, come together again	John and Marsha fight, but they always kiss and make up.
make up for	repay, compensate	Please let me make up for my mistake. Let me help you.
make up your mind	decide, choose	If you will make up your mind, we can order our dinner.
make war	fight with troops and planes and bombs	To make war is to be greedy or insane—or both.
make waves	(See **don't make waves**)	

ENGLISH IDIOMS

Idiom	Meaning	Example
make whoopee	kiss and hug, **get it on**, **make love**	Tony and Victoria were making whoopee when we walked in.
make your bum hum	excite you, please your senses, **turn you on**	Anchovies on a banana split— that'll make your bum hum!
make your hair stand on end	cause you to be afraid, **petrified**, **scared stiff**	Strange sounds began coming from the closet. It was enough to make your hair stand on end.
make your head spin	confuse you, amaze you, **boggle your mind**	All the numbers on this sheet will make your head spin.
make your mark	be known for an invention or an achievement, **set the world on fire**	If you want to make your mark, do it for humanity. Think of a cure for hate and war.
make your mouth water	cause you to salivate, cause you to be hungry	Your carrot cake smells so good it makes my mouth water.
make yourself at home	relax, feel as though you are in your own home	Lee's mom welcomed us, saying, "Please, make yourself at home."
make yourself scarce	leave, do not stay, **get lost**	If you see a bull in the pasture, make yourself scarce.
make yourself to home	(See **make yourself at home**)	
makes no difference	will not affect or change something	The color of the car makes no difference to me. I don't care.
makings of	(See **the makings of**)	
malarkey	(See **a bunch of malarkey**)	
man of few words	(See **a man of few words**)	
man of the cloth	(See **a man of the cloth**)	
mark my words	listen carefully, **pay attention**	A California team will win the Super Bowl. Mark my words.
match wits	compete with someone's wit or humor	Don't try to match wits with Pat. He has a reply for everything.
mean business	is serious or determined, **no nonsense**	At work or play she means business. She is a serious person.
mean streak	being unkind at times, having cruel traits	Kurt has a mean streak in him. Did you see him kick his dog?
mean well	wants to help, has good intentions	Kay is a gossip, but she means well. She tries to be a friend.

Idiom	Meaning	Example
measure up	do enough work, achieve high quality	With more training, he'll improve. He'll measure up to our standards.
meet up with	meet, encounter	In Montreal, he met up with a young singer named Celine.
meeting of minds	mutual agreement, consensus	We agreed to share the cost of the project. It was a meeting of minds.
megabucks	a lot of money, thousands of dollars	Her personal computer system cost megabucks. It was very expensive.
melt in your mouth	fine bread or pastry, food with a fine texture	Aunt Carol's muffins are so good! They just melt in your mouth!
mend fences	solve political problems, listen to voters	Every summer the politicians go home and try to mend fences.
mental block	(See **a mental block**)	
mess up	do a bad job, ruin it, **screw up**	The manager messed up. He spent too much money on advertising.
mess with	challenge, fight with, **mix it up** with	We learned not to mess with the Mafia. Their revenge is deadly.
messed up	depressed, dependent on drugs, not coping with life	At that point in his life, he was messed up on drugs and alcohol.
mete out	administer, give according to the law or policy	It was his duty to mete out justice in the colony.
middle ground	a position that is fair to both sides, a compromise, **keep an open mind**	The minister tried to find some middle ground between the nurses and the administrators.
middle of the road	moderate, not extreme	Our education policy is middle of the road. The majority like it.
middleman	(See **the middleman**)	
milk it	take all it will give, get all you can from it, **seize the opportunity**	I learned the mail-order business and milked the idea for all it was worth. I earned a lot of money.
milk run	airline route that stops at small cities	From Vancouver, we took the milk run through Kelowna.
mince words	(See **doesn't mince words**)	
mind boggling	too many to count, more than you can imagine	The potential for profit is mind boggling—too large to believe.

Idiom	Meaning	Example
mind games	control people's feelings, **play games**	He plays mind games with me— he tries to control my feelings.
mind go blank	cannot think what to say, **lose your tongue**	When the Prime Minister stopped to talk to me, my mind went blank.
mind in neutral	not thinking, **vegetate**	Some of our employees stand around with their minds in neutral.
mind of his own	independent thinker, **his own man**	Fu doesn't copy the work of his friends. He has a mind of his own.
mind over matter	believing you can do it, using the mind's power	When your brain controls your heart rate, it's mind over matter.
mind the store	manage the store, serve customers	Dana, please mind the store while I go to the post office.
mind your manners	be polite, be courteous, **watch your P's & Q's**	At the wedding, Mom said to me, "Now, Son, mind your manners."
mind your own business	do not ask questions about my business	I asked about her plans, and she told me to mind my own business.
mint condition	new condition, original condition, **super mint**	In an old garage we found a Peugeot 403 in mint condition.
misery loves company	sad people want to be with other sad people	On the door of the jail was this sign: *Misery Loves Company*.
miss out on	not be there, not be able to attend	If I have a job, I'll miss out on the soccer games after school.
miss the boat	misjudge, misunderstand, **make a mistake**	I missed the boat on the essay question. My answer was wrong.
miss the point	not understand, not **get the point**	I missed the point of his remark. Do you know what he meant?
miss the water till...	(See **you don't miss the water till the well runs dry**)	
miss you	feel lonely because you are not here	I miss you when you go to Hong Kong. Can I go with you?
mix it up	challenge, fight, **mess with**	If you mix it up with a street fighter, you could get injured.
mix up	become confused or puzzled	He gets mixed up when we all give advice. He gets confused.
mix you up	confuse you, **boggle your mind**	Too much information will just mix you up—confuse you.

Idiom	Meaning	Example
mixed feelings	feeling both positive and negative, happy and sad; bittersweet	I have mixed feelings. I'm happy about the new job, but sad about leaving my friends.
moment of truth	(See **the moment of truth**)	
money doesn't grow on trees	money is not easy to get, we value our money	Father said, "Money doesn't grow on trees, boy. You earn it."
money is the root of all evil	money is the cause of bad things	If money is the root of all evil, why do you want to be rich?
money talks	money causes action, **grease my palm**	If you want service, money talks. When you pay, they serve.
money to burn	lots of money, **filthy rich**	They've got money to burn, so why do they drive that old car?
moneybags	rich person, **loaded** person	We used to call him *moneybags*. He always had money on him.
monkey business	nonsense, foolishness, **funny stuff**	I've had enough of your monkey business. No more foolishness.
monkey off my back	(See **get this monkey off my back**)	
monkeywrenching	trying to ruin a project, sabotaging, **throw a monkey wrench into...**	The members of Green Peace were accused of monkeywrenching the whale hunt. They tried to stop it.
monkey's uncle	(See **I'll be a monkey's uncle**)	
month of Sundays	(See **a month of Sundays**)	
moola	money, cash, **scratch**	Without moola, we can't travel. We need money for air fare.
moon them	show them a bare **bum**, show your bare buttocks	They booed him for dropping the ball, so he mooned them.
moonlighting	working at a second job in the evening	Bernie is very tired these days because he's moonlighting.
moonshine	homemade liquor, **hooch, screech**	Art invited us over to taste his moonshine—homemade wine.
mop the floor with us	perform so well the audience wants more	We loved the Gagnon concert. He mopped the floor with us.
mop up	correct mistakes, **clean up** a mess left by others	The manager told us he would not mop up after us. We have to fix our own mistakes.

Idiom	Meaning	Example
moppie	<u>m</u>obile <u>o</u>ffice <u>p</u>rofessional, ambitious business people	A lot of moppies lost their jobs when the oil industry declined.
more money than brains	rich but not intelligent, **money to burn**, **moneybags**	He bought a house but didn't use it, rent it or sell it. He has more money than brains!
more power to you	you deserve more support, we hope you succeed because you are kind	When she told him about her plan to help abused children, he said, "More power to you, Ms. Wah."
more than meets the eye	(See **there's more than meets the eye**)	
more than welcome	we invite you, please come to our place, **feel free**	Mary invited them to stay. "You are more than welcome to sleep at our place," she said.
more than you can shake a stick at	a lot, too many, **oodles**	Alfreda has more cats than you can shake a stick at—over 30!
mothball	put away, put on a shelf	The boss mothballed the report. The owners never saw it.
Mother Nature	nature, natural forces and causes	Mother Nature provided the basic foods: wild vegetables and water.
motherhood and apple pie	statements about mom and home etc.	The audience wants news and facts, not motherhood and apple pie.
motherlode	the largest amount, the main supply	He played poker for six hours before he won the motherlode.
motormouth	one who talks fast but says very little, **disk jockey**	Listen to that motormouth! He talks fast but says nothing.
mount a comeback	begin to score goals or points while losing, **snatch victory from...**	Our soccer team was losing 4-1, but they mounted a comeback and won the game 5-4.
Mounties	Royal Canadian Mounted Police (RCMP)	The Mounties, Canada's police force, were once called *Redcoats*.
mousy	worn and faded, **shabby**	This shirt is kind of mousy, but I love to wear it.
mouth off	tell a secret, talk about private information	Why did you mouth off about the accident? I was going to tell Dad.
move it	go, go faster, **get going**	"Move it!" said the guard. "Get in your cell!"

Idiom	Meaning	Example
move over	move a little, move to the next chair, **make room**	I asked him if he would move over so I could sit beside him.
move you to tears	cause you to feel sadness or sympathy, **touch you**	The songs in Gorecki's Third Symphony will move you to tears.
movers and shakers	owners, investors, **wheeler dealer**	We invited all the big investors: the movers and shakers.
much obliged	very thankful, very grateful, **thanks a million**	"You can stay with us until your wounds heal," she said. "Much obliged, Ma'am," I replied.
muckrake	gossip, tell bad stories	If you talk about your opponent, try to avoid muckraking.
mudsling	insult, criticize	The Liberal leader lost my vote when he began mudslinging.
mugged	stopped and robbed, **held up** by robbers	If you walk down Cordova Street at night, you could get mugged.
mull over	think about, consider, **think it over**	I've been mulling over what you said about love. I believe it's more spiritual than physical.
mum's the word	do not tell anyone, this is **on the QT**	She told us the secret. Then she whispered, "Mum's the word."
Murphy's Law	"Anything that can go wrong will go wrong." **it never fails**	Have you planned for failure? Remember, Murphy's Law applies to all projects.
muscle in	force yourself between two people	He didn't want to go to the end of the line, so he tried to muscle in.
music to my ears	good news, a message that makes me happy	When she called my name, it was music to my ears.
my ass	I doubt it, that is not true	"It's our right to own a gun." "My ass! It's a privilege!"
my eye	I do not believe it, that did not happen	You ate fifteen blueberry pies? My eye!
my old man	my husband, my man	My old man is babysitting while I have a weekend holiday!
my old man	my father, my dad	My old man gets mad if I don't come right home from school.

Idiom	Meaning	Example

N

nada	nothing, none, zero, **diddly squat**, **zip**	"How much for the baseball cap?" "Nada—it was free."
nag	horse, race horse	Pat bet on a nag in the sixth race and it came in second!
nag	complain too much, **bug**, **hassle**	Poor Erik. His wife nags him about his first marriage.
nail down	get a clear answer, **find out**, **pin down**	I've checked the books, but I can't nail down the reason for the loss. I can't find the error.
nail him	hit him, hurt him, stop him	They want to nail him because he beat up on Tommy.
nail in your coffin	(See **another nail in your coffin**)	
nail it down	complete it, finalize it, **close a deal**	Don't spend too long on a sale. Try to nail it down quickly.
nail-biter	(See **a nail-biter**)	
naked as a jay bird	no clothes on, bare naked, **in the nude**	A boy had taken my clothes, so there I stood, naked as a jay bird!
naked eye	(See **the naked eye**)	
name dropper	one who implies famous people are his friends	What a name dropper! He spoke of Gordon Lightfoot as his friend.
name is cleared	name is not involved in a scandal or a crime	The lawyer thinks I should leave town until my name is cleared.
name is mud	name is bad, name is not respected	If you don't pay for the support of your child, your name is mud.
nary a word	not a word, nothing	When I asked the boy a question, he said nothing—nary a word.
natural high	feeling good from having nutritious food or exercise	After swimming, she would often experience a natural high.

205

Idiom	Meaning	Example
nature calls	need to go the washroom, **have to go**	When nature calls, just say you have an important appointment.
neat	fine, well designed, **cool**	What a neat car! It's small but roomy—and comfortable!
necessity is the mother of invention	our needs cause us to invent devices, **build a better mousetrap**	Do you think the invention of TV proves that necessity is the mother of invention?
neck	kiss and hug, **make out, make whoopee**	For me, necking is a memory from my teenage years.
neck of the woods	area, part of the country, **in these parts**	In our neck of the woods, a man doesn't hit a woman.
necktie party	(See **a necktie party**)	
need money to make...	(See **you need money to make money**)	
needle	ask bothersome questions, **bug, hassle**	She needled him with questions about his former girlfriends.
needless to say	it is obvious, **it goes without saying**	Needless to say, there are many idioms in the English language.
neither fish nor fowl	not clearly separated, a little of both	Our experiment produced a being that was neither fish nor fowl.
nerd	weird person, **nut**	That nerd! He spit on my toe!
nerves of steel	able to speak or act calmly when facing risk or danger	Percy has nerves of steel. He persuaded the gunman to leave.
nervous breakdown	(See **breakdown**)	
nest egg	money for retirement, life savings	After selling the farm, they had their nest egg—about $200,000.
net surfer	a person who frequently uses the **Internet**	Lisa is a net surfer. She can help you get on the Internet.
never say die	never quit, never **give up**	Set your goals and try to achieve them. Work hard. Never say die.
new blood	different person, someone with new ideas	Armid retired because he feels the company needs new blood.
new kid on the block	new person in the office or in the class etc.	I'm the new kid on the block. I come from Portugal.
new lease on life	(See **a new lease on life**)	

Idiom	Meaning	Example
new legs	young runners or players, rested players	The Geritols have a lot of old players. They need new legs.
new money	money earned recently, money that is not inherited	Bill's got a million or two— it's mostly new money.
new wave	new trend, the latest idea or fashion	Tony loves new-wave music. He buys only new-wave CD's.
Newfie	person from **The Rock**; from Newfoundland	Is Gordon Pinsent a Newfie? Was he born in Newfoundland?
next of kin	closest relatives, members of the family	The police are trying to find the man's next of kin—his family.
nine lives	avoiding death often, lucky to survive	Some race-car drivers have nine lives. They often escape death.
nine times out of ten	90% of the time, very often	Jack wins at cribbage nine times out of ten. He's very lucky.
nip and tuck	a close race, having just enough to win or finish	It was a close race—nip and tuck all the way—but we won!
nip it in the bud	stop it before it grows, prevent it from spreading	If the students plan a revolt, we'll nip it in the bud.
nitpick	find unfinished details or small errors	Deborah can find the errors. She likes to nitpick.
nitty-gritty	(See **the nitty-gritty**)	
no bloody way	(See **no way**)	
no bones about it	(See **make no bones about it**)	
no business	(See **got no business**)	
no can do	we cannot do it, **no way**	We can't sell you a pet tiger. Sorry, no can do.
no chancy	there is no chance of it, it cannot be done	When I asked Bill for a loan, he said, "No chancy."
no contest	one player or team wins easily, **hands down**	Compare the speed of light to the speed of sound. It's no contest.
no dice	no, not approved, **no way**	I asked Dad if we could use the car, but no dice.
no doubt	it is certain, without a doubt, **no question**	No doubt, you will inherit his fortune. You are the only heir.

Idiom	Meaning	Example
no fair	it is not fair, one person or team has an advantage	You have six players and we have five. No fair!
no fucking way [B]	(See **no way**)	
no great shakes	not special, not superior, **not so hot**	I've tasted Granny apples. They're no great shakes.
no guff	it is the truth, **no kidding**, **no shit** [B]	I swam across the lake. No guff.
no hard feelings	no feelings of anger or resentment, no grudges	Dad and Paul argue about politics but there are no hard feelings.
no holds barred	try anything, no rules apply	In a street fight, it's no holds barred. There are no rules.
no kidding	I am serious, I am not joking	Keith's my brother. No kidding. I'm telling you the truth.
no let-up	continuing strong, not diminishing	There was no let-up in the traffic. The cars kept coming.
no love lost	(See **there's no love lost**)	
no match for	not as strong as, not an equal competitor	European basketball teams were no match for the Dream Team.
no matter how you slice it	it does not matter how you look at it	No matter how you slice it, we have to hire more help.
no news is good news	if there is no news there is still a chance of good news	The doctor hasn't phoned. No news is good news.
no nonsense	serious, not joking, **strictly business**	Gil is a very serious person— a no-nonsense kind of guy.
no offence, but...	do not be insulted but..., **don't get me wrong**	No offence, but I was here first. I hope you understand.
no pain, no gain	to improve, exercise until your muscles ache	A sign on our gym wall reads *No Pain, No Gain!*
no problem (no prob)	it was not a problem, **don't mention it**	"Thank you," I said. "No problem," she replied.
no qualms	no doubts, no hesitation	She has no qualms about dating married men. She doesn't care.
no question	it is certain, **no doubt**	"No question of its quality," he said, examining the watch.

Idiom	Meaning	Example
no questions asked	you will not be asked to explain or pay	If he returns the stolen car, there will be no questions asked.
no rest for the wicked	wicked people must work long hours as a penalty, **what did I do to deserve...**	When I told the men there was another truck to unload, Bo said, "No rest for the wicked, eh."
no rhyme or reason	no sense, no logical plan	There's no rhyme or reason to the game of golf. It's stupid!
no shit [B]	it is true, **no kidding**	We drove from Calgary to Regina in seven hours—no shit.
no shrinking violet	a bold woman, not a timid woman	Barb will defend her rights. She's no shrinking violet.
no skin off my nose	no bother to me, will not hurt me	If he doesn't come to my party it's no skin off my nose.
no slouch	quite skilled or talented, **not half bad**	Cora doesn't brag, but she's no slouch when it comes to tennis.
no sweat	not a problem, no trouble, **no prob**	"Thanks for the help, Ryan." "No sweat, man."
no use for	no respect for, no desire to own	I have no use for STAR products because they are not reliable.
no way	no, do not try, it is not possible	When he told me to jump off the train, I said, "No way, man."
no word	no news, no reply, no phone call or letter	We've had no word from Denise and Guy. I hope they're okay.
no-show	someone who does not attend	There were two no-shows on the class list. All but two attended.
nobody's fool	wise or intelligent person, **been around**	Joe is nobody's fool. He's intelligent and experienced.
none of your lip	do not be rude, **don't talk back**	"You can't boss me," Bobby said. "None of your lip, boy!" I replied.
none the worse for wear	not hurt or damaged, still in good condition, **okay**	The immigrants were none the worse for wear after their wagon trip across the prairie.
nookie [B]	sex, **poontang**	My man! All he wants is nookie!
nope	no, **nay**	"Want to paint the fence?" "Nope."

Idiom	Meaning	Example
nose is out of joint	she is upset, he is not pleased	Ed's nose is out of joint because the Liberals lost the election.
nosebag	food, something to eat, **fill your face**	I'm hungry. It's time to put on the nosebag.
not	not a good idea, **forget it**	"Maybe we should buy a Lada." "Not."
not a question of	(See **it's not a question of**)	
not all it's cracked up...	(See **all it's cracked up to be**)	
not all there	retarded, slow to learn, **one brick short...**	Sometimes Vincent acts kind of strange—like he's not all there.
not at all	it was no trouble at all, **don't mention it, no prob**	"Thank you for helping us find our dog," Dad said. "Not at all," the man replied.
not by a long shot	very little chance, **not likely**	That horse won't win, not by a long shot. It's old and slow.
not by any stretch of the imagination	not adding to the story, not **stretching it**	Gigi wasn't his only girl, not by any stretch of the imagination.
not feeling myself	not feeling well, **under the weather**	I'm not feeling myself these days. I'm tired all the time.
not for all the tea in China	no; never; not if you gave me all the tea in China	"Would you like to live in space?" "No. Not for all the tea in China!"
not half bad	quite good, better than expected	Have you seen *Honey, I Ate The Kids*? It's not half bad, actually.
not likely	very little chance, improbable, **slim chance**	"Do you think we'll win the prize?" the boy asked. "Not likely," his dad replied.
not long for this world	soon will die, do not have long to live	When Lee had the flu, he said, "I'm not long for this world."
not on your life	no; it is dangerous; **no way**	"Can I shoot your gun?" I asked. "Not on your life," she replied.
not on your tintype	no, never, **not on your life**	Mom said, "You're not going to Vegas—not on your tintype!"
not playing with a full deck	not rational, **not all there**	People say he's not stable—that he's not playing with a full deck.
not so hot	not special, not superior, **no great shakes**	I went to hear Le Gang last night. They're not so hot.

Idiom	Meaning	Example
not speaking	not friendly, not speaking to each other	Emily and Pam had a fight. They're not speaking.
not to worry	do not worry, **no sweat**	"I dropped my ice cream!" "Not to worry. There's more."
not too shabby	quite good, better than average	Have you seen the new Camaro? It's not too shabby.
not with it	not feeling right, **out of it**	I'm just not with it these days. I lack energy and confidence.
not worth a plugged nickel	worthless, good for nothing	In 1930, stocks weren't worth a plugged nickel—nothing!
notch below	(See **a notch below**)	
nothing succeeds like success	one success leads to more success	This is the first rule of learning: *Nothing succeeds like success.*
nothing to it	(See **there's nothing to it**)	
nothing to sneeze at	of good quality, do not ignore it	That was a nice apartment— nothing to sneeze at.
nothing to write home about	not special or spectacular, **no great shakes**	He's a nice guy, but nothing to write home about.
nothing ventured, nothing gained	if you try nothing, you will gain nothing; **go for it**	We've decided to start a business. As the old saying goes, *Nothing ventured, nothing gained.*
now or never	(See **it's now or never**)	
nuke	heat in a microwave oven, **zap**	If you nuke a potato, it cooks in about seven minutes.
nukes	nuclear arms, nuclear weapons	He opposes the building of more nukes—like nuclear bombs.
number is up	(See **your number is up**)	
number one	the best, the winner, **top dog**	"We're number one!" the crowd shouted when we won the game.
numbskull	idiot, foolish person, **dimwit, dipstick**	Why did he call me a numbskull? I'm not stupid.
nut	a person who acts crazy or foolish	You nut! Wearing that wig makes you look like a British judge.
nut bar, nut case	(See **a nut case**)	

Idiom	Meaning	Example
nut house	mental hospital, insane asylum, **loony bin**	They took Hans to the nut house when he taped paper wings to his arms and tried to fly.
nuts	crazy, **around the bend**, **off your rocker**	If that phone rings once more I'll go nuts!
nuts	oh no, **darn**, **rats, shucks**	When he doesn't catch the ball, he says, "Nuts!"
nuts about	likes a lot, passionate, **crazy about**	Helen is nuts about Mozart. She loves his piano concertos.
nutty as a fruit cake	funny, **kooky**, **mad as a hatter**	Do I know Karl? Yes, I do. He's nutty as a fruit cake!

Idiom	Meaning	Example

O

odd one	(See **the odd one**)	
odds and ends	small pieces that are not used, **loose ends**	When you build the fence, save the odds and ends to make toys.
odds-on favorite	(See **the odds-on favorite**)	
of course you can	you can do it; yes, you can	"I can't read this fat book." "Of course you can, Johnny."
of the lot	of the group, of the bunch	This rug is the best of the lot. It's nicer than the others.
of two minds	having two opinions, **mixed feelings**	Speaking of abortion, I'm of two minds: pro choice and pro life.
off	sour, spoiled	The cream tastes a bit off. I think we should buy fresh cream.
off color	bad, dirty, impolite	His wife gets so embarrassed when he tells an off-color joke.
off key (music)	not at the right pitch, not **in tune**	He has a beautiful voice, but was he singing a bit off key?
off kilter	off balance, not straight, **out of whack**	One of the poles was off kilter. It was leaning toward the road.
off my back	(See **get off my back**)	
off the bat	(See **right off the bat**)	
off the beaten track	not on the main road, **out of the way**	I like to explore places that are off the beaten track—wild places.
off the cuff	quickly, without thinking	Off the cuff, I'd say there are 75 applicants. That's my guess.
off the deep end	(See **go off the deep end**)	
off the hook	not charged with a crime, not obligated, **let off**	The police found the murderer, which lets Louis off the hook.

Idiom	Meaning	Example
off the kitchen etc.	leading from the kitchen, attached to the kitchen	The laundry room is off the kitchen—very convenient.
off the mark	not correct, wrong	His answer is a bit off the mark. Canada Day is July 1, not July 4.
off the record	not to be reported, not official	What the President said is not to be printed. It's off the record.
off the shelf	from the store shelf, **run of the mill**	It isn't a special gift, just an off-the-shelf radio with batteries.
off the top of my head	without thinking carefully, **off the cuff**	Off the top of my head, I believe the US has 50 states.
off the wagon	drinking again, drunk again	He's off the wagon again. He started drinking last night.
off the wall	unrelated, unusual, **off topic**	His idea of selling time is really off the wall—quite strange.
off to a bad start	not a good start, a poor beginning	The class got off to a bad start because the teacher was sick.
off to a good start	a successful beginning, **away to the races**	Jim's off to a good start in math. He has the basic skills.
off to the races	moving quickly ahead, **off to a good start**	When we get our business loan, we'll be off to the races.
off topic	not on the chosen topic, not related to the topic	If you're writing about dogs, flowers are off topic.
off with	remove clothing or a covering	Off with your overcoat, Ben. Stay and visit awhile.
off with you	leave, go, **skedaddle**	Off with you, girl, or you'll be late for school.
off your high horse	(See **get off your high horse**)	
off your rocker	crazy, not rational, **around the bend**	You gave away your piano? You're off your rocker!
off-beat	different, unusual	His condo has an off-beat design. There's a shower in the kitchen.
offer I couldn't refuse	(See **an offer I couldn't refuse**)	
offhand	casual, without much thought, **off the cuff**	I didn't think before I spoke. It was an offhand remark.

Idiom	Meaning	Example
offside (hockey)	going into the opponent's zone ahead of the puck	Wayne scored a beautiful goal, but Kurri was offside.
oh my gosh	oh no, oh dear, **darn, rats**	Oh my gosh! I've lost my keys!
oilpatch	the local oil industry, the oil business	Calgary's oilpatch does not control the price of oil and gas.
okay, OK	fine, good, **cool**	It's okay with me if your friends come to play.
okay, OK	yes, alright	"Can I borrow your sweater?" "OK — if I can use your cellular."
Old Boys' Club	a group of wealthy old men with political power	For City approval, talk to Craig. He's in the Old Boys' Club.
old coot	an old man, **geezer**	That *old coot*, as you call him, is a person with feelings.
old flame	a former lover, an old sweetheart	In Toronto, I met an old flame. We were lovers many years ago.
old goat	an old man, a cranky man	Henry Wilson—that old goat— told the kids to get off his lawn.
old hat	an old idea or fashion, **passé**	Sunday picnics are old hat. They're not popular now.
old man	(See **my old man**)	
old money	an inheritance, money that has been in the family for decades	She bought that property with old money—money that her great-grandfather saved.
old wives' tale	a myth, an old story that contains little truth	One old wives' tale says that goose fat will cure a cold.
on a lark	carefree, happy in a natural way	It's fun to be with him when he's on a lark—when he's carefree.
on a pedestal	in the position of a hero, in a high place	If you put your girlfriend on a pedestal, she won't respect you.
on a roll	having good luck, **lucky streak**	I'm gonna play bingo all night. I'm lucky—I'm on a roll!
on a silver platter	like a beautiful gift, served in style	Success won't come on a silver platter. You have to work for it.
on a string	controlled by a person, **wrapped around his...**	He's got you on a string, Bonny. Are you thinking for yourself?

Idiom	Meaning	Example
on about	(See **going on about**)	
on all fours	on your hands and knees, crawling around	There was Julie, on all fours, looking for her contact lens.
on approval	taking a purchase home to decide if you want it	I buy clothes on approval so I can return them if they don't fit.
on behalf of	representing a group, acting for a group	He presented the award to me on behalf of the community club.
on board	loaded on a vehicle, riding on a boat etc.	Two thousand passengers were on board the ship to Canada.
on cloud nine	very happy, **riding high**	When Bev received her diploma, she was on cloud nine.
on deck	next in order, next to bat	Gary's at bat; Tim's on deck.
on drugs	using drugs, **do drugs**	"Do you know he's on drugs?" "Yes. His eyes look blank."
on edge	not relaxed, nervous, anxious, **edgy**	Gina's a little on edge. She gets her test results back today.
on even terms	having equal skills, having the same ability	When we play chess, we're on even terms. We're both average.
on fire	eager, energetic, **all fired up, gung-ho**	When he began working here, he was on fire—very enthusiastic.
on good terms	in a good relationship, able to talk and work with	Steve is on good terms with all his co-workers. They like him.
on his last legs	very tired or old, at the end of his career	Gordie was on his last legs, but he could still shoot hard.
on his tail	following him closely, chasing him	The thief knew the police would follow him. They'd be on his tail.
on in years	(See **getting on in years**)	
on loan	borrowed, **sign**ed **out**	The book you want is on loan to someone else until May 12.
on moral grounds	based on what is right and wrong	We refuse to accept money from drug dealers—on moral grounds.
on my back	criticizing me, **on my case, ride me**	The coach is on my back about missing the game last week.

Idiom	Meaning	Example
on my case	looking for my mistakes, criticizing me	The coach is on my case again, yelling at me to play harder.
on my good side	to become my friend, **in my good books**	He says nice things to me, hoping to get on my good side.
on my plate	on my schedule, on my list of duties or tasks	I have too much on my plate right now. I'm too busy.
on my way	continue my journey, departing	Before I leave, I'd like a cup of coffee. Then I'll be on my way.
on our last legs	nearly dead or bankrupt, nearly **done for**	Financially, we were on our last legs. We couldn't get a loan.
on parade	walking in a parade, displaying	When Jack's on parade, he marches straight and tall.
on parole	still supervised, not free of prison	He's on parole now. He can leave the prison during the day.
on pins and needles	waiting anxiously, worried	Mom will be on pins and needles until we arrive. She'll be worried.
on probation	becoming a permanent employee, **proby**	As an employee on probation, you will be learning new skills.
on purpose	for a reason, intentional	Did she drop her glove on purpose—so he would find it?
on queer street	dizzy or stunned, not acting normal	After he hit me I felt like I was on queer street—I was dazed.
on schedule	within the dates on the plan, **on target**	They arrived on Mars on June 11, which means they're on schedule.
on short notice	without much warning, **at a moment's notice**	Can you come to work on short notice? Within a day or two?
on side	for our side, supporting our group	In order to have a majority, we need to bring the clerks on side.
on speaking terms	not friendly but saying hello etc.	Louise and I are not friends, but we're on speaking terms.
on tap	available from the tap on a keg of beer or ale	There was a red neon sign in the window: *COLD BEER ON TAP*
on target	done by the planned date, **on schedule**	If we can complete the drawings by Monday, we'll be on target.
on tenterhooks	carefully, cautiously, afraid to move	He's cautious since his accident. He drives around on tenterhooks.

Idiom	Meaning	Example
on the back burner	to be done later, not as important	The playground project is on the back burner until next spring.
on the ball	smart, intelligent, **bright**, **sharp**	Max has a lot on the ball. He can solve our problem.
on the bandwagon	helping, supporting, **on side**	Get on the bandwagon, folks! Our man is going to be Premier!
on the books	listed, accounted for	Is it legal to sell items that aren't on the books—that aren't listed?
on the bright side	positive, optimistic	Chan is positive. He always looks on bright side of things.
on the brink	close, almost there, **on the verge**	Their marriage is failing. They're on the brink of divorce.
on the button	correct, accurate, **dead on**, **spot on**	When Fern guessed my age, she was right on the button: 39.
on the carpet	asked to explain a mistake, **give me the third degree**	Tom's on the carpet because he lost company documents.
on the cutting edge	(See **the cutting edge**)	
on the dole	receiving employment insurance cheques, **pogey**	If you are looking for a job, it's okay to be on the dole.
on the dot	exactly on time, not early or late	The concert started at 7:30 on the dot.
on the double	quickly, now, **move it**	Coach Keyser said, "Sutton, get over here—on the double!"
on the edge of your seat	very interested in a movie, feeling suspense in a story	The movie *The Firm* will have you on the edge of your seat.
on the fence	(See **sit the fence**)	
on the fringe	not familiar, radical, not **mainstream**	The Canasaurus Party is new— definitely on the fringe.
on the fritz	not operating, broken, **out of order**	The VCR is on the fritz again. We can't watch videos tonight.
on the go	busy, not stopping to rest	We've been on the go all day, shopping and preparing food.
on the heels	immediately after, following	On the heels of the typhoon was a five-day rain.

Idiom	Meaning	Example
on the lam	running away from the police, **lay low**	When he's not in jail, he's on the lam—always running.
on the limp	limping, walking with a leg injury	Norman is on the limp today. He sprained his ankle playing ball.
on the loose	free, running around, not in a pen or cage	The zoo notified the media that a giraffe is on the loose.
on the make	looking for romance or sex	Most of the men in the bar were on the make, looking for action.
on the mark	accurate, correct, **dead on**, **spot on**	Your answer is right on the mark. Canada became a country in 1867.
on the market	ready to sell, for sale, **up for sale**	Yes, our house is on the market. We want to sell it by October 1.
on the mend	healing, becoming healthy again	Jake's had open-heart surgery, but he's on the mend.
on the money	correct, accurate, **on the mark**, **spot on**	Your answer is on the money. You win a new Honda!
on the move	moving, going from place to place	The caribou are on the move again, migrating to find food.
on the outs	not friendly, **not speaking**	Amy and Pat are on the outs. They had a fight.
on the QT	as a secret, not to be told to anyone	I'm telling you this on the QT. Please don't tell anyone.
on the rails	operating smoothly, **on track**	Troy helped me get back on the rails when I was depressed.
on the rise	increasing, growing	The number of female engineers is on the rise—more every year.
on the road	going toward, improving, **on the mend**	Jill is feeling much better today. She's on the road to recovery.
on the run	very busy, having much to do, **on the go**	I've been on the run since early this morning. What a busy day!
on the run	running from the police, running from a problem	He's been on the run ever since he robbed a bank in Tulsa.
on the same wavelength	understanding each other, communicating clearly	I understand Ted's beliefs. We're on the same wavelength.
on the shit list [B]	on the list to be punished, **in your bad books**	Greg's on the shit list because he missed the sales meeting.

Idiom	Meaning	Example
on the side	extra, in addition, **under the table**	By typing reports and resumes, I earned a few dollars on the side.
on the sly	secretly, illegally	Phil was selling cigarettes to his friends on the sly.
on the spur of the moment	immediately, impulsively	On the spur of the moment we decided to drive to Banff.
on the stand	on the witness stand, testifying in court	Jack was on the stand today. He told the court what he saw.
on the table	offered, proposed	Our offer is on the table: a 7% increase in salary for the clerks.
on the take	stealing, robbing	A week after he got out of jail, he was on the take again.
on the throne	sitting on the toilet, in **the john**	Archie's on the throne. He'll be down in a few minutes.
on the tip of my tongue	almost able to recall, beginning to remember	Her name is on the tip of my tongue. It begins with *K*.
on the up and up	legal, within the law, not **underhanded**	If a company gives away cars, can it be on the up and up?
on the verge	close, nearly, almost doing it	Our baby is on the verge of talking. She said, "Da-da."
on the wagon	not drinking liquor, not getting drunk	The old man is on the wagon. He promised he wouldn't drink.
on the wane	decreasing, diminishing	The number of men who smoke is on the wane. It's decreasing.
on the whole	generally, considering the whole group or situation	On the whole, women are making progress toward equal status.
on the wing	flying, in flight	Canada geese were on the wing, going south for the winter.
on the wing	without a plan, creating as you go, **wing it**	Paul can perform on the wing— he has a great imagination!
on thin ice	in a risky position, barely surviving	His grades are very low in this course. He's on thin ice.
on time	not late, at the scheduled time	Mary is always on time. She is very punctual.

Idiom	Meaning	Example
on top of	informed, prepared, **up on**	Addie stays on top of math by doing problems every day.
on track	in the right direction, **on the rails**	After a few problems, our project is back on track.
on trial	in court as a defendant, defending your actions	The man charged with the assault is on trial now. He's in court.
on vacation	having a holiday from work or school	I don't feel like getting up early when I'm on vacation.
on your ass [B]	wrong, misinformed, **all wet**	He doesn't know how to manage a business. He's on his ass!
on your deathbed	very ill, nearly dead	When I get a cold, you think I'm on my deathbed. Relax.
on your guard	careful, cautious	Be on your guard when you buy a used car—don't buy a **lemon**.
on your own	independent, supporting yourself	When you're on your own, you can stay out all night if you wish.
on your side	supporting you and your efforts	"I'm on your side," Kelly said. "I want you to pass this course."
on your toes	ready, alert	I have to be on my toes in her class. I have to listen and think.
on your way	traveling, leaving, on the road home	You can be on your way as soon as the tire is repaired.
once over	(See **the once over**)	
one and the same	the same as, not different, **part and parcel**	Some people believe abortion and murder are one and the same thing.
one born every minute	many easy customers, lots of **suckers**	"There's lots of suckers," he said. "There's one born every minute!"
one brick short of a full load	mentally slow, **not all there**	I'm okay, but you may be one brick short of a full load. Ha ha.
one false move	one move to get away or call for help	"One false move and you're dead," the gunman said to his hostage.
one fell swoop	(See **in one fell swoop**)	
one for the money, two for the show...	prepare to go or run, children's countdown	Before bedtime, Dad would say, "One for the money..."

Idiom	Meaning	Example
one for the road	one drink or kiss etc. before you leave	If you have one for the road, have a cup of coffee (or a kiss).
one man's garbage is another man's art	each person has different likes and dislikes, **to each his own**	You pick up what somebody throws away, so one man's garbage is another man's art.
one man's meat is another man's poison	one person likes what another person hates, **to each his own**	Some people love his music; others hate it. One man's meat is another man's poison.
one of the boys	a typical member of the group, **a regular guy**	Roger is one of the boys, eh. He's always ready to play or help.
one-track mind	tendency to think about only one subject	My son has a one-track mind these days. He thinks only about cars.
onto something	found some important information	Nick looks very confident. I think he's onto something.
onto us	knows that we are doing bad things, **wise to us**	The doorman is onto us. He knows we didn't buy a ticket.
oodles	lots, more than we need, **scads**	"Do we have enough salad?" "Yes. Oodles!"
open a window	find a new way of looking at a topic or problem	That idea opens a window on the causes of war. What do you see?
open and shut	easy to judge, not complex	If either spouse admits adultery, divorce is an open and shut case.
open mind	(See **keep an open mind**)	
open season	legal to hunt or kill at this time	Nancy said there should be an open season on sex offenders.
open some doors	provide opportunities, help someone succeed	I'm hoping my college diploma will open some doors.
open to criticism	in a position that can be criticized, vulnerable	If you become a politician you will be open to criticism.
open to question	not clearly correct, debatable	Your decision to allow liquor at the party is open to question.
open up	talk openly, express feelings	When we become friends, I'll open up with you—I'll share.
other fish to fry	(See **bigger fish to fry**)	
ounce of prevention	(See **an ounce of prevention**)	

Idiom	Meaning	Example
out and out	bold, not hidden, **bare-faced lie**	The advertisement was an out-and-out lie. It contained no truth.
out cold	unconscious, **knocked out**	Liam is out cold. A baseball hit him on the side of the head.
out for blood	trying to defeat or hurt, seeking revenge	The Jets are out for blood tonight because they lost 7-0 last night.
out in left field	not logical or sensible, **all wet**	Don't listen to his advice. He's out in left field.
out in the cold	not included in a group, not invited	He was left out in the cold because of his religious beliefs.
out loud	loud enough to hear, spoken clearly	Dad was very angry, but he didn't swear out loud.
out of	have no more, have none, **run out**	Stop at the bakery, please. We're out of bread.
out of bounds	off the playing field, across boundary lines	Ramone kicked the soccer ball over my head and out of bounds.
out of breath	short of breath, puffing, **winded**	She was out of breath after climbing the stairs.
out of circulation	not visiting, don't **get around**	I've been out of circulation. I've been studying.
out of commission	not operating, **out of order**	My brain is out of commission. I can't think today.
out of context	taken out of the sentence, missing important words	Brian's comment, "Roll of the dice," was taken out of context.
out of control	not managed, wild, not **under control**	The crowd was out of control. People were fighting and looting.
out of hand	not controlled or disciplined	The children got out of hand. I couldn't control them.
out of harm's way	out of danger, in a safe place	Jerry parked the car off the road—out of harm's way.
out of here (outa here)	going, leaving	When I get paid, I'm outa here.
out of his element	not trained, **too deep for** him	He was out of his element when they began discussing DNA.
out of hock	not having debts, not owing any money	We paid off our mortgage today. It feels good to be out of hock.

Idiom	Meaning	Example
out of it	not feeling right, not **with it**	For some reason, I'm out of it today. I have no energy.
out of joint	(See **nose is out of joint**)	
out of kilter	(See **off kilter**)	
out of line	not showing respect, not polite	Ty was out of line when he called you a hooker.
out of luck	nothing left for you, **shit out of luck** [B]	We're out of luck. There are no tickets left.
out of my hair	not bothering me, not a problem for me	Next week the kids will be back at school—out of Mom's hair.
out of my head	crazy, **out of your mind**, **wacko**	I must have been out of my head to lend him my car. I was crazy.
out of nowhere	without warning, without an introduction	Out of nowhere a motorcycle passed us, going like a bullet.
out of order	not operating, broken	The stamp machine is out of order. I think it's broken.
out of our hands	not able to change or control the result	The decision is out of our hands. The voters will decide who wins.
out of patience	having no more patience, **lose patience**	I'm out of patience with the kids. They're fighting all the time.
out of place	in the wrong place, not appropriate	I felt out of place wearing shorts in the dining room.
out of pocket	expense paid from personal funds	Larry is out of pocket for the team lunch at McDonald's.
out of range	too far away, not close enough	The FM station is out of range of my radio. The signal is weak.
out of sight	too far away to see, not visible anymore	He watched the plane until it was a speck. Then it was out of sight.
out of sight (outa sight)	too much, too high	The price was outa sight! They wanted $200 for a nylon jacket.
out of sight, out of mind	if you do not see it you will forget about it	When I moved away, I forgot her —out of sight, out of mind, eh.
out of sorts	feeling negative, **down**	Andre is out of sorts because he didn't get enough sleep.

Idiom	Meaning	Example
out of step	not with the others, not designed for today	Your business plan is out of step with the 21st century. It's old.
out of the ball park	not close to the correct number or price	Few people will buy your product if the price is out of the ball park.
out of the blue	not expected, not on topic	Then out of the blue, he says, "What color are your shorts?"
out of the closet	not hiding your sexual orientation or secret	Jay decided to come out of the closet—to tell people he's gay.
out of the corner of my eye	at my far right or left, to the side	Out of the corner of my eye, I saw something move. It was the cat.
out of the goodness of my heart	because I am kind, because I want to help	I help her out of the goodness of my heart. I don't want to be paid.
out of the norm	not normal, not common	Having six husbands at the same time is out of the norm, eh.
out of the picture	not a factor, not competing or playing	Mario returned to Italy, so he's out of the picture. He's gone.
out of the question	not possible, **no way**	Because of the storm, traveling by car is out of the question.
out of the way	off the road or path, not blocking or obstructing	"Get out of the way!" he shouted. "Here come the runners!"
out of the way	done, no longer a problem, **over with**	Our Christmas shopping is finally done—out of the way.
out of the way	off the main road, **off the beaten track**	Rumsey is an out-of-the-way town, just east of the river.
out of the woods	out of difficulty, not in danger any more	Pedro survived the heart surgery, but he's not out of the woods yet.
out of the woodwork	from hidden places, from unknown places	Gas at 40¢ per litre will bring customers out of the woodwork.
out of this world	excellent, very delicious	Naomi is an excellent cook. Her carrot cake is out of this world!
out of touch	not communicating, not **in touch**	I'm not sure where Diane lives. We've been out of touch.
out of touch	not aware of reality, **head in the clouds**	He's been doing drugs. He's completely out of touch.
out of tune (music)	not at the correct pitch, not **in tune**	The violins were out of tune, but I enjoyed the singing.

Idiom	Meaning	Example
out of whack	not aligned, poorly constructed	The door doesn't close properly. Something is out of whack.
out of wind	short of breath, winded, **out of breath**	After running the race he was out of wind—exhausted.
out of work	not employed, unemployed	Lyle is out of work, so he stays at home with the kids.
out of your depth	not having the knowledge, **over your head**	I was out of my depth talking about genetics with the doctors.
out of your gourd	(See **out of your mind**)	
out of your mind	not thinking logically, crazy, **crackers**	You must be out of your mind to lend him money. You're crazy.
out of your tree	crazy, loony, **nuts**, **out of your mind**	You're out of your tree if you think I'm going sky diving.
out on a limb	in a dangerous place, **taking a chance**	I went out on a limb and said that you would donate $1000.
out on the town	enjoying the city's entertainment	On Saturday night, let's go out on the town and have a good time.
out to get you	wanting revenge, waiting for a chance to **get even**	Ever since I beat him at table tennis he's been out to get me.
out to lunch	not working effectively, not **with it**	The Service Manager is out to lunch. He's not helpful.
out to win	wanting to win, competitive	When Jon plays checkers, he's out to win. He's a competitor.
outdo yourself	perform better than before, do your personal best	Don't try to outdo yourself every time you run. Just jog sometimes.
outplay	play better than the opponent	The Flames outplayed the Kings in the third period of the game.
over and done with	done and forgotten, **out of the way**	We were glad when the trial was over and done with—finished.
over and out	message complete, **sign**ing **off**	"Over and out," the radio operator said when he completed his call.
over easy	eggs fried on both sides without breaking the yolks	"How would you like your eggs?" "Over easy, please—on toast."
over my dead body	do not try to do it, I'll stop you	"I want to marry your sister." "Over my dead body!"

Idiom	Meaning	Example
over my head	I do not understand, **too deep for me**	That lesson went over my head. Did you understand it?
over the edge	become ill or unable to cope, **around the bend**	Poor Ernst went over the edge when his twin brother died.
over the hill	too old, **on his last legs**	At 35, he was over the hill— too old to play pro soccer.
over the hump	past the difficult part, into an easier phase	After saving $2000, I was over the hump. I could pay the tuition.
over the rainbow	eccentric, weird, **a bit off, spinny**	Aunt Freda? She's been over the rainbow for years, poor lady.
over with	completed, finished, **over and done with**	Now that the trial is over with, we can return to a normal life.
overdo it	work too hard, become too tired	The doctor said I can work in the garden if I don't overdo it.
owly	cranky, unco-operative	When Herb gets drunk he gets owly—kind of stubborn.
own medicine	giving what you got, **tit for tat**	She hurt me so I'll hurt her—give her some of her own medicine!
own up	admit a mistake, **come clean**	If Jason is involved in the crime, he'll own up. He'll tell the police.
own worst enemy	create our own problems, prevent our own success	A smoker is his own worst enemy. He's harming himself.

Idiom	Meaning	Example

P

P's and Q's	(See **watch your P's and Q's**)	
pack a punch	hit hard, have a strong effect	Here's a word that packs a punch: *guilty*.
pack a rod	carry a hand gun, have a gun on a belt	The boys knew that one of the students was packing a rod.
pack it in	quit, leave, **pull the pin**	"What if you don't get paid?" "I'll pack it in. I'll quit."
pack uzis	carry automatic rifles, have powerful weapons	The news report stated that the soldiers were packing uzis.
pad	apartment, **digs**	You have a nice pad, Nora. I love your leather furniture!
pad an expense account	claim more money than spent, add false expenses	How can I pad my expense account if I don't have receipts?
paddle your own canoe	be an individual, be independent	*Love many, trust few, but always paddle your own canoe.*
pain in the ass [B]	(See **a pain in the ass**)	
paint a picture	describe in detail, portray with words	The speaker painted a picture of a ghetto with kids on the streets.
paint the town red	have a party downtown, go **out on the town**	During the carnival they paint the town red—have a great time.
paint with the same brush	include in the same group, generalize	He was with the gang, but can we paint him with the same brush?
pair off/pair up	find a partner, organize people in two's	The coach asked us to pair off and practise passing the ball.
pale by comparison	is not as good, is not as beautiful or talented	Most European parks pale by comparison to Banff.
pan out	succeed, go as planned, **work out**	Blair's ideas usually pan out. His suggestions are practical.

Idiom	Meaning	Example
pardon me	what did you say? please repeat it	Pardon me? Did you say you grew up in Hong Kong?
part and parcel	the same as, similar, **one and the same**	Socialism and communism are part and parcel of the same thing.
part company	separate, go in different directions, **split up**	Mel and Brad parted company after they arrived in Halifax.
part with	sell, allow someone else to own, **let go of**	Papa won't part with his Peugeot. He'd never sell it.
partners in crime	people who plan and commit crimes together, **boozing buddies**	As kids, Andy and I took apples from a neighbor's tree. We were partners in crime, so to speak.
party-pooper	one who leaves a party, **stick-in-the-mud**	You party-pooper! Stay here and dance with us.
party to that	(See **a party to that**)	
pass around	pass from person to person in the room, **hand out**	The speaker passed around a sheet of paper for us to sign.
pass away	die, **pass on**	Grandma passed away in 1974. She was 92.
pass for	appear similar to, look like	In that uniform, you could pass for a police officer.
pass off	offer as real or genuine, use a fake object or paper	If you pass off counterfeit money, you can be charged with a crime.
pass on	die, **bite the dust**, **kick the bucket**	Before her dad passed on, she visited him every day.
pass out	faint, become unconscious	He passed out after running the marathon. He fell on the road.
pass the buck	blame others, refer the problem to others	I won't pass the buck. I won't blame others for our problems.
pass through	drive or travel through a town or city	When we were passing through Regina, I called my cousin.
pass up	not take an opportunity, not do it when you can	Do not pass up this opportunity to go back to school.
pass water	urinate, **take a leak**[B], **take a pee** [B]	The nurse came in and asked him if he'd passed water yet.

Idiom	Meaning	Example
pass wind	let out gas, **let a fart** [B]	Mother says it's not polite to pass wind while you are eating.
passé	old fashioned, dated, **old hat**	It's passé to say *beg your pardon*. We don't hear that now.
pat answer	(See **a pat answer**)	
patch things up	agree to stop fighting, become friends again	Jon and May fight a lot, but they patch things up and go on.
paths will cross	(See **cross paths**)	
pave the way	make it easier to do, prepare a path	A $5000 scholarship paved the way for her career in medicine.
pay a compliment	say nice things about, say you did a good job	Tony paid you a compliment, Rita. He said you have a lovely garden.
pay a visit	go to visit someone, **drop over**	I must pay her a visit. I want to see her before we move.
pay attention	watch and listen, **listen up**	Pay attention to my words. Please listen carefully.
pay back	repay, return money that was borrowed	He said he would pay back every cent he borrowed from us.
pay down	pay more, **pay off**	Interest rates are high, so let's pay down our mortgage.
pay him back	do what he did to you, **get revenge**	Sally paid Harry back by going on a date with Jim.
pay in kind	(See **repay in kind**)	
pay my respects	attend a ceremony or send a symbol of your respect for someone	Remembrance Day allows us to pay our respects to the people who defended our country.
pay off	pay all that you owe, pay the balance	I want to pay off my loan now— pay the whole balance.
pay off	reward you, give you what you want	Studying pays off. You get higher grades.
pay the penalty	pay a fine, endure, receive punishment	He paid the penalty for his laziness: failure.
pay the price	work hard, endure, suffer	To be an Olympic athlete, you have to pay the price: pain.

Idiom	Meaning	Example
pay the shot	pay the whole bill, pay for everybody's ticket etc.	Uncle Sammy paid the whole shot for our trip to Europe.
pay through the nose	pay high rates for rent or service, **cost an arm...**	If you rent a condo in Dover, you'll pay through the nose.
pay tribute	show that you respect or admire a person, honor someone	In a letter to Ms. Lee, the City paid tribute to her for service to her community.
pay up	pay what is owed, pay a bet you lost	When I see Todd, I'll ask him to pay up. He owes me $20.
pay your dues	work hard and learn, be loyal for years	In the sport of rodeo, you have to pay your dues to get respect.
pay your way	pay your share of the expenses	"I don't want charity," she said. "I pay my way."
pay-off	reward, profit	We invested in property, hoping for a pay-off when we sell it.
peace of mind	freedom from worry or guilt	If you want peace of mind, you should buy insurance.
peaches-and-cream	beautiful skin, clear complexion	This new lotion will give you a peaches-and-cream complexion.
peachy	fine, great, wonderful, **neat**	When I asked Ko if she liked her job, she said, "Yes! It's peachy!"
pecking order	from strongest to weakest, **line of authority**	The first thing to learn about a company is the pecking order.
pedal her ass [B]	sell sex, become a prostitute	Jane used to joke about pedaling her ass to earn extra money.
pedal to the metal	accelerator all the way down, **flat out**	He always drives fast—pedal to the metal all the time.
peek-a-boo	peek through the fingers with hands covering eyes	Shelly was playing peek-a-boo with the baby.
peer sneer	an unfriendly look from a person who is the same age	When the manager praised my work, Vic gave me a peer sneer.
pell-mell	in a wild manner, in panic, **harum-scarum**	When the fire alarm sounded we ran pell-mell down the hall.
pen those words/lines	write those words or lines, compose that line	*The medium is the message*: Do you know who penned that line?
penny for your thoughts	(See **a penny for your thoughts**)	

Idiom	Meaning	Example
penny pincher	(See **a penny pincher**)	
people who live in glass houses shouldn't throw stones	people who have faults should not criticize others	Perfect people can be critical, but people who live in glass houses shouldn't throw stones.
perfect stranger	(See **a perfect stranger**)	
perk up	show interest or enthusiasm	When we mention girls, he perks up. His eyes sparkle.
pernickity/persnickety	fussy, critical of details, perfectionistic	When Dale was teenager, he was pernickity about his hair.
pet	touch intimately, kiss and caress	Petting is a prelude to sex. It is the touch of passion.
peter out	gradually lose power, reduce, **run out**	After 6, sales began to peter out. We had fewer customers.
petrified	very frightened, **scared stiff**	Gigi was petrified when a spider crawled up her leg.
phase me	bother me, affect me	When the man said I had won the lottery, it didn't phase me. Much.
phase me out	confuse me, surprise me, **throw me for a loop**	The new expressions phased me out. They confused me.
phone-in	a radio/TV show that invites phone calls	The topic for the phone-in show was *Animal Rights*.
phooey	oh no, **darn it**, **nuts**, **rats**, **shucks**	Phooey! I hit my golf ball into the water again!
photo op	photo opportunity, chance to have your photo taken	Then Brian shook hands with students to create a photo op.
piano tied to your ass [B]	something preventing you from moving	If you want coffee, make some! There's no piano tied to your ass.
pick a fight	start a fight, begin an argument	If Jamie tries to pick a fight with you, just walk away.
pick holes in	criticize, look for errors or faults, **nitpick**	Grant won't show you his work because you pick holes in it.
pick on	criticize, tease, get **on my case**	Why is everybody picking on me? I feel like a victim.
pick up	learn, understand, **catch on**	We pick up the street idioms faster than the grammar, eh.

Idiom	Meaning	Example
pick up	improve, increase	If business doesn't pick up soon, we'll need another loan.
pick up the pace	go a little faster, **step on it**	We're walking rather slowly. Can we pick up the pace?
pick up the pieces	put together again, mend	After her husband died, she tried to pick up the pieces of her life.
pick up the tab	pay the bill, **pay the shot**	Who picked up the tab for the hotel rooms? Who paid?
pick you up	give you a ride in a car, **give you a lift**	I'll pick you up at 6:45 and we'll drive to the mall.
pick you up	make you feel better, make you happy or **high**	Here, have a cup of tea. That will pick you up.
pick your brains	learn what you know, ask you questions	Maria wants to pick your brains about Freud and Jung.
pick yourself up	do not quit, persevere, **roll with the punches**	Don't let a failure stop you. Pick yourself up and try again.
pick-me-up	(See **a pick-me-up**)	
picky	fussy, looking for the perfect one	Don't be so picky, Dennis. Just choose a candy and eat it.
piddly	little, small, tiny	"What a piddly car!" "Yes. It's a Micra."
piddly-assed [B]	(See **piddly**)	
pie eyed	drunk, intoxicated, **hammered**	Byron was pie eyed when we got to the party. He was drunk, man.
pie in the sky	unrealistic, not practical, **hairbrain**, **half-baked**	When first invented, the car and phone were pie-in-the-sky ideas. Now we have phones in cars.
piece of ass [B]	(See **a piece of ass**)	
piece of cake	(See **a piece of cake**)	
piece of me	(See **want a piece of me**)	
piece of my mind	(See **a piece of my mind**)	
pig	police, **cop**, **flatfoot**, **fuzz**	Rocky says, "There was pigs on every corner. We couldn't move."

Idiom	Meaning	Example
pig in a poke	(See **a pig in a poke**)	
pig out	eat a lot, **fill your face**	Then we went to the Dairy Queen and pigged out on soft ice cream.
piggy bank	glass or porcelain pig used for saving coins	The little girl was counting the money in her piggy bank.
piggyback	carried on someone's back, riding on someone's back	Jurgen loved to ride piggyback when his dad walked in the park.
piggyback	succeed on the efforts of others	A catering firm piggybacked to success on United Airlines.
pill	(See **the pill**)	
pimple pole	youth with pimples, teenager with **zits**	Hey, pimple pole! You left your locker door open.
pin down/pin him down	get a direct answer, obtain the facts	Jed won't answer my questions. He's difficult to pin down.
pin money	extra money, money to spend on candy etc.	Janet used to earn pin money by painting signs.
pin your hopes on	hope for one big chance, hope without planning, **all your eggs...**	If you pin your hopes on some horse winning a race, you will probably be disappointed.
pinch	steal, rob, take what does not belong to you	When he was a boy he pinched pennies from his mom's purse.
pinch an inch	pinch an inch of fat on your body	"If I can pinch an inch, am I fat?" "No. Just pleasantly plump."
pinch hitter (baseball)	substitute batter, extra batter	Gomez is the best pinch hitter on the team. His average is .372.
pinch of coon shit [B]	(See **a pinch of coon shit**)	
pinch of salt	(See **a pinch of salt**)	
pinch off a loaf [B]	have a bowel movement, **drop a log**	"Where were you?" "In the can, pinching off a loaf."
pinch to grow an inch	(See **a pinch to grow an inch**)	
pinhead	one who does not use his brain, **dipstick**	"Who broke your glasses?" "Some pinhead sat on them!"
pinpoint	locate the exact place or point, determine the time	Lawrence is trying to pinpoint the time of the plane crash.

Idiom	Meaning	Example
pins and needles	(See **on pins and needles**)	
pipe down	do not be so noisy, be quiet, **keep it down**	The teacher opened the door and said, "Pipe down, Grade 7."
pipe dream	a dream based on luck, **pie in the sky**	Do you have a pipe dream or a plan? There's a big difference.
pipes	voice, **carry a tune**	K.D. Lang has great pipes, eh.
pipsqueak	tiny person, weak man, **potlicker**, **wimp**	Keith was a pipsqueak until he started lifting weights.
piss away [B]	waste, spend on liquor	He pissed away a lot of money when he was an alcoholic.
piss in the pickles [B]	ruin a project, wreck a piece of work	Plans for a school were OK until the Premier pissed in the pickles.
piss like a race horse [B]	have to urinate, **back teeth are floating**	I hope this mall has a washroom. I have to piss like a race horse.
piss off [B]	leave, go, **beat it**, **take off**	"If you don't like cigar smoke," he said, "you can piss off."
piss on them [B]	who cares about them? they are worthless	When Scotty heard you quit the team, he said, "Piss on him!"
piss parade [B]	a group of people pissing together	On bus trips we stopped for a piss parade every two or three hours.
piss poor [B]	of poor quality, not well made	Grandpa said, "That's a piss-poor tractor. Don't buy it."
piss pot full [B]	a lot, very many, more than expected	After the poker game, Sammy had a piss pot full of loonies.
piss your pants [B]	become very frightened, be very scared	The House of Horrors is so scary you'll piss your pants!
pissed [B]	angry, upset, **teed off**	She was really pissed when you told her to carry your luggage.
pissed [B]	drunk, **hammered**, **sloshed**,	When I saw her walk, I knew she was pissed. She nearly fell down.
pissed off [B]	angry, mad, **pissed**, **ticked off**	He'll be pissed off if I leave him. He'll be mad.
pissed to the gills [B]	drunk, **plastered**, **snapped**	He was pissed to the gills, so we sent him home in a taxi.

Idiom	Meaning	Example
pissing into the wind [B]	working at a hopeless job, feeling futile about a task	Cleaning up an oil spill is like pissing into the wind—hopeless!
pit of my stomach	(See **the pit of my stomach**)	
pit stop	a brief stop to buy gas or go to the washroom	Excuse me. I have to make a pit stop before we go to the movie.
pits	(See **the pits**)	
place on a pedestal	(See **on a pedestal**)	
Plan B	the substitute for Plan A, an alternative plan	Plan A depends on getting a student loan. What is Plan B?
plastered	very drunk, **hammered, looped, sloshed**	After losing the fight, Jock went and got plastered.
plastic	credit cards, bank cards	I like to use plastic when I travel. I don't feel safe carrying cash.
plate is full	too much to do, cannot do any more	I'm busy writing exams. My plate is full.
play a big part	do much to help, be a main factor	The nice weather played a big part in the success of our festival.
play a bit part	be a minor actor in a movie or a stage play	Irene played a bit part in a movie last year. She's a good actor.
play a joke on	fool or trick someone, **play a prank on**	I played a joke on Ty. I phoned and said he'd won the lottery.
play a mean game	play very well, play to win	Ingrid may beat you. She plays a mean game of chess.
play a part	be a cause, affect the result	His drinking played a part in his dismissal. Drinking was a cause.
play a prank on	arrange a surprise for you so people will laugh	Ty played a prank on me. He left a message to call the President.
play a trick on	deceive you for fun, **play a joke on**	We played a trick on Liz. We sent her picture to a beauty contest.
play along	pretend to believe, **go along with, let on**	Lisa played along with the joke on Mark. She didn't tell him.
play around	have other mates, **sleep around**	She knows he's playing around, but she won't confront him.
play dead	pretend to be dead, lie down as if you are dead	If a grizzly bear attacks you, play dead and it may go away.

Idiom	Meaning	Example
play dirty	play rough, **break the rules, play hardball**	Even if his opponents cheat and lie, Pat won't play dirty.
play dumb	act as if you do not know, **play along**	Play dumb when she tells you I won. Pretend you don't know.
play fair	play using rules, give everyone an equal chance	A referee will help us to play fair, to play according to the rules.
play games	deceive people, not be sincere, **mind games**	He's been playing games with us. We can't believe what he says.
play hard to get	pretend you do not care; you do not want him	When Tom invites you to go on a date, you could play hard to get.
play hardball	play tough, try to hurt the opponent, **play dirty**	If the manager wants to play hardball, show him that you are tough.
play havoc with	interfere with, cause sudden changes	The wind played havoc with the ball, causing it to rise or fall.
play hooky	not attend classes, stay away from school	One spring day, some of us played hooky. We went fishing.
play into his hand	do as he planned, **fall into his trap**	By accepting a ride in Paul's car, you played right into his hand.
play it by ear	play without a plan, improvise, **jam**	If our plans fail, we can play it by ear. We'll be creative!
play it cool	be calm, do not become excited, **chill out**	If Lisa tells you she's pregnant, play it cool. Don't become angry.
play it for all it's worth	get the most out of it, dramatize it, **ham it up**	When Uncle Saul tells a story, he plays it for all it's worth.
play it safe	be careful, do not **take a chance**	Play it safe when you go out in a boat. Wear a life jacket.
play it up	act like it is important, make it a **big deal**	If there's an argument, he plays it up. He makes it worse.
play my cards right	behave in the best way, do the right things	If you play your cards right at the interview, you should get the job.
play on my heart strings	cause me to feel emotional, make me feel sentimental	The movie *Hey Jude* will play on your heart strings—make you cry.
play on words	(See **a play on words**)	
play out	become tired or exhausted, become winded	After two sets of tennis, Ling said, "I'm played out!"

Idiom	Meaning	Example
play out	happen, conclude, **pan out**, **work out**,	Nina used to work for Ed. Now Ed works for Nina. I want to see how this plays out.
play second fiddle	accept a lower position, **take a back seat**	Kirk won't play second fiddle to her. He wants to be the boss.
play the field	**date** many people, go out with various men/women	After a long relationship with Sue, he began to play the field.
play the fool	pretend you are a fool, act simple or foolish	If you play the fool, people will often tell you secrets.
play the ham	act for an audience, **ham it up**	After a couple of drinks, he likes to play the ham—to be a clown.
play the heavy	be the strong man or tough guy	In our gang, Don plays the heavy. He talks and acts tough.
play the ponies	bet on horses at the race track	He's lost a lot of money playing the ponies. He bets on every race.
play the stock market	buy stocks and shares, sell stocks and shares	At first he invested in real estate; then he played the stock market.
play to the crowd	play a sport just for the crowd, **hotdog**	The coach wants us to play to win, not play to the crowd.
pleased as punch	very pleased, happy about	Our minister is pleased as punch when there's a large offering.
plug away	work slowly and steadily, **slug away**	If you plug away at physics, you will eventually understand it.
plug into	become familiar with, learn to use	If he wants to be a dentist, he'll have to plug into the sciences.
plug the product	(See **put in a plug for**)	
plug the team	add the best players from other teams	The Flyers plugged their team with star players from the league.
plumb loco	completely crazy, **crackers**	After several crop failures, one farmer went plumb loco.
plump full	very full, full to the top, **chock full**	Johnny's glass was plump full— so full he spilled some milk.
pocket of resistance	(See **a pocket of resistance**)	
pogey	cheques from employment insurance, **on the dole**	Some guys work all summer and collect pogey all winter.

Idiom	Meaning	Example
point is well taken	opinion is true, statement is logical	Your point about smoking is well taken. It *is* expensive.
point of no return	(See **the point of no return**)	
point of view	opinion, what you think of it	This is my point of view: Religion is a private matter.
point out	tell, show, indicate	The teacher pointed out that the word *run* has several meanings.
point-blank range	close range, only a few feet away	The report stated that the gorilla was shot at point-blank range.
poke fun at	laugh at, **make fun of**	Would you poke fun at someone who can't speak Chinese?
poker face	(See **a poker face**)	
polish off/polish it off	eat all of it, drink it all	Somebody polished off the last few cookies. Who ate them?
political football	a program or issue used by politicians to get votes, **play** political **games**	A day-care program is a political football. Politicians use it to get the votes of parents with babies.
politically correct	appropriate, not racist or sexist	Advertise for a sales*person*. Use the politically correct term.
polluted	very drunk, **loaded**, **plastered**, **wasted**	Every Friday night he goes to the bar and drinks till he's polluted.
pony tail	tying the hair at the back leaving a *tail* of hair	Stan pulled on Judy's pony tail as he walked past her desk.
poontang [B]	sex, intercourse, **nookie**	Listen, guys, poontang should be measured in *quality*, not *quantity*.
poor as a church mouse	(See **as poor as a church mouse**)	
poor house	(See **in the poor house**)	
pop in	visit without warning, **drop in**	When I'm in your part of town I'll pop in for a visit, okay?
pop over	visit for a few minutes, **drop over**	Why don't you pop over and see our wedding pictures?
pop the question	ask an important question, ask someone to marry you	In the old days, a man would buy the ring and then pop the question.

Idiom	Meaning	Example
pop up	appear, occur, be visible	The name *M. Greig* kept popping up in the company records.
pop your buttons	feel very proud, be full of pride	When you received the award, did you pop your buttons?
popcorn brain	one who has not learned to think, **airhead**	When I forgot my phone number they called me *popcorn brain*.
pope's nose	(See **the pope's nose**)	
positive	certain, very sure, **dead certain**	Are you positive it was Ming? Do you know for sure it was him?
pot	marijuana tobacco, **reefer**	The room smelled of tobacco, like someone had been smoking pot.
pot calling the kettle black	a guilty person accusing another guilty person	When thief accuses robber, it's the pot calling the kettle black.
pot of gold	a fortune, a lot of money	Isy believes there's a pot of gold buried in every acre he buys.
potato sack	loose fitting jacket or clothing	Potato sack looks good on Ken. Baggy clothes suit him.
potlicker	a little person, a small competitor	George—that potlicker! I can beat him with my little finger!
pound of flesh	revenge, **an eye for an eye**	For that insult, Simon will get revenge—his pound of flesh.
pound the pavement	look for a job, walk from company to company to find a job	Carrying several copies of his resume, Tang was pounding the pavement in Vancouver.
pour it on	praise a lot, compliment too much	When Harry starts pouring it on, I know he wants something.
pour out your soul	tell your private feelings, **tell all**	When Zora visits, she pours out her soul to me about her lover.
pow	a word to describe a hit or a punch, **bam**	Then pow! This guy hits Cody in the stomach.
power play (hockey)	five skaters against four or three	The Canucks scored twice on their five-minute power play.
power play (business)	a show of power, a grab for power	If a general manager demotes two managers, it's a power play.
power to burn	very powerful, lots of horsepower	That old Chev has a 454 motor. It has power to burn.

Idiom	Meaning	Example
power trip	showing power, showing authority	Last week he went on a power trip and told us to work harder.
power user	a person who uses a computer a lot	Jay uses the computer about 12 hours a day. He's a power user.
powers that be	(See **the powers that be**)	
practice what you preach	do what you say people should do	If you want to hear truth, tell the truth. Practice what you preach.
prairie oyster	the testicle of a young bull or bull calf	Do you believe that some folks in Alberta eat prairie oysters?
praise him to the skies	praise him a lot, **sing his praises**	Wade is an excellent student. His teachers praise him to the skies.
pre-menstrual syndrome	emotional crises the week before menstruation, pms	Judy says pms causes most of her personal problems.
prepare like crazy	prepare thoroughly, be ready for an event or test	Before I go to a job interview I prepare like crazy.
preppy	a youth who wears trendy clothes, **clean cut**	Brad is a preppy. He wears Polo sweaters and drives a Celica.
presence of mind	ability to think clearly and act appropriately, **cool under pressure**	When the bear charged the car, Jill had the presence of mind to sound the burglar alarm.
press charges	ask the police to charge someone with a crime	The police asked her if she wanted to press charges against the thief.
press into service	required to help, forced to serve	The young men were injured, so the old men were pressed into service.
press on	continue traveling, **keep on** going	Dumont wanted to stop at Batoche, but he pressed on to Fort Carlton.
press the panic button	become very scared, panic, **freak**	If a dog growls at me, I press the panic button. I scream and run.
pretty as a picture	very pretty, beautiful	"How do I look in my new dress?" "Pretty as a picture, my dear."
pretty penny	(See **cost a pretty penny**)	
price out	check the price of, **find out** the price	Before we buy a European car, we should price out parts and service.
price you have to pay	(See **the price you have to pay**)	

Idiom	Meaning	Example
prick [B]	penis, **dork**, **hoo-haw**	When the doctor asked me where it hurt, I pointed to my prick.
prick [B]	foolish man, **jerk**	Only a prick would feed liquor to his pet.
pride goeth before a fall	you lose self-respect before you do an evil deed	Is this saying in the Bible? *Pride goeth before a fall.*
prima donna	one who expects special treatment or privileges	A prima donna on our team might upset the other players.
Prince Charming	the perfect man, the ideal mate	Colin is not Prince Charming, but I love him and he loves me.
proby	an employee who is on probation, a new employee	When I was a proby, I tried to impress my supervisors.
promise the moon	promise that everything will be perfect	If you promise the moon, the kids may be very disappointed.
pronto	now, immediately, **right away**	You'll miss your bus if you don't leave now. Pronto!
proof of the pudding...	(See **the proof of the pudding is in the eating**)	
psych out	lose confidence, not be able to concentrate	If I think about making a mistake, I get psyched out.
psyched/psyched up	prepared, excited, **pumped**, **up for it**	Claire was psyched for the exam. She was ready for the challenge.
pub crawl	drink at many pubs in one day, **bar hopping**	If you go on a pub crawl today, you'll have a headache tomorrow.
public property	what everybody knows, public information	If you tell Zora about the plan, it'll be public property.
puddle-jumper	a small car, a subcompact	"Why buy a puddle-jumper?" "It gets good gas mileage."
pull a face	wrinkle your face, **make faces**	Lyle is 14, but he's still a boy. He pulls a face when he's upset.
pull a few strings	help by talking to powerful people, **it's not what you know...**	My application was late, but a friend of mine pulled a few strings and got me an interview.
pull a muscle	injure a muscle, strain a muscle	One of our best players pulled a muscle and can't play tonight.
pull for	support, cheer for	We were pulling for your team. We're glad you won.

Idiom	Meaning	Example
pull in your horns	not be so aggressive, stop attacking or criticizing	Father's advice is to pull in your horns or you could be dismissed.
pull it off	cause it to happen; succeed, win, **snatch victory...**	With Jean as leader of the party, the Liberals can pull it off. They can win the election.
pull it out	win just before the end; before it is too late	The score was tied, but we pulled it out with a last-minute goal.
pull out all the stops	work as hard as possible, **go all out, go for broke**	You're losing this match. If you want to win, you'll have to pull out all the stops.
pull punches	talk nice, **ease up, take it easy** on you	If the service is poor, he doesn't pull punches. He complains.
pull that	do that, do something wrong, **try that**	She reached for the phone to call the police, but the thief said, "Don't try to pull that."
pull the goalie (hockey)	remove the goaltender and use an extra skater	After our coach pulled the goalie we scored and tied the game.
pull the pin	quit, resign, leave, **pack it in**	If the company doesn't give us a raise in pay, I'm pulling the pin.
pull the plug	stop working on a project, not support any more, **leave you in the lurch**	When Zoe lied to Social Services they pulled the plug on her. They stopped paying her expenses.
pull the rug out	take away your help, remove your support, **leave you holding the bag**	Some insurance companies pull the rug out from under you when you file a claim.
pull the wool over your eyes	deceive you, trick you, fool you	Don't let him pull the wool over your eyes. He's not at the office.
pull through	recover, get well, **get over** the operation	The doctor didn't think he'd pull through, but he's feeling fine.
pull together	work together, co-operate	If we pull together, we can complete this project on time.
pull up stakes	move away, go to live in another place	We pull up stakes when winter comes. We move to Arizona.
pull up your socks	do better, improve	He'll have to pull up his socks in math—if he wants to pass.
pull your chain	ask you what you think, ask for your opinion	If we want your opinion we'll pull your chain. We'll ask you.

Idiom	Meaning	Example
pull your leg	fool you, tell you a false story as a joke	If he said Canada has a tropical climate, he was pulling your leg.
pull your weight	do your job, do your share of the work	If we all pull our weight—do our share—we can achieve our goals.
pull your wire [B]	masturbate, **jerk off** [B]	"Why do you pull your wire?" "Because it feels good."
pull yourself together	control your sadness, **get a grip** on yourself	It's difficult to pull yourself together after a divorce.
pumped/pumped up	excited about performing, ready to play	John's pumped for today's game. He really wants to play.
punch your lights out	hit you, knock you down, **knock you out**	If you try to kiss my girlfriend I'll punch your lights out.
puppy	a name for someone or something familiar	Your old Honda? Don't sell that puppy. It's **a keeper**.
puppy love	young love, love between children or teenagers	Puppy love is sweet, but it's just a step on the path to mature love.
pure luck	just luck, not skill or talent	Hank won the fishing contest, but it was pure luck, not skill.
push me (to the limit)	put pressure on me, **bug** me too much	Don't push me. One more insult and I'll punch you.
push the right buttons	say the right things, do the right things	The players want to play for Pat. She pushes all the right buttons.
push your luck	(See **don't push your luck**)	
pusher	a person who sells illegal drugs	The judge sentenced the pusher to ten years in prison.
pushing fifty	nearly 50 years old, 48 or 49 years old	Bart is pushing fifty, but he looks much younger.
pushing up daisies	dead and buried in a graveyard, **deep six**	Old Tom's pushin' up daisies. He died a long time ago.
pussy whipped	controlled by his wife, afraid his wife will **cut him off**	Tim loves his wife, but he's not pussy whipped. He has a mind of his own.
put 'em up	raise your hands, **reach for the sky**	Merv sticks his finger in my ribs and says, "Put 'em up."

Idiom	Meaning	Example
put 'er there	let us shake hands, I want to shake hands with you	After the argument, I apologized and said, "Put 'er there, eh."
put a bug in my ear	told me secretly, **a little bird told me**	"Who told you I need a wallet?" "Mom put a bug in my ear."
put a different slant on it	change the way you see it, change your view, **put things in perspective**	If you called the police because you thought I needed help, that puts a different slant on it.
put a hex on me	bring a curse upon me, put me **under a spell**	I haven't won a game of cards today. Did you put a hex on me?
put a lid on it	do not be noisy, **keep it down**	When we shout, he says, "Put a lid on it. Not so loud, eh."
put all your eggs in...	(See **all your eggs in one basket**)	
put an end to	stop or end it, cause it to stop	The policeman came and put an an end to the fighting.
put away	eat or drink, **pig out**	Dennis has a good appetite. He put away ten pancakes!
put down	criticize, **knock, put-down**	Those poor kids are put down all the time—criticized and yelled at.
put down	kill, shoot, dispatch, **put out of its misery**	The horse had to be put down because it was badly injured.
put down roots	live in one place for years, buy land and raise a family	After moving from town to town, we put down roots in Moose Jaw.
put her there	let us shake hands, I want to shake hands with you	After the argument he apologized and said, "Put 'er there."
put him in his place	tell him he is wrong— that he is **out of line**	Dwaine has insulted all of us. I hope Dad puts him in his place.
put in a good word for	tell the employer that you are a good applicant	If you apply for a job with us, I'll put in a good word for you.
put in a hard day	work hard all day, **hard day**	You've put in a hard day, Fran. Let's have supper at a cafe.
put in a plug for	advertise free, promote free	When you speak on TV, please put in a plug for my book.
put in time	be there a lot, **hang out, spend time**	Raj puts in a lot of time at the piano. He practises a lot.
put it	say it, express it	She said, "He's my favorite cowboy." That's how she put it.

Idiom	Meaning	Example
put it on the bill	charge a purchase, **charge it**, **run a tab**	When I buy something at the grocery store, I put it on the bill.
put me on	(See **putting me on**)	
put my finger on it	(See **can't put my finger on it**)	
put my foot down	say no, say you cannot do that, **no way**	When the kids ask if they can go to a restricted movie, I put my foot down.
put my neck on the line	risk my job or safety, **stick my neck out**	As a manager, I'll put my neck on the line for a good employee.
put off	upset, unhappy, **put out about**	He was put off when Nola refused to go out with him.
put off	do it later, postpone	We've put off the wedding until Chad completes his education.
put on a pedestal	(See **on a pedestal**)	
put on airs	pretend you are better or richer or smarter	Martha would never put on airs. She is very sincere.
put on the dog	use your finest dishes or clothes etc.; **show off**	When we visit Mame, she likes to put on the dog—get dressed up.
put out	do, function, perform	Vern's crew really puts out. They do a lot of work in a day.
put out	unhappy, upset	Was he put out when you asked for more money? Was he upset?
put out about	bothered, annoyed, **ticked off**	What's Jan put out about? She seems irritated.
put out feelers	discover indirectly, ask subtle questions, **through the grapevine**	I'm not really looking for a new job, but I'm going to put out a few feelers and see what happens.
put out of its misery	kill because it is suffering, **put down**	One of our dogs had diabetes, so we put it out of its misery.
put stock in	believe in, have faith in	An atheist doesn't put much stock in the Bible.
put the finishing touches on	add the last details or trimmings	Lan decorated the cake—she put the finishing touches on it.
put the heat on	cause someone to feel pressure or stress	The cops put the heat on them by asking a lot of questions.

Idiom	Meaning	Example
put the kibosh on	prevent, stop	The manager put the kibosh on our dental plan. He said no.
put them up	put your hands up, **stick them up**	The outlaw drew his gun, saying, "Put 'em up, folks, or I'll shoot."
put things in perspective	see things as they are, see the actual size	A few days after the flood, I was able to put things in perspective.
put to bed (print media)	put in a box when it is ready to print	The editor always checks the paper before he puts it to bed.
put to death	killed, shot, hanged, **put down**	If a soldier deserted the army he was put to death.
put to rest	not think or worry about it any more	It's time we put to rest our quarrel over Dad's will.
put to shame	defeated very badly, feel ashamed of losing	Our baseball team was put to shame by the Cubans: 11-0.
put to the test	be tested, be challenged	Your computer skills will be put to the test in your new position.
put too fine a point on	be too precise, **split hairs**	If you want to put too fine a point on it, the color is actually russet.
put up or shut up	pay for or be quiet, do instead of talk	If you brag about your cooking we'll ask you to put up or shut up.
put up the money	pay for, finance, **front me**	If I start a new business, will you put up the money?
put up with	tolerate, endure, not get frustrated	Alice puts up with a lot of complaining from Jackie.
put you at ease	cause you to relax, **break the ice**	An embarrassing moment can sometimes put you at ease.
put you away	defeat you, **knock you out**	If the score is tied, he must win two points to put you away.
put you in a bad mood	cause you to feel upset or unhappy	The violence in that movie put me in a bad mood. I dislike violence.
put you off your game	cause you to play poorly, cause you to make errors	Wearing a helmet will put me off my game. It will bother me.
put your best foot forward	try to do your best work, present yourself well	If you put your best foot forward, the employer will be impressed.

Idiom	Meaning	Example
put your foot in it	say or do something that causes an argument	He really put his foot in it when he said that doctors are underpaid.
put your foot in your mouth	say something that causes pain or embarrassment	If you speak the truth, you will often put your foot in your mouth.
put your heart into it	try hard, do your best, **give it your best shot**	If you hope to succeed in life, you have to put your heart into it.
put your money where your mouth is	pay what you offered, **put up or shut up**	I accept your offer. Now put your money where your mouth is.
put your shoulder to the wheel	begin to work	If you want a share of the profits, put your shoulder to the wheel.
put yourself out	give too much, sacrifice, **go to a lot of trouble**	When I visit, don't put yourself out. Don't do anything special.
put yourself through college	earn money to pay for your college education	You need a good summer job to put yourself through college.
put-down	criticism, disapproval	His speech was a put-down of our policies—very negative.
putting me on	joking, fooling me, **kidding** me	You won a Nobel Prize? You're putting me on!
putting on the ritz	dressing fancy or classy, doing things high class	She's dining and dancing in Paris. She's putting on the ritz!

Idiom	Meaning	Example

Q

quake in his boots	feel afraid, be scared, **scared spitless**	When the war began, it was scary. We were quaking in our boots.
question of	(See **a question of**)	
quick and dirty	fast or easy, instant, **short cut**	I know a quick and dirty way to calculate interest. It's easy.
quick like a bunny	very quick, without delay	Get into bed now—quick like like a bunny!
quick on the draw	quick to speak or shoot; **get the drop on**	Think before you speak. Don't be so quick on the draw.
quicker than you can say Jack Robinson	very quickly	The ghost was gone—quicker 'n you can say Jack Robinson!
quickie	(See **a quickie**)	
quick-study	(See **a quick-study**)	
quit this place	leave, go away from here, **blow this joint**	I'm bored. Let's quit this place. Let's get out of here.
quit while you're ahead	quit before you begin to lose, **don't push your luck**	If he lets you have the car, don't ask for his credit card. Quit while you're ahead.

Idiom	Meaning	Example

R

'round the clock	all hours, twenty-four hours	We worked 'round the clock to harvest the crop before it snowed.
rabbit died	(See **the rabbit died**)	
rabbit food	lettuce, carrots, cabbage etc.	Dad says salad is tasteless. He calls it rabbit food.
rabble-rouser	a person who makes noise and causes problems	A bunch of rabble-rousers were fighting at the football game.
rack my brain	think hard, try to remember	I've racked my brain, but I can't remember where I saw that man.
rack up	compile, increase, **build up**, **run up**	He racked up a lot of points with his first hand of cribbage.
rad	radical, weird, **on the fringe**	What a rad video! The singer's head was sitting on a table!
rags	clothes, **threads**	I need some new rags. My clothes are old and worn.
rags to riches	(See **from rags to riches**)	
ragtop	convertible car, **soft-top**	In the summer, Pam drives a ragtop—a Fiat Spyder.
railroad	push a plan, force a person	No, I didn't want to resign. I was railroaded into it!
rain check	using a service later, credit for a product	The store had sold all the CD's, so they gave me a rain check.
rain on their parade	ruin the party, spoil the fun, **piss on them** [B]	When Barb found out she wasn't invited to the wedding, she said, "I hope it rains on their parade."
raining cats and dogs	raining hard, raining heavily	You need a raincoat, Dear. It's raining cats and dogs!

Idiom	Meaning	Example
raise a stink	complain a lot, cause an argument or a bad scene	Gunter raised a stink by accusing the chairman of stealing funds.
raise an eyebrow	(See **raised eyebrows**)	
raise Cain	shout and make noise, cause a disturbance	They were having a wild party upstairs—really raising Cain.
raise hell [B]	make noise, disturb the peace, **raise Cain**	The neighbors are drinking and raising hell again.
raise money	earn or request money for a project or a charity	The Boy Scouts are raising money to pay for a trip to China.
raise your hand against	hit someone, hurt someone	If you ever raise your hand against her, I'll call the police.
raise your spirits	help you feel positive, help you feel happy	If you want to raise your spirits, just have a visit with Kari.
raised eyebrows	shock, surprise, disapproval	When Chuck and Di separated it caused some raised eyebrows.
raisins	old folks, seniors	Let's invite the raisins to our concert. They're a great audience.
rake in the dough	receive a lot of money, earn a large salary or profit	When he played pro basketball he was raking in the dough.
rake you over the coals	lecture you, scold you, ask you to explain	I got raked over the coals for taking the car without asking.
raking it in	(See **rake in the dough**)	
ralph	vomit, puke, **barf**, **hork**, **throw up**	In the washroom, someone had ralphed all over the floor.
ram down your throat	(See **shove down my throat**)	
rant and rave	yell and cry out, preach and complain	The old man was ranting and raving about his lost goats.
rap your knuckles	(See **get your knuckles rapped**)	
rat on	tell the police or the authorities, **squeal**	Billy won't rat on me. He won't tell the teacher.
rat race	fast pace, busy schedule, living/working in the city	What a rat race! I want to leave the city and live in the country.
ratch	damage, wreck, **trash**	Who ratched the gears on my bike? I can't shift into low!

Idiom	Meaning	Example
rats	oh no, **darn**, **nuts**	Rats! We have a flat tire!
rattle my chain	annoy me, anger me, **get under my skin**	That woman rattles my chain, the way she gossips about me!
rattle on	continue to talk, ramble, **hold forth**	The professor was rattling on about Canadian culture.
rattle sabres	threaten to attack, appear to be preparing for war	The workers are rattling their sabres, but they won't strike.
razzle-dazzle	spectacular show, dazzling display	Grandpa said the rodeo had too much razzle-dazzle—too fancy.
reach for the sky	raise your hands, **put them up**	The cowboy drew his gun and said, "Reach for the sky, mister!"
reach me	phone me, contact me	You can reach me by leaving a message at my brother's place.
reach me	cause me to feel your message	The minister said he was trying to reach the kids through a film.
reach out	offer to help, let people know that you care	Magdalena reaches out to the children in violent families.
read along	read with the leader, read together	The instructor asked the class to read along in their text books.
read between the lines	see what is not written, read the implied message, find the hidden meaning	If we read between the lines, the memo says the company is going to be sold.
read into	add your own meaning, see what you hope for	Teri reads love into every letter you write to her.
read it over	read it, **go over** it	Read it over and tell me what you think it says.
read me (CB radio)	hear my voice, hear my message	"Do you read me?" she asked. "Yes. Loud and clear," he replied.
read my lips	my lips are saying what you are hearing, believe it	Edie said, "Read my lips, people. We have no more money."
read them and weep	check your cards and cry about your poor hand	After dealing the cards, Walt said, "Read 'em and weep, boys."
read up on	read about, study, **look up**	I'm going to the library to read up on Louis Riel.
read you	see what you're thinking or feeling	You have an expressive face. Anybody can read you.

Idiom	Meaning	Example
real McCoy	(See **the real McCoy**)	
realize your potential	be the best you can, **come into your own**	If you work for a good company, you can realize your potential.
really deaf	not willing to listen, not wanting to hear about	When you talk about smoking, he's really deaf.
ream out	scold, **give you hell**, **tie into**	He reamed me out for driving too fast. He said I could have caused an accident.
reap what you sow	(See **you reap whatsoever you sow**)	
rear end	buttocks, posterior, **backside, butt**	"Where did she pinch you?" "On my rear end—my bum."
rear-end	bump a car in the back, **run into** the rear of a car	"Your back bumper is dented." "Ya, some guy rear-ended me."
red carpet	(See **roll out the red carpet**)	
red herring	a false issue, **make a mountain...**	She said, "Fluoride is a red herring. It's not important."
red tape	government forms and procedures	An immigrant faces a lot of red tape—many interviews, forms.
red-letter day	(See **a red-letter day**)	
redneck	(See **a redneck**)	
reduce to tears	ask hurtful questions until someone cries	The lawyer's hurtful questions soon reduced Karla to tears.
reefer	marijuana cigarette, **pot**	After smoking two reefers, he laughed at anything they said.
regular guy	(See **a regular guy**)	
reject out of hand	reject without thinking, throw away quickly	If the apples aren't from B.C. he rejects them out of hand.
relate to that	know about that, have experienced that	He said he was afraid to speak in public. I can relate to that.
rented lips	lips that mispronounce, lips that say strange words	Did I say *ossifer*? I meant *officer*! Excuse my rented lips!
repay in kind	give the same as you get, help one who helped you	If you help a neighbor, he may repay in kind.

Idiom	Meaning	Example
rest assured	be sure, be certain, **count on**	If Johnny said he would vote for Kim, you can rest assured he will.
rest his soul (God rest his soul)	may his soul rest in peace; I hope his soul is peaceful	I remember when Jock Reynolds (rest his soul) saved Pete's life.
rest my case	have no more arguments, have completed my work	After speaking for abortion for an hour, he said, "I rest my case."
rest on your laurels	depend only on past success to help you, **you're only as good...**	If you win an award, you can rest on your laurels, or you can set new goals.
rhyme or reason	(See **no rhyme or reason**)	
ride herd	try to control a group; supervise children	When my wife goes shopping, I have to ride herd on the kids.
ride his coattails	depend on his success, use his success	My dad was a great doctor, but I don't want to ride his coattails.
ride me	continue to remind me of a duty or habit	You can stop riding me about doing my homework. It's done.
ride the clutch	drive a car with your foot on the clutch pedal	If you ride the clutch, we will soon have to replace it.
ride the wave	use luck or success to achieve more success	Enjoy your success. Ride the wave to a better life.
riding high	feeling great, **on cloud nine**	Jane is riding high after getting an *A* in math.
right as rain	as welcome as rain, naturally good	We always enjoyed Uncle Mel's visits. They were right as rain!
right away	now, immediately, **on the double**, pronto	If you leave right away, you can get to school on time.
right, left and center	(See **left, right and center**)	
right off the bat	at the start, the very first thing	Right off the bat she says, "Are you married?"
right on	that's good, great, **okay**	When I told him he passed the test he said, "Right on, man!"
right on the money	(See **on the money**)	
rigmarole	(See **what a rigmarole**)	
rile up	become afraid, upset, **worked up**	The horses get all riled up when they smell smoke.

Idiom	Meaning	Example
ring a bell	remind you, cause you to remember	Does the name Kurelek ring a bell? Have you heard of him?
ring leader	leader of a gang, leader of some criminals	The ring leader, Tony Amano, helped the prisoners escape.
ring me	phone me, call me, **give me a ring**	Ring me when you get home from work. Tell me about your day.
ring off the hook	receive many phone calls	We put an ad in the paper. Now the phone's ringing off the hook!
rip-off	(See **a rip-off**)	
rip-snorting mad	very angry, violent	The bull got rip-snorting mad when he missed the toreador.
ripped off	cheated, **taken**	Dar paid too much for the watch. He got ripped off.
rise and shine	wake up and be happy, get out of bed smiling	"Rise and shine," he called to us each morning—at 6 a.m.!
rise to the occasion	be able to do what is needed at the time	When we need a speaker, Ed rises to the occasion. He speaks well.
risky business	a risky plan, a gamble	Being a peacemaker is risky business. You could get shot!
road apple	a frozen horse turd used as a puck for road hockey	Let's play hockey. You get the sticks and I'll find a road apple.
road to hell is paved...	(See **the road to hell is paved with good intentions**)	
Roaring Twenties	the decade following World War I (1920-1929)	In the Roaring Twenties, ladies had short hair with kiss curls.
rob Peter to pay Paul	move money from one part of a budget to another	If we use grocery money to buy gas, we rob Peter to pay Paul.
rob the cradle	court a person who is too young, **date** a minor	You're seeing Lisa? She's only 17! That's robbing the cradle!
Rock	(See **The Rock**)	
rock	shock, cause a personal change, **shake him**	*Killing Fields* is a powerful movie. It will rock you.
rock bottom	(See **hit rock bottom**)	
rock the boat	disturb or upset things, **make waves**	If you rock the boat, you may be asked to leave the project.

Idiom	Meaning	Example
rocks in your head	(See **got rocks in your head**)	
rocky road	difficult path, **rough going**	In life, he traveled the rocky road. He always chose the difficult way.
rodchester	single armrest between two airplane seats	The woman beside me rested her arm on the rodchester.
roll around	future becomes present, future date arrives, time passes	By the time your birthday rolls around, I'll have no money to buy you a present.
roll in the hay	(See **a roll in the hay**)	
roll off the tongue	natural to say, easy to pronounce	Podnzilowicz is a name that doesn't roll off the tongue.
roll out the red carpet	welcome in a special way, show lots of hospitality	We roll out the red carpet when the Queen comes to Calgary.
roll over and play dead	not try, not compete hard, **give up**	The coach said, "Don't expect the Jets to roll over and play dead."
roll their eyes	eyes express boredom or disapproval	When he told the joke again, the students began rolling their eyes.
roll with the punches	be a flexible competitor, **pick yourself up**	In politics you learn to roll with the punches and keep going.
rolling in it	rich, wealthy, **filthy rich, loaded**	"Is Erica rich?" "My dear, Erica is rolling in it."
rolling in the aisles	laughing so hard they fall out of their chairs	Robin Williams made us laugh. We were rolling in the aisles.
root for	cheer for, **pull for**	Who are you rooting for—the Leafs or les Canadiens?
root of the problem	(See **the root of the problem**)	
rope into	be asked to help, **talk into** helping	We got roped into delivering posters because we have a car.
rot gut	homemade liquor, **hooch, moonshine**	If you drink that rot gut, you'll get sick. It tastes awful!
rotten to the core	all bad, corrupt	Hitler's regime was rotten to the core—corrupt.
rotter	one who cheats or lies, **dirty rat**	Hank, you rotter! You sold me a car that won't start.

Idiom	Meaning	Example
rough and ready	strong and willing, **a game one**	For the oil-well crews, we need people who are rough and ready.
rough going	difficult work, **tough sledding**	It was rough going the first year. We had financial problems.
rough up	beat a little bit, push and slap	The leader roughed me up a bit because I lied to him.
round the clock	(See **around the clock**)	
round up	bring together, chase into a herd	Will you round up the kids and tell them to come inside?
row of beans	(See **a hill of beans**)	
royal pain	(see **a royal pain**)	
royal treatment	special hospitality, **roll out the red carpet**	We received royal treatment when we visited our relatives in Sweden.
rub elbows	work beside, associate with	Fran and I used to rub elbows when we worked at the fish plant.
rub salt in the wound	cause it to be worse, aggravate, **add insult to injury**	If you criticize a student's work in front of the class, you are rubbing salt in the wound.
rub shoulders with	work with, associate with	Art dealers rub shoulders with people from all the professions.
rub the wrong way	bother, irritate, **bug**	That waiter rubs me the wrong way. He's too impatient.
rubber match	final game, showdown	Each team has won a game. They play the rubber match today.
rubberneck	listen to a conversation on a party (co-op) phone line	Grandma used to rubberneck so she could hear the local news.
rube	rural man, **hick**, **square, yokel**	Axel Nelson is a rube—a farmer. He doesn't know about city life.
ruddy	awful, **cotton-picking, darn, friggin**	I can't find the ruddy light switch! Ouch! Here it is. Now we can see.
ruffle your feathers	annoy you, bother you, **get your dander up**	Don't let that insult ruffle your feathers. Don't let it upset you.
rug up	dress warmly, **bundle up**	Rug up, my dear. It's winter in Winnipeg!

Idiom	Meaning	Example
rule of thumb	general rule, guideline	The rule of thumb for a resume is *Don't exceed two pages.*
rumor has it	people say that, **through the grapevine**	Rumor has it you're moving to Tuktoyaktuk. Is that true?
run a red light	go through an intersection when the light is red	The driver of the stolen car ran a red light and hit a truck.
run a tab	charge your purchases, **put it on the bill**	You can run a tab for groceries at my store if you pay every month.
run a tub	turn on the tap and fill the bathtub with water	When you're finished your bath, will you run a tub for me?
run across	discover, happen to see, **run into**	While I was in Vancouver, I ran across an old friend of yours.
run amuck	not go smoothly, **go haywire**	We ran amuck when Gus joined the band. He can't play the tuba!
run an errand	deliver something, go and get something	Paul, please run an errand for me. Take this bread to Aunt Matty.
run circles around you	run faster than you, win easily	Billy can run circles around any boy in school. He's very fast.
run down	go to, walk to	Lu, please run down to the store and get an onion.
run down	check, **look over**, **run through**	Run down the list before we go to the store. Did I miss anything?
run down	criticize, **put down**	Fred doesn't run down his staff. He never says negative things.
run down	tired, in poor condition, **worn out**	His car was a run-down Buick. It belonged in the junk yard.
run for office	be a candidate in an election	I do not plan to run for office this year. I'm leaving politics.
run for the hills	run away to a safe place, run and hide	A tiger has escaped from the zoo! Run for the hills!
run for your money	(See **a run for your money**)	
run into	bump, crash into	My car slid on the ice and I ran into a mail box—knocked it down.
run into	meet by chance, **bump into**, **run across**	Did you run into anyone you know? See any old friends?

Idiom	Meaning	Example
run it by me again	tell me again, **come again**	I didn't get the postal code. Would you run that by me again.
run its course	go until it stops, **take its course**	We don't have a cure for a cold. It will just have to run its course.
run of the mill	average, common, **off the shelf**	It was a run-of-the-mill novel, the story of a man who returns to the place he was born.
run off	make copies at a photocopier	Please run off extra copies of her resume before the job interview.
run off at the mouth	talk a lot, talk when you should be quiet	Why do you run off at the mouth and disturb this class?
run out	use all, not have enough, **run short**	Dad, we've run out of coffee. Will you make some more?
run out of patience	(See **lose patience**)	
run out of town	chase out of town, **the bum's rush**	If you don't pay property taxes they'll run you out of town.
run rampant	spread quickly, go **out of control**	A disease can run rampant in a ghetto. It's difficult to control.
run roughshod	force his way, **step on people**	The foreman is mean. He'll try to run roughshod over you.
run short	have less than you need, **run out**	First we ran out of coffee. Then we ran short of wine.
run the gamut	look at what is available, check the range of choices	We ran the whole gamut of colors but she didn't like any of them.
run the gauntlet	run past the enemy, go through a dangerous area	After three job interviews, I felt like I'd run the gauntlet.
run the risk	be at risk, be unable to control the risk or danger	When you invest in stocks, you run the risk of losing money.
run the show	manage the project, **call the shots**	Talk to Luc if you want to change anything. He's running the show.
run through	practise, read, **go through**	Let's run through the answers again. I want to know them well.
run up	drive to, go to, travel to	I have to run up to Edmonton tomorrow. Do you want to come?
run up	increase, add to a total, **charge it**	Ming lets us run up a bill if we pay it once a month.

Idiom	Meaning	Example
run you out	force you to leave, **the bum's rush**	If they find drugs in your room they'll run you out of the hotel.
run you ragged	make you feel tired, **wear** you **out**	Grade 8 students use up all your energy. They run you ragged.
run-in	argument, fight	Doug had a run-in with the boss yesterday. They had an argument.
runaround	(See **the runaround**)	
running water	tap water, water from a pressure system	At the cabin in the woods we don't have running water.
runt of the litter	the smallest of all the baby animals in one litter	I like the runt of the litter— the smallest kitten.
rush	(See **what a rush**)	
rush hour	the hour of heavy traffic, **bumper to bumper**	During rush hour, many drivers become impatient and angry.
rust out	become rusty, be ruined by rust	Nobody wants that car because it's all rusted out.
rustbucket	a car that is very rusty, **beater**	Can you fix my rustbucket? Can you repair the rusty fenders?
rye	Canadian whisky, whisky made from rye	"What's your favorite drink?" "Rye and Coke."

Idiom	Meaning	Example

S

Idiom	Meaning	Example
sabre-rattling	(See **rattle sabres**)	
sack of hammers	(See **a sack of hammers**)	
sack out	sleep, **catch some z's**, **crash**	If you bring your sleeping bag, you can sack out on the floor.
sacred cow	protected part, the part that must not be changed	If our company is going to change, *everything* should be evaluated— no sacred cows.
sacred moose	(a **sacred cow** in Canada)	
sad sack	(See **a sad sack**)	
saddle up	put a saddle on a horse, place a saddle on a horse	Let's saddle up and ride our ponies to the river.
saddled with	burdened with, responsible for	She doesn't want to be saddled with a bus load of teen-age boys.
salt away	save a little money each month, save tiny amounts	By the time Jake died, he had salted away about $50,000.
salt of the earth	common people; honest, hard-working people	The Swensons are plain, decent people—salt of the earth, eh.
Saskatchewan pheasant	magpie, black and white bird	Two Saskatchewan pheasants flew out of the bush.
Sasquatch	(See **Bigfoot**)	
sassy	rude, impolite, **cheeky**, **lippy**	"I won't go to church!" he said. "Don't be sassy!" Mama said.
save a bundle	save a lot of money, save **big time**	If you buy a new car through a broker, you can save a bundle.
save face	prevent embarrassment, prevent more shame	To save face, the accused member should resign. It's embarrassing.

Idiom	Meaning	Example
save for a rainy day	save money for a time when you really need it	Ed and Vi spend little money. They're saving for a rainy day.
save your bacon	save you from failure or disaster, **save your skin**	If the boat sinks, a life raft may save your bacon.
save your skin/neck	save you from risk, dismissal or death	The dog saved your neck. His barking helped us find you.
saw off a chunk [B]	have sex, have intercourse	I could hear the couple upstairs. They were sawing off a chunk.
saw sawdust	review a decision or failure too many times	"Don't saw sawdust," said the old man. "Don't live in the past."
saw-off	tie game, even score	The game ended in a saw-off: Leafs 3, Flames 3.
say jump...how high	(an idiom to show how one person controls another)	Fritz is afraid of Olga. When she says *jump*, he says *how high*?
say my piece	say what I think, say my **two cents' worth**	When everyone else had spoken, I said my piece.
say the word	say yes or no, tell us when you want to begin	We're waiting for you. Just say the word and we'll start working.
say what	what did you say? **pardon me**?	Say what? Did you insult my pet pig?
say what's on your mind	say what you are thinking, **speak your mind**	Now, Mother, say what's on your mind. Give us your opinion.
say your piece	state your opinion, tell us what you think	OK, Vic, say your piece. Then we can vote on this offer.
scads	lots, many, **oodles**	"Are there any cookies left?" "Yes, scads of them."
scarce as hen's teeth	not many of them, few or none	Rural doctors are scarce as hen's teeth. Doctors like the city life.
scared shitless [B]	very frightened, scared, **petrified**	When I woke up and saw a light on, I was scared shitless.
scared spitless	very frightened, **scared stiff**	Believe me. I was scared spitless when the wolves started to howl.
scared stiff	very frightened, **frightened to death**, **petrified**	"Are you afraid of heights?" "Yes. I'm scared stiff of anything higher than a bicycle seat."

Idiom	Meaning	Example
scared to death	very scared, very anxious, **scared stiff**	I was scared to death that your plane had crashed. I was worried.
scaredy-cat	a person who is afraid, a coward, **fraidy-cat**	The girls will say I'm a scaredy-cat if I don't go in the water.
school of hard knocks	(See **the school of hard knocks**)	
school's out	school is finished for the day or for the year	When the bell rings at 3:30, school's out! Yea!
scoff	steal, **pinch**	People who scoff books from the library are thieves.
scoop	news report, story	What's the scoop on the murder? Do you know who did it?
scoop them	get news before they do, print the story first	The reporter said, "We scooped them all on the Harding story."
score to settle	(See **a score to settle**)	
scot-free	free of work or discipline, not asked to pay, **get off**	Four members of the gang were convicted, but two went scot-free.
scout's honor	what I say is the truth; **the gospel truth**	We didn't take your golf ball — scout's honor.
scrape by	have just enough to live, **get by**	We can scrape by if we sell the car and the TV.
scrape me off the ceiling	help me become normal or recover from shock	If I win a million dollars, you'll have to scrape me off the ceiling.
scrape the bottom of the barrel	use the last ones or the worst ones, **seconds**	He's a bad referee. We scraped the bottom of the barrel to find him.
scratch	money, cash, **bread, moola**	If we sell these bottles, we'll have enough scratch to buy cigarettes.
scratch	remove from the list, cancel	I saw the list of players on the team. I've been scratched.
scratch the surface	barely begin, uncover only a few facts	His first lecture on Stravinsky only scratched the surface.
scratch your head	feel confused, wonder who or why	They're still scratching their heads about who assassinated Kennedy.
screech	homemade liquor, **hooch, moonshine**	We can't afford a bottle of gin, so I bought a jug of screech.

Idiom	Meaning	Example
screw [B]	have sex with, **make love**	When he heard the bed squeaking he knew they were screwing.
screw loose	(See **a screw loose**)	
screw up	perform poorly, ruin it, **blow it**	I hope I don't screw up when I take my driver's test.
screw you [B]	the worst to you, **up yours** [B]	After I defeated him, he said, "Screw you." He hates to lose.
screw-up	a careless mistake, a bungled job	Those screw-ups were his fault. He forgot to order materials.
scrut	oh no, **darn**, **nuts**, **rats**	Scrut! My bike has a flat tire!
scum/scumbag	unpleasant person, **dirty rat**, **slimebucket**	"Scum!" he shouted at the man who had attacked his daughter.
search me	I do not have the answer, I do not know	"Who took my Coke?" "Search me. I don't know."
second fiddle	(See **play second fiddle**)	
second guess	guess what people think or what they will do	Don't try to second guess people. Ask them what you need to know.
second nature	natural ability or interest, talent	Skating is second nature to Paul. He's got natural skating ability.
second wind	a feeling that your energy is returning as you run	In a 10 K race, I usually get my second wind after 15 minutes.
seconds	second-rate products, products with flaws	For work, I buy seconds—shirts and pants with minor flaws.
seconds	second helpings of food, more food on your plate	Mom, can we have seconds? This is great apple pudding!
see	**date**, **go out with**, **hang out** with	Derek is seeing Angie. Aren't they a nice couple?
see a man about a dog	go to the bathroom or washroom	Excuse me. I have to see a man about a dog.
see eye to eye	agree, have similar views or opinions, **on the same wavelength**	Bob and Sue don't see eye to eye on religion. He's an atheist and she's a Christian.
see fit	decide it is right, decide it is good	I hope you will see fit to approve their request for assistance.

Idiom	Meaning	Example
see hide nor hair	not see a person because he has gone	You won't see hide nor hair of him after he borrows money.
see it through	work until you finish, **follow through**	If you renovate the kitchen, please see it through. Finish it.
see me for dust	not see me because I leave so fast, **tail lights**	If a sumo wrestler chased me, you wouldn't see me for dust.
see red	become angry, **burn up**	When she interrupts me, I see red. I get really angry.
see the light	understand, become aware	Now I see the light. I understand. You multiply first, then divide.
see the light of day	be exposed, be revealed	The treasure was buried, never again to see the light of day.
see through	see the real reason, see your motive	Mom saw through me. She knew I wanted the money for cigarettes.
see to it/see to that	be certain that it is done, be responsible for doing it	The doors should be open at 7. Ken, will you see to that?
see you/see your	match your bet, bet as much as you did	I'll see your $50 and raise you $100. That's my bet.
see you stuck	(See **won't see you stuck**)	
see you through	allow you to survive, help you pay the bills	Here's $100. Will that see you through till the end of the month?
see your way	be able to, afford to	Can you see your way to give $50 to the Food Bank?
seeing things	imagine that you see things, hallucinate	If John said there's a ghost in the house, he must be seeing things.
seek revenge	try to hurt a person who hurt you, **get back at**	If a dog bites you, there are many ways to seek revenge.
seen better days	not in good condition, **worn out**	This jacket has seen better days. Look how the sleeves are worn.
seen dead in	(See **wouldn't be caught dead in**)	
seize the opportunity	act now to gain most, **take advantage of**	He seized the opportunity to invest in gold. He didn't wait.
self-made man	one who succeeds by his own efforts	Ming built his business by himself. He's a self-made man.

Idiom	Meaning	Example
self-starter	a person who will begin to work without a supervisor; **a go-getter**	We're looking for self starters— people who can begin a job and work by themselves.
sell like hotcakes	sell many, sell fast	Hockey cards sell like hotcakes. The kids collect them.
sell out	sell a business, sell all assets	Grandpa was 60 years old when he sold out and moved to Victoria.
sell out	sell information or support	The Bible tells us that Judas sold out to the bad guys.
sell the farm	over-react, sell everything to invest in a new venture	They've discovered diamonds in B.C., but don't sell the farm, eh.
sell yourself short	not mention some of your skills or qualifications	If the employer asks about your awards, don't sell yourself short.
selling point	best feature, nicest part	The Peugeot's strongest selling point is comfort.
send a bouquet	compliment a person, announce a compliment	I would like send a bouquet to the volunteers at the Food Bank.
send him flying	trip him, cause him to fall, **ass over teakettle**	His motorcycle hit a rock and sent him flying into the ditch.
send him up	send him to prison, find evidence to convict him	The criminal threatened to kill the policeman who sent him up.
sense of humor	knowing what is funny, ability to see a joke	He has a broad sense of humor. He laughs at himself and others.
sentence to death	say that a person will be killed because he is guilty	After the jury said he was guilty, the judge sentenced him to death.
serious coin	a lot of money, **big bucks**	Membership in the Pines Golf Club will cost you serious coin.
serve notice	state your plans, say what you will do, **spread the word**	If you enter the novel contest, you are serving notice that you are a serious writer.
serve the purpose	do the job, accomplish the task	If you don't have an organ, a piano will serve the purpose.
serve them right	give them what they deserve	If they cheat on a test, it serves them right if they get an *F*.
set a spell	sit down for awhile, **visit a spell**	Hannah had to set a spell after doing the chores. She rested.

Idiom	Meaning	Example
set about	begin, start	After we found the problem with the car, we set about fixing it.
set fire	start a fire, light a fire	A child playing with a cigarette lighter set fire to the curtains.
set foot	walk, step, come for a visit	He hasn't set foot in this house since his mother died.
set for life	have enough money to last a lifetime	He inherited a lot of money. He's set for life.
set in	begin, start	He had a cold. Then pneumonia set in, and it nearly killed him.
set in her ways	having old habits, not able to change easily	After living alone for fifty years, Florence was set in her ways.
set of wheels	vehicle, car, truck, **wheels**	The Ford needs a lot of repairs. I need a new set of wheels.
set off	start, trigger	Who set off the fire alarm? Who pushed the button?
set out	place where you can see it, put where it can be used	Tomorrow we go to the lake, so set out your swim suit and towel.
set out for	leave, embark	Then we set out for Pluto, where it's much colder than the arctic.
set out to	plan to, hope to	"What did you set out to do?" "I wanted to change the world."
set the table	set plates and cutlery on the table	If you will set the table, I won't ask you to wash the dishes.
set the world on fire	do great things, achieve fame and wealth	I don't want to set the world on fire. I just want a career.
set up shop	organize a place to do business, buy a store	You could set up shop and sell this pizza. It's delicious!
set you back	pay, pay for, cost you	That looks like a fine camera. How much did it set you back?
set you straight	give you the facts, tell you how it is	If you want to know who's got the gold, Pat will set you straight.
set you up	cause you to appear guilty, **frame** you	We know you didn't steal your friend's car. He set you up.
set your mind at ease	help you to stop worrying, cause you to relax	Here is some news to set your mind at ease: the kids are safe.

Idiom	Meaning	Example
set your price	choose a price for an item you want to sell	If you want to sell it quickly, set your price lower than the others.
set your sights	choose a goal, decide what you want to get	If you set your sights on being a doctor, I will help you.
set your teeth on edge	irritate, irk, **bug**	Some songs set my teeth on edge—really bother me.
set-to	argument, fight	After playing cards, the brothers had a set-to. They argued.
set-up	plan, scheme	Here's the set-up: You buy the tickets; I'll collect the money.
settle down	be calm, relax, **chill out**	Let's wait until the baby settles down. Then we can eat.
settle down	live in one town or city, **put down roots**	We moved from place to place before we settled down in Guelph.
settle in	become comfortable in a new house or apartment	We'd like to get settled in before we have visitors.
settle it	decide what is fair, work for an agreement	If the dispute is about property lines, a survey will settle it.
seven come eleven	7 followed by 11 are lucky numbers	"Seven come eleven," he whispered as he threw the dice.
shabby	worn, torn, ragged, **lousy, mousy**	I love these shabby old slippers. They're ragged but comfortable.
shack up [B]	live together before you get married, live common-law	"Tarzan and Jane are shacked up." "Oh, I hope they're happy."
shades	sunglasses, tinted glasses	Erica looks cool in her shades. She looks like a model.
shades of	like, similar to	That building looks familiar— shades of our old school.
shady deal	unfair business deal, **a rip-off**	Cal is a good salesman, but he's put together some shady deals.
shaft	cheat, swindle, **screwed** [B]	Tom got shafted. He only got 3% commission on his sales.
shagging wagon	a van designed for relaxing and having sex	Tony's van has a bar and a bed. It's his shaggin' wagon.

Idiom	Meaning	Example
shake a habit	quit a habit, **kick a habit**	It's difficult to shake the habits you learn as a child.
shake a leg	hurry, **move it**	Shake a leg or you'll be late for work. Hurry!
shake a stick at	(See **more than you can shake a stick at**)	
shake hands	be friends after a fight, agree the fight is over	They argue for hours, but they always shake hands afterward.
shake him	make him nervous, cause him to lose confidence	Even the divorce didn't shake him. He didn't change at all.
shake on it	shake hands to show you agree on a price or a deal	After they agree on a price, they shake on it. It's a deal.
shaky ground	(See **on shaky ground**)	
shape up	improve, reform, **get it together**	The coach told us to shape up— to come to practice on time.
shape up or ship out	improve your work or go away, **if you can't cut it...**	"Soldiers must obey orders," the officer said. "You will learn to shape up or ship out."
shareware	computer programs that people share	Shareware will help us to save money. We'll share software.
sharp	intelligent, quick to learn	Geoff is a sharp kid. He's doing calculus at the age of twelve.
sharp	sarcastic, abrupt	Even when Anne was tired, she never gave you a sharp reply.
sharp	at a specific time, **on the dot**	The preacher began the service on time—at 11 a.m. sharp.
sharp as a tack	quick to understand, able to think quickly	He may be 85, but he's sharp as a tack—plays chess every day.
sharpen up	think carefully, use your intelligence	If I make a mistake, I don't want him telling me to sharpen up.
sharpen your pencils	be ready, be prepared	Let's sharpen our pencils, gang. We have to set some goals.
shekel	dollar, coin, **buck, loonie**	He earns a few shekels a day by selling bottles that he finds.
shed a little light on	explain, enlighten, help you understand,	To shed a little light on the topic of idioms, we'll read this book.

Idiom	Meaning	Example
shed a tear	cry, weep	He hides his emotions. When his dog died, he didn't shed a tear.
shell out	pay money for, **fork over**	How much did you shell out for that calculator? Thirty dollars?
shellack	defeat in a game, win by many points	The Bears were shellacked by the Pirates. The score was 19-2.
shirty	impolite, rude, **cheeky**, **lippy**	Brad has an attitude. He gets a little shirty with teachers.
shit disturber [B]	a person who tries to cause problems	Cal is a shit disturber. He tries to embarrass the boss at meetings.
shit faced [B]	very drunk, **plastered**, **polluted**	He goes to the bar every day and drinks until he's shit faced.
shit hit the fan [B]	(See **the shit hit the fan**)	
shit hot [B]	very skilled, talented	I've played golf with him. He's not so shit hot.
shit list [B]	(See **on the shit list**)	
shit myself [B]	so surprised or scared that I shit in my pants	When lightning struck the tree beside me, I nearly shit myself.
shit out of luck [B]	have no more, none left for you	There are no tickets left. We're shit out of luck.
shit-head [B]	stupid or foolish person, **dipstick**, **jerk**	What a shit-head! He put water in the gas tank!
shitting bricks [B]	very frightened, **scared to death**	When my parachute didn't open, I was shitting bricks!
shitty [B]	bad behavior, awful, **crappy**	He borrowed your car and took your girl? That's pretty shitty.
shmooze	visit with, be friendly, **rub shoulders with**	You don't have to sell wine. Just shmooze with the clients.
shmuck	foolish person, **jerk**, **nerd**	You shmuck! Stop squeezing toothpaste on me!
shoe-in	(See **a shoe-in**)	
shoot	tell me, say it, I am listening, **fire away**	"Do you have any news?" "No. Just a rumor." "Shoot. I love rumors."

Idiom	Meaning	Example
shoot it out	shoot at each other, shoot until one is killed	The thief decided to shoot it out with the police.
shoot the breeze	talk, visit, chat, **chew the fat**	Hank and I were drinking beer and shooting the breeze.
shoot the shit [B]	visit, have a conversation, **a chin wag**	The ladies went shopping, and the men sat around shootin' the shit.
shoot up	inject an illegal drug, get **a hit, do drugs**	One of the addicts was in the bathroom shooting up.
shoot up	shoot guns to celebrate and scare people	The cowboys used to get drunk and shoot up the town.
shoot your mouth off	talk without thinking, **blab, squeal**	Moe won't shoot his mouth off. He won't tell anybody.
shoot your wad	spend all your money, use all you have	If you shoot your wad today, what will you spend tomorrow?
shoot yourself in the foot	ruin your chances, **cut off your nose... your own worst enemy**	If you want the job, don't be late for the interview. Don't shoot yourself in the foot.
shoot-out (sports)	taking shots at each goal to determine the winner	Sweden won the gold medal by defeating Canada in a shoot-out.
shoot-out	a gunbattle, a duel	Two men died in the shoot-out: one **cop** and one robber.
shoot-up	shoot guns in the air without aiming	Do you remember the shoot-ups in the old western movies?
shooting fish in a barrel	a task that is too easy, a game without challenge	We won 18-2. It was like shooting fish in a barrel.
shooting match	(See **the whole shooting match**)	
shoplifting	stealing products from a store while you shop	He's charged with shoplifting. He stole some cigarettes.
short cut	a shorter path, a quicker method, **quick and dirty**	To become an actor, you learn the skills and work very hard. There are no short cuts.
short end of the stick	(See **the short end of the stick**)	
short one	(See **a short one**)	
short temper	quick to become angry, **hot tempered**	Dr. Jones has a short temper. He gets mad very quickly.

Idiom	Meaning	Example
short with me	cross, abrupt, curt, **cut me off**	Mrs. Gore was short with me. I wonder if she's angry.
shortchange	not return enough money to the purchaser, **a rip-off**	I gave the clerk $10 for a book costing $6.95 and got $2.05 back. Was I shortchanged?
shortfall	loss, deficit	Shoplifting is one of the reasons for the shortfall—for the deficit.
shot	worn, broken, ruined, **had it**	When they returned my bike, the gears were shot—worn out.
shot in the arm	(See **a shot in the arm**)	
shot in the dark	(See **a shot in the dark**)	
shoulder the blame	accept the blame, **take the rap**	The managers agreed to shoulder the blame for the error? Sure.
shoulder to shoulder	working beside him/her, **side by side**	Poet and peasant stood shoulder to shoulder during the war.
shoulder to the wheel	(See **put your shoulder to the wheel**)	
shove down my throat	force me to accept it, force me to agree to that, **eat that**	The preacher said that babies are sinners. He's not going to shove that down my throat.
shove it	put it away, **forget it**, **stuff it**	If that dental plan pays only half the cost, they can shove it.
show promise	show some of your ability, show that you will develop	Len shows promise as a teacher. He is patient and articulate.
show up	attend, go to class or work	Vi shows up every week for her lesson. She's always on time.
show you around	show you where things are, guide you	When we get to the ranch, follow me. I'll show you around.
show you the ropes	teach you the first steps, **learn the ropes**	It is my duty to take you to the plant and show you the ropes.
show you up	be better than you, cause you to look inferior	If you play tennis with Martina, she'll show you up. She's good!
show your stuff	do your best, show what you can do	When it's your turn to dance, show your stuff. Impress them!
show-off	one who displays, **showboat**	Ron is the show-off in our class. He's always advertising himself.

Idiom	Meaning	Example
showboat	a person who displays, a **show-off**	The peacock is one of nature's showboats—he's magnificent!
showdown	final fight or contest, **rubber match**	Ali defeated Frazier in the boxing showdown of the '70s.
shrink/head shrink	psychiatrist, therapist	If I can't manage my personal life, I can always visit a shrink.
shrinking violet	(See **no shrinking violet**)	
shrug it off	not let it affect you or bother you	He was hurt by the remark, but he shrugged it off and kept working.
shuck on down to the fraidy hole	go to the cellar for shelter from a cyclone or tornado, hide when you are afraid	When my uncle saw the sky turn black in the afternoon, he would shuck on down to the fraidy hole.
shucks	oh dear, well, **gee heck**	Aw shucks, Beth Ann, you know I care a whole lot for you.
shut down	stop operating, quit	Without electricity, the factory will have to shut down.
shut up	do not talk, **keep quiet**	"Shut up!" he yelled at the dog. "Be quiet or I'll muzzle you!"
shut your face	stop talking, **shut up**	When I told him he was a racist, he said, "Shut your face."
shut-down	closure, end of operations	Cold weather sometimes causes a shut-down of our schools.
shut-in	someone who is ill and cannot go outside	Our priest visits the shut-ins— people who must stay at home.
shutout (sports)	no goals scored against a goal keeper in one game	Our goalie has three shutouts this season—three zeros!
sick at heart	sad, sorrowful	Papa was sick at heart after the hailstorm ruined our crop.
sick of	not interested any more, bored by, **tired of**	We're sick of his jokes because he repeats them.
sick to death	wishing for a change, **fed up**, **sick of**	People are sick to death of the debate on gun control. They've heard too much about guns.
sicko	weird person, pervert, psycho **scumbag**	"Who would pour ketchup all over my car?" "Oh, some sicko, I guess."

Idiom	Meaning	Example
side by side	standing/walking beside, **shoulder to shoulder**	The children were standing side by side on the stairs.
sight for sore eyes	(See **a sight for sore eyes**)	
sign in	sign your name to show you are in the building	Be sure to sign in. We want to know that you are safe inside.
sign off	say good-bye, close, stop writing or talking	"I'll sign off now, but I'll write again soon. With love, Kim."
sign out	sign your name to borrow something, **on loan**	If you want to sign out a book you will need a library card.
sign up	sign the list, enrol, enlist	"Did you sign up for lessons?" "Yes. My name is on the list."
silence is golden	silence is wonderful, silence is peaceful	After a day of teaching grade two students, silence is golden.
silkhead	bald person, **chromedome**	If you were a silkhead, would you wear a toupee?
silver spoon	(See **born with a silver spoon in his mouth**)	
silver-tongued	nice-talking, **smooth talker**	A silver-tongued salesman sold me this car, but I can't drive!
sin bin (hockey)	(See **the sin bin**)	
sing his praises	praise him a lot, talk **in glowing terms**	His mom is always singing his praises, saying he's a good boy.
sing up a storm	sing loud, sing vigorously	After dinner we gathered around the piano and sang up a storm.
single out	choose one person from a group	Why does the priest single me out for extra duties? Why me?
sinking feeling	feeling of failure; despair	When I saw the ambulance at our house, I got a sinking feeling.
sit in judgement on	judge someone's actions, evaluate	Gary is afraid because you sit in judgement on whatever he does.
sit the fence	not choose either side, try to be in the middle	People don't like politicians who try to sit the fence.
sit tight	not move, wait here	I'll go and buy the hotdogs. You sit tight until I get back.
sit with you	relate to you, appeal to you	If we build a fence on your land, how would that sit with you?

Idiom	Meaning	Example
sitting duck	(See **a sitting duck**)	
sitting pretty	in a good position, in favorable circumstances	Rich in oil and timber resources, Alberta was sitting pretty.
six bits	seventy-five cents, 3 x **two bits**	Grandfather told us that he used to pay six bits for a hotel room.
six of one, half a dozen of the other	nearly equal, about the same, like twins	Panasonic and Quasar are very similar—it's six of one, half a dozen of the other.
sixes and sevens	(See **at sixes and sevens**)	
size up	evaluate, **check over**	The teacher sized up the new student. He looked scared.
skaters	skate boarders, boarders	The skaters were asked to leave the downtown area.
skedaddle	leave, go, **off with you**, **vamoose**	"Get out of here! Skedaddle!" the old man shouted at the boys.
skeleton in the closet	unpleasant secrets, old scandals	Every family has a skeleton in the closet—a dark secret or two.
skids	drug users, **heads**, **heavy metal types**	A few skids were playing video games at the mall.
skinhead	youth with a short haircut, member of the Nazi Party	Three skinheads shouted "Heil!" as they marched up the street.
skinny dip	swimming naked, in the buff	They took off their clothes and went for a skinny dip in the lake.
skip classes	miss classes, not attend classes, **play hooky**	Riza had low grades in history because he skipped classes.
skunk	not score one goal, **goose egg**	In the final game we got skunked 6-0. We were humiliated.
slackass [B]	lazy person, **lazybones**	Larry, you slackass, get over here and help us load the truck!
slam	criticize, insult, **knock**, **put down**	The newspaper article slammed the government for being slow to help the flood victims.
slammer	(See **in the slammer**)	
slash and burn	reduce and cut programs without care or mercy	To save money, the Government used slash-and-burn policies.

Idiom	Meaning	Example
sleep around [B]	sleep with and make love to many partners	Harry was sleeping around before his wife divorced him.
sleep in	sleep until late in the morning	Don't call me until after lunch tomorrow. I'm going to sleep in.
sleep it off	sleep until you are sober, sleep until you feel normal	"That medicine made me drowsy." "Go to bed and sleep it off."
sleeper	ordinary device with surprising skill or power	The Taurus SHO was a sleeper. It looked slow, but it was fast!
sleepy head	a child who is tired or sleepy	Go to bed, sleepy head. I'll see you in the morning.
slim chance	(See **a slim chance**)	
slimebucket [B]	crude, immoral person; **scumbag**	Only a slimebucket—a pervert— would molest a child.
slip	become lower, **lose ground**	My grades slipped last semester. My average dropped from B to C.
slip a notch	be less skilful, not perform as well	After the age of 30, your physical skills may slip a notch or two.
slip away	go away quietly, sneak out	While the men watched the fight, the boys slipped away unnoticed.
slip away	die, **pass away**	Grandma slipped away during the night. She was gone by morning.
slip of the tongue	(See **a slip of the tongue**)	
slip out	leave quietly, **slip away**	I'll slip out and check the parking meter. Be right back.
slip out	speak carelessly, say it without thinking	I didn't mean to answer, Sir. The words just slipped out.
slip up	cause a small mistake, **make a booboo**	The singer didn't slip up once— not even a little mistake.
slip your mind	forget, not remember	I met her at church last Sunday but her name slips my mind.
slippery slope	dangerous path, a path that leads to problems	When you assume that people are bad, you are on a slippery slope.
sloshed to the gills	very drunk, **loaded**, **plastered**,	She was sloshed to the gills and singing very badly.

Idiom	Meaning	Example
slow as a dead snail	(See **as slow as a dead snail**)	
slow as molasses...	(See **as slow as molasses in January**)	
slow day	a day with few customers, a day with little activity	We had another slow day at the theatre—only six customers!
slow down	go slower, **ease up**	Please slow down for the bumps. You're driving too fast.
slowpoke	a person who is working slower than the others	I'm a slowpoke! I've done only one question; you've done six!
sluff off	not do, avoid doing	I've been sluffing off. I'm behind in my assignments.
slug away	work slowly but steadily, **plug away**	When we returned, Annie was still slugging away at her math.
slug of	(See **a slug of**)	
smack dab in the middle	directly in the middle, in the center	The ball landed smack dab in the middle of the pizza.
smack of	is similar to, **shades of**	Even the phrase *person of color* smacks of racism. Don't use it.
small potatoes	unimportant things, insignificant matters	Don't worry about a few broken dishes. They're small potatoes.
small talk	talk about unimportant topics—the weather etc.	Winnie is good at making small talk with strangers.
smart ass [B]	a person who tries to be witty, **cocky**, **lippy**	"What do you want to drink?" "Do you have breast milk?" "Don't be a smart ass!"
smarten up	be smarter, do not be stupid	People who drink and drive should smarten up.
smarts	intelligence, mental ability	Jen gets good grades. She has the smarts to win a scholarship.
smashed	drunk, **hammered**, **wasted**	She gets smashed on gin and dances around the living room.
smashing	very beautiful, very attractive	Nicole looks absolutely smashing in that red dress.
smell blood	sense victory, be aware of an opponent's weakness	Michael is a fierce competitor. When he smells blood, he wins.
smidge/smidgeon	(See **just a smidgeon**)	

Idiom	Meaning	Example
smithwright it	throw it in the garbage, **chuck it**, **junk it**	If the drawing isn't perfect, we smithwright it—throw it out.
smoke and mirrors	false impressions, deceit, trickery, **bafflegab**	His speech about new projects is just smoke and mirrors. The company is bankrupt.
smoke like a furnace	smoke a lot of cigarettes, **chain smoke**	He died of lung cancer. He used to smoke like a furnace.
smoking gun	weapon used, evidence, **caught red-handed**	The company told me to dismiss the employee, so I was holding the smoking gun.
smooth out	solve a problem or argument	The counsellor smoothed out our problem. We're friends again.
smooth sailing	easy job, an operation that has no problems	After we paid the bank for our loan, it was smooth sailing.
smooth talker	one who says nice words, **butter wouldn't melt...**	Janet is such a smooth talker! She should be in politics.
snag	problem, difficulty, **glitch**	If you plan a project carefully, there will be fewer snags.
snap	(See **it's a snap**)	
snap a picture	(See **take a picture**)	
snap at	speak in a harsh tone, answer sharply	If I talk to you while you're watching TV, you snap at me.
snapped	drunk, **loaded**, **looped**	Whenever he gets snapped, he wants to fight.
snatch victory from the jaws of defeat	win when it appears that you will lose, **mount a comeback**	The opinion polls showed we were losing, but we snatched victory from the jaws of defeat.
snazzy	stylish, **neat**, **way cool**	That's a snazzy suit, George. It looks great on you.
snootful	(See **a snootful**)	
snotty-nosed kid	a child, a boy with a dirty face	I was just a snotty-nosed kid when I got my first job.
snow job	(See **a snow job**)	
snow them	fool them, tell them a false story	You can't snow them. They know if you're telling a lie.

Idiom	Meaning	Example
snowball	grow, become bigger, spread to other people	Among students, discontent can snowball. It can spread rapidly.
snowbirds	Canadians who go south for the winter	It's November, and the snowbirds are leaving Alberta for Arizona.
snug as a bug in a rug	warm and comfortable, **cocoon**	In this nice apartment, you'll be snug as a bug in a rug.
so and so	a person you dislike, a name you forget	Who invited that so and so to the party? I don't like him!
so far, so good	doing fine this far, good this far	After I had read one page, she said, "So far, so good."
so help me	I will need help to stop, I will need help if I do it	If that dog barks tonight, so help me, I'm going to get the shotgun!
so long	good-bye, see you later	So long, my friends. I have to leave you now.
so much as	this much will anger me, very little will anger me	If that cat so much as touches the baby, I'll tie up its tail!
so quiet you can hear a pin drop	very quiet, very still	The teacher said, "Class, try to be so quiet you can hear a pin drop."
so small you could barely swing a cat	very small room, narrow room	The bedroom was so small you could barely swing a cat in it.
so small you had to back out to change your mind	very small, tiny, as small as a phone booth	I've seen small apartments, but this one was so small you had back out to change your mind.
so to speak	using idioms, expressions, & sayings when speaking; to use metaphors	Ron was up the creek, so to speak. He'd promised to marry Suzy, but he was already married to Joan.
sob story	a sad story, a story about love lost or misfortune, **cry the blues**	Have you heard Keiko's sob story? She lost her boyfriend and her cat on the same day.
sober up	become sober, wait until you are not drunk	Give him a few hours to sober up. He'll be okay after he has a rest.
sock it to me	tell me, give it to me, **hit me**, **shoot**	"It's bad news," he said. "Sock it to me," I said.
soft in the head	foolish, crazy	If you quit your job at Gulf Oil, you're soft in the head.

Idiom	Meaning	Example
soft market	a period when sales are few and prices are low	The real estate market is soft now. Don't try to sell your house.
soft pedal	say it is not important, **downplay**	The government is trying to soft pedal their failures.
soft spot	(See **have a soft spot for**)	
soften up	cause a person to be more co-operative	Ty is stubborn about his right to smoke. You can't soften him up.
soften your stance	cause you to change your opinion or position	If his friends go against him, he may soften his stance.
software	computer programs, **courseware**	This accounting software is very easy to use.
sold on	believe in, convinced of	I'm sold on this new herbal drink. It gives me energy.
soldier on	continue working; serving well; **carry on**	When the others quit searching, the family soldiered on, hoping to find their lost girl.
some attitude	a little ego or anger or **lip**, some of your bad side	When you play this part, give us some attitude. Be a bit of a rebel.
some chick	beautiful **chick**, great woman	Gloria is some chick! Will you introduce me to her?
something borrowed, something blue	two of the things required for a happy wedding and successful marriage	The bride borrowed a blue garter, so she has something borrowed, something blue!
something is haywire	something is wrong or broken, **haywire**	Something is haywire with my back. I can't move.
something is rotten...	(See **there's something rotten in Denmark**)	
something snapped	the brain broke, the mind failed	Something snapped when he was in the war. Now he can't speak.
sometimes life is a bucket of shit and the handle is inside [B]	sometimes life is very unpleasant, **life is not all guns and roses**	The junk dealer had a poster on the wall of his shack: *Sometimes life is a bucket of shit, and the handle's inside!*
Sophie's choice	choosing between the death of you or your child	He was facing a Sophie's choice: Lose his son or lose his own life.
soul mate	one who is your natural and compatible mate	I thought Carson and I were soul mates, but we disagree a lot.

Idiom	Meaning	Example
sound asleep	sleeping peacefully, **dead to the world**	When Tara went to check the baby, he was sound asleep.
sound bite	radio advertisement, a few seconds of radio time	I advertise our hotel on the radio using ten-second sound bites.
sound off	complain, **get it off your chest, speak out**	He was sounding off about our papers—how bad they were.
sounding board	a person who listens to ideas or plans	Cliff used Linda as a sounding board for his business plans.
sour grapes	feeling negative because you did not win	If she loses, she complains about the referee. It's just sour grapes.
sour puss	one who is feeling sad, an unhappy person	Don't be such a sour puss. Let's have fun.
southpaw	left-handed person, **lefty**	Our baseball team needs another pitcher—preferably a southpaw.
sow wild oats	live a wild life as a young person	As a youth he lived a reckless life. He sowed a few wild oats.
spaced out	feeling strange or unreal, **stoned**	After falling, Jeff was spaced out. He looked dazed and limp.
spade work	first stage of the work, preparation for later work, **pave the way**	Paul did the spade work for our food bank. He asked each of the merchants for a donation.
spare me	please do not tell me, do not bore me with	Spare me the gross details of your love affairs. I'm not interested.
speak highly of	praise, say that a person is great or excellent	Angela's former teachers speak very highly of her.
speak out	say what you think, **speak your mind**	Did you speak out at the meeting? Did you tell them what is wrong?
speak up	speak louder, **crank it up**	Please speak up so everyone can hear you.
speak volumes	tells a lot, reveals much	Your smile speaks volumes about your career. You like it.
speak your mind	say what you think or feel, **speak out**	We want you to speak your mind on this issue. State your opinion.
speed up	go faster, accelerate, **step on it**	Don't speed up when you come to an intersection. Slow down!

Idiom	Meaning	Example
spell disaster	cause an accident, lead to a tragedy	An error in the design of a car could spell disaster for the driver.
spell out	explain carefully, explain each word or step	If I don't understand a question, I ask him to spell it out for me.
spell you off	do your job for you, allow you to rest	When you get tired of shoveling, I'll spell you off for awhile.
spend holidays	do during your holidays, go for your holidays	"How'd you spend your holidays?" "We drove to Texas and Tijuana."
spend time	wait, **hang out**, **put in time**	I spend a lot of time at her place. I'm there every day.
spending money	extra money, money for fun, **pin money**	Wayne earns spending money by washing the neighbors' cars.
spice of life	(See **the spice of life**)	
spice up	add spices or flavor, **jazz up**	The chili tastes good, but let's spice it up a bit.
spiffy	clean and tidy, groomed, **tiddly**	Grandpa, your car looks real spiffy. Did you polish it?
spike a drink	put alcohol in a drink of juice or pop or coffee	Somebody must have spiked my drink. I feel quite dizzy.
spike the ball	hit the ball sharply over the net	Gary's ability to spike the ball gives our team an advantage.
spill the beans	tell a secret, tell others about it, **spill your guts**	Don't tell Sammy about our plan. He'll spill the beans.
spill your guts	tell everything you know, **spill the beans**	Don't spill your guts to your mom. Don't tell her about our problems.
spin a yarn	tell a story, **make up** a story	We love to hear Norman spin a yarn. His stories seem so real.
spin crew	speech-writing crew, hired writers	The spin crew will tell me if I should say *racial* or *ethnic*.
spin doctor	a speech writer, an advisor to a politician	The spin doctor told us to say *disability*, not *handicap*.
spin the bottle	a game to decide who is to kiss whom	When we played spin the bottle, Mavis always got to kiss Ron.
spin your wheels	waste effort, not progress	If you don't have a career goal you'll just spin your wheels.

Idiom	Meaning	Example
spinny	a little crazy, eccentric, **batty**	Their family is kind of weird. Even the cat is a little spinny.
spinork/spinorky	attractive, **cool**, **groovy**, **neat**	That's a spinork sweater, Ted. It looks great on you.
spirit away	take away mysteriously, steal secretly, **into thin air**	Somebody or something spirits away my fingernail clippers. I wonder where they are.
spitting mad	very angry, **pissed off** [B]	Mom was spitting mad when you ran across her flower garden.
spitting nails	very angry, very mad, **hot, pissed** [B]	Art was spitting nails when my dog scratched the paint on his car.
splashback	reaction from the public, **fallout**, **feedback**	"Is there any splashback on the new income tax policy?" "Yes. It's all positive."
split	depart, go, leave	I gotta split. Class starts in two minutes.
split a gut	laugh very hard, **crack me up**	I nearly split a gut watching a John Candy video—hilarious!
split hairs	be very fussy, notice small differences	Clyde likes to work on research that requires him to split hairs.
split second	small difference in time, a fraction of a second	Many Olympic athletes win their events by a split second.
split the difference	divide the difference between the prices	Your price is $100. I'm offering $80. Let's split the difference.
split up	separate, **part company**	Charles and Di split up in the 90s. They were separated when she died.
spoil for a fight	try to begin a fight, **chip on his shoulder**, **cruising for a bruising**	Bud was spoiling for a fight with me. He said, "You're too chicken to fight, ain't you?"
spoiled brat	a child who always gets what he wants	Sure he's a spoiled brat. His mom gave him whatever he wanted.
spoilsport	one who will not play, **party-pooper**	You spoilsport! Why won't you play strip poker with us?
spot of tea	(See **a spot of tea**)	
spot on	correct, **bang on**, **dead on, right on**	Your answer is spot on! There are 1000 meters in a kilometre.

Idiom	Meaning	Example
spotcheck	check anytime, inspect whenever you wish	The prison guard did spotchecks on the men during the night.
spread like wildfire	spread quickly, **go public**	News of the assassination spread like wildfire.
spread out	lie down with your arms and legs apart	When you spread out on the sofa, there's no room for me.
spread the word	tell everybody, **get the word out**	The teacher asked us to spread the word about the school concert.
spring for	pay for, **pay the shot**	"Who will spring for the pizza?" "Jack will. He just got paid."
spruced up	(See **all spruced up**)	
spur on	encourage, motivate	Her refusal of his gifts seemed to spur him on. It challenged him.
square	not sophisticated, not **cool**, **rube**	What a square! He thinks Rolex is some kind of cereal!
square	(See **call it square**)	
square deal	fair to the purchaser, value for money spent	You get a square deal when you buy a tractor at Al's Machinery.
square meal	full meal: meat, bread, vegetables and milk	We need at least one square meal each day. Do you agree?
square off	face each other ready to fight, have a fight	If Joe and Bud square off, it will be an interesting fight.
square one	the beginning, **back to square one**	If you answer incorrectly, you have to start at square one.
square shooter	fair dealer, honest person	Sidney is a square shooter. He won't cheat you.
square up	pay a debt, pay your share	Cal told me you owe him $50. He's wants you to square up.
square up	leave prostitution or life on the street	I've heard there's a group that helps prostitutes square up.
squat	a place to stay, a shelter for street people, a shack	"Where's your squat?" "Across the tracks in a deserted service station."
squeaky clean	very clean, innocent	I've checked Todd's record. He's clean—squeaky clean.

Idiom	Meaning	Example
squeal	tell the police, **rat on**	Robbie won't squeal on us. He'll never tell what we did.
squealer	one who tells the police or authorities, **canary**	Jason, you squealer! You told the teacher I copied your work.
squirrel away	save, hide, put in a safe place, **salt away**	You can have your own pension if you squirrel away a few dollars each month.
stack up	compare with, **pale by comparison**	The Lincoln is a nice car, but how does it stack up against the Lexus?
stacked	having large breasts, having big **boobs**, **sweater girl**	"Please describe the woman." "She was tall, blond and, well, you might say she was stacked."
stag	party for a man who will soon be married	Let's have a stag for Greg. It's his last party as a single man.
stand behind	repair or replace, guarantee	Our company stands behind its products. We offer a guarantee.
stand by me	be my friend, be loyal to me, **be there for** me	I know you like me, but will you stand by me if I get in trouble?
stand corrected	admit a mistake or error, **own up**	The square root of 4761 is 69, not 68. I stand corrected.
stand for	believe in and represent, be the symbol for	Vicki stands for social justice. She supports public health care.
stand for	endure, tolerate, **put up with**, **stand it**	My parents won't allow us to smoke. They won't stand for it.
stand in	replace, substitute, **take my place**	I can't coach the soccer team today. Will you stand in for me?
stand it	endure it, bear it, **put up with** it	There's a very strong gas odor in here. How can you stand it?
stand on ceremony	expect everyone to know manners and customs	Leave your cap on if you like. We don't stand on ceremony.
stand out	appear different, not be the same as the others	Dick's voice stands out because it is lower than the others.
stand to lose	may lose, could lose	If my son fails to make a loan payment, I stand to lose $4000.
stand up	not meet you as planned, not attend an appointment	Jerry said he would take Rita to the movies, but he stood her up.

Idiom	Meaning	Example
stand up and be counted	say you support and will vote for it, **stand up for**	If you really believe in gay rights, you will stand up and be counted.
stand up for	support, protect, **speak out** for	I'm not afraid to stand up for our rights. I'll ask to see a lawyer.
stand up to	challenge, not **back down**	Please stand up to the bully. Tell him to stop hitting us.
standoffish	not friendly, not sociable	Brett appears to be standoffish, but he's really quite friendly.
stark raving mad	completely crazy, **out of your mind**	Ophelia went stark raving mad after Hamlet rejected her.
start a fire under him	motivate him, get him started	Somebody started a fire under Kent. He's skating hard tonight.
start from scratch	start from the beginning, go **back to square one**	After the flood, we all had to start from scratch—to rebuild our lives.
start out	start, begin, leave on a journey	Fill the tank with gas and check the oil before you start out.
start over	begin again, go to **square one**	If I make a mistake, I start over. I go right back to the beginning.
start up	start, begin, organize, begin a business	Before you start up a business you should write a business plan.
start with a bang	start well, start fast, **off to a good start**	The party will start with a bang if Elton arrives by hot-air balloon.
state of mind	mood, mental attitude, **frame of mind**	My state of mind improves when I read a book by Northrop Frye.
state of the art	most advanced, **cutting edge**	Many state-of-the-art devices use the LASER beam.
stay abreast	be aware of developments, stay current, **keep pace**	Can you stay abreast of changes in computer technology?
stay alive	win enough to continue, continue in a series	To stay alive, the Leafs must win the next two games.
stay awake	not sleep, be alert	I can't stay awake any longer. I can't keep my eyes open.
stay in line	obey the rules, behave well	Stay in line, young man. We expect you to obey orders.
stay put	stay where you are, do not move	He took his dog out of the store and said, "Sit! Stay put!"

Idiom	Meaning	Example
stay up	not go to sleep, **wait up for**	We stay up until the kids come home—if it isn't too late.
steal the show	be the favorite performer, receive the most applause	The little Peterson girl stole the show with her fine tap dancing.
steal your heart	cause you to like or love, **win the hearts**	The kittens will steal your heart. They're so cute and playful.
steal your thunder	tell your news, reveal your main message	If I mention the new product, will I steal your thunder?
steam up	upset, excited, worried	Poor Emil would get all steamed up when his car wouldn't start.
steamy	portraying lots of sex, full of love scenes	*Love In The Park* is a steamy movie. There's lots of action.
steer clear	avoid, not go there	I advise you to steer clear of the bridge. There's been a flood.
step aside	resign, quit so someone else can do the job	If Jon will step aside, Harvey can become president.
step down	resign, leave a position, **bow out**	It was time for Pierre to step down—time for him to resign.
step on it	go faster, step on the gas, **pedal to the metal**	Father said, "Step on it, son. We don't want to be late."
step on people	hurt people to get ahead, use people to succeed	I want wealth, but I don't want to step on people to get it.
step on their toes	offend them, upset them	When I mentioned their debt, did I step on their toes?
step out of line	do something bad, misbehave	If John steps out of line again, I'll remind him of the rules.
stick in my craw	irritate me, **gets to me**	That decision really sticks in my craw. How could he sell Gretzky?
stick it out	stay until you finish, **hang in there**	Can you stick it out until six? Can you work until then?
stick it up your ass [B]	put it away, **forget it**, **shove it**	You can take your useless truck and stick it up your ass!
stick my neck out	risk my safety to help, **put my neck on the line**	Why should I stick my neck out when you disobey your father?

Idiom	Meaning	Example
stick out like a sore thumb	not fit or blend, look **out of place**	The ugly painting stuck out like a sore thumb in the art gallery.
stick them up	put your hands above your head, **hands up**	The man took out a gun and said to the clerk, "Stick 'em up!"
stick to it	stay at a tough job, **hang in there**	If you stick to it—practice every day—you will be a fine pianist.
stick to your guns	not change your belief, be firm	If you testify in court, stick to your guns. Tell the same story.
stick up for	support, encourage	Will you stick up for me if I get in an argument?
stick-in-the-mud	one who does not go out, **party-pooper**	Farley, that stick-in-the-mud! He never goes to a party.
stiff	not pay for, leave without paying	The cab driver told a policeman that a lady had stiffed him.
stiff	person, man	You lucky stiff! You won a TV!
stiff upper lip	(See **keep a stiff upper lip**)	
still wet behind the ears	still quite young, **the tender age of**	When we moved to Boston, you were still wet behind the ears.
stink the joint out	play very poorly, perform badly	In Chicago, we stunk the joint out, losing 7-1 to the Hawks.
stitch in time	(See **a stitch in time**)	
stock in trade	main product, **bread and butter**	Our stock in trade is tires. We sell more tires than oil or gas.
stone dead	very dead, no sign of life, **dead as a door nail**	When we finally found the goose, it was stone dead.
stone unturned	(See **leave no stone unturned**)	
stone's throw	(See **a stone's throw**)	
stoned	drugged, **high** on drugs, **spaced out**, **wasted**	If he's stoned, he shouldn't drive. Let's hide his keys.
stonewall	block, prevent, not allow	The president stonewalled every one of our plans. He said no.
stop at nothing	do anything to succeed, not stop until you win	The Indians will stop at nothing. They will get a reservation.

Idiom	Meaning	Example
stop on a dime	stop very quickly, stop exactly where you wish	With antiskid brakes, this car can stop on a dime. See?
stop you cold	stop you quickly, **grind to a halt**	One look from the old witch will stop you cold. What a fierce gaze!
stop you in your tracks	cause you to stop, prevent you from going further	You know what will stop you dead in your tracks? A bear, that's what.
straight	(See **go straight, square up**)	
straight away	(See **right away**)	
straight cash	all cash, using only cash	When I go shopping I pay straight cash. I don't use my credit cards.
straight dope	(See **the straight dope**)	
straight face	(See **keep a straight face**)	
straight from the horse's mouth	directly from the person who said it or did it	I want to hear the story from Ty, straight from the horse's mouth.
straight goods	(See **the straight goods**)	
straight talk	the truth, the facts, **the straight goods**	My son and I believe in straight talk. We communicate.
straight up	without stopping, not reduced, **full strength**	I do ten minutes of exercise; then I run 5 km straight up.
straight up	truthfully, the way it is	Give it to me straight up— exactly what she said.
straighten you out	tell you the facts or the truth, **set you straight**	Talk to the teacher. She'll straighten you out.
strapped	having very little money, nearly **broke**	I can't afford to go to a concert this month. I'm strapped.
street smarts	knowing how to survive, **worldly wise**	You need street smarts to be a police officer in Toronto.
street wise	wise about street life, **been around**	Let's ask Sal to go downtown with us. He's street wise.
stretch the dollar	spend carefully, buy the most for each dollar	We have a large family. I stretch the dollar as far as I can.
stretch the envelope	extend the boundaries, **expand your horizons**	I've set some goals that stretch my envelope—challenge me.

Idiom	Meaning	Example
stretch the truth	add to a true story, include lies with the truth	Al was stretching the truth. He said the waves were 60 feet high.
stretching it	saying it was bigger or better than it was	To say the mosquitoes are as big as starlings is stretching it.
strictly business	very serious, not joking, **no nonsense**	When he conducts the band, he's strictly business. He's serious.
strictly for the birds	(See **for the birds**)	
strike a bargain	find a satisfactory deal or price	After discussing the price of the carpet, we struck a bargain: $15.
strike it rich	earn or win a lot of money, find a gold mine	People came to the Yukon hoping to find gold—to strike it rich.
strike me	causes me to pause, impresses me	What strikes me is the color of the leaves. They're crimson.
strike out (baseball)	fail to hit the ball while at bat	This time he'll hit the ball. Last time at bat he struck out.
strike out on your own	leave home and support yourself, be independent	I was eighteen when I struck out on my own and found a job.
strike up a conversation	begin a conversation with a stranger	Uncle Ho is sociable. He strikes up a conversation with anyone.
strike up the band	begin conducting the band, give the downbeat	Maestro, strike up the band. We want to hear some music.
strike while the iron is hot	do it before it is too late, now is the time to act	In business, timing is important. You strike while the iron is hot.
strike your fancy	interest you, appeal to you, **turn your crank**	Do you see anything on the menu that strikes your fancy? Lobster?
string a line	create a story, **make up** a story	He was stringing you a line. A dog wasn't driving the car.
string along	pretend that you believe, **go along with**	When Franz talks about shark fishing, I just string along.
string bean	thin person, **bean pole**	You string bean, Kenny! You're too skinny to hit the ball!
strip mall	a row of stores with a small parking lot in front	Does the Langdale strip mall have a video store?
stroke of genius	a very intelligent idea, a unique solution	Using laser light for surgery— now that's a stroke of genius.

Idiom	Meaning	Example
stroke of good luck	a fortunate event, **a lucky break**, **the fickle finger of fate**	Then, by some stroke of good luck, a car horn scared the lion and it ran away.
stroke your ego	cause you to feel confident or proud	Compliments are wonderful because they stroke your ego.
strung out	ill or weak because of drug abuse, **hung over**	When she's strung out on cocaine she won't talk to her family.
stubblejumper	grain farmer, Saskatchewan folk	My uncle is a stubblejumper. He owns a farm near Kuroki.
stuck on	focussed on, obsessed with	Jack is stuck on Vicki, but she doesn't care about him.
stuff it	put it away, **forget it**, **shove it** [B]	I don't want her money. She can stuff it!
stumbling block	obstacle, problem	A strip of land is in the way of peace. It is the stumbling block.
stump me	ask me a question I cannot answer, puzzle me	The question on the names of the Great Lakes stumped me.
such a card	quite a joker, such a clown	Greg tells the funniest stories. He is such a card!
suck	an immature person, **wimp**	Chad, that suck! He tells his mother everything we say.
suck eggs	have a bad experience, go, leave, **up yours** [B]	When I told him not to swear, he said, "Go suck eggs, man."
suck it up	pull in your stomach, get ready	Suck it up, Kerry. I'm going to take your picture.
suck off [B]	(See **give head**)	
suck the hind tit [B]	receive less than others, not get as good service, **the short end of the stick**	Who is sucking the hind tit of government services? Some people say it's the seniors.
suck up to	be nice for personal gain, **brown nose** [B]	Why is Ken sucking up to me? Does he expect a raise in pay?
suckbucket	student's briefcase, valise	Zen carries his suckbucket to impress the teachers, eh.
sucked in	deceived, cheated, **led to believe**, **taken in**	"You believed his story about working late at the office?" "Ya, I got sucked in."

Idiom	Meaning	Example
sucker	a person who is gullible; easy to persuade	"Who will buy that painting?" "Oh, a sucker will come along."
sucks	is poor quality, does not satisfy me	This radio sucks! I can't get my favorite station!
suffer a setback	lose a game, fail a test, become injured or ill	Italy's soccer team suffered a setback losing to Ireland.
suicide pass	(See **a suicide pass**)	
suit you	look good on you, **become you**	Red and black suit you. You look great in those colors.
suit yourself	you choose, choose what you like	"I prefer tea." "Suit yourself."
Sunday best	best clothes, **glad rags**	Father was in his Sunday best— in his three-piece, navy suit.
sunset years	senior years, over 65, **golden years**	Will you still love me when I'm old—in my sunset years?
super mint	excellent, the best quality	The photograph of the baby is super mint! It's excellent!
supercharge	boost the power, **hop up**, **tweak**	We supercharged the engine in a Datsun 510, doubling its power.
super-duper	very large, exciting or powerful, **totally awesome**	After class, Julie went to the cafe and ordered a super-duper sundae with a cherry on top.
superstar	very talented athlete or performer, the best player	Hockey's superstars include Richard, Howe, and Gretzky.
sure bet	(See **a sure bet**)	
sure thing	(See **a sure thing**)	
surf the Net	survey the **Internet** or global computer network	Olga is surfing the Net again— looking for a boy in the US.
swallow that	believe that, **buy that**, **eat that**	He said the company is bankrupt, but don't swallow that!
swallow your pride	do not let your pride stop you, control your pride	Swallow your pride. Accept the offer to return to your old job.
swear by	believe in a product and say that it is good	Joel swears by Chrysler cars. He's driven a Dodge for years.

Idiom	Meaning	Example
swear off	quit using, abstain from	Zack has sworn off beer until Christmas. He quit completely.
sweat bullets	worry, be very concerned or afraid or nervous	I was sweating bullets when I heard your plane went down.
sweat it	(See **don't sweat it**)	
sweat it out	wait and worry, **on pins and needles**	While the jury discussed a verdict, the prisoner was sweating it out.
sweater girl	girl with big breasts who wears a tight sweater	Jody was the sweater girl in our class. She was sexy.
sweep under the carpet	hide problems, cover mistakes	Don't sweep your problems under the carpet. Try to solve them.
sweep you off your feet	impress you, cause you to love them quickly	Andre is very charming. He will sweep you off your feet.
sweet on	like, love, **got a crush on**, **stuck on**	You act kind of funny when Barb is here. Are you sweet on her?
sweet spot	(See **the sweet spot**)	
sweet tooth	a need to eat candy, a craving for sweets	A piece of dark chocolate will satisfy my sweet tooth. Yum!
sweeten the pot	add more good things, make it worth more	If we sweeten the pot with a trip to Paris, we'll sell more tickets.
swelled head	feeling too proud, **let it go to your head**	If I win the talent contest, I promise not to get a swelled head.
swift	intelligent, smart, **bright**	I'm not very swift when I try to do calculus. I usually fail.

Idiom	Meaning	Example

T

Idiom	Meaning	Example
tail between his legs	running away in defeat or fear, retreating quickly	When the bear followed me, I ran with my tail between my legs!
tail lights	gone, departed, could not **see me for dust**	When I heard the police siren, I was tail lights. I was gone.
tail wagging the dog	(See **the tail wagging the dog**)	
tailgate	drive too close to the car in front, **on his tail**	The instructor told me not to tailgate—to leave more space.
take a back seat	say you are not as good, **play second fiddle**	You are good at chess. Don't take a back seat to anyone!
take a boo	look at, **take a look**	Take a boo with my telescope. See the dust on the moon?
take a bow	bow to the audience, show you like applause	The crowd is clapping because you played well. Take a bow.
take a break	rest for a few minutes or days or weeks	You've been working hard. Do you want to take a break?
take a bullet	accept blame or injury to protect someone	Pat said she was responsible for our mistake—she took a bullet.
take a chance	gamble, **try your luck**	I'm going to take a chance and buy gold. It's a gamble, but....
take a dive	plan to lose, **throw a game**	The boxer was paid to take a dive. He allowed his opponent to win.
take a drive/trip	travel, go for a drive, go on a trip	They take a drive in the country every Sunday afternoon.
take a dump [B]	shit, **drop a log [B]**, **take a shit [B]**	I looked out the window and saw a dog taking a dump on my lawn.
take a flight	go, leave, **take off**	If you don't like the way I live, you can take a flight.

Idiom	Meaning	Example
take a gander	look at, **feast your eyes**, **take a boo**	Take a gander at that valley! Just look at it!
take a guess	guess, try to answer, **hazard a guess**	"How old are you?" "Take a guess."
take a hike	go, leave, **get lost**	When her old boyfriend moved in with us, I told them to take a hike.
take a joke	not be mad if the joke is about you, **a good sport**	Let's tell the story about Steve getting lost. He can take a joke.
take a leak [B]	urinate, **take a pee** [B], **take a whiz**	We asked the bus driver to stop so we could take a leak.
take a load off your feet	sit down, **grab a chair**, **have a seat**	Jim pointed to a chair and said, "Take a load off your feet."
take a look	look at, see that, **take a boo**	Take a look at that pumpkin! It's monstrous!
take a pee [B]	urinate, **take a leak** [B], **take a whiz**	"Where can I take a pee?" she whispered to her friend.
take a picture	photograph, **snap a picture**	In Regina, he took a picture of the statue of Louis Riel.
take a piss [B]	urinate, **take a leak** [B], **take a pee** [B]	A drunk was taking a piss in the alley behind the hotel.
take a poke at	punch, hit with your fist	First he pushed Tom, then he took a poke at me.
take a poke at	say something negative in a humorous way	The speaker took a poke at women who want everything men have.
take a poll	record opinions, find out how people will vote	Take a poll before the election so you can predict the winner.
take a powder	pretend to lose, **take a dive**, **throw a game**	When I wrestle with my sons, I sometimes take a powder just to give them confidence.
take a round out of	defeat in a fight, win a fight	Johnny is a tough guy. He took a round out of Pete, you know.
take a shine to	like, show interest in	At four, Raj took a shine to the piano. Now he's a great pianist.
take a shit [B]	have a bowel movement, **take a dump** [B]	She wrote a book that explains how to take a shit in the woods.

Idiom	Meaning	Example
take a shot	criticize or insult, **put down**, **take a poke at**	When he spoke about abortion, he took a shot at the government for not changing the laws.
take a shot	shoot a gun at, aim and shoot a rifle	Uncle was looking for a target, so he took a shot at a tin can.
take a snap shot	(See **take a picture**)	
take a stand	say what you believe, state your position, **take sides**	The teacher doesn't want to take a stand on the Young Offender Act until we've written our essays.
take a strip off	scold, lecture, **give you hell**	The foreman took a strip off me for driving too fast. He was mad.
take a whiz	urinate, **take a leak** [B], **take a pee** [B]	I have to take a whiz before we get on the plane. I'll be right back.
take action	act in a deliberate way, act with a purpose	Before I take action, I'll ask Bing if he was aware of the rules.
take advantage of	act at the best time, **seize an opportunity**	I took advantage of the low price of gasoline. I bought 500 litres.
take advantage of	hurt or abuse someone who trusts you	I feel very angry toward people who take advantage of children.
take after	have similar traits, have the same personality	Kyle is calm; he takes after me. Kris is active, just like his dad.
take after	chase, try to catch	If he catches the football, you take after him as fast as you can.
take by storm	rush in, win by force, overwhelm	The Vikings landed on the beach and took the village by storm.
take calls	answer the phone, receive calls	Karen isn't taking calls because she's in a meeting.
take care	be careful	Take care. See you tomorrow.
take care of	care for someone or something, **look after**	I'll take care of Taea while you go shopping. I'll stay with her.
take care of business	do what needs to be done, do my job	"You scored a beautiful goal!" "Just taking care of business."
take charge	be in control, supervise	Jim will take charge while I'm away. He'll be your supervisor.
take cover	hide, find a safe place	If the soldiers begin shooting, you guys take cover.

Idiom	Meaning	Example
take drugs	use drugs, **do drugs**	When I take that drug, I feel sick at my stomach.
take effect	have an effect, cause a change	In two minutes the drug will take effect and you will feel sleepy.
take exception to	be upset about, object to, complain about	Vern will take exception to any questions about ethnic origin.
take for granted	expect, assume	His support cannot be taken for granted. We must ask him.
take heart	have courage, be strong	When we had troubles, Grandpa said, "Take heart, my children."
take him down a peg	push him to a lower place, **off your high horse**	Ali was too proud. Somebody had to take him down a peg.
take him out	defeat him, eliminate him	Wei entered the tournament, but Jo took her out in the first round.
take in	make smaller, tighten	These pants need to be taken in at the waist. They're too large.
take in	attend, visit	When you come to Calgary, be sure to take in the Stampede.
take it	endure it, accept it, **stand it**	He treats you very badly. Why do you take it?
take it	understand it is true, believe it is this way	I take it you want the whole class to write a report. Is that right?
take it and run	accept the offer and be happy, be satisfied	He offered to pay $200 for the damage, so I took it and ran.
take it back	not mean to say it, withdraw what you said	I said you were a turkey, but I take it back. You're a rat!
take it easy	do not try so hard, do not work so hard	When you jog, take it easy. Rest often.
take it easy on	be less demanding, **go easy on**	When you train the dogs, take it easy on Taffy. She's just a pup.
take it for a spin	drive it, **test drive it**	Al has a new motorcycle. I hope he lets me take it for a spin.
take it in stride	continue without delay, cope with	Lilian is so steady. If there's a problem, she takes it in stride.

Idiom	Meaning	Example
take it like a man	be brave when hurt, do not complain about problems	They told him not to cry when he was hurt—to take it like a man.
take it or leave it	take this offer or refuse it; no bargaining	I'll give you $150 for the sofa— take it or leave it.
take it out on	express anger toward an innocent person	Vince gets angry at work; then he takes it out on his kids.
take it personally	believe you are being attacked or accused	He was criticizing the whole class; don't take it personally.
take it the wrong way	misunderstand, feel bad; **no offence, but...**	He stares because he is curious. Don't take it the wrong way.
take it to heart	believe it is said to you, feel it is meant for you	When he said we'll burn in hell, Ella cried. She took it to heart.
take it with a grain of salt	do not believe all of it, some of it is not true	When Brian talks, take it with a grain of salt. Believe very little.
take its course	develop naturally, go through a process, **willy nilly**	We can control many parts of our environment, but the weather just takes its course.
take leave of your senses	act like a fool, not think clearly, **off your rocker**	If you wear your bathing suit to church, people will think you've taken leave of your senses.
take me seriously	be serious about me and what I say and do	I'm not joking about going to a psychic. Please take me seriously.
take my hat off to	show respect for someone, praise a person's work	I take my hat off to Roger. He has promoted business in our town.
take my head off	shout at me, say angry words to me	You don't have to take my head off when I ask where you're going.
take my place	sit or park where I usually sit or park	Mommy, he took my place! He's sitting in my seat!
take oath	say that something is true, give my **word of honor**	He took an oath that he is the child's father. I believe him.
take off	leave by plane, depart on a plane	Our plane takes off at 10:35. We have to go to the airport.
take off, eh	go, leave, **beat it**, **buzz off**, **get lost**	When he asked for my phone number, I said, "Take off, eh."
take offence	be hurt, feel offended	Jan takes offence easily. Don't be critical of her poetry.

Idiom	Meaning	Example
take on	fight, challenge	Mac wanted to take on Ted, but Ted didn't want to fight.
take on	agree to do, accept a responsibility	I'm very busy. I can't take on any more work right now.
take on	employ, hire, **hire on**	AmCorp is taking on workers. Should we apply for a job?
take on a new light	have a new meaning, see a different meaning	The music takes on a new light if you know the composer.
take out	court, date, **go out with, see**	He was taking her out when they went to college. They were lovers.
take over	do someone's job, become the new manager	Please take over the bookkeeping while I'm away. Thank you.
take pains	try hard, take extra time or care	Mr. and Mrs. Wilson take pains to find families that are truly in need.
take part in	join, be a worker or a participant	She takes part in many activities, including gardening.
take place	happen, occur	The race will take place at the university track at 10 a.m.
take possession	receive the keys as the new owner	"We bought a house in Parkland." "When do you take possession?"
take revenge	hurt one who hurt you, **get even**	If your car is stolen, report it to the police. Don't take revenge.
take sides	support one person or group in an argument	The mayor refused to take sides in the fight to save the hospital.
take solace	find peace, find comfort	It was a bad fire, but I take solace in the fact that no one died.
take that	you deserve that, you **have it coming**	Take that, you devil! And that! I'm very angry at you!
take the blame	receive the blame, accept the blame, **take the rap**	Sometimes innocent people offer to take the blame for crimes.
take the bull by the horns	control the problem, be firm, **take charge**	If the class is noisy, the teacher must take the bull by the horns.
take the bus/plane	ride on the bus or plane, **catch a plane**	Lee never takes the bus. He prefers to ride his bicycle.
take the cake	is the worst or the weirdest or the funniest etc.	Of all the people I've met, you take the cake! You're the wildest!

Idiom	Meaning	Example
take the chill off	make the room warmer, start the furnace/fireplace	An electric heater will take the chill off in the evening.
take the flack	listen to the complaints, **take the heat**	When children cause trouble, their parents take the flack.
take the heat	listen to the questions from the police or public	Vern took the heat, but Al stole the drugs. They blamed Vern.
take the pulse	discover the feelings of the people	Before you change the flag, see how people feel. Take their pulse.
take the rap	receive the blame, **take the blame**	Jeremy took the rap for the crime. He alone was sent to prison.
take the stage	go onto the stage, be the performer on the stage	When Bob Goulet took the stage we heard some great singing.
take the stand	sit in the witness chair in a courtroom	You witnessed the crime, so you will have to take the stand.
take the trouble	do extra work, do special tasks, **take pains**	Maria always takes the trouble to bake my favorite pie.
take this job and shove it [B]	I quit, you can keep this job	Jim said to the boss, "Take this job and shove it! I'm outa here!"
take time to smell the roses	use some time to relax and enjoy the scenery	Yes, pursue your goals, but take time to smell the roses.
take umbrage	feel hurt, feel offended, **take offence**	If you refuse her invitation to her party, she'll take umbrage.
take up	begin a hobby or activity, learn a skill	First, Alice took up karate. Then she learned how to meditate.
take up the slack	do somebody's work, **fill in**	When I'm away, Hal takes up the slack. He does my job.
take with a grain of salt	(See **take it with a grain of salt**)	
take you down a peg	(See **knock you down a peg**)	
take you for all you've got	take all your money by suing you or cheating you	If she divorces you, she could take you for all you've got.
take you in	give you shelter and food, **take care of**	Will your relatives take you in if you lose your job?
take you to court	sue you, bring a lawsuit against you	If you don't pay for the damage, they could take you to court.

Idiom	Meaning	Example
take you to task	ask you to explain, haul you up **on the carpet**	Did Reverend Klinck take you to task for drinking beer?
take you to the cleaners	defeat you badly, win by many points	If you play checkers with Lars, he'll take you to the cleaners.
take your lumps	endure bumps and hits, suffer through injuries	To play hockey, you have to learn to take your lumps.
take your pick	choose one, say which one you prefer	You can have Coke or Pepsi. Take your pick.
take your pulse	measure your heart rate, check your pulse	When you visit the health clinic, the doctor will take your pulse.
take your seat	sit in your chair or desk, be seated	Judy, please take your seat so we can begin the exam.
take your word for it	believe what you say, not ask for proof, **the benefit of the doubt**	You say you are eighteen. Since you don't have your ID card, we'll have to take your word for it.
take-out restaurant	a restaurant that serves food to be taken outside	There's a take-out restaurant. Let's buy some food and go to the park.
taken	cheated, **ripped off**	If he paid $1500 for that car, he got taken.
taken for a ride	tricked, deceived, **taken in**	We were taken for a ride. We lost thousands of dollars.
taken in	deceived, fooled, **taken for a ride**	I was taken in by their ads. I believed what they said.
takes one to know one	(See **it takes one to know one**)	
talk a mile a minute	talk fast, talk quickly	Mimi talks a mile a minute. It's hard to understand her.
talk about	if we are talking about, if you want to discuss	Talk about cold! Last winter it was -43° Celsius!
talk away	continue talking, talk and talk	The baby was talking away, but no one could understand her.
talk back	reply without respect, **lip off**	In China, kids don't talk back to their parents, do they?
talk big	brag, exaggerate, promise a lot	Bert talks big *before* a game. He's more humble afterwards.
talk into	persuade, convince	Try to talk him into buying a new car. His Fiat is rusty.

Idiom	Meaning	Example
talk is cheap	talk is not action, saying is easier than doing	He says he's going to pay his debt, but talk is cheap.
talk it over	discuss it, **hash it over**	I don't agree with you, but let's talk it over before we decide.
talk it up	talk with enthusiasm, tell people about it	If we want to build an arena, we have to talk it up with the people.
talk shop	talk about jobs, talk about what we do at work	I don't like to talk shop when we have visitors. It's too boring.
talk the leg off the lamb of God	talk a lot; persuasively; have **the gift of the gab**	Minerva was a talker. She could talk the leg off the lamb of God!
talk through your hat	talk without logic, say unbelievable things, **hot air**	If you tell Dad about building a home in outer space, he'll say you're talking through your hat.
talk turkey	discuss a fair deal, negotiate seriously	If the owner really wants to sell, he'll talk turkey.
talk your ear off	talk too much, talk all the time	Polly is only three years old, but she can talk your ear off.
talk your head off	talk a lot, say too much	You can talk your head off, but I won't change my opinion.
tall one	(See **a tall one**)	
tall tale	a story that is partly true, an exaggerated story	Fishermen love to tell tall tales. They lie a little, eh.
tangle with	fight against, have a fight with	I wouldn't want to tangle with Vince. He's strong—and mean!
tank	a drunk, an alcoholic, **lush**, **wino**	Percy—that tank! He drinks a case of beer every day.
tank	(See **in the tank**)	
tanked/tanked up	drunk, **polluted**, **sloshed**, **wasted**	After an evening at the tavern, the sailors were tanked.
tar with the same brush	(See **paint with the same brush**)	
taste of his own...	(See **give him a taste of his own medicine**)	
teach an old dog...	(See **you can't teach an old dog new tricks**)	

Idiom	Meaning	Example
teach you the tricks of the trade	teach you how to do it, teach you the easy way, **learn the ropes**	Welcome to the company, Ken. Paul will work with you and teach you the tricks of the trade.
team player	an employee who works well with other employees	Team players—that's what we need in our company.
team up	play together, form a team	If you team up with Lana, we can play bridge, okay?
tear a strip off	scold, lecture, criticize, **give you hell** [B]	Kasan's father tore a strip off him for missing a day of school.
tear around	go fast, run here and there, drive around	When Ty was young, he liked to tear around town in his car.
tear me apart	criticize me or my work, find all my faults	If you waste tax dollars, the voters will tear you apart.
teed off	upset, cross, **ticked off**	She was teed off about the errors in the balance sheet.
teed up	ready to operate, ready to use	"Is your presentation ready?" "Yes. All teed up, ready to go."
tell a soul	(See **won't tell a soul**)	
tell all	tell everything you know, **pour out your soul**	In a job interview, I answer their questions, but I don't tell all.
tell him a thing or two	tell him he caused a problem, **tell him off**	If Sid took my keys, I'm going to tell him a thing or two.
tell him off	tell him you are angry, tell him he is wrong	If he mentions my toupee once more, I'm going to tell him off.
tell him where to get off	tell him what you think of him, **tell him off**	If he complains about the meals, tell him where to get off.
tell him where to go	tell him to **go to hell** [B], **tell him off**	If he criticizes the way I drive, I'll tell him where to go!
tell me another one	tell me another excuse, tell me another lie	You say the spaceship took you away. Sure. Tell me another one.
tell me straight	(See **give it to me straight**)	
tell on	tell a secret, tell about a crime, **squeal**	Will Robbie tell on us? What if he tells the police we did it?
tempest in a teapot	(See **a tempest in a teapot**)	

Idiom	Meaning	Example
ten-four (CB radio)	yes, I hear you, **okay**	"See you in Memphis, big fella." "Ten-four, good buddy."
tender age of	(See **the tender age of**)	
test drive	drive to evaluate, **try it out**	I test drove the new Harley on Saturday. What a bike!
test the water	check people's feelings, **take a poll**	Wilson always tests the water before he introduces a budget.
thank goodness	I am thankful or relieved, **thank heavens**	Thank goodness you're here. We were worried about you.
thank heavens	thank the gods, **thank goodness**	When we phoned Mom, she said, "Thank heavens you're safe!"
thank your lucky stars	(See **you can thank your lucky stars**)	
thanks a bunch	thanks very much, thanks a lot	When I deliver the groceries, she says, "Thanks a bunch, Teddy."
thanks a million	thanks very much, thanks a lot	Thanks a million for all you've done for us. We do appreciate it.
that a boy/that a girl	good work, well done, **'at a boy, 'at a girl**	Whenever I get a good grade, she says, "That a boy, Reid!"
that is that	(See **and that's that**)	
that takes the cake	that is the strangest or loudest or wildest etc.	I've seen big pumpkins, but that takes the cake! It's fifty pounds!
that'll be the day	that will never happen, **not on your life**	Me? Wear a ring in my nose? That'll be the day!
that'll be the frosty Friday	that day will never come, **don't hold your breath**	Canada become part of the US? That'll be the frosty Friday!
that's a corker	that is unusual, that is amazing	"The baby weighed 12 pounds." "Wow, that's a corker!"
that's all she wrote	that is the end of the story, the story ends here	At the end of the lesson he said, "And that's all she wrote."
that's cool	that is good/fine/OK, that is **groovy**	When we gave Fonzie a leather tie, he said, "That's cool."
that's his bible	that is his rule book, code or main reference	The Oxford English Dictionary— that's her bible.
that's life	that is the way life goes, **c'est la vie**	Whenever Maurice has bad luck, he says, "Ah, that's life."

Idiom	Meaning	Example
that's stretching it	that is adding to the story, **stretching it**	Did he say there were fifty flying saucers? That's stretching it.
that's that	(See **and that's that**)	
that's the spirit	good work, good attitude, **way to go**	"That's the spirit," the Captain shouted as we scrubbed the deck.
that's the ticket	that is the answer, that is the solution	I said, "Can we share the job?" Mr. Tse said, "That's the ticket!"
that's the way the ball bounces	that is fate, **that's life**	If Jon got the job, good for him. That's the way the ball bounces.
that's the way the cookie crumbles	that is fate, that is the way things happen	You didn't win the prize? That's the way the cookie crumbles.
the air was blue	there was much swearing, someone said bad words	When Dad discovered the dent in his Cadillac, the air was blue.
the apple doesn't fall far from the tree	kids are like their parents; **a chip off the old block; like father, like son**	I looked at the father, then at the son, and I thought, *The apple doesn't fall far from the tree.*
the apple of his eye	his favorite girl, the girl he desires	Susie was his sweetheart, the apple of his eye.
the balance of power	the deciding votes; votes that cause the winner, **tip the scales**	He will try to get the support of the workers because they hold the balance of power.
the ball's in your court	you speak or act now, **it's your turn**	She offered to pay $1900 for your car, so the ball's in your court.
the be-all, end-all	the best, the greatest, **his nibs, world beater**	Brian believes he's the be-all, end-all in politics, but wait until he loses the next election.
the bee's knees	the best, superior, **the cat's meow**	Kay was voted best citizen. Now she thinks she's the bee's knees.
the benefit of the doubt	fair judgement when some of the facts are not known, **take your word for it**	If money is missing, we give you the benefit of the doubt. We assume you didn't take it.
the best of both worlds	the best parts of two cultures or styles etc., **two heads are better...**	If you have Italian design and German engineering, you have the best of both worlds, eh.
the best-laid plans of mice and men go oft astray	plans are not guaranteed, plans sometimes do not **work out**	If this boat sinks, we'll say, "The best-laid plans of mice and men go oft astray."

Idiom	Meaning	Example
The Big Apple	New York City, New York, USA	Guess what! My friend and I are going to live in The Big Apple!
the big 0	zero, nothing, **zip**	You won a car. I got the big 0.
The Big O	Olympic Stadium in Montreal	We watched Diane compete in the pentathlon at The Big O.
the big picture	all parts together, the whole plan, **can't see the forest...**	Look at the big picture. Doing two jobs will have a negative effect on your family.
the bigger they are the harder they fall	we can beat the big guys, big players fall harder, **mind over matter**	"Look at all their big players!" "Don't worry. The bigger they are, the harder they fall!"
the bitter end	the end of a long struggle, the end of a difficult time	On a ranch you work till a job is done. You stay till the bitter end.
the blind leading the blind	the leader is ignorant or incompetent	With Filbert as President, it's the blind leading the blind.
the bottom fell out	the project stopped, the business failed, **the wheels fell off**	When the price of oil dropped, the bottom fell out of the oil industry in Alberta.
the bottom line	the final number, the conclusion	The bottom line is this: we can't afford to buy another store.
the breaking point	the time you cannot go on, the point where you quit	My job was so stressful I reached the breaking point. I had to quit.
the brush-off	refusal, rejection	The first time he asked her for a date, she gave him the brush-off.
the buck stops here	I am responsible for what we do—no one else; **pass the buck**	"The buck stops here," the new manager said to us. "We don't blame others for our problems."
the bum's rush	being chased away, **run out of town**	If you tell us to pay more tax we'll give you the bum's rush.
the burning question	the main question, what we all want to know	Who drove the car into the lake? That's the burning question.
the butt of the joke	the person who is laughed at, **the goat**	Frank is so sensitive. He hates to be the butt of a joke.
the call of duty	the feeling that you have to work, **duty calls**	When the group needs a secretary I answer the call of duty.

Idiom	Meaning	Example
the calm before the storm	the quiet time just before anger or an attack	The enemy is planning an attack. This is the calm before the storm.
the can	toilet, washroom, **the john**, **the loo**	Who's in the can? Please hurry! I have to go!
the cart before the horse	backwards, back to front	Having dessert before dinner is putting the cart before the horse.
the cat's ass [B]	the best, **number one**, **the bee's knees**	Since Val won the beauty contest, she thinks she's the cat's ass!
the cat's meow	somebody special, **a hot shot**	When Vi wears diamonds, she thinks she's the cat's meow.
the cat's out of the bag	the secret has been told, people know the secret	We know about your affair with Brad. The cat's out of the bag.
the crack of dawn	(See **at the crack of dawn**)	
the crunch	the difficult time, the day we have less money	The crunch is coming—when we have one salary instead of two.
the crux of the matter	the main point, the real issue	Uncle Bert is too old to drive the car. That's the crux of the matter.
the customer is always right	satisfy the customer, agree with the customer	Now let's discuss an old saying: *The Customer's Always Right.*
the cutting edge	the latest technology, **state of the art**	Compact discs are no longer the cutting edge in recorded music.
the devil makes work for idle hands	if a person is not busy he will do evil things, **work ethic**	The protestants believe children should be busy because the devil makes work for idle hands.
the downside	the negative side, the disadvantages, the bad points	The downside of abortion is that some women use it as a method of birth control.
the dying seconds	the last few seconds in a game	The score was tied 3—3 in the dying seconds of the third period.
the early bird gets the worm	the one who arrives first gets the reward etc.	I want to go to the sale at 8 a.m. The early bird gets the worm!
the end justifies the means	any method is fine if the result is good	If a person steals food to survive, does the end justify the means?
the end of the line	the time to leave, the place to get off	When the group began to gossip, it was the end of the line for me.
the end-all, be-all	(See **the be-all, end-all**)	

Idiom	Meaning	Example
the eye of a needle	the hole in a needle, the opening for the thread	The hole in the tube was smaller than the eye of a needle.
the eye of the storm	the center of the storm, the middle of the storm	The eye of the storm is directly over Lake Simcoe.
the F-word	fuck [B], **friggin**	Mommy, Mommy! Charles said the F-word!
the family jewels	the male genitals (the source of future progeny)	Sure I wear a jockstrap—to protect the family jewels!
the fat hit the fire	the trouble got worse, people began fighting	Kate accused Maude of lying— that's when the fat hit the fire.
the fickle finger of fate	the chances in life, the way life changes unpredictably, **that's life**	Our lives were saved because a dog barked. We were saved by the fickle finger of fate.
the fifth column	the column in a newspaper that tells about the media	The fifth column often comments on the need for fair reporting.
the first leg	the first part (of a journey), **a leg up**	The first leg will take us to Paris. Then we'll go on to Rome.
the gift of the gab	the ability to talk, **a way with words**	Bev can speak to the parents. She has the gift of the gab.
the gloves are off	the fight is beginning, **play hardball**	The candidates have insulted each other. The gloves are off!
the goat	the person who is blamed for a problem	Ken is the goat, but all he did was open the door for the students.
the going gets rough	the task becomes harder, it is a **rocky road**	In the second year, you study law. That's when the going gets rough.
the going rate	the standard price or fee, the usual price	The going rate for car repairs is about $60 an hour.
The Golden Rule	*Do unto others as you would have them do unto you.*	If everyone lived by The Golden Rule, you may not like the way you are treated.
the gospel truth	the real truth, as true as the gospel	I opened the package to count the cookies—that's the gospel truth!
the grass is greener on the other side of the fence	things look better from a distance, it is natural to desire a neighbor's things	When you look at other homes, the grass is often greener on the other side of the fence.

Idiom	Meaning	Example
The Great One	Wayne Gretzky, "Gretz"	The Great One was the heart of the Edmonton Oilers.
The Great White Hope	Caucasian boxer who could win the heavyweight title	In the 1970s, George Chuvallo was The Great White Hope.
The Great White North	Canada, *the true north...*	Millions of Americans enjoy their holidays in The Great White North.
The Grim Reaper	an executioner; a person who decides your fate, position, grades, etc.	Old Mason was The Grim Reaper. He showed no mercy when he failed students.
The Group of Five/ The Regina Five	artists K. Lockhead, A. McKay, D. Morton, T. Godwin, R. Bloore	The Group of Five are famous for their bold, abstract paintings.
The Group of Seven	Canadian painters who formed a group in 1917	Do you know the names of the artists in The Group of Seven?
the handwriting is on the wall	the message is clear, the conclusion is obvious	I tell my students the handwriting is on the wall: *learn how to learn.*
the hard way	the difficult method, **the rocky road**	If we plan, we can avoid doing our work the hard way.
the heat is on	there is pressure to win, we must succeed	When you compete for a career position, the heat is on.
the hell you say	I do not believe it, **get out, go on**	Harper won the election? The hell you say!
the in's and out's	knowledge and experience, **know**ing **the ropes**	He knows the in's and out's of the car business. He's experienced.
the in-crowd	a few special people, a clique	Cleo's part of the in-crowd—girls who play on the basketball team.
the inside story	the personal story, the story that is not published	Greg knows the inside story on the Lawson murders. He's married to Marcia Lawson.
the inside track	being close to the person who has power, **Bob's your uncle**	If your uncle works at Sears, you should have the inside track on the new job in Men's Wear.
the jig's up	we know what you do, we know your secret	The jig's up, ladies. We know why you buy those vibrators.
the john	the toilet, **the biffy, the can**	Where's the john? I have to wash my hands.

309

Idiom	Meaning	Example
the joke is on you	you are the one we are laughing at, **play a joke**	You got the book with blank pages. The joke's on you!
the key to success	the most important factor, best way to succeed	He said the key to success in business is customer service.
the knock against	his worst fault, his main problem	Phil is a great teacher. The only knock against him is his temper.
the lap of luxury	a lifestyle that includes the finest house etc.	Flo married a rich realtor and now lives in the lap of luxury.
the last of it	the end of it, no more of it	We've had a week of -40 weather. I hope we've seen the last of it.
the last straw	one too many problems, the one that ruins it	The break-in was the last straw. We decided to move.
the laughing stock	the person everybody is laughing at	If you ride a camel to work, we'll be the laughing stock of the town.
the lay of the land	(See **get the lay of the land**)	
the life of the party	a lively, funny person who causes people to laugh	Jerry was the life of the party — singing, joking and laughing.
the lights are on but nobody's home	the eyes are open but lifeless, **not all there**	"Hello! Hello, Pat! His lights are on but nobody's home. Ha ha."
the lion's share	the largest part, the biggest piece	Thanks to the mothers for doing the lion's share of the work.
the living daylights	the life, the consciousness	When that dog barked, it scared the living daylights out of me.
the living end	the very best, the greatest, the most beautiful	Have you heard K.D. Lang sing? She's the livin' end.
the long and the short of it	everything I know, the whole story	He ended his report with, "That's the long and the short of it."
the long arm of the law	the police, police methods	Thanks to the long arm of the law, a thief's in jail and I have my car.
the loo	the toilet, **the can**, **the john**	I'll see the kitchen later, thanks. Where's the loo?
the Lord helps those who help themselves	if you work to help yourself God will help you	If you pray, remember, the Lord helps those who help themselves.
the lowdown	the facts, the real story	Did you get the lowdown on how he died? What really happened?

Idiom	Meaning	Example
the luck of the draw	the chance that your name or number will be chosen	Plan your future. Don't depend on the luck of the draw.
the luck of the Irish	the good luck of Irish people	When Kerry wins a prize, he says, "Aye, it's the luck of the Irish."
the makings of	the potential to become, the ability to develop	Look at Debi dance. She has the makings of a ballerina.
the man in the middle	the person between two enemies	When hockey players fight, the linesman is the man in the middle.
the Man in the Moon	a myth that the moon is the face of a man	"Who will help me find my dog?" "I know. The Man in the Moon!"
the middleman	a person who buys from the producer and sells to the merchant	If we can buy from the producer, we can save the money we pay to the middleman.
the moment of truth	the time when you receive a very important message	The moment of truth has arrived. My grades are in this envelope.
the more the merrier	if more people come, we will have a better party	Tell everybody the party's at my place—the more the merrier!
the most	the greatest, the best etc., **way cool**	You are the most, man. You paint great stuff—like it's real!
the naked eye	without binoculars or field glasses	We can see Mars with the naked eye. We don't need a telescope.
the nitty-gritty	very important matters, **the crunch**	The nitty-gritty of an election is the vote itself—the numbers!
the odd one	one of a few remaining, **few and far between**	"Do you ever see any buffalo?" "Oh, the odd one."
the odds-on favorite	the one who is favored to win, the one to bet on	Orlando was the odds-on favorite but they lost the series.
the old college try	a good effort, trying hard like a college student	Let's give it the old college try, boys. We can win this boat race!
the old man	father or husband, **my old man**	Jenny said, "I'll ask the old man if I can use the car."
the once over	**(See give it the once-over)**	
the one that got away	the fish that got away, the friend you lost	Have I told you about the one that got away? Her name was Lana.
the Peter Principle	people are promoted to a job they cannot do	The manager is an example of the Peter Principle. He's hopeless!

Idiom	Meaning	Example
the picture of health	looking very healthy, **fit as a fiddle**	Rick looks very well these days. He's the picture of health.
the pill	a contraceptive pill, a contraceptive drug	Bev has religious reasons for not taking the pill.
the pit of my stomach	bottom of my stomach, deep in my belly	From the pit of my stomach came a growling sound. I was hungry.
the pits	poor quality, not good value	The music was the pits. The violins played badly.
the point of no return	a time when it is too late to stop or turn back, **change horses in...**	Our offer to purchase the business has been accepted. We've reached the point of no return.
the pope's nose	the tail of a roasted chicken	The pope's nose is too greasy. I prefer a piece of breast meat.
the powers that be	the people in power, the power brokers	I applied for a liquor license, but the powers that be said no.
the price you have to pay	what you must endure or pay or lose	Loneliness is the price you have to pay for being famous.
the proof of the pudding is in the eating	do not judge until you test the finished product, do not **jump to conclusions**	She drew a cartoon of a boy with a plum on his thumb. Then she wrote *The proof of the pudding...*
the rabbit died	according to myth, a sign that a woman is pregnant	When Pop heard I was pregnant he said, "So the rabbit died, eh."
the real McCoy	the real thing, the genuine one	This painting is the real McCoy. It's the original!
the rest is gravy	the rest is free, the rest of the money is profit	When we get the grain cheque, we pay our bills, and the rest is gravy!
the rest is history	the rest of the story is well known; you know the rest; **that's all she wrote**	Fleury took a pass from Suter, went around a defenceman, and the rest is history.
the right stuff	effective skills; the right words or actions	Harry is persuasive. He has the right stuff to become a salesman.
the road to hell is paved with good intentions	good intentions achieve nothing without action, **actions speak louder...**	Convert your charitable feelings into action! *The road to hell is paved with good intentions!*
The Rock	Newfoundland, Canada; (on the east coast)	We know a girl from The Rock. Her name is Sherry Sooley.

Idiom	Meaning	Example
the room is so small you have to go outside to turn around	the room is *very* small; **so small you could barely swing a cat**	It's not a large apartment. The bathroom is so small I have to go outside to turn around!
the root of the problem	the cause of the problem, the reason for the problem	Students don't do enough reading —that's the root of the problem.
the runaround	an indirect answer, **pass the buck, what a rigmarole**	I complained about the dryer, but they gave me the runaround. They blamed the delivery man.
the school of hard knocks	life's hard lessons, learning from mistakes, **roll with the punches**	Teachers taught me what I *should* know; the school of hard knocks taught me what I *must* know.
the shit hit the fan	people become angry, somebody starts a fight	It was a good party until Ed started a fight. Then the shit hit the fan!
the short end of the stick	the worst job, the least pay, **dump on**	When I work with Ken, I always get the short end of the stick. He gives me the hard jobs.
the sin bin (hockey)	the penalty box, **cool your heels**	For tripping, hooking or holding you get two minutes in the sin bin.
the spice of life	things that make life exciting	Romance—for many people, it's the spice of life!
the spitting image	one who looks like someone, **dead ringer**	Patty is the spitting image of her mother—same face, same hair.
the squeaky wheel gets the grease	the person who complains loudest gets served first	Our clerks put up this sign: *The squeaky wheel gets the grease!*
the straight dope	the truth, the facts, **get to the point**	The cop said, "Gimme the straight dope, Shorty. I haven't got time for your stories today."
the straight goods	the truth, the facts, **straight talk**	Gimme the straight goods— the truth—that's all.
the strong, silent type	a quiet and rugged-looking man	Doris loves men like Jeff—the strong, silent type.
the sweet spot	the best spot to touch, the spot that feels good	Keep rubbing. When you find my sweet spot, I'll purr like a kitten.
the tail wagging the dog	minority controlling the majority	If criminals get more rights, the tail will be wagging the dog.
the take	the cash, the amount of money received	The take from the New Year's dance was over $2000.

Idiom	Meaning	Example
the talk of the town	what everybody is talking about, **hot topic**	If a preacher has an affair with a hooker, it's the talk of the town.
the tender age of	the young age of, **still wet behind the ears**	He was the tender age of three when his mother died.
the tide turned	there was a change, **the turning point**	The tide turned when the baby began to nurse. He grew stronger.
the tip of the iceberg	a small part of it, about one-tenth of it	This invoice is only part of the debt—the tip of the iceberg.
the tricks of the trade	skills of an occupation, **learn the ropes**	I know the printing business. I'll show you the tricks of the trade.
the turn of the century	the beginning of a new century: the year 2000	By the turn of the century we will know the aliens who visit earth.
the turning point	the second or minute when things go better or worse, **tip the scales**	When Tanya hit the ball over the fence—that was the turning point in the game.
the underground	the hidden actions of those who fight a law or attack	Some Canadians fought the GST through the underground.
the upper hand	the advantage, **get the jump on**	Because you have graduated from college, you have the upper hand.
the way I see it	my view of it, my opinion	The way I see it, men and women aren't equal physically, eh.
the way to a man's heart is through his stomach	feeding a man good food will cause him to love you, **beauty is only skin deep**	"Do you believe the way to your heart is through your stomach?" "No, but you *are* a great cook!"
the way you hold your mouth	it is a mystery; it could be the shape of your mouth; **hold your mouth...**	"Why does the lock open for you but not for Joan?" "It's the way I hold my mouth."
the wheels fall off	it breaks, it fails, **fall apart**	When the coach is away, our team loses. The wheels fall off!
the whole ball of wax	all related things, **all that jazz**, **the whole nine yards**	Being in love means commitment, sacrifice, patience, understanding —the whole ball of wax.
the whole caboodle	(See **kit and caboodle**)	
the whole nine yards	including all the work, doing the whole job, **the whole ball of wax**	My goals include a degree, career, marriage, children— the whole nine yards.

Idiom	Meaning	Example
the whole shebang	everything, every bit/piece/person	When the cable broke, the whole shebang fell in the river.
the whole shooting match	everything, every bit/piece/person	Wagon, horses, load—the whole shootin' match disappeared.
the whole works	the whole building, all the equipment, everything	The warehouse and stock—the whole works burned in the fire.
the wolf is at the door	poverty is coming, **keep the wolf...**	A month after my husband lost his job, the wolf was at the door.
the world is your oyster	the world is small beside your talent and skill	With imagination—our greatest gift—the world is our oyster.
there are two sides to every story	two people tell different stories of the same event, **compare notes**	If you compare Mary's story with Sam's, you'll know there are two sides to every story.
there you go	you are correct, there is your example, **how about that**	"Everything is green—the grass, the trees. There's a green bird!" "Well, there you go."
there's a catch to it	there is a hidden cost or condition	If we buy the bed, we get a TV? There must be a catch to it.
there's many a slip twixt the cup and the lip	it is easy to spill what you are drinking; it is easy to make mistakes	On the side of the beer mug were these words: *There's many a slip twixt the cup and the lip.*
there's more than meets the eye	part of the story has not been told	In a government scandal, there's always more than meets the eye.
there's more than one way to skin a cat	there are many ways to do it, I know another method	For math problems, there's more than one way to skin a cat.
there's no love lost	they do not like each other, **bad blood**, **hold a grudge**	There's no love lost between Jay and Pete. They've been fighting since they were boys.
there's no tomorrow	we have to win today; if we lose, we are out; **do or die**	The Bruins will be eliminated if they lose tonight. There's no tomorrow.
there's no two ways about it	there is only one answer; cannot have two meanings	We have to get you on that plane. There's no two ways about it.
there's not much to choose between them	they are nearly equal, **it's a toss-up**	A Ford or a Mercury—there's not much to choose between them.
there's nothing to it	it is easy to do, **it's a snap**	I can solve this math problem. There's nothing to it.

Idiom	Meaning	Example
there's nothing to it	it is not true, it is a lie	I heard that Pearl had left Carlos, but there's nothing to it.
there's one born every minute	there are lots of people who will believe anything, there are lots of **suckers**	"Only a sucker would buy this car." "Right, and there's one born every minute."
there's something fishy	there is something wrong, there is something strange	There's something fishy about a 1970 car with only 5000 km.
there's something rotten in the state of Denmark	something is wrong, something is strange, **there's something fishy**	Father knew I was tricking him. He said, "Something is rotten in the state of Denmark."
these parts	these parts of the country; **neck of the woods**	In these parts, folks don't like federal politicians.
thick as a brick	slow to understand, slow to learn	We're all thick as a brick in at least one subject, eh?
thingamabob/thingamajig/ thingamadoodle	name for a strange part, **whatchamacallit**	If I can get the thingamajig in the right hole, this car may start.
things are looking up	we are feeling positive, life is better	Now that Vic has a job, things are looking up. We feel positive.
think better of it	change my decision, decide not to do it	We were going to buy a trailer, but we thought better of it.
think nothing of it	my help was nothing, **no problem**, **not at all**	"Thank you for helping us find our lost puppy." "Think nothing of it."
think over	think more about, consider	I'm going to think over what you said about keeping the baby.
think straight	think clearly, be rational	I'm so tired I can't think straight. Let me rest; then we can talk.
think tank	people thinking together, **brain storm**	Our company think tank will solve the problem.
think the world of	admire greatly, **worship the ground...**	Samson thinks the world of you. He would do anything for you.
think through	think in steps, think carefully	Before you go to the manager with an idea, think it through.
think up	imagine, create	My story is finished. Now I have to think up a title.
third degree	careful questioning, **on the carpet**	If I'm late, I get the third degree. Mom asks me a lot of questions.

Idiom	Meaning	Example
this one is on me	I will pay for this one (drink, lunch, etc.)	"This one's on me," Mr. Kirby said as he paid for my lunch.
thorn in my side	(See **a thorn in my side**)	
thrash	driven hard and fast, used carelessly	That car has been thrashed. Don't buy it.
threads	clothes, **glad rags**, **rags**	Hey, Lucy. Nice threads! I love your jacket.
three-bagger	(See **a three-bagger**)	
three sheets to the wind	very drunk, **plastered**, **pissed to the gills**	The Captain was three sheets to the wind—staggering.
three slices short (of a full loaf)	mentally disabled, **one brick short...**	If you order worm soup, they'll think you're three slices short.
through the grapevine	through gossip, **bush telegraph**	"How did you know I moved?" "I heard it through the grapevine."
through the mill	used a lot, nearly **worn out**	These jeans have been through the mill. They're ragged.
through the roof	(See **go through the roof**)	
through the wringer	experienced a lot of personal problems	Hey, I'm tough. I've been through the wringer a few times.
through thick and thin	during good and bad times, **for better or worse**	My dog Pal stays with me through thick and thin. He's a true friend.
throw a curve	confuse, deceive, surprise	Dad threw a curve at me when he asked if he could borrow $1000.
throw a game	deliberately lose a game, cause your team to lose, **take a dive**	They said that Red threw his last game of pool, but I think he's too honest to do that.
throw a kiss	kiss your hand and wave, **blow a kiss**	When Madonna threw a kiss to her fans, they cheered.
throw a monkey wrench into the works	wreck a project, **monkeywrenching**, **piss in the pickles**	The report that coffee causes cancer threw a monkey wrench into our plans to import coffee.
throw a party	invite people to a party, have a party	Connie throws the best parties. Everybody has a great time.
throw a tantrum	show your bad temper, **lose your cool**	When I refused to buy candy for Reggie, he threw a tantrum.

Idiom	Meaning	Example
throw away	put in the garbage, **throw out**	I threw away those old magazines. I hope you didn't want them.
throw caution to the wind	live or act carelessly, not be cautious	Let's throw caution to the wind and buy ten dresses!
throw chunks	vomit, puke, **barf, hurl, woof your cookies**	One look at those oysters and she started throwing chunks. Yuk!
throw cold water on	discourage, cause you to lose interest	Don't be negative. Don't throw cold water on our travel plans.
throw down your arms	stop fighting or arguing, **bury the hatchet**	It's time to throw down your arms and forgive him.
throw good money after bad	spend more on a failure, repair a poor product	If we fix that TV again, we'll be throwing good money after bad.
throw in the towel	quit fighting, **give up**	Don't throw in the towel. One more year and you'll graduate.
throw insults	say rude things, insult someone	When you don't get what you want, you start throwing insults.
throw me for a loop	confuse me, **phase me out**	The question on parliamentary procedure threw me for a loop.
throw on a dog for you	cook a wiener for you, make a **hotdog** for you	Hal was cooking wieners on the barbecue. "Can I throw on a dog for you?" he asked.
throw out	put in the garbage, discard, **throw away**	Do you want these old magazines, or should I throw them out?
throw some light on	explain, give information, **shed a little light on**	Martin, can you throw some light on the DNA? Explain it to us?
throw that in	mention that, suggest that	Don't forget to add the sales tax— just thought I'd throw that in.
throw the baby out with the bath water	throw away something good with the waste, discard everything	Keep the good subjects when you revise the course. Don't throw the baby out with the bath water!
throw the book at	punish to the maximum, **come down hard**	Drunk drivers deserve the full penalty. Throw the book at them!
throw up	vomit, puke, **barf, ralph, upchuck**	The baby will throw up if you bounce him after he's eaten.
throw you	cause you to forget or stumble	Don't let the large crowd throw you. Focus on your music.

Idiom	Meaning	Example
throw you to the dogs	let you fight alone, let you fight the bad guys	Let us help you. The pimps will throw you to the dogs.
throw your weight around	use power to scare you, **power trip**	Bud throws his weight around— tells everybody what to do.
thrown in	added to a list, recipe etc.; included afterwards	The weather will be cloudy, with a shower or two thrown in.
titch	(See **just a titch**)	
ticked off	a little upset, annoyed, **teed off**	Fred gets ticked off at people who throw butts out the window.
tickety-boo	operating well, **A-OK**	After they gave him insulin, everything was tickety-boo.
ticketed	known as, named, labeled	If you do something funny, you'll be ticketed as the team clown.
tickled pink	happy, very pleased	Aunt Sophia was tickled pink to receive a photo of the family.
tiddly	neat, tidy, clean and shiny, **spiffy**	The ship is ready for inspection. Everything is tiddly.
tide turned	(See **the tide turned**)	
tie in	connect, relate	Can you tell me how lasers tie in? How do lasers apply to surgery?
tie into	scold, lecture, **give you hell** [B]	When we were alone, he tied into me. He said I caused the problem.
tie one on	drink a lot of liquor, become very drunk	At Cayla's wedding, Uncle Ben tied one on. He got really drunk.
tie up	tie a string or piece of rope around	If you tie up the parcel I'll take it to the post office.
tie up loose ends	finish a project, complete the details of some work, **finishing touch**	"Have you finished the survey?" "Just about. I have to tie up some loose ends and print the report."
tied to your mother's apron strings	still dependent on mom, needing your mom's help	He has to ask his mother. He's still tied to her apron strings.
tied up	busy, unable to help	I'm tied up right now. I'm busy with a client.
tight/tight fisted	not generous, unwilling to spend, **cheap**	People say he's so tight he'd sell a gift and bank the money.

Idiom	Meaning	Example
tight race	close race, **down to the wire**	It was a tight race for the mayor's position. Kutz won by ten votes.
tight spot	uncomfortable position, **between a rock and a hard place**	At the interview Vic was in a tight spot. They asked him, "Why were you dismissed from three jobs?"
tight-ass [B]	stingy person; **tight fisted**	Mason is a tight-ass! He collects rent from his old grandmother.
tighten our belts	not spend as much, be careful with our money	We'll have to tighten our belts when Stan goes on pension.
till hell freezes over	until the end of time, until the end of the world	You can wait till hell freezes over but they won't pay their bill.
till the cows come home	for a long time, for days or weeks	A letter from Dave? You'll be waiting till the cows come home!
till you're blue in the face	until you are very tired, until you look sick	You can train a flea till you're blue in the face, but he won't learn.
time and again	many times, repeatedly	I've told that boy time and again not to fight, but he won't listen.
time flies when you're having fun	time goes quickly when you are playing, **how time flies**	Ho looked at his watch, yawned and said, "Time flies when you're having fun, eh."
time is money	time is valuable, time is equal to money	Employers who pay hourly wages know that time is money.
time is of the essence	it is important to work as quickly as possible, **make hay while...**	When you're paying $75 an hour for a lawyer's services, time is of the essence.
time off	days off work, holidays	I've been working too hard. I think I need some time off.
time on your hands	time to relax or do what you wish, **time to kill**	If you have time on your hands, read the novel *Fifth Business*.
time out	stop for a minute to discuss or plan	We need a time out to look at the map. I think we're lost.
time ran out	there was no more time allowed for the game etc.	Time ran out before I could complete the exam.
time to kill	time to relax or rest, **kill time**	We had some time to kill while the car was being repaired.
time to time	(See **from time to time**)	

Idiom	Meaning	Example
time's a wasting	we are wasting time, we should be working	Time's a wasting. Let's finish our work and then rest.
time's up	there is no more time for the test or game etc.	The coach checked his watch and said, "Time's up. Stop running."
times were hard	it was a time of poverty, **hard times**	It was 1850. Times were hard in Sweden then.
tin ear	unmusical ear, unable to appreciate music	With my tin ear, I couldn't say if she was singing flat.
tin Lizzie	car, old car	You can park your tin Lizzie over there beside the barn.
tip a few	drink a few beer etc., **bend your elbow**	Chuck used to tip a few when he was younger. He drank with us.
tip of my tongue	(See **on the tip of my tongue**)	
tip of the iceberg	(See **the tip of the iceberg**)	
tip the scales	change or influence a decision, **the upper hand**	If you speak two languages, it could tip the scales in your favor when you apply for a job.
tip the scales at	cause the scale to go up, **weigh in at**	Elmer tips the scales at 135 kilos. He's a heavyweight.
tip your hand	reveal your plan, show your strategy	Don't tip your hand in a game of chess. Surprise the opponent.
tipsy	a little bit drunk, slightly drunk, **buzzed**	After her third glass of sherry, Mona was a little tipsy.
tired of	bored, not interested	I'm tired of that song. I hear it every morning.
tired out	tired, weary, **dog tired**	When our visitors left, I was tired out. I slept for hours.
tit for tat	equal response, **an eye for an eye**	Gerry hit Ross. Then Ross hit Gerry, and it was tit for tat.
tits and ass (T & A) [B]	sexual stimuli for men, **cheesecake**	The men's parties have a lot of T & A—dancing girls.
tits up [B]	dead, not operating, **kaput**	The tractor's tits up again— the clutch is broken.
to a fault	doing it too much, **go overboard**	May gives most of her money to charity. She's generous to a fault.

Idiom	Meaning	Example
to a man	every man or person, not one person disagreed	We asked the team who should be coach. To a man, they chose you.
to be perfectly honest	to tell you the truth, to tell you exactly how I feel, **as a matter of fact**	"Your cat's up in the tree again." "To be perfectly honest, I don't care. Let him come down alone."
to beat the band	with lots of energy, **like crazy**, **like mad**	Aunt Jemima was making pancakes to beat the band.
to blame	at fault, guilty	Who's to blame for starting the fire? Who did it?
to boot	in addition to, plus	We'll trade you the car for the truck and give you $500 to boot.
to coin a phrase	to create a new phrase, to **make up** a phrase	To coin a phrase, "Life is just book of idioms!"
to each his own	we like different things, **one man's garbage...**	She likes the Rolling Stones, but he likes Mozart—to each his own.
to go	remaining, left to do	We've cleaned five rooms. Just one to go.
to go	to take with you	One large pizza—to go, please.
to heart	(See **take it to heart**)	
to hell with that [B]	that is not a good idea, **no way**	"You could plead guilty." "To hell with that!"
to the best of my knowledge	I believe this is true, **as far as I know**	To the best of my knowledge, Barrie and Bonnie are twins.
to the max	to the greatest amount, **groaty to the max**	You should see this video. It's grungy to the max!
to top it off	to complete it, to finish it	To top it off, they presented us with Olympic pins.
to-do	(See **make a big to-do**)	
toast	in a lot of trouble, **catch hell** [B], **history**	Ferris, if you drive your father's Porsche, you're toast.
toe the line	do what you are told to do, **follow the rules**	The Military expects you to toe the line—to do as you are told.
together	happy, successful; **get it together**, **with it**	Cathy is really together. She's knows how she wants to live and she's doing it.

Idiom	Meaning	Example
toke up	smoke marijuana, smoke pot	Does it matter if some of our politicians used to toke up?
token gesture	(See **a token gesture**)	
ton of bricks	(See **like a ton of bricks**)	
tone down	make softer or nicer; not so harsh	"What do you think of the letter?" "I'd tone it down. It's too harsh."
toney neighborhood	a district that has expensive houses	The Kitigawas bought a large house in a toney neighborhood.
tongue in cheek	fooling, joking, **kidding**	Most of what Bob said was tongue in cheek. He was joking.
tongue-lashing	(See **a tongue-lashing**)	
tons	lots, very much/many, **a holy pile**	There were tons of people at the wedding—and tons of food!
too bad	a little bit sad, unfortunate	Too bad Annie won't be home when I visit. I'd like to see her.
too big for his britches	too proud, **cocky**, **swelled head**	I promise not to get too big for my britches if I win the award.
too deep for me	too complicated, too complex	The DNA theory is too deep for me. I can't understand it.
too far gone	not able to stop a disease, **a goner**	Several doctors tried to treat the cancer, but it was too far gone.
too little too late	not enough effort or work when it was needed, **make hay while...**	The Roughriders scored two touchdowns in the fourth quarter, but it was too little too late. They lost.
too many chiefs and not enough Indians	too many directors and not enough workers, **too many cooks...**	Everybody tried to be the boss. We had too many chiefs and not enough Indians.
too many cooks spoil the broth	too many managers cause problems, **too many chiefs...**	The structure failed because it was designed by a group of architects. Too many cooks spoil the broth.
toodles/toodle-oo	bye, good–bye, **so long**	"Toodle-oo," she said, smiling. "I must go now."
tool around	play, **fool around**, **goof off**	The students were tooling around because they had no assignment.

Idiom	Meaning	Example
toot your own horn	brag, talk about your own success	Since Ted won the bowling trophy he's been tooting his own horn.
tooth and nail	(See **fight tooth and nail**)	
top dog	boss, leader, **head honcho**	Kruger is top dog now, but he could lose the next election.
top drawer	excellent, **first class**	Amy's report is top drawer. It deserves a high grade.
top it off	finish it, add the last piece or statement	He topped it off by saying we would get a big bonus this year.
top it up	fill it to the top, fill it to the mark	Check the oil every week and top it up if necessary.
top-notch	very good quality, **first class**	Claret Sol is a top-notch wine, but it's very dry.
top of the morning	good morning, have a good morning, the best of the morning	Old Tweedsmuir would say, "Top o' the morning to you," as we walked to school.
top that	do better than that, improve on that	"Top that!" the farmer said, holding up a six-pound potato.
toss it around	discuss it, consider it	We like your idea. Can we toss it around for awhile? Discuss it?
toss-up	(See **it's a toss-up**)	
total stranger	(See **a total stranger**)	
totally awesome	excellent, fantastic, **far out**	The Band was totally awesome! They were excellent!
touch a drop	drink a drop of liquor, have a drink of liquor	Steve was a heavy drinker, but he hasn't touched a drop in years.
touch and go	between life and death, **nip and tuck**	I recovered from my heart attack, but it was touch and go for awhile.
touch base	contact again, **keep in touch**	Touch base with me in a month or so. Call me about May 10.
touch it with a ten-foot pole	reply, answer, comment on it, **beat around the bush**	If anyone in your audience asks a question about religion, don't touch it with a ten-foot pole.
touch of	(See **a touch of**)	

Idiom	Meaning	Example
touch off	start an argument or a fight, **set off**	His remark about gun control touched off a heated discussion.
touch on	speak briefly about, mention	Ms. Lee spoke on sales, then touched briefly on service.
touch up	add details, make small changes	I touched up the painting in a few places. Does it look better?
touch wood	hoping that our good luck continues	We've never had a flat tire on this car—touch wood.
touch you	cause you to feel love or sorrow or regret	Did Mom's letter touch you? Do you feel sorry for her?
touched	(See **touched in the head**)	
touched in the head	a bit crazy, **a bit off**, **funny in the head**	People will think you're touched in the head if you wear that Superman suit to work.
touchy	sensitive, ready to argue, **edgy**	Barb is kind of touchy about her weight. Don't comment on it.
tough act to follow	(See **a tough act to follow**)	
tough bananas	it is a problem for you, **too bad**, **tough luck**	"I had to *walk* to school!" "Well, tough bananas!"
tough call	(See **a tough call**)	
tough customer	a determined person, one who fights hard	Remember John Ferguson? He was one tough customer.
tough luck	that is bad luck for you, **tough bananas**	"I lost $100 betting on Ali." "Tough luck, guy."
tough on me	makes me work hard, **hard on me**	My supervisor is tough on me— never satisfied with my work.
tough row to hoe	(See **a tough row to hoe**)	
tough sledding	hard work, slow progress, **heavy going**, **rough going**	We've had tough sledding on our building projects. Rainy weather has caused a lot of problems.
tough tarts	(See **tough bananas**)	
tough titty	(See **tough luck**)	
toughen up	become tougher, grow stronger	The army will toughen him up. They'll develop his stamina.

Idiom	Meaning	Example
tower of strength	(See **a tower of strength**)	
toy with	not be serious about me, not **take me seriously**	I love her, but she's just toying with me—playing with me.
track record	list of achievements, summary of career work	Lou's track record is excellent. She was top seller last year.
trade insults	insult each other, say rude things to each other, **mudsling**	When the two men couldn't agree on the cause of the problem, they began trading insults.
trade secret	a business secret, a special recipe or formula	I won't tell how Paula makes her pizza. It's a trade secret.
traffic jam	traffic that is not moving, many vehicles on one road	I was late for class because of a traffic jam. Honest!
train of thought	(See **lose my train of thought**)	
tranny	transmission of a car or truck	When you buy a used car, check the condition of the tranny, eh.
trash	wreck, ruin, **ratch**	That puppy trashed one of my slippers—chewed it to pieces!
trash the place	wreck a room or building, **a bull in a China shop**	If you invite the Casey boys, they'll trash the place.
trendy	fashionable, at the beginning of a trend	That's a trendy coat she's wearing. I've seen it in fashion magazines.
trial and error	learn by correcting errors, **hit and miss**	We learned to make pizza by trial and error. We gradually improved.
trickle-down economics	a system that depends on government spending to help the economy	Private enterprise is better than trickle-down economics because profit motivates people.
tricks of the trade	(See **the tricks of the trade**)	
tried and true	tested and proven, reliable, **true blue**	When Sven chops wood, he uses a Sandvik axe. It's tried and true.
trifle with me	be careless about my feelings, **mind games**, **toy with me**	When John forgot that he asked me to go to the dance, I felt he was trifling with me.
true blue	loyal, faithful	Moe is true blue. We've been good friends for forty years.
true colors	real beliefs, true values, principles	In the debate on abortion we'll see her true colors—her beliefs.

Idiom	Meaning	Example
try it	try to do it, **try your hand at**	After I sing the song, you try it. See if you can sing it.
try it on	wear a garment to see if it fits	If you like that dress, you can try it on in one of our fitting rooms.
try it out	use it for awhile, test it, **test drive**	This is our new life-time pen. Would you like to try it out?
try me	ask me, see what I say; challenge me, **find out**	"You wouldn't call the police, would you?" "Just try me."
try out	try to become a member of a team	Let's try out for soccer this year. Let's play on the team.
try that	try to do that, **pull that**	When I reached for the phone, the thief said, "Don't try that."
try that on for size	see if you like that, consider that	This TV has a 48" screen. Try that on for size.
try your darndest	try very hard, **bend over backwards**, **go the extra mile**	I try my darndest to be fair to customers, but some are never satisfied.
try your hand at	try to do, **try it**	Would you like to try your hand at washing dishes? It's fun!
try your luck	see if you can win, you **take a chance**	They won a prize. Do you want to try your luck?
tube head	a person who watches TV a lot, **couch potato**	In the winter he's a tube head— always watching hockey on TV.
tube him	leave him, **drop him**	He was a bore so I tubed him.
tubular	nice, fun, **cool**	The lounge was totally tubular, a great place to take her friends.
tuckered out	short of breath, panting, puffing	Timmy was tuckered out after jogging with his father.
tune in	adjust the tuning knob on a radio or receiver	The announcer said, "Tune in tonight at 8 for our Talk Show."
tune me out	stop listening to me, not **pay attention** to me	If you speak in a boring way, students will tune you out.
tune up	improve the operation, improve performance	After Fred tunes up the Mercedes the motor will run smoother.

Idiom	Meaning	Example
tuned in	able to understand, **on the same wavelength**	If you're tuned in, you know who I've been talking about.
tunnel vision	looking straight ahead, not seeing other directions	Our president has tunnel vision. He believes in only one plan.
turf it	cut it, delete it, **throw out**	If students don't enrol in the program, we'll have to turf it.
turkey	fool, **dumbo**, **jerk**	You turkey! Why did you put jelly on my pizza?
turn a blind eye	see a problem but not act, **look the other way**	The teacher knows that I come in late, but she turns a blind eye.
turn a profit	profit from, **make money**	It will be a year before we turn a profit on this new product.
turn about is fair play	the same rules apply to both sides, **what goes around...**	You tripped him; he tripped you. Turn about is fair play.
turn down	refuse, not accept	Sal turned me down when I asked her to go to a movie. She refused.
turn in	give to the manager, **hand in**	When you leave our company, please turn in your uniform.
turn in	go to bed, **crash**, **hit the hay**	I'm going to turn in now. I'm very tired.
turn into	become, change into, convert	If you eat any more hotdogs you'll turn into a wiener!
turn of the century	(See **the turn of the century**)	
turn on a dime	turn sharply, turn quickly, **do a 180**	A Celica has excellent steering. It can turn on a dime.
turn on you	turn against you, change from friend to enemy	If you preach your religion, they may get mad and turn on you.
turn out	happen, develop, **end up**	How did your cake turn out? Is it a good recipe?
turn out	attend, **show up**	Only 40% of the population turned out to vote.
turn over a new leaf	begin living by a new set of rules or values	Since Bob stopped drinking he's turned over a new leaf.
turn the corner	achieve part of a goal, progress toward a goal	Lan was very ill, but she's turned the corner. She's recovering.

Idiom	Meaning	Example
turn the other cheek	accept hurt twice, not fight back	He is a passive man. He will turn the other cheek instead of fight.
turn the other way	look away or ignore, **look the other way**	When I come in late, he turns the other way. He tries not to notice.
turn the tables on	begin to defeat the person who was defeating you, **mount a comeback**	When I learned how to return his serve, I turned the tables on him and won the set.
turn ugly	become uncivilized, begin fighting	When Buddy insulted Ted's wife, things turned ugly.
turn up	attend a meeting, **show up**	Only fifteen people turned up at the Block Parents' meeting.
turn up	be found, be seen	We can't find the ring now, but I'm sure it will turn up soon.
turn up your nose at	say it is not good enough, reject it	If you turn up your nose at country music, you may lose some friends.
turn you around	help you begin a new life, **turn over a new leaf**	His new friends helped to turn him around. He's much nicer now.
turn you on	arouse you, cause you to feel excited	"What turns you on?" "Good books and nice girls."
turn your crank	interest you, inspire you	Classical music turns his crank. He likes the great symphonies.
turn your stomach	make you feel sick, cause you to feel ill	Watching you eat those oysters turns my stomach. Yuk!
turn yourself in	walk into a police station to tell them what you did, **own up**	If you tell your counsellor about the shooting, he'll advise you to turn yourself in.
turn-on	something that excites or arouses you	Her voice was a turn-on for me. She has a sexy voice.
turning point	(See **the turning point**)	
turnout	the number of people, the size of the group	There was a good turnout at the Writers' Club today: 20 people.
tweak	increase the power, **hop up**, **supercharge**	If we tweak the engine in this old Cortina, we'll have a sports car.
twerp	small child or person, **knee high to a grass...**	Ricky is just a twerp. He can ride on Grandpa's knee.

Idiom	Meaning	Example
twig to that	think of that, realize that	His uncle Ralph is the Premier! I just twigged to that.
twiggy	slim person, as slim as a twig on a branch	Kim is a gymnast. She's slim and agile—a real twiggy.
twilight years	senior years, over 70, **golden years**	Grandma wants to keep her own home during her twilight years.
twist my arm	persuade me, convince me	I really don't like pie, but if you twist my arm, I'll have a piece.
twist of fate	the way fate works, the way things happen	Then, by a twist of fate, a plane flew over and the pilot saw us.
twist your words	change the meaning of what you say, **put a different slant...**	When she gave her testimony in court, the lawyer tried to twist her words to mean something else.
twit	fool, **airhead**, **dipstick**	What a twit! He thinks a busboy is a kid who rides the bus!
two abreast	two people standing or walking side by side	The children were walking two abreast on the way home.
two bits	.25¢, twenty-five cents, a quarter	Can you lend me two bits? I have to phone home.
two for one	two products for the price of one	Want a milk shake? We can buy two for one at Toy's Ice Cream.
two left feet	awkwardness, poor coordination	When it comes to dancing, I have two left feet. I stumble a lot.
two pee holes in the snow	small holes, tiny holes	He looks very tired. His eyes are like two pee holes in the snow.
two sides to every story	(See **there are two sides to every story**)	
two's company, three's a crowd	two people are happier than three, the third person is not welcome	Jill asked, "Can I invite Ginger?" Jack replied, "Two's company, three's a crowd."
two-cents' worth	opinion, comment	Want to hear my two-cents' worth? Want my opinion?
two-fisted attack	strong verbal attack, much argument, **rattle sabres**	If you protect the wolves, you can expect a two-fisted attack from the ranchers.
typo	error in typing, **nitpick**	The interviewer said my letter of application has a few typos.

Idiom	Meaning	Example

U

U-turn	turn and go the opposite direction, **do a 180**	The driver of the truck made a U-turn and drove back into town.
uh-huh	yes, **yep**	"Do you want a piece of cake?" "Uh-huh."
uh-uh	no, **nope**	"Have you done your homework?" "Uh-uh."
under a spell	controlled by a spirit or magic, **cast a spell**	She danced when she saw the cat. She seemed to be under a spell.
under arrest	stopped and taken away by the police, **busted**	"Jean, you are under arrest." "What for, sir?" "For stealing a loaf of bread."
under control	order restored, control returned	The prisoners caused a riot, but things are now under control.
under fire	being asked many difficult questions	After your speech, you will be under fire from reporters.
under his own steam	by himself, without help	Although Don was injured, he left the field under his own steam.
under my belt	completed, finished	With an accounting course under my belt, I can do the bookkeeping.
under my breath	whispered, not spoken loud enough to hear	When the teacher asks questions, I often answer under my breath.
under my care	cared for by me, **look after**	The house is under my care until the owner returns from Europe.
under my skin	in my thoughts, in my feelings	I can't stop thinking about Paul. I've got him under my skin.
under my wing	having my protection and help and guidance	I am Anna's guardian. She'll be under my wing until she's 18.
under oath	after promising to tell the truth in court	At the trial you will be asked to tell your story under oath.

Idiom	Meaning	Example
under pressure	feeling of too much to do, feeling a lot of stress	Gabor is under a lot of pressure now. He's working at two jobs.
under the influence of alcohol	partly drunk, **buzzed**	Is he under the influence now? Is he drunk?
under the table	hidden, not recorded, not **above board**, **on the side**	"Do you get paid for bringing customers to the store?" "I don't get a cheque—just a little money under the table."
under the weather	not feeling well, ill, sick, not **feeling myself**	Dan's been under the weather lately—sick with the flu.
under the wire	just before the end, before closing, **just in time**	"Did you receive my application?" "It arrived on the last day of the competition, just under the wire."
under way	started, commenced	The concert is under way. The band is playing *O Canada*.
under wraps	secret, not advertised, **on the QT**	I know the name of the winner, but I have to keep it under wraps until tonight.
under your thumb	under your control, doing your wishes	Willie is under your thumb now. He does what you tell him to do.
underdog	the player or team that is not likely to win	The Canucks are underdogs this year. People say they won't win.
underhanded	not legal, not according to rules, not **above board**	Some people say the government was underhanded in dealing with the Indians.
unsung hero	great person who has not been honored or praised, **behind the scenes**	The mothers of the graduates are the unsung heroes. The mothers are Homework Supervisors!
until you're blue...	(See **till you're blue in the face**)	
up a storm	(See **sing up a storm**)	
up against	competing against, trying to defeat	"Who were you up against?" "Gaetan Boucher, the Champion."
up against it	poor, not able to pay the bills, **hard up**	We were up against it that year. The crop had failed, we had lots of bills, and none of us had a job.
up and coming	starting to develop ability, showing potential	Lisel has won six junior trophies. She's an up-and-coming athlete.

Idiom	Meaning	Example
up and running	operating, working	Andre is repairing the copier. It will soon be up and running.
up for grabs	available, can be bought	The estate will be sold by auction. Even the antiques are up for grabs.
up for it	ready, prepared to play, **pumped**	Tonight's game is important. Every player has to be up for it.
up for sale	advertised for sale, **on the market**	The Wongs must be moving. Their house is up for sale.
up front	at the beginning, **level with** beforehand	He was up front with me. He told me about the interest charges *first*.
up in arms	angry, ready to fight, **hot**	The smokers are up in arms about the no-smoking bylaw.
up in smoke	burned, destroyed by fire	The barn went up in smoke before the fire truck arrived.
up in the air	not decided, not settled	They aren't sure who killed the President. It's still up in the air.
up on	aware of, informed about, **on top of**	Are you up on the latest computer games? Have you played UFOX?
up shit creek [B]	in a bad situation, **in a fix**	If we lose our matches, we're up shit creek. We need a campfire.
up the ante	increase the payment, increase the deposit	If they up the ante to $50, I won't enter the hockey pool this year.
up the creek	in a predicament, in difficulty, **in a jam**	Without insurance, you could be up the creek if there's a fire.
up the stump [B]	pregnant, **a bun in the oven**	She didn't use a contraceptive, so she's up the stump again.
up to	planning, doing	What are you up to? Are you planning another fishing trip?
up to date	recent, current	The radio reports events as they happen. The news is up to date.
up to it	have enough energy to do it, **up for it**	"Would you like to play another game of badminton?" "No, I don't think I'm up to it."
up to my ears	have too many, **coming out of our ears**	You're selling books? I'm up to my ears in books!

Idiom	Meaning	Example
up to no good	doing bad things, causing problems	Tom's up to no good these days— stealing drugs and selling them.
up to par	good enough to pass, up to a standard	This woodwork is not up to par. It's below our standard.
up to scratch	good enough, **up to par**	The cloth in these jeans is poor quality. It's not up to scratch.
up to snuff	good quality, **measure up**	We expect quality photographs— every picture must be up to snuff.
up to something	trying to make a deal, planning a joke	David is up to something. He has a look of mischief in his eye.
up to speed	at normal speed, feeling healthy again	Tim's recovered from his surgery but he's not up to speed yet.
up to you	your choice, your decision	Whether you go or stay is up to you. It's your decision.
up with	support it, this is good	Millie was waving a flag and shouting, "Up with fluoride!"
up your alley	what you like to do, what interests you	Sewing—that's right up your alley. It's one of your hobbies.
up your sleeve	hidden, ready to use if asked	When I write an exam, I like to have a topic up my sleeve.
up yours [B]	I hope you have an accident, **screw you**	When she told him to get out of the house, he said, "Up yours!"
upchuck	vomit, puke, **barf**, **hork**	Please hand me the paper towel. Baby upchucked on my sweater.
uphill battle	difficult work, **rough going**, **tough sledding**	We've asked the government to protect children's rights, but it's an uphill battle all the way.
upper crust	upper class, high class, aristocracy	Kurt acts like upper crust because his ancestor was a German baron.
upper hand	(See **the upper hand**)	
upset the apple cart	cause a major problem, stop progress	You will upset the apple cart if you tell your folks we're moving.
upside	positive side, good news	If war has an upside, it would be that it's good for the economy.

Idiom	Meaning	Example
uptight	tense, nervous, not relaxed, **worried sick**	"What are you uptight about?" "I'm not sure. It could be fear of losing my job."
use up	use all of it, use all you have	We've used up all the shampoo. Please buy some more.
used to	accustomed to, having felt it often	Lynn is used to being alone. Henry is away from home a lot.
useless as a fifth wheel	(See **as useless as a fifth wheel**)	
useless as the tits...	(See **as useless as the tits on a boar**)	
user friendly	easy to learn or use, easy to operate	Cars with automatic transmission are user friendly—easy to drive.
uzi	(See **pack uzis**)	

Idiom	Meaning	Example

V

vamoose	leave quickly, go, **get going, hit the road**	We better vamoose, my friend, or we'll be late for our appointment.
variety is the spice of life	a variety of experiences makes life interesting, **to each his own**	On the sign above the door were these words: GENERAL STORE *Variety is the spice of life!*
vegetate (veg out)	not do anything, be a **couch potato**	After work he just vegetates— just sits there and says nothing.
VIP	Very Important Person, **big boys, big wig**	Only the VIP's—the president, and members of the board— are invited to the dinner.
virgin territory	untouched or unexplored area	The island was virgin territory. There were no signs of humans.
virtual reality	a "real" experience created on a computer	Virtual reality allowed me to experience space travel.
visit a spell	visit for awhile, **set a spell**	Well hello, Charlie. Come in and visit a spell.

Idiom	Meaning	Example

W

Idiom	Meaning	Example
wacko	crazy, **bonkers, nuts**	If I eat worms, will people think I'm wacko?
wacky	silly, foolish, **kooky, nutty as a fruit cake**	Lucy sometimes does wacky things—like, one time she sent ice cream in the mail.
wait a minute	pause for a short time, think about this, **hold it**	Wait a minute. Before we visit Doris, let's phone her.
wait a sec	wait for a second, **wait up**	Wait a sec, Mag. I'll be right there.
wait around	wait to see what will happen, **hang around**	Let's wait around and see if the bird returns to its nest.
wait for the other shoe to drop	wait for the final step, wait for the conclusion, **leave me hanging**	He said he'd make two changes. First, he resigned. I'm waiting for the other shoe to drop.
wait on customers	serve customers in a restaurant or store	Please wait on the customers in the lounge. Take their orders.
wait on tables	(See **wait on customers**)	
wait on you hand and foot	serve you, bring everything you want, **suck up to**	Anna says she's tired of waiting on you hand and foot. She won't be your slave anymore.
wait up	wait for me, wait until I **catch up**	Danny, wait up. I want to talk to you.
wait up for	not go to bed until the kids come home at night	Mom always waits up for us when we go to a party.
wait with bated breath	wait with suspense, want to know what happens	We waited with bated breath for news of the fallen climber.
wake up	awaken, rouse from sleep	On Saturday I usually wake up around noon. **I sleep in.**

Idiom	Meaning	Example
wake up	be alert, stop daydreaming	Wake up, Walter. It's your turn to deal the cards.
wake up and smell the coffee	be more aware, **get with it**	You don't know about the Net? Wake up and smell the coffee!
wake with a start	wake suddenly, jump out of bed	I woke with a start when Santa Claus landed on our roof.
walk	not have to pay a fine or go to jail, **get off**	They couldn't prove that Don was guilty, so he walked.
walk a straight line	walk without staggering, show that you are sober	If you can't walk a straight line, don't drive a vehicle.
walk down	walk along, walk on	We walked down the road to the lake. It was a nice day for a walk.
walk of life	lifestyle, occupation, vocation	People from all walks of life eat at Fabio's Restaurants.
walk on eggshells	be very careful, **watch your step**	Your son is so afraid of making a mistake he's walking on eggshells.
walk the talk	do what you talk about doing, **practice what you preach**	If we advise people to recycle, *we* should recycle. We have to walk the talk.
walk through	read or perform slowly, practice slowly	At our first rehearsal we walked through the first act of the play.
walk up	walk along, walk on, walk in	They walked up and down the hall, waiting for the doctor.
walk-through	inspect the house you are buying just before you become the owner	The day before we moved into our new home, we did a walk-through with the real estate agent.
wall flower	a girl who is not invited to dance, **shrinking violet**	I won't go to the party because I feel like a wall flower when the boys don't ask me to dance.
warmed over	warmed on a stove, reheated	For supper we had warmed-over waffles. They tasted okay.
want a piece of me	want to hurt me, want revenge, **have at me**	I wrote a letter to the local paper criticizing the hockey team. Now everybody wants a piece of me.
want it so bad I can taste it	want it very much, **die for**	I want that trophy. I want it so bad I can taste it.

Idiom	Meaning	Example
want to make something of it	do you want to argue or fight about it?	Yes, I did kiss Millie Watkins. Wanna make something of it?
warm up	begin to exercise, exercise slowly	To warm up, she walks about a kilometre; then she jogs.
warped sense of humor	thinking that weird things are funny, **sense of humor**	If you laugh at cruelty, you have a warped sense of humor.
wash	(See **a wash**)	
wash down	wash by letting water run down, **hose down**	If the kids play in the bathroom I'll have to wash down the walls.
wash it down	drink to help you swallow, drink after eating	Have a donut—and some coffee to wash it down.
wash it off	spray water to clean it, **hose it off**	If you spill latex paint, you can wash it off with water.
wash out	become clean, **clean up**	"Will this stain wash out?" "Yes, if you use bleach."
wash your hands of it	not be involved anymore, withdraw from a project	If you don't believe in the union, wash your hands of it.
wash-out	(See **a wash-out**)	
washed up	ruined, unable to continue in business	I can't believe Max is washed up. He was a successful businessman.
wasn't born yesterday	wise from experience, **been around**	Pat can survive in the workplace. She wasn't born yesterday.
WASP	White Anglo-Saxon Protestant	Don's a WASP and I'm a WASP, but we have different beliefs.
waste no time	hurry to do it, do not delay	After the meeting, I left. I wasted no time leaving that dirty city.
waste not, want not	if you do not waste, you will not be needy	Melinda's motto is *Waste Not, Want Not*. She's very efficient.
wasted	drugged, **high**, **stoned**	He acts weird when he's wasted. Drugs do strange things to him.
wasted	badly injured, bruised, **beat up**	Tom was wasted by the C-Train Gang. He's in the hospital.
watch out	be careful, **look out**	Watch out! There's a truck!
watch out for	watch and care for, **keep an eye on**	Jamie, you watch out for Cathy. Hold her hand at the crosswalk.

Idiom	Meaning	Example
watch over	care for, protect, **look after**	"Who watches over you, Kari?" "My Guardian Angel, that's who."
watch your language	do not swear, do not use crude language	Watch your language. There are children in the room.
watch your P's and Q's	be polite, **mind your manners**	At the banquet, remember your manners. Watch your P's and Q's.
watch your step	watch where you step, be careful	Watch your step, Grandfather. The sidewalk is icy.
watch your step	stay out of trouble, **keep your nose clean**	The referee told me not to fight. "Watch your step," he said.
water down	add water to make it weaker, dilute	The cherry drink is too strong. It should be watered down.
water under the bridge	the past, history	That failure is water under the bridge. Let's not live in the past.
water-cooler talk	office news, gossip	I believe water-cooler talk— unless it's about me.
watering hole	bar, pub, licensed premises	The St. Louis Hotel is Ralph's favorite watering hole.
wax eloquent	speak beautifully, make a speech using nice words	When we talk about art, Uncle Jonas begins to wax eloquent.
wax poetic	become poetic, begin to recite poems	Whenever you read the Psalms, Andy begins to wax poetic.
way cool	very nice, very **cool**	His voice is way cool, eh. I love listening to him.
way out (away out)	not close to the answer, wrong by a large amount	Your guess was way out. My age is 49, not 41.
way out of line (away out of line)	very inappropriate, not acceptable	When the teacher hit you, he was way out of line.
way to go	good work, **good for you**, **good going**	When Kelly scores a goal, we yell, "Way to go, man!"
way you hold your...	(See **the way you hold your mouth**)	
weak-kneed	not strong in character, lacking will power	Marvin yielded to temptation. He appears to be weak-kneed.
wear down	become dull or weak, use until worn	Confinement in a prison began to wear down his spirit.

Idiom	Meaning	Example
wear off	not have as much effect, not affect as much	The effects of the drug began to wear off, and the pain returned.
wear out	use until thin or full of holes, **shabby**	If you wear out your gloves, we'll provide a new pair.
wear out your welcome	stay or visit too long, not be welcome anymore	If we stay more than three days, we'll wear out our welcome.
wear the pants	make the decisions, control everything	Betty wears the pants in the Cheong family. She's the boss.
wear your heart on your sleeve	show your emotions, reveal your true feelings	If you wear your heart on your sleeve, he'll know you love him.
weasel word	vague or ambiguous word, a word that deceives you	Show that contract to your lawyer. She can find the weasel words.
weather the storm	survive a crisis, live through **tough times**	Pat lost his job and I had surgery, but we weathered the storm.
weed out	remove, delete, **get rid of**, **turf it**	We have to weed out the courses that people don't need, such as *Caring For Your Polar Bear*.
weigh in at	measure the weight of a person, **tip the scales**	Teddy weighed in at one hundred kilograms. He's a heavy man.
weirdo	strange person, pervert, **creep**	This weirdo started following us around the park. It was scary!
wekabi	personal evil spirit, personal devil	His wekabi told him to steal the statue of the Ethiopian ruler.
well heeled	wealthy, rich, **well off**	The Clarks were well heeled, wealthy enough to hire servants.
well hung [B]	having a large penis and testicles	That stallion is well hung. He's very well equipped.
well off	wealthy, **well to do**	Ken's family is fairly well off. They can afford a few luxuries.
well taken	true, significant	Your statement is well taken. The Canadian family *has* changed.
well to do	wealthy, rich, **loaded**	Many well-to-do families send their children to private schools.
went through the roof	(See **go through the roof**)	
went to bat for	(See **go to bat for**)	

Idiom	Meaning	Example
went under	(See **go under**)	
went wild	(See **go wild**)	
wet behind the ears	(See **still wet behind the ears**)	
wet the bed	urinate while in bed, urinate during sleep	Some kids wet the bed because they have emotional problems.
wet your whistle	have a drink, quench your thirst	If you're thirsty, have some apple cider to wet your whistle.
whack off [B]	(See **jerk off**)	
whale of a game	(See **a whale of a game**)	
what a brain	what an intelligent person, what a **bright** girl	What a brain! She got 98% on her math test.
what a dish	what a beautiful girl	Julia Roberts—what a dish!
what a rigmarole	what a process, what a **hassle**	To get a refund, I had to answer 50 questions. What a rigmarole!
what a rush	what a thrill, what a great feeling	After riding in Paul's Corvette, Rita said, "What a rush!"
what came over me	what happened to me, what caused me to change	I couldn't remember my name. I don't know what came over me.
what did I do to deserve this	why am I being punished? **no rest for the wicked**	Working in the sewers, I thought, "What did I do to deserve this?"
what gives	what is happening, **what's going on**	Jerry walks in and says, "What gives? Where is everybody?"
what goes around comes around	you get what you give; our actions are passed on until they return to us	Wise folks have learned that you eventually get what you give— what goes around comes around.
what if	(See **what-if**)	
what in tarnation	what is this? **what the hell** [B]	What in tarnation? Where did you get that dinosaur?
what in the name of heaven	what is that? **what's going on**	You built a gazebo? What in the name of heaven is that?
what in the world	what is happening, what is it?	What in the world is that? It looks like a space ship!

Idiom	Meaning	Example
what it boils down to	what it really means, **the bottom line**	What it boils down to is this: we don't have enough money.
what the dickens	where did it go? how do you explain it?	What the dickens did you do to your hair? Who cut it off?
what the hay	who cares? why worry?	The hood blew off my car, but what the hay—who needs a hood?
what the heck	why bother? it does not matter	Bing and Ko are getting married. What the heck. I don't care.
what the hell [B]	why? how? **what the heck**	What the hell is he doing with my diary? Where did he get it?
what the Sam Hill	what happened, what is it?	What the Sam Hill did you do to my bike? The gears won't shift.
what you don't know won't hurt you	if you do not know about a problem, you do not worry	Don't tell Dad I'm gay. What he doesn't know won't hurt him.
what's cooking	what is happening, **what's going down**	What's cooking with the kids? They're too quiet.
what's eating you	what is bothering you? are you upset?	"What's eating you, Darryl? You look kind of mad."
what's going down	what is happening, what is going to happen	The students want to know what's going down—where the teacher is.
what's going on	what is happening, **what's going down**	I want to know what's going on. Who wrote this note?
what's good for the goose is good for the gander	rules that apply to the wife also apply to the husband, **turn about...**	If you need a holiday, so do I! What's good for the goose is good for the gander.
what's in it for me	what will I receive? how will I benefit?	Before I give you the information, what's in it for me. Do I get paid?
what's new	what is new in your life? what is happening	"Hi, Pearl. What's new?" "Lots. I have a baby!"
what's the big idea	why are you doing that? who said you could do that?	What's the big idea? Who said you could chop down that tree?
what's the poop	what is the news? what did you hear? **what's going down**	When Holly wants to know what happened, she says, "Well, what's the poop?"
what's up	what is happening? what is the latest news?	Bugs Bunny says to Elmer Fudd, "A bee 'n a bee! What's up, Doc?"

Idiom	Meaning	Example
what's your beef	what is your complaint? why are you upset?	What's your beef, Mark? I can see that you're upset.
what's your poison	what do you like to drink? which liquor do you like?	Come over to the bar and I'll buy you a drink. What's your poison?
what's-his-face	what is his name, I cannot remember his name	Nobody can park here, not even old what's-his-face—the judge.
whatchamacallit	what do you call it, **thingamajig**	To finish the job, I need a what-chamacallit. A trowel!
what-if	plan, theory, hypothesis	We did a what-if on the computer to see when the world will die from pollution.
wheatbelt	wheat-producing area, **breadbasket**	Farmers in the wheatbelt pray for rain for their crops.
wheeler-dealer	a person who is good at making sales and deals, **a closer**	Cliff is a wheeler-dealer in the energy industry. He brings buyers and sellers together.
wheels	vehicle (car, truck etc.), **set of wheels**	Jeff, can I borrow your wheels? My sister needs a ride to the mall.
wheels fell off	(See **the wheels fell off**)	
when in Rome, do as the Romans do	when you are a visitor do the same things as your hosts do	When I visit an Asian country, I learn the customs, and do as the "Romans" do.
when it comes to	when this is the topic, when we talk about this	When it comes to cars, I like GM. I would buy a Chev or a Pontiac.
when push comes to shove	when people fight, when the fighting begins, **when the going gets tough**	The workers are demanding a fair wage. When push comes to shove, we may have to call the police.
when the chips are down	when the right decision must be made, when you must win	When the chips are down—when we are losing—we play better. We need to be challenged.
when the crunch comes	when there is less money, when the economy fails	When the crunch comes, we'll have our mortgage paid off!
when the dust settles	when the fight is finished, when it is calm again, when the lights go on	Abortion is a serious issue, but when the dust settles, women will be able to choose.
when the going gets tough	when there are problems, when progress is difficult	When the going gets tough, we need people with a good attitude.

Idiom	Meaning	Example
where angels fear to tread	where even the angels fear to go, where danger is	They were using a Ouija board— going where angels fear to tread!
where do they get off	where do they get the right? **how come?**	Where do they get off telling me to slow down? Who asked them?
where it's at	where important things are happening, where the action is	China—that's where it's at today. Their society is changing; their economy is growing.
where the rubber hits the road	where the theory is tested, when the action begins; **the nitty -gritty**	In the workplace, you apply what you've learned—that's where the rubber hits the road.
where there's a will, there's a way	when we are determined we find a way to succeed, **when the going gets tough**	The manager of the charity held up this sign: WHERE THERE'S A WILL, THERE'S A WAY!
where's the loo	where is the bathroom? where is **the can?**	When Bev looks for a bathroom she says, "Where's the loo?"
whet your appetite	improve your appetite, cause you to be hungry	Would you like to order a salad to whet your appetite?
whip you	defeat you, beat you in a game, **wipe you**	Jason says he can whip you in a game of tennis. Can he beat you?
whip you into shape	help you become fit, improve your fitness	These aerobic exercises will whip you into shape.
white elephant	a purchase that was not used, a useless object	Should we take the statue of Stalin to the White Elephant Sale?
white knuckles	a tense feeling, acute worry	Driving through fog is scary— it's white knuckles all the way.
white lie	a small lie, a **fib**	"You said you were 39, not 40." "Yes. I told a white lie."
whiz	urinate, pee, piss,[B] **have to go, take a leak** [B]	A few minutes after the concert began, my daughter whispered, "Mommy, I have to whiz."
whole hog	every effort, all your energy, **gung-ho**	When I play racquetball, I work hard. I go whole hog.
whole shebang	(See **the whole shebang**)	
whole shooting match	(See **the whole shooting match**)	
whore blossom	pimple, cold sore, **zit**	Every time I eat shortbread, I get whore blossoms on my chin.

Idiom	Meaning	Example
whup you	(See **whip you**)	
why in the name of...	why, **why in the world**	I want to know why in the name of heaven she bought that gun.
why in the world	why, why is it? **for the life of me**	Why in the world would anyone want to live in the desert?
wicked	exciting, terrific, **cool**	"Wicked!" Dawn said when she saw my haircut. "It looks great."
wide awake	fully awake, alert	After the bear stuck his head in our tent, I was wide awake.
wild	exciting, awesome, **rad**	"Do you like my new shirt?" "Ya, man. It's wild."
wild about	like a lot, **crazy about**, **mad about**	I'm just wild about Harry, but he doesn't care about me.
wild and woolly	uncivilized, like an animal	When cowboys are on the range, they become wild and woolly.
wild goose chase	(See **a wild goose chase**)	
willy-nilly	whether you want it or not, without choice	I continue to receive junk mail— willy-nilly—like it or not!
wimp	weak person, **chicken**	Tiny Tim is not a wimp, but he looks thin and weak.
wimpy	weak, lacking courage, like a **wimp**	Sean acts kind of wimpy, but he's a strong, decisive leader.
win big	win a big prize, win a lot of money	You can win big with Lotto 649. You can win millions!
win by a nose	barely win, win by one point or part of a second	In the final race, we won by a nose. Our boat was just in front.
win going away	win by going ahead near the end of a race or game	Scoring four goals in the third period, the Leafs won going away.
win the hearts	win the approval, cause people to like you	Elvis won the hearts of the crowd when he sang *Love Me Tender*.
wind up	conclude, finish, **end up**	What time will the meeting wind up? When should I pick you up?
wind up	see this result, see that ending, **end up**	If you are a strong leader, you could wind up as our president.

Idiom	Meaning	Example
windbag	a person who talks a lot, a person who brags	Kerry is bragging about Ireland again. What a windbag!
window of opportunity	(See **a window of opportunity**)	
window on the world	the place where you can see the world	For some people, TV is their only window on the world.
wing it	improvise, change your plans, **play it by ear**	If I am asked strange questions at an interview, I wing it. I give the best answers I can think of.
wing nut	a person who acts crazy, **a nut**	Jerry, you wing nut! How did you get that horse in the elevator?
wingding	wild party, **bash**	We went to Happy Harry's wingding. It was a great party.
wingy	wild, crazy, **wacko**	Leon drove his car into the lake again. That guy is really wingy!
winner take all	the winner of the game gets all the money	Bert said, "Let's play one more game of poker, winner take all."
winning isn't everything; it's the only thing	winning is the only thing that matters, **get it straight**	It was Vince Lombardi, a football coach, who said, "Winning isn't everything—it's the only thing."
winning streak	winning game after game, **make a clean sweep**	The Expos have won nine games— their longest winning streak.
wino	an alcoholic, a drunk, **lush, tank**	See that wino over there. He used to be the president of GASCO.
wipe out	lose control of a car/bike so that it spins or rolls	Larry wiped out on the last corner. His car is in the ditch.
wipe that smile off your face	stop smiling, do not smile, **cut it out**	Reg, tell Peter you're sorry and give him a big kiss. Gail, wipe that smile off your face.
wipe you	defeat you by many points, **blow you away**	Tran has won every spelling contest. She'll wipe you.
wired	very excited, **pumped**	Jay didn't sleep last night. She's really wired for her exam today.
wired for sound	ready to operate, prepared for use	"Is the hall decorated and ready?" "Yep. It's wired for sound."
wise to us	know what we are doing, **onto us**	Your husband knows you're seeing me. He's wise to us.

Idiom	Meaning	Example
wishful thinking	believing it is true because you wish it was true	Roy says that he is going to marry Dawn, but it's wishful thinking.
wishy-washy	not able to decide, saying yes and no	I like you because you're decisive, because you're not wishy-washy.
with all my heart	with all my feeling	I love Canada with all my heart.
with bated breath	with worry and tension, with suspense, **leave me hanging**	With bated breath, they waited for news of the men who were trapped in the mine.
with bells on	happy to come, ready to have fun	I'd love to come to your wedding. I'll be there with bells on!
with his tail between his legs	running away in fear, retreating like a coward, **run for the hills**	When he saw the bear, he turned around and ran with his tail between his legs.
with it	informed, sophisticated, **cool, in the know**	In the fashion world, Brad's really with it. He knows fashion.
with the naked eye	without binoculars or a telescope	The comet cannot be seen with the naked eye. It is too small.
with wings	to take out, to take with you, **to go**	"Can I take your order?" "I'll have a Big Mac, a large fries and a Coke—with wings."
within earshot	close enough to hear, **under my breath**	Lil was within earshot of the radio during the newscast. She heard it.
without a doubt	for sure, **without question**	Without a doubt, Toyota has the best record. It's the most reliable.
without a full deck	mentally unbalanced, **one brick short...**	At times he acts strange—like he's playing without a full deck.
without a hitch	without a problem, **smooth sailing**	Except for one flat tire, the trip went without a hitch.
without a word of a lie	without any lies, **the gospel truth**	Without a word of a lie, that fish was five feet long.
without batting an eye	without pausing, looking calm and natural	Without batting an eye, she gave him a false name and address.
without question	certain, **no doubt**	Lee sang best, without question. She has an excellent voice.
wolf down	eat quickly, **inhale**	The boys wolfed down their lunch and ran out to play soccer.

Idiom	Meaning	Example
wolf in sheep's clothing	(See **a wolf in sheep's clothing**)	
won't see you stuck	will help if necessary, will not refuse firmly, **leave the door open**	"Will you judge our pie contest?" "I'd rather not do it, but I won't see you stuck."
won't tell a soul	will not tell anyone, **keep it to yourself**	You can tell me your secret. I won't tell a soul.
wonky	dizzy, confused, **woozy**	After falling off the horse, Pedro was feeling a little wonky.
woof your cookies	vomit, puke, **barf, hork**	If you eat bananas, anchovies and cheese, you'll woof your cookies.
woozy	feeling a little bit sick in your stomach, **wonky**	I've had the flu and my stomach is still a bit woozy.
word for word	quoted exactly, verbatim	He repeated her message word for word—exactly as she had said it.
word is good	you can believe it, you can count on it	Artur's word is good. You can believe what he says.
word is out	I have heard, people are saying, **rumor has it**	Word is out that you're moving to Denver. Is it true?
word of honor	solemn promise, **take oath**	He gave me his word of honor that he will pay me on Friday.
word of mouth	(See **by word of mouth**)	
word to the wise	(See **a word to the wise**)	
work	is right, is fine, is appropriate	*Plaintive*—that's the right word! It works!
work cut out for	a lot of work to do, difficult tasks to do, **a tough row to hoe**	If you want to be a chartered accountant, you have your work cut out for you.
work ethic	belief that you must work; that work is good for you	Do you believe that Canadians have a strong work ethic?
work it out	solve it, try to agree	My teacher and I disagree about my grade, but we can work it out.
work my buns off	work hard every day, **work your ass off** [B]	I work my buns off while he sits around and makes phone calls!
work my fingers to the bone	work so hard that I become thin and weak	I worked my fingers to the bone to help my kids get an education.

Idiom	Meaning	Example
work of art	beautiful painting or carving etc.	Every rug she weaves is a work of art.
work out	succeed, go as planned, **pan out**	Did the recipe work out? Did the cake taste good?
work things out	discuss a problem and find a solution, **work it out**	Maria and Paulo had a fight, but they worked things out.
work to rule	do only as much work as you have to do, **draw the line**	The teachers are working to rule because they are not satisfied with their salaries.
work up a sweat	work or exercise hard, perspire, **break a sweat**	When I skip, it takes me ten minutes to work up a sweat.
work up a thirst	become thirsty, work or play until you are thirsty	Digging trenches at midday, the men soon worked up a thirst.
work your ass off [B]	work very hard, **work my buns off**	Why do you work your ass off for such a small salary?
work your buns off	work hard, work steadily	If you work your buns off, you can learn these idioms!
workaholic	one who loves to work; who is addicted to work	Gary is a workaholic. He even works on weekends!
worked up	excited, upset	Now, Dad. Don't get worked up about the war. Don't get upset.
world beater	a person who tries to be the best in the world, **set the world on fire**	My coach said, "You don't have to be a world beater. Just be the best you can be."
world is your oyster	(See **the world is your oyster**)	
World Wide Web (www)	a network of computers in all parts of the world, **Internet**	Some people use the Web to find information; others use it to find friends.
worldly wise	knowing how to survive, having **street smarts**	You've lived on the streets of LA. You're worldly wise. You're **hip**.
worlds apart	not close to agreement, very different	Israel and Palestine are neighbors but they're worlds apart.
worn out	(See **wear out**)	
worn out	very tired, **bushed**	Whew! I'm worn out from all that walking! How far did we walk?

Idiom	Meaning	Example
worried sick	very worried, extremely anxious	Velma is worried sick about her son. He's using cocaine.
worse for wear	(See **none the worse for wear**)	
worship the ground she walks on	love her very, very much; **crawl on my hands...**, **mad about** her	"Does Anthony love Cleopatra?" "He adores her. He worships the ground she walks on!"
wouldn't be caught dead	would not like to do it, would rather die than do it	Have you seen Lulu's miniskirt? I wouldn't be caught dead in that.
wouldn't miss it for the world	I would rather attend it than see the world	"Are you coming to my wedding?" "I wouldn't miss it for the world!"
wouldn't say shit if her mouth was full of it [B]	would not say a bad word, would not swear	Vi is so sweet. She wouldn't say shit if her mouth was full of it.
wound up	excited, **pumped**	Before Nadia sings, she gets all wound up. She can't relax.
wow	oh, awesome, **gee whiz**	Wow! I can see every star in the universe tonight.
wrap around his finger	controlled by him, **on a string**	I do whatever she wants. She's got me wrapped around her finger.
wrap it up	finish it, end it, **bring to a close**	They played some new songs but they wrapped it up with a hit.
wrap up	end, conclude	The Olympics wrap up on Sunday. Closing ceremonies are at 1 p.m.
wrap your mind around	understand, comprehend, **get your mind around**	Val's niece is also her half sister. Wrap your mind around that!
wrap-up	closing, conclusion	During the wrap-up, the speaker thanked everyone for coming.
wreak havoc	damage, destroy, **lay waste**, **trash the place**	If the workers get mad, they'll wreak havoc in the warehouse. They'll wreck the place.
write it off	say it is a financial loss, call it a business expense, deduct it from income	Don't worry about the cost of my plane ticket. I can write it off as a business expense.
write up	record in writing, prepare a written account	I've been asked to write up a list of the winners for the newspaper.
writer's block	being unable to think of something to write	I told the teacher I couldn't do the paper because of writer's block.

Idiom	Meaning	Example
written all over your face	showing on your face, **body language**, **read you**	When you heard that Italy lost the World Cup, disappointment was written all over your face.
written in blood	like a law, binding, cannot be changed	Now that his name is written in blood, he's a member of our gang.
written in stone	written in final form, like a commandment	Our agreement isn't written in stone; it can be changed.
wuss	(See **wimp**)	
wysiwyg	*w*hat *y*ou *s*ee *i*s *w*hat *y*ou *g*et (if you are lucky)	The printer is supposed to print what you see on the computer screen — wysiwyg!

X

X Generation	(See **Generation X**)	
x marks the spot	look for x, begin at x, x is important	Someone had written on the map "X marks the spot where we were abducted by aliens."
X-rated	for adults, for a mature audience	*Born Loose* is an X-rated video. It contains nudity and sex.
XL	extra large or very large, extra luxury or extra power; shirt — size XL, car — 300 XL	"This shirt is marked XL. What does that mean?" "It means extra large. On cars, XL means extra luxury or power."

Idiom	Meaning	Example

Y

ya	yes, **yep**, **yo**, **uh-huh**	"Did you graduate from high school?" "Ya. I got a diploma."
yada	idle talk, chatter	He's always talking—yada, yada!
yak	talk a lot, visit, **chew the fat**, **chin wag**	When I went to bed, Kate and Mom were still yakking away about the children.
yawner	(See **a yawner**)	
yellow	lacking courage, afraid to defend, **chicken**	Some fans think he's yellow because he doesn't fight.
yellow belly	a coward, a person who is afraid to do something	Smith, you yellow belly! Jump in the water and swim!
yeow	oh, **wow**, **yikes**	Yeow! That stove is hot!
yep	yes, **uh-huh**, **ya**, **yo**	"Do you like country music?" "Yep. I like the hurtin' songs."
yeppers	yes, **afraid so**, **uh-huh**, **ya**, **yo**	"Do I *have* to come home by 9?" "Yeppers, that's what we agreed."
yikes	oh, **gee**, **gosh**, **yeow**	Yikes! There's a spider on me!
yin-yang	an opening or space, everywhere, **all over hell's half acre**	Australia has too many rabbits. They have rabbits coming out of their yin-yang.
yo	yes, hello, I hear you, **okay**	When they call to you, just answer, "Yo!"
yokel	(See **local yokel**)	
you and the horse you rode in on	you and your horse go, both you and your horse, **screw you** and the horse	"Did you say I should leave?" "Ya, you and the horse you rode in on. Git!"
you bet your boots	believe it, certainly, you can **count on** it	The cowboy said, "You bet your boots I'm going to the rodeo."

Idiom	Meaning	Example
you betcha	that is correct, right; **you got it**	When I asked, "Are you coming?" she said, "You betcha."
you can bet your bottom dollar	you can be sure of it, you can bet your last dollar on it	If Terry knows about the dance, you can bet your bottom dollar he'll be there.
you can lead a horse to water but you can't make him drink	you can provide what they need but you cannot force them to use it	We provide information, but I wonder if they read it. You can lead a horse to water....
you can run but you can't hide	you can run away but you cannot hide from your past or your problems	When I told a priest I was going away to forget my past, he said, "You can run, but you can't hide."
you can thank your lucky stars	you were lucky, be thankful you are safe	He can thank his lucky stars that a doctor was there. He nearly died.
you can't make a silk purse out of a sow's ear	you cannot improve the quality of junk; cannot make gold from iron	When Hal put a Mercedes star on his Ford, I said, "You can't make a silk purse out of a sow's ear."
you can't teach an old dog new tricks	old dogs and old people do not like to change or learn, **die hard**	Our senior employees don't like computer training—you can't teach an old dog new tricks.
you can't tell a book by its cover	the cover or surface does not reveal its contents, **beauty is only skin deep**	If you buy a car because it looks nice, remember this: you can't tell a book by its cover.
you don't miss the water till the well runs dry	you do not appreciate some things until they go away or become extinct	Now we have only memories of of our song birds. You don't miss the water till the well runs dry.
you don't say	that is surprising, **how about that**	"We have ten kids," the man said. "You don't say!" my mom replied.
you got it	you have the answer, you are doing it right	"You got it, kid!" the coach said. "That's the way to score!"
you had to be there	to understand, you should have been there with me; it was funny then	When I said, "Goo!" everybody laughed and clapped. I guess you had to be there.
you have to be good to be lucky	people with ability cause their own good luck, **prepare like crazy**	Athletes don't wait for good luck. They try to improve, knowing you have to be good to be lucky.
you need money to make money	you have to spend money to make a profit, **nothing succeeds like...**	If I had money, I would invest in real estate. It's true that you need money to make money.

Idiom	Meaning	Example
you reap whatsoever you sow	you will see the long-term effects of your actions, **chickens come home...**	Youthful passion can produce a lifetime of consequences. We reap whatsoever we sow.
you snooze, you lose	if you are not alert you will lose an opportunity, **seize the opportunity**	Store clerks sometimes charge too much for a product. If you snooze, you lose.
you're full of it [B]	you are a liar, you are full of shit [B]	If you think I'm joining that cult, you're full of it.
you're kidding	you are joking, you are not serious	You're kidding. Jen wouldn't take off her clothes and climb a tree.
you're not kidding/ you aren't kidding	you are right, you are not joking	"It's really cold today," Jen said. "You aren't kidding!" he replied.
you're on	you have a deal, you have a date	When she suggested they go out for dinner, he said, "You're on."
you're only as good as your last shift	you are judged by your most recent work, don't **rest on your laurels**	If you believe that you're only as good as your last shift, you should do your best every day.
you've got to be kidding	you must be telling me a joke, **get out of town**, **you're kidding**	"The manager wants me to give him a massage every afternoon." "You've got to be kidding!"
young at heart	feeling or thinking that you are young, youthful	Sarah is over sixty, but she's young at heart.
your goose is cooked	(See **goose is cooked**)	
your lip	your sharp words, your bad replies	I don't want any more of your lip, Son. Don't say *no* to me.
your number is up	the time has come, it is your turn to die	When your number's up, you go. That's how I feel about dying.
your own worst enemy	hurt yourself, **shoot yourself in the foot**	If you use cocaine, you'll be your own worst enemy.
your turn	your chance, your try	The clerk said, "Wait your turn. Wait until I can serve you."
yours truly	me, myself, the writer or speaker	The announcer said, "This is yours truly, Danny Burrows, saying good-bye for now."
yoyo	fool, **dipstick**, **jerk**, **nerd**	I was parking my car when this yoyo on a motorcycle started driving in circles around me.

Idiom	Meaning	Example
yuk	awful, gross, ugly	When Jenny cooks beef liver, the kids say, "Yuk!"
yum	it tastes good, I like it	Yum! This soup is good!
yummy	delicious, tasty	I don't like J-Bars, but the kids think they're yummy.
yuppie	young, upwardly-mobile, professional person	The yuppies are buying BMW's, but can they afford them?

Z

zap	heat in the microwave oven, **nuke**	I zapped my hotdog. It was ready in 30 seconds!
zig when you should zag	move the wrong way, move left instead of right	I had an accident because I zigged when I should've zagged.
zilch	zero, none, nothing, **diddly**, **nada**, **zip**	"How much did you win?" "Zilch. Not a penny."
zinger	strong statement, sarcastic words, **get off a few good ones**	Randi says kind things, except for the occasional zinger. Like today she called Tom a beast.
zip	close, shut tight	Mom told me to zip my lips while the preacher is talking.
zip	go quickly, run	After we deliver the flowers we can zip over to the bank.
zip/zippo	nothing, zero, **nada**	The Smiths have paid nothing on their account—zippo.
zipperhead	business person, administrator	What musicians hate is to have a zipperhead controlling the arts.
zit	pimple, blemish	I'm not going to the party because I have zits on my face.
zonked	tired, exhausted, **falling asleep**	After playing soccer in the park, I needed a rest. I was zonked.
zoom in	move the camera closer, magnify the subject	Now zoom in for a photo of the baby. Get a close-up of her face.